Perhaps one in these:

Salinger   31-41, 50-55

Lee, 62-71

Politics in China

The CERI Series in International Relations and Political Economy

Series Editors, Christophe Jaffrelot and Christian Lequesne

This series consists of works emanating from the foremost French research center in international studies, the Paris-based Centre d'Etudes et de Recherches Internationales (CERI), part of Sciences Po and associated with the CNRS (Centre National de la Recherche Scientifique).

Founded in 1952, CERI has about sixty fellows drawn from different disciplines who conduct research on comparative political analysis, international relations, regionalism, transnational flows, political sociology, political economy and on individual states.

This series focuses on the transformations of the international arena, in a world where the state, though its sovereignty is questioned, reinvents itself. The series explores the effects on international relations and the world economy of regionalization, globalization (not only of trade and finance but also of culture), and transnational flows at large. This evolution in world affairs sustains a variety of networks from the ideological to the criminal or terrorist. Besides the geopolitical transformations of the globalized planet, the new political economy of the world has a decided impact on its destiny as well, and this series hopes to uncover what that is.

Politics in China
Moving Frontiers

Edited by
Françoise Mengin and Jean-Louis Rocca

POLITICS IN CHINA
© Françoise Mengin and Jean-Louis Rocca, eds, 2002

First published 2002 by
PALGRAVE MACMILLAN™
175 Fifth Avenue, New York, N.Y.10010 and
Houndmills, Basingstoke, Hampshire, England RG21 6XS
Companies and representatives throughout the world

PALGRAVE MACMILLAN is the global academic imprint of the palgrave macmillan division of St. Martin's Press, LLC and of Palgrave Macmillan Ltd. Macmillan is a registered trademark in the United States, United Kingdom and other countries. Palgrave is a registered trademark in the European Union and other countries.

ISBN 0–312–29578–2

Library of Congress Cataloging-in-Publication Data
available at the Library of Congress

A catalogue record for this book is available from the British Library.

Design by Newgen Imaging Systems (P) Ltd., Chennai, India.

First edition: November 2002
10 9 8 7 6 5 4 3 2 1
Printed in the United States of America.

CONTENTS

Contents

NOTES ON THE CONTRIBUTORS

DELIA DAVIN is Professor of Chinese Studies at the University of Leeds. She lived in China for two years in the 1960s and is still a regular visitor. She now works on gender and migration issues in China. She is the author of *Internal Migration in Contemporary China* (Macmillan, 1999).

GRANT EVANS is a Reader in Anthropology at the University of Hong Kong. He has written extensively on Southeast Asia, and in particular on Laos. His latest book is *A Short History of Laos; the Land In-between* (2002).

GILLES GUIHEUX completed a Ph.D. in History and Civilization at the Ecole des Hautes Etudes en Sciences Sociales (Paris) in 1996. Since then, he has been Senior Lecturer in Contemporary Chinese History. He is currently Researcher at the French Centre for Research on Contemporary China (Hong Kong). His most recent works focus on private entrepreneurship in Mainland China; he is the author of *La main invisible de la prospérité. Grands patrons et grandes entreprises privées à Taiwan* (forthcoming).

HUA LINSHAN, Historian, Associate Researcher at the Center for Studies on Modern an Contemporary China in Paris. Publications include *Les années rouges* (Seuil, 1987), *Enquête sociologique sur la Chine, 1911–1949* (Presses universitaires de France, 1996) with Isabelle Thireau (awarded the Drouin de Lhuys award from the French Academy of Political and Moral Sciences in 1997).

CHING KWAN LEE is Assistant Professor of Sociology at the University of Michigan. Her research interests include labor, ethnography, China, socialism and post-socialism. She is the author of *Gender and* the South China Miracle (University of California Press, 1998), and is currently working on a book entitled In the Twilight of Socialism: Trajectories of Labor Struggles in Reform China.

FRANÇOISE MENGIN, Political Scientist, is Research Fellow at the Centre for International Studies and Research (Sciences Po, Paris). Her most recent works focus on the re-mapping of the Greater China space in the context of globalization. She is the author of Trajectoires chinoises: Taiwan, Hong Kong et Pékin (Karthala, 1998).

TAK-WING NGO teaches Chinese Politics at Leiden University, the Netherlands. He is the Editor of the journal China Information and co-editor of the NIAS Press (formerly Curzon Press) book series on Democracy in Asia. His most recent publications include The Cultural Construction of Politics in Asia (with Hans Antlöv, Curzon 2000) and Hong Kong's History: State and Society under Colonial Rule (Routledge, 1999).

JEAN-LOUIS ROCCA is Research Fellow at the Centre for International Studies and Research (Sciences Po, Paris) and Visiting Professor at the People's University in Beijing. He is also responsible for a new program of academic exchanges between French and Chinese researchers in social sciences. He is currently working on the unemployment, employment and social welfare policies in China, their impact on Chinese society, and the reactions of urban population to these policies. He is doing extensive field studies on these topics in order to compare situations in three different Chinese regions: northeastern China, Sichuan and Shanghai. He is a member of a Sino-European network sponsored by the European Commission that aims at comparing unemployment and employment policies in China and in some European countries. Jean-Louis Rocca has published papers related to these topics in collective books and academic journals in French and English.

DOROTHY J. SOLINGER, Professor of Political Science at the University of California, Irvine, and Senior Adjunct Research Scholar, East Asian Institute, Columbia University. She is the author of a number of books on contemporary China, most recently, Contesting Citizenship in Urban China: Peasant Migrants, the State, and the Logic of the Market (University of California Press, 1999), the winner of the 2001 Joseph R. Levenson Prize of the Association for Asian Studies. Her current work is on urban unemployment.

ISABELLE THIREAU, Sociologist, Researcher at the Center for Studies on Modern and Contemporary China in Paris. Has recently published *Disputes au village chinois. Formes du juste et recompositions locales des espaces normatifs* (Editions de la Maison des Sciences de l'Homme, 2001) edited with Wang Hansheng.

DAVID L. WANK is Associate Professor of Sociology, Sophia University, Tokyo. After undergraduate study of History and Chinese Language and Literature (B.A. Oberlin College, 1980) he taught English for two years (1980–1982) in Shanxi Province. Immersion in a Chinese work unit stimulated his curiosity about state power and social relations and led him to pursue graduate study in political sociology and institutional change (Ph.D. Harvard University 1993). He has authored *Commodifying Communism: Business, Trust, and Politics in a Chinese City* (Cambridge University Press, 1999), coedited *Social Connections in China: Institutions, Culture, and the Changing Nature of Guanxi* (Cambridge University Press, 2002), and is coauthoring a book on the politics of China's Buddhist revival since the Cultural Revolution.

Introduction: Analyzing Changes through Overlapping Spheres

FRANÇOISE MENGIN AND JEAN-LOUIS ROCCA

China as an Exception?

For many years now, numerous and significant field and case studies on Chinese society have been undertaken. Empirical knowledge has unquestionably improved and been extended compared to the pre-reformist period. Theoretical approaches have gone hand in hand with the improvement in empirical knowledge on China. These works very often conclude with paradoxical statements: China has a communist regime and a capitalist economy, an authoritarian state and a dynamic society, a neo-traditionalist substratum and an entrepreneurial spirit, China is a unified nation but is the victim of centrifugal forces. But, the issue at stake, now, is how to go beyond these paradoxes? Therefore, the starting point of this book was not to propose a new set of concepts, but to explore new paths.

This volume is the result of a conference that was held in Paris in December 1999[1] bearing such questioning in mind. We tried to escape two mainstream approaches, the culturalist one and the functionalist/evolutionist one. The first paradigm is based on the irreducibility of China: in this view, because of its cultural characteristics, Chinese society should not be compared to other societies. It follows that China is unique and its evolution can only be described according to Chinese specificities. The works of Lucian Pye on political culture are apposite examples of this line of reasoning.[2] Perhaps ironically, growing communication and exchange between Mainland China and other Chinese societies such as Taiwan, Hong Kong, or Overseas Chinese communities—whose trajectories have been quite different from that of the PRC—would seem not to have deprived this line of reasoning of its salience. At the time the Chinese Mainland was welcoming Overseas capital, be it of financial, human, or of a symbolic nature, the reference to some all-encompassing notion of "Asian values" has subsumed all "Chinas" in one that cannot be characterized otherwise but by reference to its supposed "Chineseness."[3]

In fact such an approach is not limited to those who claim to draw their research from the culturalists. In trying to explain the specificities of Chinese society, some authors rely upon cultural features that are not questioned in turn. Culture is considered as a given "substance," objectively confining individuals and groups within an unquestionable vision of the world. For example, Mayfair Yang and the numerous works based on her findings perceive traditional networks as the essence of true Chinese society, which is opposed to the "political" and artificial apparatus. These "natural" relations could compensate for the weakness of "civil society" as an element of resistance against the monopolization of power by the party-state.[4] Of course, the point is not to deny the importance of such works, but to question a culturalist starting point, even if it is not claimed as such.

However, the complexity of contemporary Chinese culture combining a traditional heritage, socialist background (the preservation of social differentiation between urban dwellers and rural inhabitants for example), the tremendous impact of modernity on lifestyles (the importance of nuclear families in urban areas, influence of consumption, and so on), and the obligation for individuals to straddle across these different worlds shows that the cultural dimension cannot be reduced to a well-defined set of norms and values. This moving aspect of culture is well illustrated by Delia Davin, who argues in one of the chapters of this book that the maid is typical of female migrants: despite the traditional nature of domestic service as an occupation for women, in contemporary China it can be a force for modernity with the potential to transform the lives of individuals and their communities. Indeed, because they are unique among migrants for their close contacts with urban people during their sojourns in the cities, maids may do more to bring new ideas on lifestyles, family life, and consumption to the villages than other returned migrants who have had less contact with urban people.

Besides, using the concept of "loose state," Yves Chevrier has shown that the traditional state in China has been historically and not culturally produced. In certain periods of time, the state revealed its ability to change relations with society, and allowed the latter to develop spaces of autonomy, calling into question its traditional way of governance.[5] More specifically, within the framework of a larger study on democracy and authoritarianism in Asia, the dialectical process linking culture and politics has been aptly analyzed in a recent volume edited by Hans Antlöv and Tak-Wing Ngo. When exploring the relationship between the normative/moral order and the actual political order, the book looks at "how certain values are mobilized and articulated in a way that sustains, produces, or modifies a particular political system. It also examines how these values and systems are interpreted as being 'democratic' in a specific sense in different countries."[6] For these authors: "cultural norms are politically sanctioned as much as political acts are evaluated by use of culturally perceived categories."[7] In other words, culture and politics are constantly linked, as practices of politics are constituted through cultural perceptions and historical experiences.

As for modernization theories based on the functionalist/evolutionist paradigm, their applications to China are, at first glance, more salient as they lead to more subtle conclusions. Chinese society is analyzed through normative concepts—privatization, democratization, rationalization, publicization, formalization—which are supposed to allow scholars to put China somewhere along the historical process of "development." Even when it is argued that China "in transition" does not look like other cases of transition—or that the transition in China has taken a specific form—the notion of transition itself and then of paths of evolution is still given first place. The underlying principle is that there are models of modernization that can be grasped as linear models along which the only pertinent question would be which place to give the studied entity, in this case China. As long as modernity is set as a universal form and is opposed to tradition, a cleavage between the "Western world" and the rest is inevitable, the latter being forced to mobilize "values" that preexisted before Western modernity. Besides, Western modernity is posited both as monolithic, and as a turning point more than as a process. As process, modernity implies adjusting tactics. It thus produces junctions, that is changes, that undermine any linear vision of history.

Fundamentally, for the proponents of modernization theory, economic development creates the preconditions for modern societies due to two ruptures.[8] First, modern societies would be formed of independent and clearly delineated spheres: religious, public, private, politics, economics, representation, reality, and so on. This structure is the direct opposite of the holist one of the so-called traditional society in which the different aspects of social life are inextricably interlinked. Modern societies would be social systems constituted of subsystems with their own characteristics and developing particular types of relationships with the other subsystems. Second, in contrast to traditional societies, modern societies would be characterized by the rationality of behavior and organization, based on interests not only individual but also public. The leap from imaginary to rationality would symbolize the path to modern civilization.

Again, the point at stake is not only to pinpoint works that explicitly claim such an approach, but also those that are *implicitly* based on it. For example, numerous authors use the concept of "civil society," though such a mechanical transposition comes up against the specificities produced by the contemporary context.[9] As in China—as well as elsewhere[10]—it is impossible to draw a clear cut between society and state, and it is difficult to talk about an autonomous sphere. On the contrary, the most dynamic change seems to take place in the very overlapping between state and society.

The use of the functionalist/evolutionist paradigm leads to a series of paradoxes. It seems unable to encapsulate the significance of the evolution of Chinese society. For example, if we use the theory that considers the separation of spheres as a main element of the modernization process, China is still an inscrutable country. Instead of being clearly delineated, the frontiers between the so-called spheres seem blurred. For example, most studies on the Chinese economy insist on the influence of political power on economic life in urban[11] as well as in rural sector.[12] Markets are still underdeveloped and play a less important role than political protection in economic success. Of course, it is possible to consider that the results would have been better in the context of a market economy and observers argue that the Chinese economy is compelled to take the road in that direction.[13] Nonetheless, the crucial element is that, despite the phenomenon of straddling between the economy and politics, most analysts agree on the fact that China's economy has experienced an exceptionally high level of growth in recent years. Religious revival that has gone hand in hand with economic growth in Taiwan is also an apposite example. The strong utilitarian orientation of folk religion has motivated people to accumulate wealth. But economic growth has led to an enrichment of temples, which, in turn, has reinforced people's commitment to folk religion with a utilitarian orientation.[14]

In modernization theories, relations between spheres are supposed to correspond to clear patterns. For example, economic development must open the path toward political pluralism. In the Chinese case this sequence does not seem to function. The discrepancy between the "development" of the economic sphere and the "underdevelopment" of the political sphere has been constantly noted. Whereas a "modern economy"—although not a standard liberal one—is emerging in China, the political system seems to be dominated by the intrusive power of the Communist party. Moreover, economic modernization has not led to the waning of "corruption" but, on the contrary, to its increasing impact.[15] Whatever the reason given to explain these different anomalies, they call into question the validity of the modernization theories.

The following chapters illustrate these different hypotheses, calling into question the existence of clear frontiers between "spheres," antinomical features, and territories. As to the market mechanisms themselves, Gilles Guiheux's chapter on enterprises, entrepreneurs, and social networks in Taiwan show that cooperation and competition simultaneously coexist among small enterprises. He also shows that economic activity does not rely only on rational objective criteria, but also on personal relationships between individuals. As to the dichotomy between state and business, Guiheux insists on the key role played by the state in Taiwan in the construction of a transnational high-technological industrial community formed by engineers from both sides of the Pacific. Ching Kwan Lee, when analyzing three patterns of working-class transition in urban China, shows that with the intertwined processes of capitalist globalization and market reform, not only do systems or institutions undergo transformation, but classes and class relations are made and remade, and that modes and terms of labor struggles too change in the process. In another chapter, David Wank studies power conversion in the making of China's rentier entrepreneur élite, and shows that it is not the private ownership of productive means that determines such an élite, but wealth accumulation that itself relies on access to state agents, that is, state resources. Thus the emerging entrepreneur élite is being defined not only by different business lines, business size, and social backgrounds, but by the variations these create regarding perceptions of the need for state power and ties with officialdom in the conduct of business. Therefore, categories that were previously discrete and unrelated have instead become in some senses symbiotic. Wank provides as a case study the example of a Xiamen entrepreneur that illustrates the entwining between private and public strategies. The entrepreneurial talent of this businessman lies in developing the necessary ties to pursue new opportunities in successive policies, rather than in spotting new business opportunities. Hence, more than a dichotomy between state and business, Wank's chapter suggests that the analysis should focus on the distinction between structural and practical power. While all entrepreneurs rely on practical power conversion techniques to varying degrees, these enable entrepreneurs from lower social structural positions to compensate for their low levels of social capital by forging more efficacious ties, though such a business strategy is especially risky.

Likewise, the cleavage between state and society at the local level is less and less relevant. In this book, Isabelle Thireau and Hua Linshan show that the decreasing dependence of villagers on rural officials supports the development of all kinds of formal and informal discussions concerning village affairs, and eventually of criticisms of the official decisions taken. The cooperation needed between officials and those "who matter in the village" requires negotiations in order to establish compromises favoring all the different parties' interests. The new institutional forms transmitted from the upper levels are often contradictory, difficult to interpret and implement, or needing some adjustment to the local context. Such adjustment is made through discussions held in various arenas. From the same perspective, according to Jean-Louis Rocca, the labor crisis has extensively changed the state/society relationship in urban areas: urban China seems to experience a double process of "statization of society" and of the "socialization of the state," in the sense that political action is more and more concerned by the "rise of the social," a process that Jürgen Habermas relates to the process of modernization of the State, accumulation, income, consumption, investment, poverty becoming the main targets of political action. Statization of society occurs as the State structures more and more formally the "social" through a welfare system. The role of the Social State is to "forestall" the potential conflict between labor and capital and to protect individuals.

Similarly, in the field of international relations, the authors of this volume do not draw a clear frontier between the State and transnational actors. Françoise Mengin for example shows in this volume that although Sino-Taiwanese links are an apposite case of transnational relations that, as such, would indicate the primacy of economic interests over national identification, they are still participating in the formation of the state. Growing transnational relations go hand in hand with a state-building process because of the interweaving of transnational factors and governmental action. In another chapter, Grant Evans underlines in his study of the Southern Chinese borders, that because of local complexities, among others, borders, however fixed they seem, are always involved in broader social and economic processes that constitute these borders over time. And he concludes that from the micro-movements of an ethnic minority, to the macro-movement of the Mekong, the Southern borders of China remain in a state of flux.

Besides, social behavior in contemporary China is far from being driven by rationality and the satisfaction of individual interests. For example, it seems impossible to understand the forms taken by "economic

modernization" without taking into account the role of moral values.
Economic activities take place within a social environment organized
around a certain conception of the world and based on a common experience. In particular the importance of the notion of "group" (whatever
their "grounds": familial, clientelist, affinitary, and so on) must be rein-
troduced at the center of our analysis and without neglecting the nonu-
tilitarist and purely imaginative aspects of the collective entities.[16] Social
behavior cannot be reduced to clear patterns as utilitarist and authentic
motivations cannot be separated. It is particularly true in the case of relations (*guanxi*) that play such an important role in socioeconomic life. As
Kipnis states: "In *guanxi*, feeling and instrumentality are a totality."[17]

Is the West an Exception? Problems of Methodology

The incapability of the evolutionist/functionalist approach to go beyond
paradoxical explanations gives a very strange image of Chinese society.
It is considered as an exception to all others. But more fundamentally, it
could be fruitful to call into question bluntly the very validity of this
paradigm to analyze changes at large. In other words, does this approach
fit into the context—the Western world—from which it has emerged?
The answers given by some authors to this question are far from being
positive. In particular, historical sociology and economic sociology tend
to show that these norms can be questioned even for Western countries.
The "openness" of the thinking of some of the prominent representatives of this school is particularly useful for those who want to go beyond
the evolutionist/functionalist/culturalist paradigms. Polanyi for example
highlights the "overlapping" between political power and economic
development all along the emergence of capitalism in Great Britain. For
him capitalism is politically instituted:

> It can be personified as the action of two organizing principles in
> society, each of them setting itself specific institutional aims, having
> the support of definite social forces and using its own distinctive
> methods. The one was the principle of economic liberalism, aiming
> at the establishment of a self-regulating market, relying on the sup-
> port of the trading classes, and using largely *laissez-faire* and free
> trade as its methods; the other was the principle of social protection
> aiming at conservation of man and nature as well as productive
> organization, relying on the varying support of those most imme-
> diately affected by the deleterious action of the market—primarily,
> but not exclusively, the working and the landed classes—and using

protective legislation, restrictive associations, and other instruments of intervention as its methods.[18]

In clear opposition to a discourse that emphasizes the role of legal procedures in Western societies, Wallerstein insists on the importance of the use of violence and illegal means in the functioning of capitalism,[19] while Thompson lays stress on the role of a "moral economy" to explain economic behavior.[20] In capitalist societies, economic rationality is determined by immaterial purposes, and not only by material purposes.

Yet, the approach of historical sociological studies is not limited to the stresses put on facts, which contradict orthodoxy. They propose new elements of methodology. According to Theda Skocpol, the authors involved in historical sociological studies can be defined by the following points: "[T]hey ask questions about social structures or processes understood to be concretely situated in time and space. Second, they address processes over time, and take temporal sequences seriously in accounting for outcomes. Third, most historical analyses attend to the interplay of meaningful actions and structural contexts, in order to make sense of the unfolding of unintended as well as intended outcomes in individual lives and social transformations. Finally, historical sociological studies highlight the *particular* and *varying* features of specific kinds of social structures and patterns of change. [...] For them, the world's past is not seen as a unified development story or as a set of standardized sequences. Instead, it is understood that groups or organizations have chosen, or stumbled into, varying paths in the past. Earlier 'choices,' in turn, both limit and open up alternative possibilities for further change, leading toward no predetermined end."[21]

Thompson remarks that there is a silence "as to cultural and moral mediations, as to the ways in which human being is imbricated in particular, determined productive relations, the way these material experiences are handled by them in cultural ways, the way in which there are certain value-systems that are consonant with certain modes of production and productive relations which are inconceivable without consonant value-systems."[22] In other words, productive relations and cultural values are dependent variables. Polanyi insists on the necessity to consider all human behaviors as socially shaped by material and ideal interests, which are impossible to distinguish. Social arrangements are generated by belief systems and different structural possibilities.[23]

The contributions of the economic sociology are very close to those of historical sociology. For Mark Granovetter and Richard Swedberg, the common core of the central propositions of economic sociology are the following: "1—Economic action is a form of social action; 2—economic action is socially situated; and 3—economic institutions are social constructions."[24] Such an approach is particularly useful in examining China. The first proposition points out that, from a sociological perspective, "economic action cannot, in principle, be separated from the quest for approval, status, sociability, and power."[25] Its relevance is demonstrated in this book by Dorothy Solinger's chapter, though she does not refer explicitly to Granovetter and Swedberg. According to Solinger: "The transition from the state allocation of labor to labor deployment by market demand has been path-dependent." When explaining this paradox, she shows that the State has to deal with contradictory and noneconomic objectives "to reduce the drain on the state's resources while honoring an elite within the furloughed workforce." As a consequence, policies introduce a "system of quotas" for unemployment and reemployment, which leads to a multiplication of the categories of unemployed. "The reliance on command-economy methodologies means, then, that there is no necessary relationship between who should be cut and who is cut, nor between who needs welfare relief and who gets it." Likewise, Thireau and Hua criticize in this volume the fact that the new independence provided to rural inhabitants by institutional changes is often stressed from the economic perspective. For them, it should be remembered that such independence stems also from the major political changes introduced at the end of the seventies and without which such reforms would have been unthinkable such as the abandoning of the concept of class struggle.

Swedberg and Granovetter also state that economic action is socially situated in the sense that it "is embedded in ongoing networks of personal relationships rather than being carried out by atomized actors. [...] An action of a member of a network is *embedded* because it is expressed in interaction with other people."[26] In the field of international relations, Mengin shows in this volume that transnational activities are no exception to social activities generally. For instance, although Taiwanese businessmen, as atomized actors, try to free themselves from governmental regulations when investing on the Chinese Mainland and therefore call into question Taipei's Mainland policy, they also partake in the working-out of the latter as they form interest groups articulating policy demands. Therefore, she suggests that rather than focusing on the forming of a transnational society, one should analyze the various processes that alter individual strategies into collective ones, as well as the embedding of the latter in power relations.

One can also refer here to Solinger or to Rocca when they show that policies aiming at sacking workers of the public sector are far from being based on a purely economic rationality. They are largely influenced by extra-economic goals such as the necessity to respect social stability and official ideology.

Finally, the third proposition of Swedberg and Granovetter states that "economic institutions are social constructions" and are not systematically the most efficient from the point of view of economic rationality. They are constructed by mobilization of resources through social networks. From these central propositions, the different studies related to economic sociology lay stress upon different topics, which are usually neglected. In particular, they insist on the influence of networks on the functioning of "markets" and on the role of irrational choices in economic activities.[27] For instance in this volume, Guiheux shows that the embeddedness of economic activity in social relationships has proved to be capable of producing its own sources of allocative efficiency. The "family" firm is not a type of organization doomed to be replaced by more modern organizational types: close relational bonds allow the creation and the management of large and modern firms. Furthermore, he shows that social ties can be contracted and extended: networks have no explicit boundaries and the absence of clear boundaries allows a person to extend his or her network ties to another person with whom they have no preset relationship. Here again, this case study confirms that capitalism pours into traditional social relations without abrupt change.

More generally, there is also an embeddedness of cultural constructs into power relations. In Manuel Castell's words: "[C]ultural codes are embedded in the social structure in such a way that the possession of these codes opens the access to the power structure."[28] In this respect, and studying how nation-states articulate with capitalism in late modernity, Aihwa Ong explores the flexible practices, strategies, and disciplines associated with transnational capitalism and seeks to identify the new modes of subject making, the new kinds of valorized subjectivity. In a more Foucauldian approach, the embeddedness of cultural constructs into power relations is also at stake when Castells postulates "new styles of governmentality, in which different categories of citizens are treated according to their ability to serve market competitiveness."[29]

Furthermore, it is also useful to take into account the analysis done by Cornelius Castoriadis of what he calls "the imaginary institution of the society." For him, a society is determined by the "imaginary" of its members. The imaginary is not an image or a production of social realities; on the contrary to a certain extent it creates the realities: "History is impossible and inconceivable outside of the productive or creative imagination [...] as this is manifested indissolubly in both historical *doing* and in the constitution, before any explicit rationality, of a universe of *significations.*"[30] The imaginary is itself a production of the previous societies, of the natural element of the human condition, and of the social imaginary of the period. As a consequence it is not possible to "theorize" a society from an external point of view from this society. Moreover, as all aspects of social life are determined by the imaginary of the time, it is impossible to distinguish different spheres and to assume the existence of a hierarchy between them. For example, the category of "market economy" is neither the expression of the real nature of the economy nor the best solution found to create wealth; rather it is the production of a social imaginary historically defined:

> What is capitalism? An innumerable host of things, facts, events, acts, ideas, representations, machines, institutions, significations, results— that we can, somehow or other, carry back to a few institutions and to a few nuclear or germinal significations. These institutions and these significations, however, are—would have been—effectively impossible outside of the actual temporality established by capitalism, outside of this particular mode of society's self-alteration that irrupts with, in and through capitalism and that, finally in a sense *is* capitalism.[31]

This imaginary presents two indissociable levels:

> On one level of its actuality, capitalist time is the time of incessant rupture, of recurrent catastrophes, of revolutions, of perpetually being torn away from what already exists. [...] On another level of its actuality, capitalist time is the time of accumulation, of universal linearization, of digestion-assimilation, of making the dynamic static, of the effective suppression of otherness, of immobility in perpetual 'change,' of the tradition of the new, of the shift from 'ever more' to 'more of the same,' of the destruction of signification, of powerlessness at the heart of power, of a power that empties itself out as it extends over a wider range.[32]

This vision of capitalism fits perfectly with the feeling of a modernization process dominated by contradictory phenomena. The introduction of capitalist norms is also the introduction of the contradiction of capitalism between a constructive side and a destructive side, between the importance of tradition and the acceleration of change. In contemporary China, the introduction of the imaginary of capitalism has led to a fantastic acceleration of time and then a series of insoluble contradictions.

As Rocca states in this volume, the permeability of China to external economic patterns and economic changes and the rapidity of the indigenous modernization process lead the Chinese economy to experience at one time the three stages of the evolution of capitalist labor, that is to say: primitive capitalism, industrial capitalism, and postindustrial capitalism. At the very moment one form is emerging, a new one calls it into question. Not only does this simultaneity contribute to deeply reshaping the overall structures of the society, but it also creates contradictions within employment policies and political discourse, and between social groups.

The danger that emerges from the "work" of calling into question the functionalist/evolutionist approach is to limit the reflection to a deconstruction. In this case, it is difficult to avoid the postmodernist tautology describing societies as aggregations of networks and of flows of relationships, while individuals are "floating" from one network to another one. Here, we are not very far from the discourse of the disappearance of reality and the triumph of virtuality. In parallel, stresses on the "imaginary" or the "moral economy" could also lead to a return to a culturalist approach.[33]

In order to avoid this pitfall, it is important to lay stress on different points: the intertwining between the imaginary and reality; the central part played by struggles between social actors; the persisting hierarchization of powers. Firstly, the imaginary is not floating over reality. As Migdal states, "Attempting to distinguish whether peasants act according to a 'moral economy,' emphasizing the symbolic configurations, or are 'rational actors' driven only by material needs is a futile exercise; it loses sight of the integration of the material and the moral. [...] All people combine available symbols with opportunities to solve mundane needs for food, housing, and the like to create their *strategies of survival*."[34]

The imaginary contributes to structure the reality through the active role of models of action. For example, the functional state is not determined by its functions, but by a certain model of state's action. Even if the complete control of the state on society is a utopia, this utopia has an influence on the reality. Still, even if "the markets" do not function on the base of the so-called market, the market ideology has undoubtedly an effect on the political economy.

Likewise, the debate over a possible "Westernization" of the world should not be understood according to a polarized view: the adoption versus the reject of so-called "Western models." A complex and often paradoxical process links models and reality. Some authors have demonstrated that what can be perceived as a rejection of alien (or "imported") models is, in fact, a complex process of hybridization that dismisses any reasoning in terms of "extraneity." In Jean-François Bayart's words, "historical fields of intra-continental and intercontinental interaction have contributed to the distinct historicity of societies in Africa and Asia; diminishing the usefulness of the over-arching binary distinctions between East and West, and North and South."[35] Even in the case of colonialists that effectively acted as a demiurge, "they did not do so *ex nihilo;* and colonial creations were also subject to multiple acts of reappropriation by indigenous social groups."[36]

In order to better understand this process of "appropriation," Jean-François Bayart lays stress on the overwhelming importance of the distinction drawn by Bruce Berman and John Lonsdale between "state building" and "state formation." The former refers to a conscious effort at creating an apparatus of control; but political change is also the result of "conflicts, negotiations and compromises between diverse groups" (i.e., state formation).[37] This distinction is, in fact, a methodological position that allows us to analyze the interaction of what comes "from above" and what comes "from below." When analyzing growing Sino-Taiwanese exchange and the apparent contradiction existing between economics and politics in a context of contending sovereignties, the chapter by Mengin uses this distinction as a methodological framework. Understanding state formation as a historical process whose outcome is a "largely unconscious and contradictory process of conflicts"[38] helps to explain the interweaving of transnational factors and governmental action, and how a nation–state (Taiwan) is reshaped by growing transnational relations rather than undermined by the latter. Dealing respectively with rural and urban areas, the chapter by Thireau and Hua, as well as that by Rocca illustrate this conflicting and moving meeting of logics from below and from above.

Secondly, the analysis must focus on struggles between social actors. Social life is not a world of soft adjustments and of fair negotiations but a struggle for social controls over political and economic wealth. Yet the actors are neither atomized individuals nor groups stifled in ossified imaginaries and practices. They are what Joel Migdal calls "social organizations": "Informal and formal organizations are the settings within which people have had structured, regularized interactions with others. These organizations—all the clans, clubs, and communities—have used a variety of sanctions, rewards, and symbols to induce people to behave in their interactions between father and son, employer and employee, landlord and tenant, priest and parishioner, and so on."[39]

The state can be considered as a social organization:

[T]he groups exercising social control in a society may be heterogeneous both in their form (for example, a small family and a sprawling tribal organization) and in the rules they apply (for example, based on personal loyalty and founded on profit maximization). [...] [T]he distribution of social control in society may be among numerous, fairly autonomous groups rather than concentrated largely in the state. In other words, the over-all sum of authority may be high in the society, but the exercising of that authority may be fragmented. In this mélange, the state has been one organization among many.[40]

It is particularly true in the contemporary period, where social concerns are put at the center of the political arena. This "rise of the social,"[41] or this interpenetration between the society and the state, leads the state to stay on the sidelines of the battlefield and, at the same time, to be a battlefield. Some chapters of the present volume show that in very different contexts, state and social strategies cannot be separated. Evans emphasizes an interweaving between state and nonstate logics in the definition of borders. Solinger and Rocca reveal the richness of the strategies of survival used by the unemployed to answer to public policies, Wank the variety of means used by entrepreneurs to obtain practical power, and Mengin the growing involvement of Taiwanese large firms in politics generated by the progressive implementation of popular sovereignty in Taiwan.

These different theoretical elements compel us in *Politics in China: Moving Frontiers* to emphasize again the importance of frontiers between the territories—certainly in a metaphorical sense—controlled by social organizations. These frontiers are continually reshaped, particularly when the structures of society are called into question by new social forces. China is precisely in that situation. Internal evolution and external influence redefine all power legitimacy, sources of power, and moral approaches to the economy, and so on. What is at stake is the control over new territories, and more specifically new frontiers as the reshaping process creates opportunities to take advantage of the blurring of the old ones. The setting in motion of social dynamics has called into question the structural segmentation of the Chinese society. The ancient separation between rural and urban population led to the emergence of two territories in geographical but also social terms (labor, status). Now, through migration, the two territories are reshaped and different

questions emerged: control over migrants, exploitation of the differential
in terms of cost of labor, control over jobless people (see the chapters by
Solinger, Davin, and Lee). For their part, Thireau and Hua in their chapter show that rural cadres cannot be considered as a coherent and homog-
enous group clearly delineated from the individuals they administer.

As to the frontier between money and politics, Tak-Wing Ngo wonders
in this volume about the surprisingly low level of popularity of the new
Hong Kong SAR government, given the fact that the SAR government
has been trying painstakingly to uphold the freedom enjoyed by the people, to maintain a good relationship with Beijing, to offer business incentives for investment, and to reform social services for the provision of
community welfare. Ngo argues that the answer lies in the fact that Hong
Kong's transition to Chinese rule has been accompanied by a change in
government-business relations: the relationship between money and
power changed from collaboration to collusion. The SAR political system
charted out by the Basic Law preserves the domination of business without institutionalizing a mechanism to check business power. Ngo shows
that not only can business interests veto pro-labor policies and marginalize popular sector influence, but they can also exchange political support
with personal gains.

Thirdly, and finally, the emphasis on the heterogeneity of social organizations presupposes a hierarchy of powers. Of course, the most fruitful
analysis of power in the modern world insists on the continuity of power
relations over the whole of society. According to Foucault, power relations take root in the whole of the social network.[42] All power relations
refer to the state as a model because of the historical process of statization of society but they do not stem from the state. For Hannah Arendt,
the concomitant destruction of public and private spheres and the
"rise of the social" characterize modern societies. Habermas identifies
modernity with a double process of statization of the society and of
socialization of the state.[43] Put like that, this approach can lead to a nonhierarchical conception of power. Whatever the social structure in
question—family, enterprise, state, and so on—power relations would be
of the same nature. The definition given by Yang of "rhizome" is a good
example of this kind of conception. For her rhizomatic networks are
nonhierarchical systems produced by circulation of constant flows of
relations between people without a leading power being in command.
Individuals are the basic cells of the different power and they come and
go freely between these nonhierarchical powers.[44]

However, the decreasing gap between state and society does not mean
that hierarchies of power do not exist anymore. First of all, the state has

not disappeared. On this point Foucault's conception is far more complex than it is usually assumed as revealed by his definition of governmentality (see above). In the concept of governmentality, political power (the power on population and territories) is the real subject of his analysis of power. The state is still a determining element of social control not anymore in term of statization of society but of "managing of population."[45]

Besides, in response to this postmodern approach of power, it must be remembered that societies are profoundly unequal. On the contrary to Appadurai, who "gives the misleading impression that everyone can take equal advantage of mobility and modern communications and that transnationality has been liberatory, in both a spatial and a political sense, for all peoples,"[46] Aihwa Ong shows that "in translocal strategies of accumulation, the migrant's ability to convert economic capital into social prestige is limited by the ethnoracial moral order of the host society."[47] In this volume, the chapter by Thireau and Hua clearly shows that, depending on his familial and personal characteristics and his relations with segments of local bureaucracy, an individual has not the same access to new "mediatisation spaces." In the same perspective, Solinger analyses the layering of statuses of the unemployed created by policies aiming at reducing public employment. From workers enjoying basic allowances and preferential reemployment treatment at the peak, to the peasants without jobs at the bottom, the gap in living conditions is immense and increasing.

The objective of this book is neither to provide a new and complete framework of analysis, nor to get the reader bogged down in eclecticism, but merely to propose paths for further research. For the time being, no conclusion, even temporary, will be drawn from the various analyses presented in this book. One can only hint that the difference vis-à-vis the pre-reformist China is maybe that the objective is less to control the frontiers than to exploit the frontiers. The mere existence of borders— between countries, systems, or administrative entities—brings about differences that in turn produce wealth through trade, investment, migration, smuggling, and social differentiation.

Notes

1. *Wealth and Labor in China: Cross-cutting Approaches of Present Developments* (Paris, Centre for International Studies and Research, Sciences Po) December 6–7, 1999. Besides the multiform assistance of this research center, this volume has benefited from the help of David Camroux whom we wish to thank here.

2. Lucian W. Pye, *The Spirit of Chinese Politics* (Cambridge, Mass. and London: Harvard University Press, 1992); *The Mandarin and the Cadre*. *China's Political Cultures* (Michigan: University of Michigan Press, 1988).

3. "The glow of Chinese Fraternity" is well analyzed by Aihwa Ong in "Chinese Modernities: Narratives of Nation and of Capitalism," in *Undergrounded Empires. The Cultural Politics of Modern Chinese Transnationalism*, eds Aihwa Ong, and Donald Nonini (London and New York: Routledge, 1997): 179–182.

4. Yang, Mayfair Mei-hui, *Gifts, Favors, and Banquets: The Art of Social Relationships in China* (Ithaca, New York: Cornell University Press, 1994).

5. Yves Chevrier, "L'empire distendu: esquisse du politique en Chine des qing à Deng Xiaoping," (The loose state: an outline of Chinese politics from the Qing to Deng Xiaoping) in *La greffe de l'Etat* (The graft of the state), ed. Jean-François Bayart (Paris: Karthala, 1996): 263–395.

6. Hans Antlöv, and Tak-Wing Ngo (eds), *The Cultural Construction of Politics in Asia* (London: Curzon Press, 2000): vii.

7. Ibid., viii.

8. Classic modernization theory is well represented by Seymour M. Lipset, "Some Social Prerequisites of Democracy and Political Legitimacy," *American Political Science Review* 53, 1 (March 1959): 69–105; Gabriel A. Almond, and James S. Coleman (eds), *The Politics of the Developing Areas* (Princeton, N.J.: Princeton University Press, 1960); and of course Barrington Moore, *Social Origins of Dictatorship and Democracy: Lord and Peasant in the Making of the Modern World* (Boston: Beacon Press, 1966).

9. See Thomas B. Gold, "Party-state versus Society in China," in *Building a Nation-State: China After Forty Years*, ed. J. K. Kallgren (Berkeley: University of California Press/Institute of East Asian Studies/Center for Chinese Studies, 1990); David Strand, "Protest in Beijing: Civil Society and Public Sphere in China," *Problems of Communism* 39, 3 (1990): 1–19; Martin Whyte, "Urban China: A Civil Society in the Making?" in *State and Society in China. The Consequences of Reform*, ed. Arthur Rosenbaum (Boulder, Co.: Westview Press, 1992).

10. On this issue see below.

11. David L. Wank, *Commodifying Communism: Business, Trust, and Politics in a Chinese City* (New York: Cambridge University Press, 1999); Margaret M. Pearson, *China's New Business Elite. The Political Consequences of Economic Reform* (Berkeley: University of California Press, 1997); Dorothy Solinger, *Contesting Citizenship in Urban China: Peasant Migrants, the State, and the Logic of the Market* (Berkeley: University of California Press, 1999).

12. Jean C. Oi, "The Role of the Local State in China's Transitional Economy," *The China Quarterly* 144 (December 1995): 1132–1149; "Fiscal Reform and the Economic Foundations of Local State Corporatism in China," *World Politics* 45 (October 1992): 99–126; *Rural China Takes Off, Institutional Foundations of Economic Reform* (Berkeley: University of California Press, 1999); Christopher C. Findlay, Andrew Watson, and Harry X. Wu (eds), *Rural Enterprises in China* (Basingstoke: Macmillan/New York: St. Martin's Press, 1994); Samuel P. S. Ho, *Rural China in Transition. Non-agricultural Development in Rural Jiangsu, 1978–1990* (Oxford: Clarendon Press, 1994); Ole Odgaard, *Private Entreprises in Rural China. Impact on Agriculture and Social Stratification* (Aldershot: Avebury, 1992); Jane Duckett, *The Entrepreneurial State in China. Real Estate and Commerce Departments in Reform Era Tianjin* (London and New York: Routledge, 1998).

13. Barry Naughton, *Growing out of the Plan. Chinese Economic Reform, 1978–1993* (Cambridge: Cambridge University Press, 1995).

14. See Chu, Hai-yuan, "Taiwanese Society in Transition: Reconciling Confucianism and Pluralism," in *The Other Taiwan: 1945 to the Present*, ed. Murray A. Rubinstein (Armonk, N.Y.: M.E. Sharpe, 1994): 93.

15. Jean-Louis Rocca, "Corruption and its Shadow: An Anthropological View of Corruption in China," *The China Quarterly* 130 (June 1992): 401–416.

16. Yang, *Gifts, Favors, and Banquets*; Andrew B. Kipnis, *Producing Guanxi. Sentiment, Self, and Subculture in a North China Village* (Durham: Duke University Press, 1997); Yan, Yunxiang, *The Flow of Gifts. Reciprocity and Social Networks in a Chinese Village* (Stanford: Stanford University Press, 1996).

17. Kipnis, *Producing Guanxi*, 23.

18. Karl Polanyi, *The Great Transformation* (New York: Rinehart, 1944): 132.

19. Immanuel Wallerstein, *The Modern World-System: Capitalist Agriculture and the Origins of the European World-Economy in the Sixteenth Century* (New York: Academic Press, 1974); *The Capitalist Word-Economy: Essays* (Cambridge: Cambridge University Press, 1979); *The Modern World-System II: Mercantilism and the Consolidation of the European World-Economy 1600–1750* (New York: Academic Press, 1980).

20. Edward P. Thompson, *Customs in Common* (New York: The Free Press, 1991).

21. Theda Skocpol, "Sociology's Historical Imagination," in *Vision and Method in Historical Sociology*, ed. Theda Skocpol (Cambridge: Cambridge University Press, 1984): 1–2. Underlined in the original.

22. Michael Merril, "Interview with E.P Thompson," *Radical History Review* 3, 4 (1976): 4–25.

23. Karl Polanyi, *Primitive, Archaic, and Modern Economies* (New York: Doubleday Anchor, 1968); and *The Livelihood of Man* (New York: Academic Press, 1977).

24. Mark Granovetter, and Richard Swedberg (eds), *The Sociology of Economic Life* (Boulder, Co.: Westview Press, 1992): 6.

25. Ibid., 7.

26. Ibid., 9.

27. Robert G. Eccles, and Dwight B. Crane, *Doing Deals: Investment Banks at Work* (Boston: Harvard Business Scholl, 1988). Olivier Williamson, *Markets and Hierarchies: Analysis and Antitrust Implications* (New York: Free Press, 1975); William Domhoff, *The Higher Circles* (New York: Random House, 1971); Mark Mizruchi, and Michael Schwatz (eds), *Intercorporate Relations: The Structural Analysis of Business* (Cambridge: Cambridge University Press, 1987).

28. Manuel Castells, *Rise of the Network Society*, volume 1 of *The Information Age* (Oxford: Basil Blackwell, 1996): 416, cited by Aihwa Ong, *Flexible Citizenship, The Cultural Logics of Transnationality* (Durham and London: Duke University Press, 1999): 159.

29. Ibid., 225. By governmentality, Foucault means three things "1—The ensemble formed by the institutions, procedures, analyses and reflections, the calculations and tactics that allow the exercise of this very specific albeit complex form of power, as its principal form of knowledge political economy, and as its essential technical means apparatuses of security. 2—The tendency which, over a long period and throughout the West, has steadily led towards the pre-eminence over all forms (sovereignty, discipline, etc.) of this type of power which may be termed government, resulting, on the one hand, in the formation of a whole series of specific governmental apparatuses, and on the other, in the development of a whole complex of *savoirs*. 3—The process, or rather the result of the process, through which the state of justice of the Middle Ages, transformed into the administrative state during the fifteenth and sixteenth, gradually becomes 'governmentalized.' " In Graham Burchell, Colin Gordon and Peter Miller, *The Foucault Effect. Studies in Governmentality* (London: Harvester Wheatsheaf, 1991): 102 and 103.

30. Cornelius Castoriadis, *The Imaginary Signification of Society* (Cambridge: Polity Press, 1997): 46.

31. Ibid., 206 and 207.

32. Ibid., 207.

33. Yang, *Gifts, Favors, and Banquets;* and Kipnis, *Producing Guanxi.*

34. Joel S. Migdal, *Strong Societies and Weak States: State-Society Relations and State Capabilities in the Third World* (Princeton, N. J.: Princeton University Press, 1988): 27.

35. Jean-François Bayart, "Finishing with the Idea of the Third World: The Concept of the Political Trajectory," in *Rethinking Third World Politics*, ed. James Manor (London and New York: Longman, 1991): 53.

36. Ibid., 52.
37. Bruce Berman and John Lonsdale, *Unhappy Valley, Conflict in Kenya and Africa* (London: James Currey, Nairobi: Heinemann Kenya, Athens (Ohio): Ohio University Press, 1992): 5. See also chapter 2 by John Lonsdale, "The Conquest State of Kenya, 1895–1905," 13–44.
38. Ibid., 5.
39. Migdal, *Strong Societies and Weak States*, 25. Underlined in original.
40. Ibid., 28–29.
41. Hannah Arendt, *The Human Condition* (Chicago and London: University of Chicago Press, 1958).
42. "[L]es relations de pouvoir s'enracinent dans l'ensemble du réseau social." Michel Foucault, "Le pouvoir, comment s'exerce-t-il?" (Power, how is it exercised?), in *Michel Foucault, un parcours philosophique, (Beyond Structuralism and Hermeneutics), 1982–1983,* Hubert Dreyfus and Paul Rabinovitch (Chicago, University of Chicago Press, 1984): 318.
43. Jürgen Habermas, *The Structural Transformation of the Public Sphere: An Inquiry into a Category of Bourgeois Society* (Cambridge: Polity Press, 1989).
44. See, in particular, Yang, *Gifts, Favors, and Banquets.*
45. Burchell, Gordon, and Miller, *The Foucault Effect,* 102.
46. Ong, *Flexible Citizenship,* 11.
47. Ibid., 25.

PART I

Reshaping Labor

CHAPTER ONE

"Three at Once": The Multidimensional Scope of Labor Crisis in China

JEAN-LOUIS ROCCA

Since 1994, due to important redundancies in state-owned enterprises, China has undergone a sharp and cumulative increase of unemployed people. In 1997, the recognition by the Party Congress of the necessity of modernizing the public sector and of making it profitable has even more accelerated the trend. However, though many journalists and scholars have mentioned this unemployment crisis as a turning point in the process of the reform policy, very few attempts have been made to evaluate the nature and the consequences of this new trend. The increase in unemployment is generally perceived as an unavoidable consequence of the growing influence of the norms of capitalism on Chinese economy. In the present "economic system," labor must respect accurate specifications in terms of quantity and quality, productivity and cost. Consequently, the socialist system of production using a nonmarketized and nonproductive workforce cannot survive. In other words, the Chinese labor force would be experiencing the same kind of transformation the European labor force did in the eighteenth and nineteenth centuries, that is to say a process of marketization.

My hypothesis is that this analysis, which fits with the ideology of liberal economy, is only a part of the story. If the present labor crisis is a consequence of the introduction of the norms of capitalist labor, it is also a product of the rapid mutation of this capitalist labor itself that, like in Western countries, seems to go through three stages. The first one has taken place in new economic sectors where "primitive capitalist" labor conditions have been introduced all along the 1980s: rural industry, private sector, foreign enterprises, and so on. In these sectors, the use of labor corresponds to a formal submission of labor to capital.[1] The workers are exploited, "as they are," and then still deeply influenced by their local origins. Labor conditions, though very different from those dominating in state-owned enterprises (SOE), remain characterized by the still determinant influence of the social origin of the workers. In particular, localistic and kinship networks are essential components of the labor market and of the organization of the labor process.[2] The production regime is very close to what Buravoy calls "market despotism" in which "labor process" and "political and ideological apparatuses of production"[3] are mainly based on the use of coercion. The reproduction of labor force takes place in the process of production with very few interventions of the state. At this stage, capitalism has been limited to enclaves while the great majority of workers—mainly SOEs workers—have escaped to the marketization of labor.

Today, after hardly two decades of development, this first stage is called into question by a global reassessment of the status of labor. First of all, the SOEs workers are not spared anymore by the introduction in China of the categories of capitalist labor. They are confronted with a process of labor rationalization that has led to massive lay-offs and, for those who have kept their jobs, new labor conditions and new remuneration systems defined by pre-taylorist principles. Secondly, in certain primitive capitalist sectors a phenomenon of intensification of labor has been taking place that contributes to a decrease in the influence of societal elements in the definition of workers' status. We are witnessing here a process of modernization of Chinese capitalism in which it goes from a formal submission of labor to a real submission of labor to capital.[5] In this process, labor tends to be less an external element of the process of production than an integrated part of the scientific technical apparatuses. At the same time, the growing intervention of the state changes the nature of the production regime. The market despotism is replaced by a "hegemonic regime" characterized by the intervention of the state in the reproduction of the labor force.[6] Through social insurance legislation and the effects of public policies aiming to develop collective bargaining, the workers' interests are coordinated to those of capital.

The process of development of capitalism is not only led by the rationality of the profit. It has an economic aspect (the integration of labor force as a mere element of scientific methods of production) but also a political side, that is to say the building of a welfare state in order to control the political aftermath of the hegemonic control. As in every other kind of society, in capitalist societies economic actions are embedded in social relations: "1—Economic action is a form of social action; 2—economic action is socially situated; and 3—economic institutions are social constructions."[7] In industrial capitalism, economic sphere does not become an autonomous deus ex machina, dominating the society; the rationality of both political and economic actions have to be found in the evolving characteristics of social relations.

The present unemployment crisis is mainly a consequence of the evolution of the Chinese capitalism to the second stage. It is not surprising if we remember that the specificities of the contradictions of "market despotism" involve the intervention of the state. According to Polanyi, although the commodification of labor is of absolute necessity for the capitalism it is also its most obvious weakness as no sooner was market society institutionalized than a counter-movement appeared that aims to protect the society from the "excess" of the market logic (in terms of remuneration, flexibility, unemployment, and so on).[8] Thus, the history of capitalism is characterized by "two organizing principles in society":

> The one was the principle of economic liberalism, aiming at the establishment of a self-regulating market, relying on the support of the trading classes, and using largely *laissez-faire* and free trade as its methods; the other was the principle of social protection aiming at conservation of man and nature as well as productive organization, relying on the varying support of those most immediately affected by the deleterious action of the market—primarily, but not exclusively, the working and the landed classes—and using protective legislation, restrictive associations, and other instruments of intervention as its methods.[9]

Consequently, the emphasis recently put on social legislation by the Chinese state can be considered as an attempt to build a welfare state in order to limit the consequences of the labor rationalization. However, the building of a welfare state in China takes place in a very specific situation. Whereas welfare states in Europe appeared in a context of (and in response to) rapid growth of employment opportunities and active resistance of workers movements against labor exploitation, the Chinese state has to build a welfare system in a situation of unemployment and a low level of "market despotism." In other terms, the question at stake in China is not the one of a transition between market despotism and hegemonic regime (Buravoy) or of the appearance of a counter-movement of the social forces affected by the deleterious action of the market (Polanyi).

The attempt made by the Chinese regime to build a welfare state takes place in a situation of impressive slow-down of the manufacturing sector as a whole and of deep change in the nature and in the role of labor in Chinese society. It seems that Chinese society is experiencing, like many developed countries,[10] the emergence of a "post-industrial capitalism." Not only does intensification in the use of labor diminish the part of labor in production cost in industry but the service sector itself is experiencing a process of rationalization of labor that limits the use of labor and particularly the use of non-highly-qualified workers. In China, labor opportunities tend to decrease to a great extent and, as a consequence, the labor force witnesses a situation of uncertainties, revealed for example by the development of petty or temporary jobs and the spreading of "flexibility" in urban areas. The workplace does not provide any more social identities and personal protection to urban dwellers.

The permeability of China to external economic patterns and economic changes and the rapidity of the indigenous modernization process lead the Chinese economy to experiment "at once" the three stages of the evolution of the capitalist labor. Not only does this simultaneity contribute to deeply reshaping the overall structures of the society but it also creates contradictions within employment policies and political discourse, and between social groups. The seriousness of the crisis makes labor and employment one of the most important questions at stake in the political arena and challenges the political equilibrium in urban areas. In particular, the postindustrial capitalism is linked to a new kind of social state whose borders are constantly changing. Here we come very close to the assessments of scholars who question the classical weberian approach of the state in terms of clearly defined public and private spheres, legal and illegal activities, and so on.[11]

Finally, my intention is not to neglect the internal agenda, even if it appears sometimes as a simple constraint according to the importance of external pressure. Chinese economy has its own pace of evolution and in terms of regional disparities, political struggles, state policies and social stratification, what had happened during the pre-reformist period is not without consequences on the present environment. The general configurations of reform policies as well as the reactions of the social actors to the new challenges constitute key elements in the process of understanding the present reshaping of labor. For example, the status of labor introduced by the socialist regime in the 50s explains to a great extent the strategy adopted by the reform policy in the first years of the reforms: "bypass" of the *danwei* system, introduction of the capitalist labor with caution and in the fringes of the economy. However, my intention is not to consider the changes in labor relations as a mere consequence of the impact of economic reforms on the socialist legacy. The Chinese "capitalism" has evolved all along the reform period in response to internal and external stimuli that can be considered only as mere consequences of socialist legacy.

Urban Workers as a Working Class?

The status of urban labor during the socialist period was very particular. First of all, workers were not treated by employers as people without means of production and then compelled to sell their capacity to work. They were both workers *and* owners of means of production. Their duty were to develop state-owned productive forces in a framework from which any aspect of exploitation is supposed to have been eradicated. Secondly, workers were entirely dependent on working units (*danwei*), mainly big enterprises, administrations, and social organizations (schools, and so on). The dependence was not limited to the payment of a salary, whose level was generally not based on the intensity of work, but were concerning all aspects of social life (housing, social insurance, and so on). The life-tenure job was the rule.

Apparently, this system of *danwei* looks like the Western welfare system, in which an important part of the national workers are protected by a series of regulations and policies. In both cases, labor appears as a fundamental element of the social life. In the context of urban society, it was the only source of income and the only source of social identity. On this ground, a working-class identity has been gradually built, based on different values: importance given to skilled labor and priority given to security and labor experience. In the Chinese case, the characteristics of these values contributed to justify the analysis of Elizabeth Perry, who sees at the origin of the *danwei* system the influence of the "urban labor movements dominated by skilled artisans"[12] and in particular personalities like Chen Yun.[13] As a consequence, the Chinese working class corresponds to the second and third "levels (layers) of class" as they have been defined by Katznelson. Level two is characterized by the existence of "ways of life" specific to the working class, both at the workplace and in the community, and the third one by the fact that workers "formed groups, sharing dispositions," having "values of justice and goodness."[14]

Nevertheless, the absence of the two other levels of class as they are defined by Katznelson prevents us from considering Chinese workers as forming a working class. "The frost level is the structure of capitalist economic development, whose main elements include an economy based on privately owned autonomous firms that seek to make profit-maximizing decisions. These enterprises employ labor for a wage and sell what they produce in the market." He adds that "capitalism is unthinkable without proletarianization" and "is impossible without a quite specific mechanism of exploitation."[15] In China, instead of an objective relation linking the owner/manager of a capital and a worker whose labor must valorize the capital in exchange for a wage, we have a sort of administrative relation through which a worker is assigned to a *danwei* and paid without any consideration for his level of productivity. Of course, it is necessary to mention the fact that a number of urban workers were working in collective enterprises in which working conditions and living conditions were far from being as good as they are in a state-owned sector. Moreover, even in state enterprises, workers with temporary status were victims at certain periods of methods of exploitation. But, these categories represented a minority and their statuses were not comparable to the ones experienced by capitalist workers. Following Buravoy, in order to characterize these categories of workers it is probably more accurate to use the term "bureaucratic despotism" (where the capacity of bargaining resources are few) which he opposes to "bureaucratic bargaining."

Instead of the private appropriation and distribution of surplus through a market, the state socialist enterprise faces central appropriation and redistribution. Instead of competition among firms in the pursuit of profit, state socialist firms bargain with central planning agencies. Enterprises have greater or lesser capacity to extend concessions to their employees according to their bargaining power with the centre, linked to their monopoly of the production of key goods. The more centralized the economic system, the more important is the bargaining and the more there develops a dualism of factory regimes: bureaucratic despotism in the weaker sectors producing low-priority goods [...] and bureaucratic bargaining in the stronger sectors producing high priority goods.[16]

The fourth level concerned the existence of collective action. "Groups of people sharing motivational constructs [...] may or may not act collectively to transform dispositions to behavior."[17] According to Thompson, the working class is a historical production: "The factory hand or stockinger was also the inheritor of Bunyan, of remembered village rights, of notions of equality before the law. The working class made itself as much as it was made."[18] "Class happens when some men, as a result of common experiences (inherited or shared), feel and articulate the identity of their interests as between themselves, and as against other men whose interests are different from (and usually opposed to) theirs that one can speak of a "working class."[19] In the Chinese case, the working class lack this political dimension, as is revealed by its inability to launch and develop collective actions. Of course, during the socialist period, conflict arose in the factories, developing sometimes from economic demands to political protests. It was the case notably in the years 1956–57 and during and after the Cultural Revolution. However, what is striking in that kind of protest movement is the inability to develop *collective* action at a general level. The reason for this phenomenon lays probably in the fact that workers cannot "feel and articulate the identity of their interests as between themselves, and as against other men whose interests are different from (and usually opposed to) theirs." Enterprises are communities in charge of all aspects of social life. The objective of each community is not to create wealth but to achieve certain productive and political tasks. The added value by the economic process is not the produce of the labor process but the result of an abstract calculation made by the state. As Walder has shown, thanks to the concept of neo-traditionalism, the interests of *danwei's* cadres and workers are very close. "Party-sponsored networks cut across all the offices and workshops and all the occupational groups within a factory. Through time, some of the relationships within these networks have come to embody personal loyalties as well as more abstract loyalties to the organization and its doctrine."[20] Consequently, Chinese workers have no "enemies of class" as the "management" cannot be identified to owners of means of production and exploiters of labor. On the contrary they constitute a privileged social category and the *danwei* interests seem to override the class interests. Sheehan is right when she says that "conflict, often originating from economic grievances, but quickly developing into a political dispute as a result of the dominance of the party within enterprises, has been a far more common feature of industrial life in China than is generally recognized."[21] But precisely, when the workers' demands go beyond some basic material benefits, as workers' status is essentially political and not economic, they immediately meet the dangerous ground of politics, demanding a kind of collective self-management.

At the same time, the workers are themselves highly divided and "divisions within the labor force created by these political networks were just as real as those based on differences in skill, pay, or geographical origins and dialect group that have served as focal points of labor mobilization in an earlier era of the labor movement, and that in many cases were still potential bases of mobilization."[22] This splitting between the different statuses of *danwei* and between the different categories of workers (young/ old workers, skilled/unskilled, permanent/temporary) and the very different relations developed by the multiples segment of working people with the cadres prevent worker protest from becoming the base of a worker movement.

First Stage: Primitive Capitalism and Bypass Strategy

Until the beginning of 1990s, the system of *danwei* was not removed drastically. As the objective of the state was to avoid a direct confrontation with the urban population, the core of the urban economy has been bypassed and the introduction of the capitalist labor has taken place in new territories. Of course, some reforms were adopted. In 1986, the Bankruptcy Law allowed the closure of enterprises that were not able to pay their debts. The same year four regulations were adopted[23] that abolished the system of life-tenure job, gave the right to enterprises to dismiss employees, introduced unemployment insurance, and enabled the enterprises to hire employees. The rationalization of methods of production, the possibility of hiring labor force, and the spreading of the relations between remuneration and labor productivity have changed the situation of labor to a certain extent.[24]

But, as the failure of the introduction of the director responsibility system has shown,[25] the reluctance of workers, management, and local governments to introduce a real capitalist labor relation has impeded any radical change until the mid-1990s. As a result, between 1980 and 1994, more than half of the urban active population increase (62.9 million people) was absorbed by the public sector (31.9 million). The urban collective sector hired 8.6 million people, the individual sector 11.4 million and the private sector (including different types of foreign-investment enterprises) 11 million. In 1994, the "employees and workers of public economic units" (*guoyou jingji danwei zhigong*) were still representing 66.7 percent of the urban active population against 76.2 percent in 1980.[26] In the manufacturing sector where the reforms would have had a great impact, the change is of minor importance, as 30.5 percent of the workforce of this sector were "employees and workers of public economic units" in 1994 against 32.4 percent in 1980.[27]

Thus, a vicious circle is emerging: the bypass strategy puts a brake on the development of a labor market whose limits reduce its capacity of absorbing labor force. Besides, the reactions of the different social groups to this strategy have not been without influence on the slow growth of the nonpublic sector. First, the reluctance of the urban society toward the private sector as well as the difficulty for urban people to mobilize financial resources have contributed to the relatively small increase of the individual sector and of the private sector. Second, it is important to notice that even in these "capitalist" sectors the marketization of labor force has been far from being completed because of the impact of local norms and values on the structuration and development of the local economy.

The first enclave is the urban private sector. It has two dimensions, as it is formed of the "real" private sector (*siying*) and the individual sector (*geti*).[28] These two sectors employ 82.6 million people in 1999 (22.2 percent of the urban active population).[29] In the first one, the labor relation and the working conditions are clearly of a capitalist nature, but the number of people it employs is small: 17 million in 1999 (8 percent of the urban active population).[30] Of course, numerous studies tend to show that a part of the collective-owned units are managed, de facto, as private enterprises. But, on the contrary, it is interesting to notice that a great number of urban collective-owned enterprises are in the same situation as the SOEs and that an important proportion of their employees have been recently laid off.[31] The number of employees of the sector have declined from 36.28 million in 1991 to 17.1 million in 1999.[32]

As for the individual sector, it has to be divided into at least two subsections, the one controlled by the urban dwellers that concerns generally the most lucrative activities (clothes shops, for example) and the one in which migrants play a dominant role.[33] It is what Hill Gates calls a *petty capitalism*[34] "producing outsourced goods for larger firms, rearing children who as adolescents are lent to the formal sector as capable and low-cost labor, supplying cheap goods and services for each other and low-wage in all sectors." Nonetheless, in both cases, the scale of activities is generally very small and, above all, activities are capitalist in a very narrow way. The role played by the kinship and the regional networks distinguishes clearly this sector from the norm of universality the industrial capitalism introduces in the labor process. In capitalism, workers were not treated as individuals, and owners of means of production have no personal relationships with the persons they employ. In "petty capitalism," we have owners and workers, but the existence of personal ties linking the two prevent us from speaking in terms of working class and capitalism even under the form of despotism or formal submission of labor.[35]

The second enclave is the one that has been created by the foreign investment along the coast and notably in Guangdong and Fujian. It is constituted by foreign funded economic units (2.94 million employees in 1998), enterprises set up by Hong Kong and Taiwan companies (2.93 million employees) and collective enterprises or state-owned enterprises working as subcontractors for foreign enterprises.[36] Here, the labor relation and the working conditions are clearly capitalist, looking very closely to the norms of despotism.[37] Most female workers are rural migrants coming from remote places who can easily be victims of harsh exploitation.[38] They are forced "to work seven days a week, 12 hours a day, earning as little as 12 to 18 cents an hour with no benefits, housed in cramped, dirty rooms, fed on thin rice gruel, stripped of their legal rights, under constant surveillance and intimidation."[39] Numerous workers have been victims of factory explosions and fires, as in Jinjiang city (Fujian) where 32 workers who were locked in dormitory were killed.[40] However, not only is the number of employees of this sector very small but the submission of labor is formal as the labor force is used as "the capitalist finds it."[41] For example, as it has been shown by Ching Kwan Lee the localistic network plays a very important role during recruitment.[42] Moreover, "the despotic labor regime was organized through localistic networks"[43] and the workers without localistic support among shopfloor leaders are given the most difficult working posts.

The last enclave concerns the township and village enterprises (TVE, *xiangzhen qiye*) that are, most of the time, controlled by local authorities. From the beginning of reform policy to the mid-1990s, it was the only nonpublic sector that had undergone a real significant growth in term of employment. The employees of TVEs were 120.1 million in 1994 against 30 million in 1980. But here also the way the society has interpreted the economic reforms has contributed to shape the new capitalist labor in a very "primitive" manner. In fact, at the first stage, the "natural" superiority of TVEs on SOEs (proximity of raw materials, flexibility, commercial dynamism, and so on) has enabled TVEs to limit the "exploitation" to a small part of the labor force and to respect the principle of "moral economy" that constrains the "elite to guarantee (or at least not infringe upon) the *subsistence claims* and arrangements of the peasants."[44] Many workers are from the districts and sometimes from the village and then are members of local networks. Because of this status they enjoy the best labor conditions and the best remuneration.[45] Only those who come from further places and who are in charge of the worst tasks are submitted to exploitation in a form very close to what happens in the second enclave.

In short, during the 1980s, even in these different enclaves, the introduction of the capitalist labor has not been completed and has not gone beyond the stage of a formal submission of labor. Not only have the employers used labor as they find it but the local actors have reinterpreted the principle of capitalism through their specific terms. The "market despotism" that is emerging in capitalist enclaves did not enable capitalism to integrate labor as a real means of the production process and then appeared in fact as an obstacle to its development.

Second Stage: Toward a Welfare State?

Since the mid-1990s, the primitive capitalism based quite exclusively on labor-intensive industries has entered a phase of stagnation. Despite the lack of details about this phenomenon, the official figures reveal it with accuracy. The nonstate nonagricultural enterprises (rural and urban) employed 236.64 million people in 1996 and 239.89 million in 1998. In every sector, the number of employees diminishes (urban collective sector) or grows far slower than gross output and profits. The most spectacular example is the one of TVEs that employed 125 million people in 1998 to a maximum of 135 million in 1996.[46] At the same time, the number of TVEs has decreased from 25 million to 20 million and the profits have increased from 135 to 197 billion.[47] In the past, the TVEs did not need to have a high rate of productivity to be profitable, but now, because of the development of national competition (and in certain sectors of international competition) the rural enterprises need to improve their labor productivity or disappear. The consequence of this crisis of growth of the nonstate sectors is their inability to absorb newcomers. It seems that the only sector that has succeeded in escaping from this intensification of the use of labor is the exporting sector. The investment remains labor-intensive oriented and "despotic" management keeps controlling labor conditions.[48]

Whatever the change in these sectors is, it is the public sector that experiments with the most violent form of the restructuring of working conditions. Since 1994, the SOEs have gradually gotten rid of their plethoric workforce in a context of neutrality of the local and national power at the beginning, and then, since 1997, with the support of the state. This phenomenon has revealed deep change in the mentality of the local authorities when they manage public enterprises. Whereas they opposed the different reforms in the 1980s,[49] now they seem to be more than favorable to the new policy of redundancies. National leaders were even compelled to put a brake on the enthusiasm of certain city bureaucracies that accelerated the laying off. Central authorities had to emphasize that the redundancies must be gradual and implemented cautiously.[50]

Even if the official urban unemployment rate[51] has not increased to a great extent—it was around 3 percent from 1994 to 2000—4.76 million people in 1994,[52] 5.53 million in 1996,[53] 5.768 million in 1997,[54] 5.71 million in 1998,[55] 5.75 million in 1999[56] and 5.95 million in 2000[57]— the situation is very serious. In order to give a true picture of the situation it is necessary to add to the registered unemployment (*dengji shiye*)[58] other categories of "non-working" that have been set up in recent years by the central authorities. The reason for this phenomenon is to prevent the official unemployment rate from increasing too sharply; the "trick" being to set up categories of people who, though without jobs, continue to own to a *danwei;* then they are not entitled to be considered as unemployed. Thus, official statistics reveal that in spite of important redundancies, the number of the "employees and workers of public economic units" only slightly decreased from 112 million to 85 million between 1994 and 1999.[59]

The main category of "non-working" people is the "laid-off" people (*xiagang*) which are persons who are not working anymore but remain employees of the *danwei* and who are supposed to receive a meager allocation from it.[60] Officially, the status of *xiagang* is temporary since the laid-off are victims of a transitional situation. Thanks to the economic development and to the emergence of a modern labor market, they are supposed to be reemployed by the same unit once it will become "modern" and profitable or to be hired by another enterprise.[61] But for the great majority of them, the opportunity of getting a new job is very small. And after having spent three years in reemployment service centers (*zaijiuyefuwu zhongxin*),[62] they become registered unemployed.[63]

It is difficult to give precise estimations of the number of *xiagang*, as the Chinese scholars themselves recognize that they are unable to collect figures,[64] but according to different sources, between 40 and 70 million people lost their job between 1994 and 2000.[65] However, the most interesting figure is not the number of fired people but the number who have been fired and not yet reemployed. The proportion of "reemployment" varies to a great extent from source to source and from place to place according to the importance of laying off and the opportunities provided by the local labor market. The national figures vary from 20 percent to 70 percent.[66] In Liaoning the proportion is only of 25 percent[67] and in Shaanxi one-third.[68] Moreover, the increase in the number of lay-off has led to an increase in time necessary to find a new job.[69]

According to different sources, the number of *xiagang* still without new jobs were 6–8 million in 1996, 4.5–12 million in 1997, 7.5–9 million in 1998, 9–15 million in 1999.[70] Some figures given by the Hong Kong press are higher.[71] During interviews some officials and researchers estimated the real number of unemployed (including registered unemployed plus *xiagang* not yet reemployed) at 20 million in 1999 and between 22 and 25 million in 2000.[72] Table 1.1 tries to sum up these different figures.

In order to give an accurate picture of the situation, it would be necessary to take into account another category of unemployed: the workers who are paid no more or only a small part (*touqian gongzi*) of their wages. They continue to be considered normal workers, and sometimes they continue to work, but because of the financial problems met by their *danwei*, the enterprise's management are unable or unwilling to pay salaries. According to different sources, 10 million were not receiving their wages anymore or only a part of them in 1995,[73] 12.8 million in 1996 and 13.8 million in the first nine months of 1997.[74] Finally, we should include in the unemployed population other categories like "early retired"—in fact forced retired (at 50 years for men and 45 years for women)—and rural migrants who have no jobs. Although we lack figures to evaluate the importance of this category, according to different sources, it seems that it concerns several million people every year.[75]

If we were able to include these different categories we would probably reach an unemployment rate of 15–17 percent, with local figures largely lower in coastal and southern provinces and much higher in central and northern provinces. In Liaoning, the provincial unemployment rate is probably as high as 20 percent and 30 to 50 percent in certain industrial cities like Fushun, Anshan, Liaoyang, Benxi.[76]

The objective of this vast movement of redundancies is not only "setting to capitalist labor" the Chinese workers but also forcing them to enter into the second stage of capitalism, in which the question is less to incorporate a maximum of workers to the production process than to rationalize the use of labor. In other terms, the objective is to introduce a real submission of labor to capital and to set up hegemonic mode of labor control. The insistence of the official discourse on the necessary

Table 1.1

Years	1996	1997	1998	1999	2000
Numbers*	13.5–15.5	14.7–17.2	16–19	15–20	22–25
Rates**	6.6–7.6%	7–8.2%	7.6–9%	7–9.3%	9.2–10.4%

* Registered unemployed plus *xiagang* not yet reemployed (million).
** "real" urban unemployment rate.

"enterprise modernization" fits with this trend. The strategy "to leave the small ones and grasp the big ones" (*fangxiao zhuada*) aims at setting up big groups able to give priority to the high-tech technology and then to cope with the transnational companies.[77] Some examples, in the textile industry[78] and the steel industry[79] show that the process of taylorization of labor is largely implemented in certain enterprises. The supremacy given to machinery vis-à-vis labor, the segmentation of productive tasks, the emphasis on intensification of labor, the use of scientific methods like "full-load work method" (*manfuhe gongzuofa*) in order "to improve productivity and reduce manning levels by using labor to the full,"[80] the complexity of the remuneration systems in order to control workers, the attempts to avoid workers turnover witness a clear orientation to "modern capitalism." Even if Zhao Minghua and Theo Nichols remark that the practices are also very close in certain aspects to more "primitive" capitalism: "lengthening of working day, restrictions on sickness leave," and so on, the objective seems clear. We are in a transitional period, and it is not surprising to notice contradictions and variations within the process of intensification. It is all the less surprising that in most of these "modernizing" enterprises we feel the influence of Hong Kong investors who bring capital, but also modes of management that are very similar to those employed in the enclaves of coastal provinces. Under such a context, labor process is logically a mixture of "primitive capitalism" and "modern capitalism."

In political terms, the collapse of state-owned labor-intensive industries has forced the state to change to a great extent the "management" of urban labor. It has clearly decided to get rid of the old system but without giving up the principle of protection of workers. The Labor Law adopted in July 1994 witnesses this will to conciliate certain aspects of the socialist regulation and the new economic constraints.[81] Still more clearly, the state has started to set up a welfare system to cope not only with the collapse of the old labor paradigm but also with the growing number of unemployed and people in need. The old age protection system (*yanglao baozhuang zhidu*) and health protection system (*yiliao baozhang zhidu*) as well as the unemployment protection system (*shiye baozhang zhidu*)[82] are based on the contributions of enterprises and workers to funds managed by local authorities. In the near future, the funds should be controlled in the framework of a universal and national system.

Besides, in industrial cities stricken by the SOEs reform, the local states have entirely taken charge (through reemployment program, policies of support for the poor, and so on) the effects of the social crisis produced by the extensive laying off. Municipal authorities and grassroots institutions have to deal with a growing flow of demands from the urban population, some of these demands being expressed through protest movements organized on a weekly and sometimes a daily basis.[83] In particular, trade unions and women's federations are now playing very important roles. They take charge of a growing part of social policies and they also play a role of lobbyists representing the interests of people in need within the state apparatus.

From a theoretical point of view, urban China seems then to experience a double process of "statization of the society" and of the "socialization of the state," a process that Jürgen Habermas identifies to the process of modernization of the State.[84] Socialization of the state in the sense that the political action is more and more concerned by the "rise of the social": "the emergence of society—the rise of housekeeping, its activity, problems, and organizational devices—from the shadowy interior of the household into the light of the public sphere";[85] accumulation, income, consumption, investment, poverty becoming the principal targets of political action. Statization of the society as the State structures more and more formally the social realm through a welfare system. The role of the social state is to "forestall" the potential conflict between labor and capital and to protect the individuals.[86] This double process is not a conscious program elaborated by the state or by the ruling class; it is the effect of the constraints of the modernization itself. Not only is the society not anymore a pure object submitted to "total" control, but it is becoming the main concern of the politics. As a consequence, the state is led both to be "invaded" by the social demands and to be involved in the "management" of the social problems.[87] It is important to insist on the fact that the concept of "socialization of social welfare," defined by Linda Wong as a process in which "people should eschew dependence on the state" and "all strata of society—local communities, mass organizations, work units, families and individuals—must be actively involved" in welfare matters is only one side of the evolution.[88] The other side is the increase in the scope of the state's interventions in welfare matters through the multiplication of state-like orientations of many para-public agencies whose funds are usually of public origin. In other words, the limit between society and state are blurred and the border of the state seems to be constantly changing.[89]

Toward a Postindustrial Labor Crisis

The least one can say about this process is that it is meeting huge obstacles. The main reason for these difficulties lays on the characteristics of the period in which the setting up of the social state takes place. First of all, whereas the emergence of a welfare state in Western countries is a consequence of a period of development of modern capitalism, in the Chinese case the mainspring of change is a crisis produced by the "setting to capitalist labor." Under such an unfavorable situation, the state is unable to reach its own objectives. For example, the different funds that are supposed to provide universal protection are in a very serious situation. The enterprises are not willing to pay the due contributions, some because they have no funds for that, and others because they prefer to save money for investment or trafficking purposes. Besides, the total wages on which the contributions are calculated are declining drastically.[90] Lastly, the funds are badly managed: it is not rare to discover that large amounts of money have disappeared or have been transferred into private accounts. In 1998, 8.2 billion yuan devoted to the payment of 1.8 million early retired were embezzled.[91] As a result, the urban population has experienced for several years a decrease in social security. Many urban dwellers do not have their health expenses reimbursed anymore.[92] *Xiagang* people and a proportion of registered unemployed do not receive money, and as we have noticed above, million of retired people are victims of delay in payment of pensions. The number of poor people has been multiplied 13 times from 1997 to 2000.[93] *Xiagang* people represent about half the total number.

Secondly, the political environment is also very different from the one fifty years ago in Western countries. During this period, the Western workers constituted a social group who played a determining role in economy as well as in political life, even if the forms taken by political participation varied to a great extent from country to country.[94] Not only were their working forces and their working skills needed by the enterprises, but their political opinions were not neglected. This is not the case in present China where the pseudo working class is in complete decay. In being excluded from the production process, workers' privileged connections with the regime have been called into question. Besides, they have lost any firm status in the society, which is impeding them from defending independent interests. The numerous protest movements that have broken down in recent years have shown that the laid off people have no other choice than to play the card of the preservation of a form of dependence toward the acting power, rather than to affirm a political autonomy. In industrial cities many ex-workers are engaged in what I called a "ritualized social bargaining" in order to get resources from local states particularly frightened by the possible occurrences of social unrest.[95]

Lastly, historical specificities of the period must not be read only through the "endogenous" glasses but also in taking into account external influences. In particular, it is important to notice the influence of postmodern capitalism, which can be characterized by a decay of industry and a dominance of the financial capitalism. As a consequence, labor tends to play a decreasing importance in economy and labor cost tends to represent a marginal element of the production cost.[96] Not only are the industrial sectors experiencing a violent restructuring of labor force through post-fordist devices like *reengineering*,[97] but the services sector is also stricken by strategies of "saving labor."[98] In parallel, the only kind of labor the new capitalism seems to need is the "intelligent" labor that is concentrated in the hands of a very small number of people. Consequently, the population of most Western countries tends to be composed of two very different and very opposed categories: one composed by managers and intellectual workers and one by a growing number of people involved in petty and temporary jobs.[99]

It clearly appears that China is also concerned by this process of post-industrialization. The economic growth creates a decreasing number of jobs. In 1997, the growth rate was 8.8 percent and the employment growth 1.1 percent. The numbers were respectively 7.8 percent and 0.5 percent in 1998 and 7.8 percent and less than 0.4 percent in 1999.[100] In particular, it is striking to remark that the most flourishing sectors of Chinese economy are largely concentrated in capital and technology-oriented activities (transports, information, electricity, finance, technical services, and so on)[101] where qualifications and wages are the highest. The attempt to create big groups able to compete with multinational firms[102] contribute to stress on high-tech labor, to the detriment of nonqualified or even qualified labor. In contrast, the collapse of the traditional manufacturing sector witnesses the decay of labor-intensive enterprises. Through a slow but steady movement of concentration, the restructuring of Chinese industry combines redundancies with emphasis on investment and technology.[103]

Another striking point is the phenomenon of polarization of income and social status. As Hu Angang remarks, one is witnessing an increasing income gap between a small number of well-paid people working most of the time in the "flourishing" sectors and huge number of people living on low wages or not working at all.[104] According to a 1997 survey, the 1.3 percent of households owning more than 200,000 yuan of assets controls 31.5 percent of total assets, the 44 per cent of poorest families owning only 3 percent.[105] Beside the well-off people, a lot of urban dwellers must engage in temporary and badly paid activities.[106] It is particularly the case of *xiagang* who not only meet great difficulties to get new jobs but also rarely get stable ones. Most of reemployed *xiagang* are involved in self-subsistence activities (*zimo zhiye*) that is to say petty, temporary and flexible jobs like peddling, repairing, shoe-shining, and so on. In 1997, of 4.8 million *xiagang* who got jobs in 1997, 2.8 million were employed in the private sector among whom 1.9 million were in the "self-subsistence sector."[107] In Shanghai, a privileged city, a survey concerning 1000 *xiagang* shows that only 9.5 percent have found relatively stable jobs and 8.7 percent are attending training courses.[108] According to Watson, the situation is very similar in Shaanxi, where "the ranks of the laid-off are likely to be dominated by those with lower skills or low likelihood of being competitive for alternative jobs."[109] The field work I did in 2001 and 2002 in Northeast provinces and in Shanghai show that 70 to 80 percent of the new jobs are temporary and unstable jobs.

In European countries, most of the new jobs or the new occupations (like attending training sessions) are sponsored by the state or by institutions sponsored by the state. The decay of the welfare state does not seem to lead to the decay of the state but to a new social state whose task is to no longer impose a modus vivendi between labor and capital, but to guarantee the reproduction of an increasing number of unemployed or half-unemployed. In China, in 1994 a "reemployment program" (*zaijiuye gongcheng*) was set up under the leadership of the local Labor Bureau (Laodong ju). The objective of the program is to stimulate the supply of jobs through different means (training sessions, organization of a labor market, creation of new jobs especially in service sector, and so on) in order to redeploy the laid-off workers.[110] Within the framework of this program the trade-unions have set up 100 technical and professional training centers. The Labor Bureaus have created 4,000 employment agencies and the mass movement streets' bureaus, and residents' committees and individuals 50,000 employment services centers.[111] In May 1998 there were 30,000 training centers in China.[112] In industrial big cities, numerous technical schools have developed training sessions devoted to young people without jobs, *xiagang*, and unemployed.[113] Thanks to this program, 4.3 million jobs have been created and 34,000 institutions have helped 8.7 million people to be reemployed. Moreover, 3 million persons have attended professional training sessions.[114]

The enterprises that hire laid-off people enjoy preferential tax policies.[115] For those *xiagang* who want to set up businesses, they can receive some help. In Shenyang and in Hunan, authorities have set up a "*xiagang* card", which gives its holders different advantages.[116] In Shenyang[117] and in Shaanxi,[118] the municipalities' governments, the women's federations, street offices (*jiedao banshichu*), the trade unions, and the residents' committees assist financially the unemployed in setting up new activities like peddling. At the beginning of 1999, a new step in the same direction seems to have been made. Different national leaders pointed out that "SOEs' laid-off workers should go to re-employment service centers, sign agreements on their basic livelihood and re-employment, and dissolve their work relationship with their original enterprises after gaining re-employment. Laid-off workers should obtain an unemployment insurance fund from a social insurance body if they cannot find re-employment upon termination of the three-year period at re-employment service centers; if they still cannot find re-employment after two-years of obtaining an unemployment insurance fund, they will be entitled to minimum living expenses provided by a civil affairs department."[119]

Besides, the Ministry of Labor and Social Security insists on the importance of the "two guarantees" (of a basic living for laid-off and of pensions paid on time) so that people "can have a peaceful and joyful Spring Festival."[120] In other terms, the state is expecting a new period and probably long period in which the problem will not be to create jobs but to "manage" unemployment. In the first nine months of 1999, 50.6 percent of the vital allocations given to laid-off workers come from the public money and 20.8 percent from the "society," that is to say the unemployment funds. The enterprises contributed only for 28.6 percent of the total. It is scheduled that public contributions will increase in the near future.[121] Moreover, except in some wealthy provinces and municipalities (Beijing, Shanghai, Zhejiang, Fujian, Guangdong, Shandong, Jiangsu), local governments are unable to collect enough money for that purpose and they ask central governments for some subsidies.[122]

Nevertheless the financial question is far from being solved. The funds raised for that purpose are huge[123] but they are not sufficient,[124] and it is asked of "enterprises, society, and financial institutions to take-up of the burden each to provide laid-off workers with basic living expenses."[125]

In short, labor is less and less a consequence of the valorization of a capital as in the period of industrial capitalism. It is no longer the result of economic activities but the result of political decisions. In most cities the main creator of labor is not the firm but the Chinese state. As a consequence of the partial disconnection of labor from economic activities, the fact that labor does not appear anymore as the main element of production threatens the very existence of a working class in China. At first glance, it seems that while the old pseudo working class is disappearing, a new (and real) working class is emerging. It is partially true that, as we have seen in the southern enclaves, the characteristics of labor are very close to those dominating in primitive capitalism. In this capitalist sector, based exclusively on the low cost of labor, workers are "floating" in a double manner. They "float" because they keep very strong connections with their native places but also because the capital of the firms in which they work can "swing" at every moment. The mentality and behaviors of the new "working class" are characterized by the importance of the "local networks," during recruitment as well as within the labor process.[126] Under such a context it is difficult for these floating workers to develop a "common experience of life" and to "share dispositions" and then to launch collective action. Besides, in the new modern capitalist sector, the fact that it is dominated by technology-oriented strategy and service-oriented activities contributes to marginalize labor in the economic realm. The low level of reemployment and the increasing importance of services activities witness this process of marginalization. The question at stake seems to be less the one of transition between an old working class and a new capitalist working class than the one of the decay of labor as it was defined in industrial states.

The marginalization of workers in the economic realm—wealth seems to be more and more created without them—reinforces their social dependency on the state and therefore worsens their political weakness. As it is shown by the analysis of the protest movements in different cities, workers (or more precisely ex-workers) seem to settle down in this position of dependents or clients of the local state, taking advantage of the fact that the scope of the unemployment problem threatens social stability. As they lose their identity as workers, they are led to emphasize their identity as urban dwellers.

Simultaneity and contradictions

In each phase of capitalism, different forms of labor control coexist at the same time and in the same place. But the case of China represents an utmost example of this rule. China is undergoing at once three stages that took two centuries to emerge and to develop in Western countries. This situation leads any observer of the labor scene to a series of puzzling paradoxes. The Chinese state affirms its intention to create a welfare state but allows the bureaucracy of coastal provinces to support openly Hong Kong and Taiwan capitalists when labor conflicts occur.[127] Labor is in a process of commodification, which is supposed to produce a growth of job opportunities, while at the same time, its importance in the production process is clearly decreasing and the new economy creates less jobs than the public institutions do. The setting of Chinese workers to capitalist labor does not contribute to generalize productive labor but to convert into labor any kind of "activity," whatever its economic usefulness. The social identity of workers based on a privileged position vis-à-vis the political apparatus is called into question by the introduction of "capitalist relationships," but leads to a new one based on territorial, pre-capitalist relationships between clients (the urban déclassé workers) and patrons (local states).

Nevertheless, from this "postmodernist" chaos three determinant elements seem to emerge. The first one is the importance of the state. Of course, as far as the weberian ideal-type is used, the borders of the state seem to shrink. Not only does state action beat a retreat from economic realm, but the institutionalization of the regime is far from being completed. Corruption, the involvement of army and bureaucracy in smuggling activities, and the development of localism appear as unavoidable consequences of this "rational–legal" vacuum. Yet, the blurring of the state borders—an effect of the formation of a social state—can be analyzed as an extension of the state. In cities, a growing number of people are dependent on public funds and on public initiatives, even though the state is not in charge of the burden as a clearly delineated body. Under such a perspective, one could analyze the evolution of the state not in terms of a retreat, but in terms of diminishing the gap between state and society. For example, it is more and more difficult to consider labor problems outside public policies and more and more difficult to analyze state power without taking into account labor crisis. In short, the institutions they are dependent on have changed (the *danwei* yesterday, the local state today), as well as the means of bargaining (the dominant position in industry yesterday, the potential ability to destroy social stability in cities), but the nature of the link between workers and power remains the same.

The second point concerns the question of workers' interests. The status of workers is called into question both by the introduction of capitalist labor relations and by the marginalization of labor in the economy. The first phenomenon could have led to the emergence of a workers' movement, which would have fit with a process of socialization of the state. As in the Western welfare state, workers could have constituted one among many interest groups contesting and lobbying for the satisfaction of their demands. But the second phenomenon impedes this process, since the workers are losing every eminent position. They only represent a negative force whose asset is to occupy a strategic place—the urban stage.

The third question emerging from the labor crisis is one of identity. Concerning urban workers, we cannot speak anymore of a common experience in the workplace and in the community. *Danwei* is no longer a place of socialization, and to be a worker does not guarantee a stable and clear identity anymore. In other words, even those people who are lucky enough to work are in a "floating" situation. As for the urban population, as a whole, the identity lays on a territorial ground and for the most "connected" people on the diverse opportunities that provide *guanxi*. This is the only specificity it has compared to the rural "floating population" (*liudong renkou*).

Notes

1. At this stage, the labor is submitted to the process of capitalist production but it is used by the capital as it finds it, in a context of craft production and of agricultural economy; see Karl Marx, *Un chapitre inédit du capital* (Paris: UGE, 1971): 191–199.

2. Ching Kwan Lee, "Disorganized Despotism: Transition From Neo-Traditionalism in Guangzhou," paper presented at the Annual Meeting of the Association for Asian Studies, March 26–29, Washington DC; Anita Chan, "Chinese Factories and Two kinds of Free-Market (Read Bonded) Workforces," paper presented at the Annual Meeting of the Association for Asian Studies, March 26–29, 1998, Washington DC; Ching Kwan Lee, *Gender and the South China Miracle. Two Worlds of Factory Women* (Berkeley: University of California Press, 1998).

3. The process of production has two moments: "First, the organization of work has political and ideological effects—that is, as men and women transform raw materials into useful things, they also reproduce particular social relations as well as an experience of those relations. Second, alongside the organization of work—that is, the labor process—there are distinctive political and ideological apparatuses of production which regulate production relations. The notion of production regime or, more specifically, factory regime embraces both these dimensions of production politics," Michael Buravoy, *The Politics of Production* (London: Verso, 1985): 7–8.

4. Buravoy, *The Politics of Production* 1985, chapter 3.

5. Marx, *Un chapitre inédit du capital* 1971: 191–199.

6. Buravoy, *The Politics of Production* 1985, chapter 3.

7. Richard Swedberg and Mark Granovetter, "Introduction" in *The Sociology of Economic Life*, eds, Richard Swedberg and Mark Granovetter (Boulder: Westview Press, 1992): 6.

8. Karl Polanyi, *The Great Transformation* (New York and Toronto: Farra and Rinehart, 1944); see also the very interesting study of Fred Block and Margaret R. Somers, "Beyond the Economistic Fallacy: The Holistic Social Science of Karl Polanyi" in *Vision and Method in Historical Sociology*, ed. Theda Skocpol (Cambridge: Cambridge University Press, 1984): 47–84.

9. Polanyi, *The Great Transformation:* 132.

10. For USA see Jeremy Rifkin, *The End of Work: the Decline of the Global Labor Force and the Dawn of the Post-Market Era* (New York: Putnam's Sons, 1995) for Europe see Dominique Méda, *Le travail, une valeur en voie de disparition* (Paris: Flammarion, 1995).

11. On this question see Béatrice Hibou, ed. *La privatisation des Etats* (Paris: Karthala, 1998); Joel Migdal, *Strong Societies and Weak Societies. State–Society Relations and State capabilities in the Third*

World (Princeton: Princeton University Press, 1988), and the papers presented at the conference *The Dynamics of States*, Ebenhausen (Germany), 12–13 October 1999.

12. Elizabeth J. Perry, "Labor's battle for political space: The role of workers in contemporary China" in *Urban Spaces in Contemporary China. The potential for autonomy and community in post-Mao China,* ed. Deborah D. Davis (Cambridge, Mass.: Woodrow Wilson Centre Press and Cambridge University Press, 1995): 302, 325; Elizabeth J. Perry, "From Native Place to Workplace: Labor Origins and Outcomes of China's *Danwei system*", in *Danwei. The changing workplace in historical and comparative perspective*, eds. Lü, Xiaobo and Elizabeth J. Perry (Armonk NY and London: M.E. Sharpe, 1997): 42–59.

13. Perry, "Labor's battle for political space: The role of workers in contemporary China" 1995.

14. Ira Katznelson, "Working-Class Formation: Construction Cases and Comparisons" in *Working-Class Formation: Nineteenth Century Patterns in Western Europe and the United States,* eds. Ira Katznelson and Aristide R. Zolberg (Princeton, Princeton University Press, 1986): 14–19.

15. Katznelson, "Working-Class Formation: Construction Cases and Comparisons": 14.

16. Buravoy, *The Politics of Production* 1985: 15.

17. Katznelson, "Working-Class Formation: Construction Cases and Comparisons": 19.

18. E.P. Thompson, *The Making of the English Working Class* (New York: Vintage, 1966): 194.

19. Thompson, E.P. Thompson, *The Making of the English Working Class* 1966: 6–10.

20. Andrew G. Walder "The Chinese Cultural Revolution in the Factories", in *Putting Class in its Place. Worker Identities in East Asia,* ed. Elizabeth Perry (Berkeley, University of California, 1996): 168–198.

21. Jackie Sheehan, *Chinese Workers. A New History* (London and New York, Routledge, 1998): 2.

22. Ibid.

23. "Temporary Regulations on the Implementations of Labor Contracts in State-owned Enterprises," "Temporary Regulations on the Recruitment of Workers in State-owned Enterprises," "Temporary Regulations on the Dismissal of Workers in State-owned Enteprises who violate Discipline," and "Temporary Regulations on Unemployment Insurance for Workers in State-owned Enterprises," See Linda Wong and Ka-ho Mok, "The Reform and the Changing social context" in *Social Change and Social Policy in Contemporary China,* eds. Linda Wong and Stewart MacPherson (Aldershot: Avebury, 1995): 1–26.

24. Greg O'Leary, "The Making of the Chinese Working Class" in *Adjusting to Capitalism. Chinese Workers and the State,* ed. Greg O'Leary (Armonk N.Y.: M.E. Sharpe, 1997): 48–74.

25. Yves Chevrier, "Micropolitics and the Factory Director Responsibility System 1984–1987" in *Chinese Society on the Eve of Tiananmen. The Impact of Reform,* eds. Deborah D. Davis and Ezra F. Vogel (Cambridge, Mass.: Harvard University Press, 1990): 109–133.

26. *Zhongguo tongji nianjian* (hereafter *ZGTJNJ*) (China Statistical Yearbook), 1995: 90–91.

27. *ZGTJNJ* 1995: 102.

28. The distinction between the two sectors is based on the number of employees: an individual enterprise owner cannot employ more than seven wage-earners.

29. Zhongguo laodong tongji nianjian 2000 (China Labour Statistical Yearbook) (Beijing: China Statistics Press, 2000): 399.

30. Ibid.

31. Hu, Angang, "Zhongguo chengzhen shiye zhuangkuang fenxi" (Analysis of the situation of unemployment in Chinese cities and towns), *Guanli shijie* 4 (1998): 47–63.

32. Zhongguo laodong tongji nianjian 2000 (China Labour Statistical Yearbook) (Beijing: China Statistics Press, 2000): 399.

33. Jean-Louis Rocca, "L'Etat entre chiens et loups. Résistance anti-taxes et racket fiscal en Chine populaire," *Etudes chinoises* XI, 2 (1992): 77–140.

34. Hill Gates, "Owner, Worker, Mother, Wife: Taibei and Chengdu Family Businesswomen" in *Putting Class in its Place. Worker Identities in East Asia,* ed. Elizabeth Perry (Berkeley: University of California Press, 1996): 127–165.

35. Dorothy J. Solinger, "The floating population in the cities: chances for assimilation?" in *Urban Spaces in Contemporary China. The potential for autonomy and community in post-Mao China,* ed. Deborah D. Davis (Cambridge, Mass.: Woodrow Wildson Centre Press and Cambridge University Press, 1995): 113–139; Dorothy J. Solinger, "Job Categories and Employment Channels Among the 'Floating Population' in *Adjusting to Capitalism. Chinese Workers and the State,* ed. Greg O'Leary (Armonk, N.Y.: M.E. Sharpe, 1997): 3–47.

36. *ZGTJNJ* 1999: 136–137.

37. Ching Kwan Lee, "From Organized Dependence to Disorganized Despotism: Changing Labor Regimes in Chinese Factories", *The China Quarterly* 155 (1999): 44–71; Anita Chan, "Chinese Factories and Two Kind of Free-Market (Read Bonded) Workforces", paper presented at the Annual Meeting of the Association for Asian Studies, March 26–29, 1998, Washington DC.

38. In the delta, 90 percent of production-line workers are migrants (Li Cheng, "Surplus Rural Laborers and Internal Migration in China," *Asian Survey,* XXXVI, 11 (1996): 1132. See also Anita Chan, "Chinese Factories and two kind of Free-Market (Read Bonded) Workforces," paper 1998, Lee, *Gender and the South China Miracle* 1998.

39. C. Kernaghan, "Behind the Label: Made in China," a special report prepared for National Labor Committee, March (1998). See also *China Labor Education and Information Centre,* "Behind the Boom. Working Conditions in the Textile, Garment and Toy Industries in China," Hong Kong, 1995, *China Labor Education and Information Centre,* "Women Workers in China," 1995; *China Labor Education and Information Centre,* "The Flip-side of Success. The Situation of Workers and Organising in Foreign-invested Electronics Enterprises in Guangdong," Hong Kong, 1996 and different information published by the Hong Kong reviews *Change* and *China Labor Bulletin,* Hong Kong. For an overall analysis see Anita Chan, *China's Workers under Assault. The Exploitation of Labor in a Globalizing Economy,* Armonk, London, M.E. Sharpe, 2001.

40. *Summary of World Broadcasts, Far East* (Hereafter *SWB*), 3016, G/6, 5 September 1997. Two similar cases have recently taken place in a Japanese-invested factory in Huizhou (Guangdong) and in a table-tennis factory in Yiwu City (Zhejiang), *CLB* 42 (May–June 1998): 17.

41. Marx, *Un chapitre inédit du capital* 1971.

42. Lee, *Gender and the South China Miracle* 1998: 84.

43. Ibid: 116.

44. James C. Scott, *The Moral Economy of the Peasant. Rebellion and subsistence in Southeast Asia* (New Haven and London: Yale University Press, 1976): 188.

45. See Christofer Findlay, Andrew Watson, and Harry X. Wu, eds. *Rural Enterprises in China* (New York: St. Martin's Press, 1994), Samuel P. S. Ho, *Rural China in Transition. Non-agricultural Development in Rural Jiangsu, 1978–1990* (Oxford: Clarendon Press, 1994).

46. *ZGTJNJ* 1999: 136–137.

47. *ZGTJNJ* 1999: 136–137 and *ZGTJNJ,* 2000: 420–422.

48. Lee, "From Organized Dependence" 1999.

49. Chevrier, "Micropolitics and the Factory Director Responsibility System 1984–1987" 1990.

50. *Zhengming* 240 (October 1997): 28–30, *Zhengming* 241 (November 1997): 12–13.

51. "Urban unemployment rate refers to the ratio of persons unemployed in urban area to total employment and unemployment in urban area," *ZGTJNJ* 1996: 133.

52. *ZGTJNJ* 1996: 114.

53. Li, Peilin, "Laogongye jidi de shiye zhili: hou gongyehua he shichanghua" (Old Industry and Unemployment Administration: Postindustrialization and Marketization), *Shehuixue yanjiu* 4 (1998): 12.

54. *SWB/FE,* 3255, S1/1–2, 17 June 1998.

55. *Zhongguo laodong tongji nianjian 1999* (China Labour Statistical Yearbook) (Beijing: China Statistics Press, 1999): 7.

56. *Zhongguo laodong tongji nianjian 2000* (China Labour Statistical Yearbook) (Beijing: China Statistics Press, 2000): 7.

57. Hu, Angang, "Creative Destruction of Restructuring: China's Urban Unemployment and Social Security (1993–2000)", paper prepared for the conference organized by the CAEC Taskforce Project 2001–2002 "Unemployment: The East Asian and European Experiences in Perspective", Bangkok, March 28–29, 2002.

58. "Unemployment refers to those non-agricultural population within working age (16–50 for male, 16–45 for female) who are able to work and willing to work but unemployed and registered in local employment service agencies (*dangdi jiuye fuwu jigou*)," *ZGTJNJ*, 1996: 133. The employment service agencies depend on Labor Bureau (*laodongju*).

59. *ZGTJNJ*, 1995: 84; and *SWB/FE*, 3423, G/8, 4 January 1998, *Zhongguo laodong tongji nianjian 2000* (China Labour Statistical Yearbook) (Beijing: China Statistics Press, 2000): 3.

60. See Zhu, Qingfang, "Chengzhen pinkun renkou de tedian, pinkun yuanyin jiekun duice" (Characteristics of urban poverty, poverty reasons and anti-poverty policies) *Shehui kexue yanjiu* 1 (1998): 62–66; Hu, "Zhongguo chengzhen shiye zhuangkuang fenxi", Antoine Kernen and Jean-Louis Rocca, "The Social Responses to Unemployment. Case study in Shenyang and Liaoning," *China Perspectives* 27 (January–February 2000): 35–51.

61. About this category see Kernen and Rocca, "The Social Responses to Unemployment. Case study in Shenyang and Liaoning," 2000; Jean-Louis Rocca, "Old Working Class, New Working Class: Reforms, Labor Crisis and the Two Faces of Conflicts in Chinese Urban Areas," paper prepared for the conference organized by EU–China Academic Network, "Economic Reforms, Social Conflict and Collective Identities in China," Madrid, 21–22 January 1999, forthcoming; Watson, A. (1998), "Enterprise Reform and Employment Change in Shaanxi province," paper presented at the Annual Meeting of the Association for Asian Studies, March 26–29, 1998, Washington DC.

62. Every enterprise laying off workers are legally compelled to set up reemployment service centers that must pay vital allocations (*shenghuofei*) to laid-off people and provide them training assistance for the search of a new job.

63. *Sichuan gongren ribao* (hereafter *SCGRRB*), 24 June 1999: 2.

64. Hu, "Zhongguo chengzhen shiye zhuangkuang fenxi" 1998.

65. *Zhengming* 245 (March 1998): 24; Zhu, "Chengzhen pinkun renkou de tedian, pinkun yuanyin jiekun duice"1998; Shen, Hong in Jiang, Liu (ed.), *Zhongguo shehui xingshi fenxi yu yuce* (China social situation analysis and prediction) (Beijing: Shehui kexue wenxian chubanshe, 1999), pp. 90–105. *Jingji cankao*, "Yao duqudao anzhi xiagang zhigong" (We must by all means find jobs for *xiagang* people), 7 February 1998; Jean-Louis Rocca, "The Rise of Unemployment in Urban China and the Contradictions of Employment Policies," *China perspectives*, 30 (July–August 2000), pp. 42–55; Hu, "Creative Destruction".

66. See *Jingji cangai bao* 1998; Laodong he shehui baozhang bu, Guojia tongjiju; Sun, Zhigang, "Bian zaijiuye wei zaichuangye" (From reemployment to setting up of enterprises) *Zhongguo gongye jingji* 5 (1998): 41–45; Ma, Mingjie, "Zhongguo chengshi zhigong shenghuo zhuangkuang baogao," (Report on living situation of workers and employees in urban China), *Gaige zongheng* 1 (1998): 36–37; Hu, Angang, "Create labor for the people: The problem of employment in China and employment strategy", manuscript, 1998; Tian, Bingnan, Yuan, Jianmin, "Shanghai xiagang renyuan de diaocha yanjiu" (Study of a survey on Shanghai *xiagang*), *Shehuixue* 2 (1997): 7–12, *Associated Press*, 28 August 1999, Watson, "Enterprise Reform and Employment Change in Shaanxi province 1998; Mo, Rong, "Zhongguo jiuye xingshi yiran yanjun" (The situation of employment in China is still very serious) in *2000 nian: zhongguo shehui xingshi fenxi yu yuce* (2000: Social situation in China: analyses and perspectives), ed. Jiang, Liu (Beijing: Zhongguo shehui kexue chubanshe, 2000), pp. 182–195.

67. Kernen and Rocca, "The Social Responses to Unemployment. Case study in Shenyang and Liaoning," 2000.

68. Watson, "Enterprise Reform and Employment Change in Shaanxi province" 1998.

69. In 1996, according to a survey, *xiagang* were without jobs three years and nine months on average; see Tian and Yuan, "Shanghai xiagang renyuan de diaocha yanjiu"1997; See also Ma, "Zhongguo chengshi zhigong shenghuo zhuangkuang baogao": 36–37.
70. See in particular "Xiagang zhigongde shenghuo zhuangkuang ji qi shehui zhichi" (Living conditions of *xiagang* and social support), *xiaofei jingji* 1 (1997: 47–51), also Ma, "Zhongguo chengshi zhigong shenghuo zhuangkuang baogao"; Fan, Hailin, "Lun shiye baoxian yu zaijiuye fuwu (Unemployment insurance and reemployment service), *Renkou xuekan* 2 (1998): 29–32; Sun "Bian zaijiuye wei zaichuangye" 1998: 41–45; *Liaowang*, 17 August 1998, 33: 22, Hu, manuscript, 1998; Li, Jianli, "Weilai sannian woguo jiuye xingshi yu duice fenxi" (Analysis of the situation of employment and countermeasures in the three next years), *Hongguan jingji guanli* 12 (1998): 12–15 and 19, Laodong he shehui baozhang bu, Guojia tongjiju, "1998 nian Laodong he shehui baozhang shiye fazhan niandu tongji gongbao" (Annual report 1998 concerning the development of labor services and social protection), *Zhongguo laodong baozhang bao*, 17 June 1999: 1; Guojia jiwei shehui fazhan yanjiusuo kejizu, "Yijiujiujiu nian woguo jiuye xingshi yuce ji duice jianyi" (Situation of employment in China in the future in 1999 and some advice on the necessary counter-measures), *Jingji gaige fazhan* 11 (1998): 20–23; Hu, Angang, "Guanyu jiangdi woguo laodongli gonggei yu tigao laodongli xuqiu zhongyao tujing de ruogan jianyi" (Some advices about necessary means to diminish the demand of labor and to increase labor supply), *Zhongguo nuankexue* 11 (1998): 37–44, Guojia jiwei hongguan jingjiyanjiuyuan ketizu, "1999–2001 nian woguo jiuye xingshi yu duice yanjiu" (Study on the situation of employment in 1999–2001 et on the necessary counter-measures), *Guanli shijie* 4 (1999): 71–81; *Zhengming* 245 (March 1998): 24, Zhu, "Chengzhen pinkun renkou de tedian, pinkun yuanyin jiekun duice"1998; "Yao duqudao anzhi xiagang zhigong;" *SWB/FE*, G/8, 13 mars 1999.
71. There were more than 28 million *xiagang* workers and people without wage in 1998; *Zhengming* 256 (February 1999: 6–7).
72. Interviews 1997, 1998 and 1999.
73. Zhu, "Chengzhen pinkun renkou de tedian, pinkun yuanyin jiekun duice" 1998.
74. Zhu, "Chengzhen pinkun renkou de tedian, pinkun yuanyin jiekun duice" 1998.
75. Interviews, Beijing 2000–2001.
76. Kernen and Rocca, "The Social Responses to Unemployment. Case study in Shenyang and Liaoning," 2000; interviews Liaoning, 2001–2002.
77. Jean-François Huchet, "Concentration and the Emergence of Corporate Group in Chinese Industry", *China Perspectives* 23 (May–June 1999): 5–17.
78. Zhao, Minghua and Theo Nichols, "Management Control of Labor in State-owned Enterprises: Cases from the Textile Industry", *The China Journal* 36 (July 1996): 1, Zhao, Minghua and Theo Nichols, "Management Control of Labor in SOE. Cases from the Textile Industry" in *Adjusting to Capitalism. Chinese Workers and the State*, ed. Greg O'Leary (Armonk, N.Y.: M.E. Sharpe, 1997): 75–100.
79. Elizabeth M. Freund, "Downsizing China's State Industrial Enterprises. The Case of Baoshan Steel Works" in *Adjusting to Capitalism. Chinese Workers and the State*, ed. Greg O'Leary (Armonk, N.Y.: M.E. Sharpe, 1997): 101–121.
80. Zhao Minghua and Theo Nichols, "Management Control of Labor in SOE. Cases from the Textile Industry" 1996.
81. Joseph Hilary K, "Labor law in 'a socialist market economy': the case of China", *Columbia Journal of Transnational Law* 33, 3 (1995): 559–581.
82. For more details, see the article in two parts written by Ge, Yanfeng, "Gaige yu fazhan guocheng zhong shehui baozhang zhidu de jianshe wenti"(The problem of construction of a system of social protection in the process of development and reform) *Shehuixue Yanjiu* 1 (1998): 98–109 and 2 (1998): 93–98, and World Bank, *China 2020, Pension Reform in China. Old Age Security* (Washington: World Bank, 1997).

83. See Rocca "Old Working Class, New Working Class: Reforms, Labor Crisis and the Two Faces of Conflicts in Chinese Urban Areas" 1998; Kernen and Rocca, "The Social Responses to Unemployment. Case study in Shenyang and Liaoning," 2000.

84. Jürgen Habermas, *The Structural Transformation of the Public Sphere* (Boston: MIT Press, 1989).

85. Hannah Arendt, *The Human Condition* (Chicago and London: The University of Chicago Press, 1958): 73.

86. Jürgen Habermas, *Après Marx* (Paris, Hachette, 1997): 249–293.

87. Arendt, *The Human Condition,* 1958.

88. Linda Wong "Reforming welfare and relief-Socializing the state's burden", in *Social Change and Social Policy in Contemporary China,* eds. Linda Wong and Stewart MacPherson (Aldershot: Avebury, 1995): 50–69.

89. Hibou, *La privatisation des Etats* 1998.

90. Ge, "Gaige yu fazhan guocheng zhong shehui baozhang zhidu de jianshe wenti" 1998.

91. *Agence France Presse,* 25 July 1998.

92. Zhu, "Chengzhen pinkun renkou de tedian, pinkun yuanyin jiekun duice"1998; Fieldworks, Jilin, 2001, Liaoning, 2001–2002.

93. Hu, "Creative Destruction" 2002.

94. Katznelson and Zolberg, *Working-Class Formation* 1986; Sean Wilentz, *Chants Democratic: New York City and the Rise of the American Working class, 1790–1850* (New York: Oxford University Press, 1984), Peter Sears, *Revolutionary Syndicalism and French Labor: A Cause without Rebels* (New Brunswick: Rutgers University Press, 1971).

95. Rocca, "Old Working Class, New Working Class: Reforms, Labor Crisis and the Two Faces of Conflicts in Chinese Urban Areas".

96. Peter Drucker, *Post-Capitalism Society* (New York: Harper Collins, 1993).

97. See James Womack, Daniel Jones et Daniel Roos, *The Machine that Changed the World* (New York: Macmillan, 1990), Benjamin Coriat, *L'Atelier et le robot* (Paris: Bourgois, 1990).

98. Jeremy Rifkin, *The End of Work: the Decline of the Global Labor Force and the Dawn Of the Post-Market Era* (New York: Putnam's Sons, 1995); see also André Gorz, *Métamorphoses du travail, Quête du sens. Critique de la raison économique* (Paris: Galilée, 1988).

99. For USA William Bridges, *How to Prosper in a World Without Jobs* (Londres: Allen and Unwin, 1995). Rifkin, chapter 11, for France see André Gorz, *Misères du présent, Richesse du possible* (Paris: Galilée, 1997).

100. See Yang, Yiyong, "2000 nian zhongguo jiuye xingshi jiqi zhengce xuanze" (About employment situation in 2000 and the choices concerning employment) in *2000 nian zhongguo: jingji xingshi fenxi yu yuce* (China in 2000: Analysis and perspectives of social situation. Blue book on economy), eds. Liu, Guoguang, Wang, Luolin, Li, Jingwen (Beijing: Shehui kexue wenxian chubanshe, 2000).

101. Hu, manuscript 1998.

102. Peter Nolan, "Large Firms and Industrial Reform in Former Planned Economies: the Case of China", *Cambridge Journal of Economics,* 20 (1996): 1–29.

103. Huchet, "Concentration and the Emergence of Corporate Group in Chinese Industry" 1999.

104. Hu, manuscript 1998.

105. Zhu, "Chengzhen pinkun renkou de tedian, pinkun yuanyin jiekun duice"1998.

106. Wang, Feiling, "Floaters, Moonlighters and the Underemployed: a National Labor market with Chinese characteristics", *Journal of Contemporary China* 7, 11 (1998): 459–475.

107. *Agence France Presse,* 2 February 1998 and 4 March 1998, *SWB,* 3168, S2/3, 6 March 1998. See also other surveys in Kernen and Rocca, "The Social Responses to Unemployment. Case study in Shenyang and Liaoning," 2000; *Shehuixue yanjiu,* "Chengzhen qiye xiagang zhigong zaijiuye zhuangkuang tiaocha" kejizu (Study group of research on the situation of re-employment of *xiagang* people from urban enterprises) "Kunjing yu chulu" (Difficulties and ways out) 6 (1997): 24–34, *Jingji cankao bao,*" Yao duqudao anzhi xiagang zhigong" 1998.

108. Tian and Yuan, "Shanghai xiagang renyuan de diaocha yanjiu"1997. For another example see Jiang, Ping, "Bu zaiye renkou tedian ji chengyin" (Composition and characteristics of unemployed population), *Funü yanjiu luncong* 1 (1998): 21–25.

109. Watson, "Enterprise Reform and Employment Change in Shaanxi province, 1998.

110. *Renmin Ribao,* 23 March 1995: 2.

111. *SWB,* 3244, S1/4–5, 4 June 1998.

112. *Agence France-Presse,* 18 May 1998.

113. For Henan see an example in *Agence France-Presse,* 9 July 1998. In Shenyang this activity is very important, see Kernen and Rocca, "The Social Responses to Unemployment. Case study in Shenyang and Liaoning," 2000.

114. *SWB,* 3255, S1/1–2, 17 June 1998 and Kernen and Rocca, "The Social Responses to Unemployment. Case study in Shenyang and Liaoning," 2000.

115. Watson, "Enterprise Reform and Employment Change in Shaanxi province" 1998; Kernen and Rocca, "The Social Responses to Unemployment. Case study in Shenyang and Liaoning," 2000.

116. *SWB,* 3104, S1/3, 17 December 1997; and Kernen and Rocca, "The Social Responses to Unemployment. Case study in Shenyang and Liaoning," 2000.

117. Kernen and Rocca, "The Social Responses to Unemployment. Case study in Shenyang and Liaoning," 2000.

118. Watson, "Enterprise Reform and Employment Change in Shaanxi province" 1998.

119. *SWB/FE,* G/4–5, 19 January 1999. See also *Zhengming* 259 (May 1999): 6–7.

120. *SWB/FE,* G/7, 12 February 1999.

121. Mo, "Zhongguo jiuye xingshi yiran yanjun" 2000.

122. Shen Qilan, Wen Xinmei, Chen Qingang, "Jiangxi xiagang zhigong shenghuofei zhifu you he wenti" (Problems for the payment of allowances to Jiangxi *xiagang, Jingjixue xiaoxibao,* 16 juillet 1999): 2.

123. 900 million in Liaoning, 156 million in Heilongjiang, 50 million in Jiangxi for issuing pensions. Different loans are allocated by the provinces to the cities. Ibid.

124. *Zhengming* 256 (February 1999): 6–7.

125. *SWB/FE,* G/8, 13 March 1999.

126. Lee, *Gender and the South China Miracle* 1998.

127. See C. Kernaghan; *China Labor Bulletin* 40 (January–February 1998): 2–6, *China Labor Bulletin* 42 (May–June 1998): 17; *China Labor Bulletin* 42 (May–June 1998): 13–15; *China Labor Bulletin* 42 (May–June 1998): 15; *China Labor Bulletin* 43 (July–August 1998): 16; *China Labor Bulletin* 43 (July–August 1998): 23.

From:

Françoise Mengin & Jean-Louis Rocca, ed.

Politics in China (Palgrave 2002).

CHAPTER TWO

Labor in Limbo: Pushed by the Plan toward the Mirage of the Market

DOROTHY J. SOLINGER

Introduction

The precipitous, unprecedented sackings of millions and millions of urban industrial workers since the Fifteenth Party Congress of late 1997 have riveted the attention of observers. The picture is of enforced idleness among the workforce, unpaid wages and pensions, and steadily escalating numbers of layoffs, accompanied by a mounting drumbeat of strikers on parade along the streets. The usual assumption is that, now that the market and its disciplines have been brought into play, those firms and laborers unable to keep up with the competition just have to go. A second frequently encountered assumption is that these workers are angry and destitute, ripe for uprising. Thus, it appears at first glance that the marketization of industrial output and of labor have produced a situation verging on desperation, both for the redundant workforce and for the state as well.[1]

There is also research on the benefits the state is providing for, and the propaganda the state is presenting to, the furloughed personnel. These efforts appear to be making the process more humane, more palatable.[2] Can both scenarios be correct? Are these abruptly jobless people really finding new placements with the aid of governmental programs and preferential policies, or sustained by state payoffs (what's called the basic living allowance)? Or are they mostly left at loose ends on the "market" and ready to rebel? And how much does the market truly drive the process?

I take no issue with the seriousness of the circumstances; nor do I challenge the views that there are bitter ex-employees, some of whom have gone on strike. And neither do I question that the state—both central and local—is concerned and helping. Instead, I provide some alternate images, and offer two observations: The first is that the command apparatus, along with the customary procedures of state planning, have been just as much or even more the pushing force in the layoffs and their alleviation as has the market, though the overall process is full of paradoxes. The second is that many discarded laborers are indeed surviving, if barely, and are neither on the brink of bursting out in strikes, nor are they relieved very much by governmental largesse. But neither can one conclude that they are absorbed into a labor market.

To begin with, I illustrate paradoxes generated by pretending to proceed in accord with market dictates while instead remaining faithful to prejudices from the time of planning. Next I explore the official explanations for this monumental rush to discharge. I go on to spell out dimensions of it that resemble the methodologies of the supposedly spent command economy, and then highlight the ways in which myths are bolstering the promotion of the market. Finally, I explore survival strategies among some laid-off Wuhan workers struggling to seek their equilibrium as they are jostled between market and plan.

The chapter is based on interviews with 30 unemployed workers and a few officials involved in the program of layoffs in Wuhan in late summer 1999; I also consulted numerous journal articles. Wuhan, an old industrial base, where traditional processing industries such as textiles labored with substandard and obsolete equipment; where the state-owned sector was particularly dominant;[3] where economic development slowed down markedly after the mid-1980s, especially in contrast to the coast, in the absence of preferential policies and flourishing foreign trade and investment;[4] and that became the refuge for hundreds of thousands of peasant workers migrating in from its densely populated surrounding rural areas, experienced the pains of unemployment more than many parts of the country.[5]

Paradoxes in Combining Plan and Market

The September streets of the city of Wuhan on the eve of the People's Republic of China's fiftieth anniversary symbolized the first of a string of ironies gracing the ongoing campaign to cut the urban workforce while simultaneously establishing a labor market: This irony is of a China preparing to be sleek, slim, and efficient, streamlining its firms by forcing their workforces into a labor market prepared for international competition. For all the while, policy eschews internal labor market contention. This contrast is apparent upon seeing former city workers freely shining shoes, pedaling pedicabs, and cruising in taxicabs in the thousands along the roads and lanes, while the peasant street merchants (the shoe-repairers, snack stallkeepers, vegetable vendors) were, temporarily—in preparation for the anniversary presentation—nowhere to be found. Hence, one senses instantly that the citizens of Wuhan were meant to patronize laid-off urban workers, but to starve out outside peasants—people who just might, if permitted to, compete for the jobs of the former.[6]

Another irony arises from the fact that anniversaries call forth memories; at this one, a policy aimed at attaining modernization through mass mobilization and institutional change is eerily reminiscent of the '50s Great Leap Forward, now roundly recognized as a disaster. For in both cases a movement geared at growth and speedy—thus, necessarily, haphazard—transformation produced widespread hunger (in the former case, of course, famine) and severe deprivation for its target population.

There is a further irony, in a prominent slogan suggested to inspire the populace at this time of celebration: this is the old Mao-era one calling to "Rely on the Working Class Wholeheartedly!"[7] This rhetorical holdover is, clearly, betrayed by the effort to build a modern corporate-based economy that discards laborers, those very individuals who were themselves once enshrined in the former regime—in a most heartless, Darwinian struggle of the fittest.

Too, Chinese people have been tutored for decades in the dictum that there is no unemployment under socialism. Now that formulation is termed a "misunderstanding," as people are told to "Get rid of the old idea of no unemployment under socialism; establish the view that within a certain degree unemployment is a normal phenomenon in a market economy." The recent celebration of China's economy as a "socialist market" allows the leadership to label the loss of work a phenomenon that is not just capitalist, but common anywhere that resource allocation is mainly carried out by the market mechanism,[8] as it is in China today.

But since the regime retains socialist mentalities and pretensions (as well as deeply rooted concerns for social peace and stability),[9] its politicians are not altogether callous. So we find yet another paradox: even as leaders dismiss and marketize, at the same time they strive to reemploy the victims, largely via bureaucratic manipulation. As expressed by a manager of a district labor market exchange: "We set up labor markets, reemployment centers, social welfare and unemployment relief precisely to keep people from reaching the state of starvation."[10] So abandonment of many, many laborers (and the floating population in the cities) is at the same time matched by favors for others among the municipal workforce. Thus, the *Workers' Daily* calls for state-led reemployment and state-supplied basic livelihood guarantees plus extra official attention and concern.[11]

And in still one more variant of the schizophrenic approach to the market, local governments press banks to provide loans for paying wages and supporting employment, and coerce firms to reabsorb their extra workers, or encourage the firms to force middle-aged workers to retire early (with inadequate pensions), so that these people are compelled to seek a second job. None of these measures will produce new jobs, nor will they reduce the labor supply on the market.[12]

Several particularly powerful lines of propaganda reflect the state's often successful effort to legitimize its market-oriented actions in this campaign: The leadership proclaims the market to be absolutely necessary for China's forward motion ("laying off is the product of system reform and it is [also] the demand of system reform"; or "without the process of laying off, we can't enter the socialist market economy and state firms can't become part of the modern enterprise system"). It also labels unemployment "a necessary demand of the market economy."

Moreover, it depicts the process as one that is ultimately benevolent— "in the long-term interest of the working class,"[13] in a constant refrain. But workers with no steady salaries (put into that position, they are told, because of their limited educational backgrounds) are in greater and greater numbers unable to afford the accelerating costs of schooling for their own children, that very future working class in whose long-term interest this campaign is supposedly being waged.

The claim of necessity has not gone unchallenged. For countercharges implicitly question the market-drivenness of the movement. As one writer commented,

There have been some strange phenomena in recent years: in 1997 the gross domestic product rose by 8.8 percent, central finance grew at 13 percent, local finance at 12.5 percent, and the population increased at only one percent. In 1998 the economy slowed down but was still at the top of the list worldwide. Normally economic development can completely eliminate unemployment. Here it not only didn't eliminate it but while the numbers of unemployed increased, those laid off also suddenly shot up: in 1997, the 11.5 million layoffs represented an increase of 44 percent.[14]

Too, massive unemployment produced insufficient demand in the market, as "people dare not spend money" out of pessimism about their future incomes and in the absence of any guarantees of new jobs. Moreover, as a number of scholars have pointed out, labor market development in China is yet "rather backward."This market is one marked by much instability and turnover, by peasants appropriating workers' jobs, and by workers plunged into downward mobility and being treated as pariahs, as urban "peasants" have been.Why, then, is there so much sudden unemployment?

Unemployment, Its Causes and Cure: The Official Story

Causes

Despite the rhetorical emphasis on marketization, discussions of the layoffs invariably attribute them at least in part to previous state policy decisions, rather than simply to market forces.[15] Historical causes begin with the planned, command economy. Under that system, labor was allocated by administrative dictat, with no reference whatever to market forces. Various "noneconomic" phenomena became attached to that model, such as a value system honoring full employment; the fact that an enterprise's administrative rank was correlated with the number of employees on its books; the welfare role of the firm (which made its workers reluctant to depart even when they were permitted to do so); and the social role some firms took on by hiring on the basis of personal relationships.

Once the reform era began, these issues were not resolved, while new difficulties emerged that only increased the extent of surplus labor.With economic powers decentralized, localities across China sponsored "blind, duplicated construction." Such activity was no doubt undertaken in part to provide placement for an area's unemployed populace (especially numerous at first, with the return of Cultural Revolution-era sent-down youth to the cities). Many of these projects became the pretext for rampant borrowing, which the firms frequently could not repay, plunging them into debt that in turn threatened workers' wages and pensions. And later, under two state-induced recessions (1988 and after 1993)—instituted to clear up inflation issuing from these practices—stiff curtailment of credit for state firms occasioned significant losses. This again complicated the enterprises' ability to sustain their workforces, which only made even more workers appear to be in excess.

By the time the mid-1990s had arrived, millions of people who had once been placed in the plants out of a concern to secure their livelihood (and to secure the regime's urban support), had little to do on the job; many scholars estimate that up to a third of the workforce or about 30 million laborers could be classified as "hidden unemployed." At the Fifteenth National Party Congress in the fall of 1997, enterprises were urged to cut back their workforces in the name of elevating efficiency. Also, mergers were encouraged while bankruptcy was to become a normal event for loss-sustaining and noncompetitive firms.[16]

Tens of thousands of small firms precipitously released "to the market," once freed from state oversight, only generated yet more unemployed, even if they were still capable of absorbing workers. And many managers, falsely believing that efficiency would rise simply by shedding workers, then neglected developing new products, improving their business management, or opening new markets, all activities that might have engaged their own laid-off employees.

Of course, market competitive forces were certainly present. The opening of the Chinese market to foreigners and the relaxation on entry into many sectors for nonstate firms did spell lethal rivalry for a large number of state firms.[17] Competition from unencumbered domestic firms, not charged with responsibility for their employees' welfare, and from challengers on the international market,[18] prompted changes in the structure of employment: Some sectors and regions suffered from the market contention, and a tumble in their profits forced them to cut their personnel.[19] This process gradually squeezed out the state–owned sector, which, from 1978 to 1997, saw its proportion of gross value of industrial output fall from 77.6 percent to a mere 26.5 percent.

Over the same period, profits culled in the state-owned enterprises (SOE) dropped while losses ballooned from 4.2 billion yuan to 83.09 billion.[20] Contacts with the global market also enhanced the technological level within Chinese industry and some enterprises were able to intensify the capital component of their investment, prompting them to fire even more workers. And the influx of labor from the countryside allegedly tightened up the metropolitan labor markets. Demographic factors also played a role. These included the pronatal policy of the Mao years, a recent rise in the labor-age population, and the disparity between the country's immense population and its relatively low level of economic development.

The State's Cure: The Reemployment Project[21]

In response to mounting numbers of layoffs, the leadership devised a "Reemployment Project," piloted in 30 cities in 1994. The project was extended nationwide the following year, and pushed continuously thereafter. Its intent displays the predicament faced by the conflicted regime: it is to "safeguard the workingclass's present and long-term interest,"[22] for, after all, "We can't just push the laid-offs out to society," in the words of President Jiang Zemin.[23] This care is meant to manifest the "superiority of socialist production and the socialist system."[24] The program is to "set up a buffer zone between the enterprise [which is shedding workers] and society," in the hope of "promot[ing] social stability"; it is also to "reduce the enterprises' burdens while lightening social pressure."[25]

But the idea behind the project is to solve the problem of unemployment and promote the reemployment of those let go at a juncture when the nation's social security system, labor market, and legal framework are all perilously incomplete and imperfect, and when the number of job posts is clearly insufficient.[26] Thus its provisions make for a curious mix of market and plan. Its content includes the goals of underwriting the basic livelihood needs of the laid-off and setting up "reemployment bases" that provide free training and jobs; collecting and computerizing information on local job markets; providing job introduction organs; and building up new marketplaces, especially night markets where the traders receive preferential policies in taxes and fees. Individual cities have their own additional programs, such as Wuhan's expanding economic development at the district and street levels to establish new positions, and running district- and city-wide reemployment "fairs" and city-wide labor exchanges.[27]

The project, moreover, demands that each firm that has laid off some or all of its workers create a "reemployment service center," to which its *xiagang* (furloughed) workers are to be entrusted for a period up to three years.[28] The center is to provide a basic living allowance [*jiben shenghuofei*], again for up to three years, using funds donated by the enterprise, and, where this is not possible, from the city's financial departments and/or banks, and, if an enterprise has contributed to the fund, from the city's unemployment insurance fund. Where necessary, a donation is to be solicited from the enterprise's management department. Second, the center is also to train the workers for a new occupation, and to help them locate new work posts. And third, the center should contribute to the pension, medical, and social security funds on behalf of each laid-off worker entrusted to it. Other prongs of the project are to use tax incentives to encourage enterprises to hire those who have lost their original jobs, and to reduce or eliminate taxes and fees for the unemployed who set up their own businesses.[29]

But there are critical limitations on this effort—namely, a scarcity of funds, the widespread dependence of the unemployed upon firms that have either gone bankrupt or that are suffering serious losses and deeply in debt,[30] and the inadequate supply of positions in the economy to employ these people.[31] Thus, though the story of China's recent surge of layoffs is officially told in terms of the pull of the market, the tale is in fact far more complex than that, both in terms of cause and cure. Indeed, instrumentalities of planning still infuse the overall effort.

Planned Unemployment and Immature Marketization
The Role of the Plan: Path-dependent Praxis

The transition from state allocation of labor to labor deployment by market demand has been path-dependent. Indeed, two critical features of the Communist party's historical approach to policy implementation continue to structure its handling of unemployment.[32] These two conventions—executing policy by means of commands and quotas and handling the working class as a several-layered status hierarchy—enable political leaders to fulfill several objectives: to reduce the drain on the state's resources while honoring an elite within the furloughed workforce. These modes of action mean that the personnel cutting campaign is probably harsher than it need be, while the reemployment project is far more restrictive than the rhetoric surrounding it promises. The reliance on command–economy methodologies means, then, that there is no necessary relationship between who should be cut and who is cut, nor between who needs welfare relief and who gets it.

Commands as Cause: The Use of Quotas

True, the late 1997 intensification of cutbacks was partly driven by the desire of many local governments to divest themselves of deadbeat firms under their ownership.[33] But it was also spurred along by habits of compliance with the orders of "upper levels" in the bureaucratic hierarchy. Many sources concur in pointing to commands from above to shed workers. Informants referred to letting people go as a "trend"; "level by level leaders demand the reduction of personnel, no matter what," explained another.

One source notes that,

> Some enterprises' results are rather good, and they really need not lay off people. There's enough work to do. But still each year, personnel are forced to leave according to a certain proportion. This occurs because their upper level gives its enterprises a quota for the

number to be laid off [and uses its fulfillment] as one basis for evaluating leading cadres' work.[34]

According to another,

> To reach the goal of cutting people, some firms raise the [production] quota, so that staff and workers can't finish their tasks. Then, on the pretext that they are unqualified, the firm cancels their labor contracts, or compels them to retire early.[35]

Though one more criticizes the use of quotas to reduce the numbers in a unit as a "deviation," such a caution is a sure sign that the practice is widespread.

Quotas are also employed in determining the number of workers from each firm permitted to enter into the care of the firm's reemployment center. One informant's company had a quota allowing only 30 people to enter the center at one time. Newly laid-off personnel, such as she, had to wait in line until those currently in the center found work, at which point the latter were to break their ties with the center. And not being within the jurisdiction of the center means that a person is not even classified as *xiagang,* though s/he might be from a state firm and meet all the other specifications. By extension, not having this status means one is not qualified to obtain a *xiagang* certificate or, in some cases, even to get any living allowance.[36] Quotas clearly serve to limit the numbers of potential beneficiaries and the extent of benefits disbursed, while they could well inflate the numbers sacked.

Curing by Categorization: A Layering of Statuses[37]

The term *xiagang* is popularly used, quite loosely, to refer to people no longer at work in their original *danwei.*[38] But in fact, the regime and local governments stratify those whose jobs have been terminated into at least seven tiers, each of which receives differential treatment. It appears in journals and in interviews that an implicit status hierarchy accords benefits or lack thereof to workers according to the following descending status hierarchy: those from relatively healthy state firms; those from poor state firms; people whose situations do not fit the criteria for *xiagang* (the "diverted," "early retired," "on long holiday") and those from wealthier collective firms; the registered unemployed; personnel from poor collectives; those in special difficulty [*tekun*]; and last, peasant migrant labor.[39] In a rough sense, these layers eerily parallel the divisions within the socialist-era working class, as described by Andrew Walder in a 1984 article.[40]

In fact, those who fully qualify as *xiagang* (according to the state's definition) stand in the top two tiers of the hierarchy, and are the only ones
counted as "laid off" and accorded benefits.

While significantly complicating any effort to achieve a true measure of
the numbers affected by the mass discharge campaign, these labels and distinctions seem to allow the government to absolve itself of the responsibility of caring for them all. And the hodgepodge of terminology somehow
justifies to the recipients that their respective treatment has a rationale.
Perhaps intentionally and perhaps inadvertently, by splitting up the workers severed from their posts into a myriad of situations, each with its own
label, this range of terms and treatments could serve to repress any unified
mobilization.[41]

These two path-dependent throwbacks to the methodologies of the
planned economy—causing cutbacks through commands and quotas, and
truly succoring only workers from the best state-sector firms—contribute
in a major way to the discrepancy between a discourse of marketization
and a reality of statist execution. These practices also help to account for
the great shortfall between a benevolent program to ease dismissed workers into society and onto the labor market and the actuality of suffering
for many. The resort to such approaches suggests that policy fulfillment by
fiat still obtains in several critical ways.

Market Lapses

While policy execution by planning is well rehearsed, the numbers in
need of work are so large and the labor market yet so imperfect that no
amount of good faith and no degree of adherence to market prescriptions
could meet the goals of at once letting millions go while also smoothing
their way into a new occupation or workpost. There are also serious mis-
conceptions and oversimplified views about the capacity of the market to
handle the massive numbers of laid-off people supposedly spilling into it.

Misperceptions include lack of understanding of the limitations of
the private sector; a misjudgment that reemployment centers could serve
as the bridge to a job; and inflated expectations about the operation of
preferential policies. There are also gross insufficiencies of funding, making it foolish to guarantee that enterprising ex-employees can begin
their own businesses or even survive at a barely acceptable level of subsistence until they do. Moreover, it is difficult to confirm that—or even
to measure if—personnel cuts automatically and by themselves lead to
greater efficiency in the firms. Below I examine the flaws in the hopes
placed in these market solutions.

The Inadequacy of the Private Sector

Since the market for manufactures atrophied in the late 1990s with falling domestic demand, some people imagine that "there is great potential for the tertiary sector," which allegedly supplied 70 percent of new jobs in 1997.[42] Premier Zhu Rongji commented in early 1998 that, "Since many industrial products are in excess supply, only the service sector can absorb labor power."[43] And yet, the Ministry of Labor and Social Security was fully aware of the weaknesses of this sector by early 1999, characterizing it as having only "limited development potential."[44] As the former vice chair of the Wuhan City People's Congress's finance and economics committee commented, a healthy service sector cannot simply thrive on its own, rather, it requires an expanding economy in which workers' incomes are rising to create a market for its business.

Besides the issue of a stagnant market, the individual thinking of setting him/herself up in business often has a low income and no real chance of obtaining a bank loan, and must face high risk and fierce competition. Many private businesses, therefore, have very short life spans. One provincial labor bureau chief even adjudged that the service sector could at best just provide just a "supplementary income" for the laid-off workforce.[45] Labor journals feature advice columns urging the furloughed to borrow only a small amount of money, and to go into trades where there are fewer competitors.[46]

Despite the wisdom of this admonition, there is little evidence on the streets that it has been heeded. Instead, particular trades in major cities, having become fads, are quickly saturated. In Wuhan this trendiness was literally omnipresent. In the pedicab trade, for instance, where not so long ago drivers could collect three yuan for peddling the shortest-distance trip, a *hanggui* (rule of the trade) had developed informally by mid-1999 only permitting them to charge two. Similarly, on one sidewalk where three different shoe-shiners contended for customers, each got only two yuan per shine. Household labor was also in oversupply by early autumn 1999. Local branches of the Women's Federation were obligated to sign contracts pledging to find work for neighborhood women laid off from state firms. But one woman told me that she was to contact that office just once a month and then wait to be called for a job. By late summer 1999 this meant she was biding her time for up to a month with nothing to do.[47] Another wore herself out uncomplainingly for more than 10 hours a day at a tiny stall on her husband's university grounds in 1995 and 1996. But as such stalls proliferated, the school administration demanded they all be dismantled.

Landing a post with a private entrepreneur is no less dicey. Most commonly a worker takes a job and then quits it quickly, once s/he finds there is no social security or welfare offered, no contract to be signed, the pay is piddling, and the boss treats him/her with contempt. One interviewee had this experience, relinquishing her post within half a month after being assigned to the storeroom, where she was warned not to steal cell phones.[48] Many do persist in these professions despite their trivial take and uncertain prospects. But one cannot conclude that, just because they are on the streets laboring, their service is one that the market demands.

Reemployment Centers' Failures to Reemploy

Even if reemployment centers were really equipped to nurture the laid-off and foster new skills, the external environment—the "labor market"—lacks the necessary job posts.[49] In part, this is because state macroeconomic policy in the mid-1990s focused on fighting inflation and efficiency, not on investing in labor-intensive trades or job creation. There has also been a serious scarcity in bank credit for the kinds of firms—small or even medium-sized—likely to employ or be started by those who have lost their jobs.[50]

But many centers do not even try to train or place their charges. Perhaps too intimidated by the meager prospects of locating jobs, many personnel expend their time soliciting and disbursing funds, or even just sending rice to the idle as a form of relief.[51] This approach lulls some former workers into a sense of security, as is apparent in warnings in the journals against allowing ex-workers to treat the center as a "blind alley" that one "only enters and never leaves." There are also workers slipping back into their original firms when their stint under the care of the center terminates.[52] When such things occur, centers simply cannot contribute to forging a labor market.

The training the centers should be supplying varies a great deal: some informants reported that their firms' centers offered helpful training programs, with courses in computer science, accounting, cooking, running small businesses, repair work, and other basic skills.[53] Other interviewees said, however, that the center in their firm merely provided a form to fill in but had nothing more to offer.[54] Even where training is available, not everyone eligible chooses to partake, some doubting it could increase their incomes. Others assume they would have to abandon their present work opportunities to participate in the classes.[55] This hesitancy no doubt is heightened when the training on offer is, contrary to regulations, not free, or when it is irrelevant to the positions on the market.[56] A late 1997 report on Wuhan's reemployment project found that, of the nearly 300,000 known laid-off workers in the city, only 16,204 (about five percent) were recorded as having received some training in the first nine months of the year.[57]

One worker admitted that her center had found some jobs for people, but "not good jobs"—just washing floors or cleaning houses; another complained that the center did nothing to help her; and a third had been dismissed by a unit with a center, but felt that even "going there is no use ... there's so many laid-off workers ... the center couldn't possibly manage to help them all."[58] Many centers failed to pay the medical insurance they were supposed to supply: in a study of over 700 laid-off workers in Wuhan, 56 percent were found to be without it.[59] And in a number of textile firms in difficulty managers were afraid to allow their laid-off staff and workers to enter a center at all, because the firm could not afford to pay the enterprise share of the center's trusteeship expenses.[60]

Given these many sorts of misses, the steps from a firm into its reemployment center and then onto the open market make for a perilous journey very frequently not preparing one for success at its end point.

The Precariousness of Preferential Policies
As noted earlier, the Reemployment Project is to grant job-seekers and employers preferential policies to facilitate the creation of new positions. The policies include reduction and elimination of taxes and fees for those setting up on their own enterprises and for firms that hire specific proportions of laid-off workers; free business licenses; bank loans at low interest; provision of sites and stalls; and "reemployment bases," sites that hire or provide space for large numbers of the recently jobless.[61] If these programs went into effect for all the unemployed, there would be a huge drop in the numbers without a post.

But for many reasons this cannot be the case. In a September 1997 study of 2,447 workers in 580 firms in 10 Hubei cities, of the 567 working in private enterprises, just 13.7 percent enjoyed preferential policies.[62] Among my own informants, one woman noted bitterly that since entering the night market established by her residents' committee, she had had to buy a business license for several hundred yuan. Another had to pay monthly taxes and fees amounting to 65 yuan, despite the fact that policy dictated eliminating these costs.[63]

Units in charge delay and resist, unwilling to relinquish the monies they could garner by ignoring the injunctions.[64] Employers sometimes manipulate the rules to their own advantage, as by firing "unemployed" people they have already hired (for which there are no inducements, in accord with the hierarchy of those out of work) and then switch to employing *xiagang* workers, a move that earns the firm a subsidy. Sometimes these firms engage the laid-off just for a trial period (long enough to collect the incentive money) and then quickly shove them out.[65] Other areas fail to publicize the policies: in one Hubei county, of 9,656 people laid off, 95 percent were not even aware that they needed to acquire a *xiagang* certificate to be eligible for these policies.[66]

Workers may choose not to avail themselves of the supposed benefits out of despair. One informant, a member of a household in special difficulty [*tekunhu*], who was therefore entitled to eight different types of favorable policies set by his district government (no taxes on business, fewer fees, cheaper schooling for his children, some reductions in medical fees, no introduction fee for finding a job, and half-price rent), had not even bothered to apply for the necessary certificate. For he had no money for rent, he was too ill to work, had no children in school, and, because of his illness, could not go into business.[67] Another had also not registered for the certificate, since, clearly depressed, she surmised that, "it can't be of any help." Thus this program promising reemployment via privileged regulations is one beset by many drawbacks.

Funding Shortages

Even with the best of intentions, state efforts to construct a labor market while sustaining the castoffs crash on the shoals of a very shallow pool of available funds. In addition to financing reemployment centers, firms with laid-off workers and their urban governments are responsible for contributing to three kinds of guarantees for the newly out-of-work: the basic livelihood allowances, unemployment insurance payments, and the urban residents' lowest livelihood guarantee [*zuidi shenghuo baozhang*].[68] But not one of these programs has a truly stable and reliable source of funding.[69]

The Ministry of Finance has made a substantial allocation for basic living allowances. But given that firms that have let go their workers are generally in serious financial straits in the first place—often unable even to pay wages—they usually cannot afford to contribute their share. Huge disparities attend the amounts available among firms and among regions as well. As one article explained,

There are great differences among areas in the level of economic development. If local financial departments are the main units in charge of funding, areas where workers need the guarantees can't get them and places where they don't need funds can't even use up the money they have.[70]

Only a minority of cities had set up special funds for reemployment as of 1998. The main sources for this capital are the unemployment insurance fund and local financial departments. But some localities instead assess a special fee to be collected for this purpose. In recent years nationwide the total outlay represented under 0.1 percent of the country's financial expenditures, while the percent of GDP used this way "was so small that it couldn't be measured."[71]

As local governments have also been charged with producing funds to meet the needs of those in special difficulty [juekun jijin] that draw upon the same capital sources, some areas question whether they need to raise money for the Reemployment Project as well.[72] An odd twist in Wuhan, not likely to be limited to that one city: while the textile trade's reemployment center was short almost half the funds it needed for worker allowances in early 1998,[73] the city was spending almost 100 million yuan on the administrative costs and wages in the city's numerous reemployment centers![74]

Unemployment insurance only came into existence in 1986, so its accumulated funds are quite limited. Moreover, only two percent of the wage fund was drawn to compose this pot until 1998, when three percent became the rule. Too, the pooling level is low, and only a portion of the funds are actually used for the livelihood relief of the unemployed.[75] In 1998, the total intake of the fund nationally was just 6.84 billion yuan, of which 5.196 billion was spent, and reemployment centers received over a quarter (1.46 billion). And, while 79.279 million persons were participating in the fund nationally, only 1.581 million unemployed people got unemployment relief, while another 1.486 million staff and workers in enterprises experiencing difficulty got one-time payments.[76] According to a survey of xiagang in dozens of cities in the second half of 1997, 96.3 percent claimed to be living in cities that provided no social relief aid at all![77]

Personnel Cuts and Efficiency
Since at least early 1997, the mantra of the Chinese leadership has been to "cut personnel, raise efficiency."[78] But just as preferential policies and reemployment centers cannot transform all jobless people into jobholders, neither can the sometimes random chopping away of personnel by itself create efficiency where there was little or none before. As one critic complained, "Some enterprises have been losing money for a long time.

If they reduce their laborers, force down their welfare benefits and then say, 'the enterprise has turned around its losses,' is this 'cutting off personnel and raising efficiency'?"[79]

Firms given leeway—even orders—to shrink their payrolls do so, but then resort to tactics that do nothing to enhance efficiency, the supposed intention behind the layoffs. These tactics include treating the workers as scapegoats for the inefficiencies of the management, taking this "reform" as one more opportunity for corruption, and using layoffs for revenge against those with whom they've had conflicts. Even as frontline production workers are sent packing, leaders bring in their relatives to replace them. Other enterprises that could still absorb labor nonetheless throw out staff and workers when their leaders' squandering and waste is what really caused the unit's losses.[80]

Sudden unemployment in this economy in transition from planning is thus clearly partially driven and structured by administrative patterns passed down from the past, while a yet nascent labor market can hardly address the needs of the dismissed.

Survival of the Sacked

Traits of the Laid-off

Studies of the laid-off population show that the majority are female, over 30 or 35, and undereducated.[81] Laid-off workers themselves are clear about the obstacle their ages present. As many women over the age of 30 remarked, "Only people under 30 can find work."[82] One would have loved to become a saleswoman, but, at 37, could not hope to be hired because she was "too old." The *xiagang* workers are also keenly aware of the liabilities of their insufficient education, usually the outcome of their having been of school age during the Cultural Revolution. One bemoaned, "All laid-off workers know they've been laid off because of their poor educational background. So I want to be sure my boy gets a good education, so he won't have to suffer like I did." And a laid-off accountant in her late 30s with a technical school diploma remarked, "I expect to find a job through acquaintances some time ... it's hard for me to apply directly—I don't have enough education for that."[83]

The 1995 national urban population one percent sample survey found that 69 percent of the furloughed had just junior-high and lower levels of schooling (whereas the figure with this amount among the employed was 63.9 percent).[84] But probably because of the much more massive firings in the next few years, official statistics for 1998 show that just

53.5 percent of those released from their posts had only a junior-high education or below.[85]

What attitudes do these people entertain? What work do they do, how do they find it and how long do they stay? What are their levels of income and means of survival financially? The overall impression is that laid-off workers are often struggling in a limbo fashioned from leftover planning-era procedures mixed with myths about what the open market can achieve.

Attitudes: Tied to the State Plan?

Governmental propaganda and even much scholarly Chinese literature chastise the jobless—those thrown out of work largely because of a sudden change in official policy after years of absolute and unquestioned state provisioning and security—for being "in love with government arrangements" and wanting only to "wait, rely, and demand"; "looking to the government instead of to the market." Such reports also disparage them as too fussy, unwilling to do the jobs that peasant migrants do.[86] Their yearning for state-bestowed sustenance has supposedly left them disinclined to venture into the market.

Surely there are people among the laid-off who fit these stereotypes. But, more importantly, there is a clear rationale behind this mindset, one long ingrained by state practice. As one writer pointed out, their "not wanting to part from their firms or do service work or set themselves up in business is not just because of a [negative] mentality. [It's because] they are weighing the costs of losing their benefits."[87] And even though the workers know that the welfare entitlements that graced their lives for decades are disappearing around them, many, even those out of work for years, "still entrust their original work unit and the government with their hopes for reemployment,"[88] no doubt under the illusion that with time these benefits might possibly somehow reappear.

Other reasonable motives for remaining out of work are feelings like those of one of my informants that, "It's because of my self-respect that I don't want to serve others [as a cleaning lady] who may think I'm a thief." She wished she could start a business of her own, but had neither sufficient capital nor the means for leaving a deposit on a loan with a bank ("You need economic power [*jingji shili*] to get a loan").[89] All this, of course, is a function of long-standing state enterprise provisioning and of state banks' lending habits.

Under the assumption that a willful choice to eschew the market keeps many out of it, official and academic surveys seem to demonstrate that huge numbers of the jobless either do not want to work or do not need to work—either because another family member is employed (for the time being), for reasons of age or health, or because of household chores. Of the 11.5 million officially counted as laid off at the end of 1997, 2.56 million (22 percent) supposedly did not want to work or were temporarily not working (as if these two categories could be conflated), while just 37.57 percent were said to be actively looking and had a pressing demand to work.[90] A Wuhan study alleged that the *xiagang* can be divided into three types: one third are reemployed; one third have gone through *neitui, tingxin liuzhi,* or *liangbuzhao;*[91] and only one third need help with their reemployment.[92]

These data are open to serious question if a 1997 six-month survey of laid-off workers in dozens of cities is accurate. It found that a full 100 percent queried wanted to find work.[93] In my own interviews, not one wanted to be without work, even though some claimed that there was household work that they needed to do, or that their spouse preferred that they not work. Others were temporarily unable to locate work or deeply discouraged, either from looking unsuccessfully or from being repeatedly let go when they clashed with the boss or when the ventures failed. Most of these people would have been incorrectly categorized as "not wanting to" or "not needing to work" in governmentally-endorsed studies.[94] This would be consistent with a state effort to reduce the drain on state coffers.

An odd blend of faith in the state and—only sometimes—anger at their unit's management is a typical state of mind for the laid-off.[95] According to one study in Wuhan, the respondents tended only to "blame the unit and the government a little: 'they don't want us to be laid off... but they can't support us.' "[96] As a pragmatic cab driver declared to me, "It's no use being angry—the whole country's being laid off[!]" A former female accountant, seemingly disconsolate, described herself as "very sad, not angry. Who is there to be angry with? I think it's just my fate, not sure whose fault it might have been. Anyway, there's nothing I can do." At her husband's prompting, she did recognize that it was in the leaders' power to determine who was cut, as he remarked that, "What makes us sad is that the leaders weren't cut too, so we're a little angry that it isn't fair."

Most surprisingly, many of those with whom I spoke appeared to have absorbed governmental rhetoric about their plight and its positive contribution to the national well-being. Two laid-off women reflected over bowls of noodles,

For China to progress, we have to go through this process, and people will be affected, like us. All developed countries have unemployment. We understand the government and the need to sacrifice for the next generation, for our own kids. People need to get culture and education so the country can get stronger. They eliminate us because the government knows that foreign firms want young, educated people. It's a necessary law of social development to eliminate people.

And a male janitor, mopping the marble pillars of my hotel at 1:30 A.M., bravely proclaimed, with tears in his eyes, "Without reform and opening up, China will remain backward. There's no future for it otherwise."[97]

And yet, despite a nostalgia for state-arranged job allocations, a large number of my informants displayed admirable pluck about working and finding work, as their words reveal:

—If you don't fear fatigue and don't fear bitterness, you can find something to do; if you've no income, you can't be choosy;

—(On being asked about a suicide case): It was his own character. A lot of people are laid off. They can't all commit suicide!

—I feel I should work. Of course I'd be upset if I never found a job.

—Even though there's a lot of people laid off in Wuhan, you can still find something to do ... if you still have two hands.

—Everyone has to eat, even the American President. It's all just a difference in the division of labor.[98]

Echoing their sentiments, a 1997 Wuhan survey of laid-off workers found that 55 percent were willing to become just ordinary workers, service or salespeople; another 35 percent were prepared to do any kind of work, no matter how dirty or tiring, if only it would enable them to meet their basic expenses.[99] Here then are people deserted by their *danwei* and by the state, but not resorting to demonstrating. Moreover, those people appear to have been written off by the plan but not to have found a place in the market.

Despite the laudable spunk, when queried about the future, the state of limbo between plan and market into which these people have been cast became painfully plain. Here are some of their replies:

—A sick man denied his *bingtui*[100] and confined to his home by his disability views "wait[ing] for my pension" as his only future;

—A couple, both of whom have lost their jobs: "Go forward a step and then see where you are [*zou yibu, kan yibu*]; don't dare think about it [*buganxiang*]";

—A cabbie, asked if it would be okay with him to drive a cab for the rest of his life: "If it's not okay, then what? I'll just have to see what comes up" [*buxing zenma ban? hai yao kan jihui*]"; and
—A night market stallkeeper: "Hard to say [*buhao shuo*]."[101]

And yet, as if their problems were all of their own making, the extremely frequent job turnover these *xiagang* experience has convinced one analyst to oppose any governmental efforts to entice firms to hire them:

Some go to work for several days and then are laid off once again. This is because the new posts are too demanding for them or the wages aren't much higher than they could get in basic livelihood allowances, they feel the conditions are inferior, or it's too far from home.[102]

If my small sample is representative, the state and many Chinese scholars, failing to understand the complexity of these people's state of mind, quite unfairly berate them for their attachment to their former firms and their inability to find or hold onto new employment in the market.

Getting Jobs and Staying with Them: How the "Market" Works

Many are, in fact, seeking jobs on their own. But can we infer from this that the labor market is working? On one point the official critique of the laid-off workers is absolutely correct: "People only feel they are employed [or, one might say, have a 'job' [*gongzuo*]] if they are in a state enterprise with stable work and full welfare benefits and guarantees."[103] Whether currently at work or not, all the once laid-off laborers I met considered themselves "*xiagang* workers." By the same token, I could never convince cabbies that driving their taxis amounted to a "job." Apparently their labor, with its instability and insecurity—no matter what their earnings— was not the equivalent of a genuine "*gongzuo*."

Moreover, "reemployed" is a slippery concept. In one of my interviews, the still securely employed friend of a woman who had been laid off three times found the definition of the term quite simple: "It means that you work and get an income again, even if it's temporary or short term, unstable." But neither I nor her presently jobless companion could calculate whether or not we should count the latter among those with that label.[104] Besides the flimsiness of "jobs" people take, the nature of many laid-offs' work life is most irregular. A late 1998 Ministry of Labor and Social Security Information Center survey of over 4,000 working-age people in four cities found that, of those furloughed who had found new work,

22 percent were laboring under 30 hours per week; another 59 percent were working 30 to 50 hours; and those at work more than 50 hours per week made up the last 19 percent. The corresponding percentages for those still in their original posts was 2.6, 93.5 and 3.9 percent, respectively. Thus, whereas 41 percent of the *xiagang* workers worked abnormal hours, only 6.5 percent of the "employed" did so.[105]

Among my sample, there was a temporary cook who made six to eight yuan per day (about US$1.00) cooking lunch for random and shifting establishments on the strength of friends' introductions. Another woman who, first let go by her own firm, had later been dismissed from a private enterprise when its business deteriorated, and was currently dishwashing at a restaurant for 12 hours per day for 300 yuan a month, or less than a yuan per hour. Another woman, on her third post-enterprise position, was charged with watching the gates at the idle plant where she had once been employed.

Then there was the woman doing housework when contacted by the Women's Federation, sometimes just once a month. When she did get this very temporary employment, she was paid by the hour, at the measly rate of 3.2 yuan (about US cents 40). A cab driver had finally determined to take up his present profession after running through a full five jobs since his layoff in 1994, including driving a pedicab, serving in a restaurant, running a small stall on the street, and working for a private firm. Shoe-shiners polish until dark falls, even through the damp chill of the winter—or, admitted one, she simply "couldn't eat." At the night markets, where stall after stall specializes in one or another of a few varieties of cheap merchandise (stationery, cosmetics, stockings, flashlights, kitchen utensils, knives), salespeople commonly take in only 200 to 300 yuan per month.[106]

In late 1998, the labor ministry's four-city investigation discovered that 41 percent of those out of work had been so from one to three years.[107] Similar data come from Wuhan: a year earlier the study of 760 laid-off persons concluded that "the absolute majority" of the 360 reemployed among them had spent more than two years looking for work.[108] Given the lack of clarity as to just what "reemployment" and "job" really mean, plus the prevalence of short-term posts, it is difficult to know how to interpret this data. But since these figures imply difficulty in finding new placements, the next question is how people manage it.

All the information suggests that in spite of the mammoth official efforts on their behalf reported by local governments, by far the greater part of the laid-off make their arrangements either "on their own" or through personal ties. In the 1997 Wuhan survey of 360 reemployed, just two percent used governmental assistance and another three percent drew on their neighborhood committee's help. A full 44 percent claimed to have achieved a new position on their own, 40 percent through the help of friends and relatives, 3.6 percent at a talent exchange center, and 21.6 percent at a professional introduction office, with 5.5 percent in an "other" category.[109]

The typical ad must surely scare off the average laid-off person: it calls for a college graduate, preferably holding a Master's degree, under the age of 30 or 35, with two or more years of work experience. As a news article admitted: "This won't work for those who couldn't get higher education because of 'historical reasons' and those middle-aged workers who have lost their jobs."[110] Nor will an electronic screen at Wuhan City's central labor market posting job openings suit their needs. For virtually all the jobs are for people under 30, some even for those under 22 years of age.[111]

These considerations lend credence to the assertion of one scholar that, "Fewer than 10 percent of the surplus personnel use the labor market for employment or reemployment."[112] The instability of the work they locate and of the earnings that go with it, combined with the unwillingness of firms to sign contracts or to offer any benefits, all add to the rapidity of quits and firings that the members of the laid-off population repeatedly experience.[113] Here again we find furloughed folk functioning, but neither serviced by the state, ensnarled in strikes, nor in demand on the market.

Financial Survival

Much writing on the laid-off censures those termed the "hidden employed." One study of 1,000 dismissed workers in eight enterprises reported that over 70 percent belonged to this category, meaning they were still collecting some "basic living allowance" from their former firm while obtaining wages from a job elsewhere.[114] Granted, this behavior apparently obstructs the development of a true labor market and further hamstrings the economic recovery of failing firms.

But material on the income and mundane miseries of these people evinces the genuine necessity of such activity for those thrust into the vacuum between the state security of the past and the very inchoate, totally insufficient social security system of the present. Such people must constantly scramble for the wherewithal for subsistence. This they do in a "market" that could clearly do without them.

The 760-respondent survey in 1997 Wuhan revealed that 57 percent of the furloughed received no allowance at all from their firms—a figure very close to the national, official one for that year[115]—and others got as little from them as 20 yuan a month.[116] Twenty-one percent of those "reemployed" were earning a mere 100 to 200 yuan a month and 36 percent between 300 and 500 yuan.[117] Of those who had not become "reemployed," a full 38 percent somehow got hold of funds amounting to less than 100 yuan a month; another 23 percent got 100 to 200, and 16.5 percent 200 to 300. According to this breakdown, over three quarters (77.5 percent) were trying to make do on less than 300 yuan a month for an entire family and 61 percent had under 200 yuan![118] Far more grim were the findings from a five-province trade union survey of 1.58 million workers from 4,494 enterprises that had stopped or half-stopped production. There 15 percent were surviving on an average income under 50 yuan![119]

And whence did such meager intake derive? In Fangxian, Hubei in 1998, 50 percent were relying on the apparently skimpy allowances from their units, 20 percent on income from odd jobs, 10 percent were "resting on their laurels," and just 20 percent had become "reemployed." In Shanghai two years earlier the percentages were quite similar.[120] In short, going to work for a second unit to supplement the generally paltry payments from their original enterprises should not be viewed as a covert or even an illicit form of behavior. In many cases it is absolutely essential, particularly in the absence as yet of any effective social security and unemployment insurance system.

These poverty-stricken people endure various hardships. In Fangxian, 75 percent of those dismissed had both their young and their elderly depending upon them.[121] Such people cannot "afford to be filial or to raise their children; they can only eat rice and pray to Buddha," quipped one commentator.[122] A study of over 28,000 children in a district of Shijiazhuang, Hebei, found that 30 percent had laid-off parents and that, because of these layoffs, 11 percent of middle school students were thinking of quitting school.[123] The State Statistical Bureau admitted that at as of the end of 1997, "most laid-off workers were without medical benefits";[124] even in prosperous Shanghai, researchers reported in 1996 that the allowances of the laid-off were so low that there was "no way to squeeze out some money to see a doctor."[125]

My interviews with laid-off people, who were nearly all engaged in some form of income-generating activity and some of whom did receive some allowance from their old firms, is quite consistent with these accounts. My disabled male worker very rarely even eats eggs and is still wearing the clothes from the time he last worked, five years ago.[126] Another man, supporting himself since he was laid off in 1996, got sick in 1998 and had to pay over 2,000 yuan for his medical bills. The factory, using the alibi that "We've got people with more serious illnesses than you," only reimbursed 400 yuan of his costs.[127]

Those with children were compelled to put out 400 to 500 yuan a year for their primary school educations, 700 to 800 for middle school and at least 1,200 for high school; to manage this, they were perforce cutting down on everything else that made up the fabric of their existence. As a middle-aged woman bemoaned with her 18-year-old daughter standing beside her at a night-market stall, "Now it takes two people just to raise one child." With no money for schooling beyond her middle school and no jobs for the girl, it was not quite clear why this sacrifice was being made.[128]

Several small incidents in the course of my patronage of the laid-offs' businesses struck me powerfully as a symbol of the grit amidst poverty of these people without "jobs." The first was the extravagant gratitude of a pedicab driver when I paid him six instead of the five yuan he asked for (the equivalent of 12 US cents extra); the second was the evident thrill on the face of a night-market stallwoman to whom I gave an extra .20 yuan (or US$.025) for a pair of scissors for which she asked 1.80 yuan. And third was the shoe-shiner who refused to take three yuan when the going rate was two, proclaiming proudly that she "still had to have a conscience."

Conclusion

Clearly those laid-off laborers still willing to work for their livelihoods—and there are many of these—have sunk from the status of the masters of their workplaces, the "leading class" of China, to a social position hardly better than that of the peasants from outside the city seen as trespassing upon the urban turf when they enter town in search of jobs. This steep decline in the workers' standing is in the first place at least in part the product not just of the market, but also of the regime's clinging to certain key facets of the command economy in order to get state goals achieved. That is, it is relying on quotas to kick people out, and concocting a hierarchy among former workers that justifies limiting the number of recipients eligible for entitlements—just as it once depended upon a similar ranking system for those at work.

Meanwhile, state leaders have convinced themselves that they are cobbling together a labor market by passing some interim preferential policies, calling for the construction of reemployment centers, and nurturing a private sector. These measures, they pronounce, should dispose of the problems of the dislocated. The stark inadequacy of such tactics forms the second part of the problem. The overall outcome is that much of Chinese labor is living in a limbo between plan and market, in a world that partakes of the worst of both models, large numbers of them surviving but just barely. Government benefits often fail them, and yet they have neither the time nor the spirit to resist the state. Instead they soldier on, neither striking nor succored. The final irony in this chapter that began with a long list of them is that China's marketizing, proto-capitalist economy is converting the country's less educated, middle-aged city folk into cheap labor and second-class citizens, thereby ever narrowing the camp of those who fully belong. So, at the same time the working class is lionized in rhetoric, its members are in actuality filling the function of the farmers cleaned away to prettify the cities' streets in celebration of "socialist" China's fiftieth anniversary.[129]

Notes

1. Antoine Kernen, "Surviving Reform in Shenyang—New Poverty in Pioneer City," *China Rights Forum* (hereafter *CRF*) (Summer 1997): 11; Andrew Watson, "Enterprise Reform and Employment Change in Shaanxi Province," paper presented at the Annual Meeting of the Association for Asian Studies, Washington, DC, 28 March, 1998; Ching Kwan Lee, chapter in this volume; and Ching Kwan Lee, "From Organized Dependence to Disorganized Despotism: Changing Labour Regimes in Chinese Factories," *The China Quarterly* (hereafter *CQ*) 155 (1999): 44–71.

2. Mark Blecher, "Strategies of Chinese State Legitimation Among the Working Class," paper presented to the Workshop on Strategies of State Legitimation in Contemporary China, Center for Chinese Studies, University of California at Berkeley, 7–9 May 1999; Jean-Louis Rocca, chapter in this volume; Antoine Kernen, and Jean-Louis Rocca, "The Reform of State-Owned Enterprises and its Social Consequences in Shenyang and Liaoning," (Ms., 1999); and Jean-Louis Rocca, "Old Working Class, New Working Class: Reforms, Labour Crisis and the Two Faces of Conflicts in Chinese Urban Areas" (first draft). Paper presented at the Second Annual Conference of the European Union–China Academic Network, 21–22 January 1999, Centro de Estudios de Asia Oriental, Universidad Autonoma de Madrid, Spain.

3. Even though the state sector's percentage of gross value of industrial output has decreased significantly in the 1990s down to 38.7 percent as of 1997 *Wuhanshi tongjiju, bian* (Wuhan City Statistical Bureau, ed.), *Wuhan tongji nianjian* (Statistical Yearbook of Wuhan, 1998) (Beijing: Zhongguo tongji chubanshe, 1998): 49, as of 1988, in a list of eight cities, only Xi'an surpassed Wuhan's 78 percent (Dorothy J. Solinger, "Despite Decentralization: Disadvantages and Dependence in the Inland and Continuing Central Power in Wuhan," *CQ* 145 (March 1996): 10).

4. Solinger, "Despite Decentralization", 1–34.

5. Si, Yuan and Zeng, Xiangmin, "Wuhan '98 hongguan zhengce shouxian mubiao—zaijiuye," (Wuhan's '98 macro policy's first objective: reemployment) *Wuhan jingji yanjiu* (Wuhan economic research) (March 1998): 55–58.

6. This same thing occurred in other cities. See Lorien Holland, "Poor, and Poorer," *Far Eastern Economic Review* (hereafter *FEER*) (21 October 1999): 26; and "Undesirable, maybe, but vital," *Economist* (16 October 1999): 41.

7. Erik Eckholm, "China to Let 50 Slogans Bloom (a Bit) and Just 50," *New York Times* (15 September 1999).

8. In *Jingji ribao* (Economic Daily) (hereafter *JRB*) (27 April 1998).

9. See, for instance, Deng, Baoshan, "Zhengfu, qiye, he xiagang zhigong zai zaijiuye gongcuozhong de cuoyong," (Government, enterprise, and laid-off staff and workers' role in reemployment work) *Zhongguo laodong* (Chinese Labor) (hereafter *ZGLD*) (March 1999): 11.

10. Interview, September 7, 1999.

11. *Gongren ribao* (Workers' Daily) (6 May 1998); and Cai, Fang, "Zhuangui shiqi de jiuye zhengce xuanze: jiaozheng zhiduxing niuqu," (Employment policy choice in a period of transition: rectify systemic distortions), *Zhongguo renkou kexue* (Chinese Population Science) (hereafter *ZRK*) (February 1999): 5–6.

12. Cai, "Zhuangui shiqi de jiuye zhengce xuanze," 5.

13. *JJRB* (27 April 1998); also see Zhu Rongji's speech in Tianjin, from *Jingji guanli wenzhai* (Economic Management Digest), in *Gongyun cankao ziliao* (Workers' Movement Reference Materials) (hereafter *GYCKZL*) (March 1998): 5.

14. Wang, Aiqun, "Dangqian jiuye xin tedian," (New characteristics of present unemployment), *Zhongguo jiuye* (Chinese Employment) (hereafter *ZGJY*) (June 1998): 29.

15. The following analysis draws upon these articles and books: Deng, Baoshan, "Zhengfu, qiye, he xiagang zhigong zai zaijiuye gongcuozhong de cuoyong," 11; Zhu, Rongji, *Jingji guanli wenzhai*, 5; Li, Peilin, *Zhongguo gaigebao* (China Reform News) (1 April 1998) in *GYCKZL*, (March 1998): 11; Hu, Angang, *Zhongguo jingji shibao* (Chinese Economic Times) in *GYCKZL* (March 1998): 12; *JJRB* (27 April 1998); *Gongren ribao* (*Worker's Daily*, hereafter *GRRB*) (6 May 1998); Wang, Aiqun, "Dangqian jiuye xin tedian," 29–30; Yang, Yiyong and Li, Jianli, "1999 nian wo guo jiuye xingshi yiran shifen yansu," (In 1999 China's employment situation is still extremely serious), *Neibu canyue* (Internal Consultations) (hereafter *NBCY*) 449 (2 October 1999): 2–7; Cai, "Zhuangui shiqi de jiuye zhengce xuanze," 3; Li, Peilin, "Zouchu guoyou qiye de renyuan guomihua luoji" (The logic of the excessive intensity of personnel in the state enterprises) *ZRK* (February 1999): 7–11; Jun, Fu, "Shixi wo guo dangqian de shiye tedian yu jiuye nandian" (Examine and analyze our country's present unemployment's characteristics and the difficulties in employment), *Shehuixue* (Sociology) (hereafter *SHX*) (January 1997): 26; Ma, Rong, "Wo guo jiuye jiegou de bianhua qushi," (The trend of the changes in my country's employment structure) *Laodong baozhang tongxun* (Labor and Social Security Bulletin) (hereafter *LDBZTX*) (April 1999): 29; Liu, Yongzhu, *Disanci shiye gaofeng* (The third high tide of unemployment) (Beijing: Zhongguo shiji chubanshe (China Book Publishers), 1998) 22: 74; Tang, Yunchi, and Liu, Yunhai, eds, *Zhuangyizhong de zhennan: zhongguo xiagang wenti zhuizong yu tansuo* (Shock in transition: tracking and exploration of China's layoff problem) (Beijing: Zhongguo laodong chubanshe [Chinese Labor Publishers], 1998): 114–117, 161, 170–171; Guo, Qingsong, "Shichang jingji tiaojianxia zhongguo chengzhen shiye renkou wenti" (The problem of China's urban unemployed population under the market-directed economy) *Renkou yu jingji* (Population and Economy) (hereafter *RKYJJ*) (May 1996): 51; and Cheng, Xi, "Dangqian wo guo de jiuye yali burong hushi," (My country's present employment pressure is hard to ignore), *RKYJJ* (January 1999): 59–61.

16. In September 1997, at the Chinese Communist Party's Fifteenth Congress, a program calling for these measures was announced and the results were immediate. For coverage and official statements, see *Summary of World Broadcast, Far East*/3023 (13 September 1997) S1/1, from Chinese Central Television, September 12, and *Summary of World Broadcast, Far East*/3024 (15 September 1997) S2/18, from Xinhua (the official Chinese news agency), September 14, 1997.

17. Barry Naughton, "Implications of the State Monopoly over Industry and its Relaxation," *Modern China* (hereafter *MC*) 18, 1 (1992): 14–41.

18. According to Tang and Liu, *Zhuanguizhong de zhennan*, 161, China's foreign trade dependency rate (ratio of trade to GDP) went up from just 12.6 percent in the early 1980s to over 40 percent by the mid-1990s, making the country quite vulnerable to influences and shocks from the world economy.

19. Ibid., 170–171, 183–184.

20. Li, Peilin, "Zouchu," 7, 8.

21. See " 'Chengzhen qiye xiagang zhigong zaijiuye zhuangkuang diaocha' ketizu," ("Investigation of urban enterprises' laid-off staff and workers' reemployment situation" project topic group), "Kunjing yu chulu," (A Difficult Pass and the Way Out) from *Shehuixue yanjiu* (Sociology Research) (June 1997) reprinted in *Xinhua wengao, shehui* (New China Draft, Society) (March 1998): 21–28; Ru, Xin, Lu, Xueyi, and Dan, Tianlun, eds, *1998 nian: zhongguo shehui xingshi fenxi yu yuce* (Analysis and prediction of China's social situation) (Beijing: Shehui kexue wenxian chubanshe, 1998): 86.

22. Tang and Liu, *Zhuanguizhong de zhennan*, 117.

23. For one example of many, see his March 1998 speech in *GYCKZL* (March 1998): 3.

24. Zhang, Fengming, no title, in *ZGLD* (April 1999): 46.

25. Wuhanshi fangzhi zaijiuye fuwu zhongxin (Wuhan city textile reemployment service center), "Wuhanshi fangzhi zaijiuye fuwu zhongxin yuncuo qingkuang huibao," (A Summary Report on the Operations Situation of the Wuhan City Textile Reemployment Service Center) (18 March 1998): 6.

26. Shen, Wenming, and Ma, Runlai, "Zaijiuyezhong de zhengfu xingwei," (The government's behavior in reemployment) *ZGLD* (February 1999): 19; Lei, Peng, "Zhigong peixun yu jiuye cuzin—chengshi fupin de zongyao," (Staff and workers' training and the promotion of reemployment—the important path in subsidizing urban poverty) *Laodong neican* (Labor Internal Reference) (hereafter *LDNC*) (November 1998): 30–31.

27. N.a., "Guanyu wuhanshi zaijiuye wenti di diaocha bao," (An investigation report on Wuhan city's reemployment question), probably written around mid-1997: 8; and Wang, Baoyu, "Zai jiuye gongcheng renzhong dao yun," (Reemployment project: The burden is heavy and the road is long). Unpublished manuscript prepared for the Wuhan City People's Congress (Wuhan, 1997): 8–12.

28. Yang, Shucheng, "Zaijiuye yao zou xiang shichanghua," (In reemployment we must go toward marketization) *ZGJY* (March 1999): 19.

29. Ibid., 30–31.

30. According to n.a., "1998 nian qiye xiagang zhigong jiben qingkuang," (The basic situation of the laid-off enterprise staff and workers in 1998) *LDBZTX* (January 1999): 10, laid-off workers let go by enterprises losing money represented 67 percent of all laid-off workers as of the end 1998.

31. Zhang, Handong, "Dangqian zaijiuye gongcheng de qi da wuqu," (Seven big misunderstandings in the present reemployment project), *Lingdao neican* (Leadership Internal Reference) (July 1998): 27.

32. The material in this section comes from Laodong he baozhang xinxi zhongxin, "Dangqian xiagang zhigong zhuangkuang ji ying yinqi zhuyi de jige wenti" (The situation of the present laid-off staff and workers and several issues that ought to lead to attention), *ZGLD* (May 1999): 18–19; *GRRB* (17 May 1998); Li, Peilin, "Shiye zhidu yu xiagang zhidu ying zhubu binggui" (The systems for unemployment and layoffs should gradually be merged), *NBCY* 452 (3 October 1999): 2; Xue, Zhaojun, "Tuoshan chuli xiagang zhigong de laodong guanxi wenti" (Appropriately handle issues of the laid-off staff and workers' labor relations), *NBCY,* 461 (12 May 1999): 20–22; Song, Xiaowu, "Dangqian jiuye he shiye baoxian cunzai de wenti yu duice," (Existing problems in present employment and unemployment insurance and measures to deal with them), *NBCY* 461 (5 December 1999): 13–14; Zeng, Linghua, "Zaijiuye gongzuo ying yu jiuzheng de jige buliang qingxiang," (Several bad situations that reemployment work should rectify), *LDNC* 7/98: 30–31; Ming, Ruifeng, and Chen, Feng, "99 yijidu laodong baozhang

xingshi tongji fenxi," (An analysis of statistics on the situation in the first quarter of 1999's labor insurance) *Laodong baozhang tongxun* (Labor and Social Security Bulletin) (hereafter *LDBZTX*) 5/99: 22–23; Zhang, Ruiying, and Zhang, Guoxiang, *Gonghui gongzuo tongxun* (Trade Union Work Newsletter) January and February 1998, in *GYCKZL* (March 1998): 13–14; Tian, Bingnan, and Yuan, Jianmin, "Shanghai xiagang renyuan de diaocha yanjiu," (Investigation research on Shanghai laid-off personnel), *SHX* (February 1997): 7–12; Wen, Wufeng, "Tiqian tuixiu toushi," (A perspective on early retirement), *LDBZTX* (January 1999): 14; and interviews in Wuhan, August–September 1999.

33. Barry Naughton, "China's Economy: Buffeted From Within and Without," *Current History* 97 [No. 620] (1998): 275–276.

34. Tian and Yuan, "Shanghai xiagang renyuan," 11.

35. Zhang and Zhang, *Gonghui,* 14.

36. Interviews, September 1 and 4, 1999. The worker I interviewed on September 4 got about two-thirds of the allowance she would get if she were in the center (140 yuan/month instead of 222).

37. See Watson, "Enterprise Reform," and Beijing daxue, zhongguo jingji yanjiu zhongxin chengshi laodongli shichang ketizu (Beijing University Chinese Economy Research Center Urban Labor Market Task Group) (hereafter, Beijing University), "Shanghai: Chengshi zhigong yu nongcun mingong di fenceng yu ronghe," (Shanghai: Urban staff and workers and rural labor's strata and fusion) *Gaige* (Reform) 4 (1998): 99–110.

38. By official definition, a "laid-off" or *xiagang* worker is one who meets three conditions: (1) those who began working before the contract system was instituted in 1986 whose jobs were formal, permanent ones in the state sector and those contract laborers whose contract term is not yet concluded, (2) those who, because of their firm's problems in business and operations have been let go, but who have not yet cut off their relationship with their original firm and (3) those who have not yet found other work in society. This is in Guo Jun, "Guoyou qiye xiagang yu fenliu you he butong?" (What's the difference between laid-off and diverted workers in the state firms?) *Zhongguo gongyun* (Chinese Workers' Movement) (hereafter *ZGGY*) (March 1999): 32, among many other places. According to official definition, an "unemployed" worker is one whose firm has gone bankrupt, so the post has disappeared altogether and thus there is no question of holding onto ties with the plant. Of these, only the "registered unemployed" are counted in official statistics. These are those who are over 18 years of age who have an urban household registration, and are registered at the labor departments but have not yet found work.

39. See, Dorothy J. Solinger, "Why We Cannot Count the 'Unemployed'," *CQ* 167 (September 2001): 671–688.

40. Andrew G. Walder, "The Remaking of the Chinese Working Class, 1949–1981," *MC* 10, 1 (1984): 3–48.

41. Thanks to Thomas Bernstein for this idea.

42. Yue, Wei, "Zaijiuye tujing you duotiao," (There are many channels for reemployment), *ZGLD* (July 1999): 14–17.

43. Zhu Rongji's speech in Tianjin, from *Jingji guanli wenzhai* Zhu Rongji, 6.

44. Laodong he baozhang xinxi zhongxin, "Dangqian xiagang zhigong zhuangkuang," 19.

45. Li, Ge, "Zaijiuye zhengce silu di zaitansuo," (A reexploration of thoughts on reemployment policy) *ZGLD* (July 1999): 8–10.

46. As, for instance, Liang, De, "Xiagang zhigong yao jue," (Laid-off staff and workers getting into business should decide) *Zhongguo gongren* (Chinese Worker) (hereafter *ZGGR*) (March 1999): 21.

47. Interview, August 28, 30, and September 3, 1999.

48. Bi, Jianghao, "Xiagang zhigong weihe wanger quebu?" (Why do laid-off staff and workers flinch?) *ZGJY* (June 1998): 18; interview, September 1, 1999.

49. Mo, Rong, "1999 nian wo guo jiuye xingshi fenxi he zhengce jianyi," (Policy suggestions and analysis of my country's 1999 employment situation) *ZGLD* (February 1999): 12.

50. Zhou, Detian, and Mao, Daiyun, eds, *Shengcun youhuan: zhongguo jiuye wenti baogao* (Subsistence suffering: A report on issues in Chinese employment) (Shenyang: Shenyang publishing company, 1998): 287–288.

51. Among others Yang, Shouye, and Xing, Lei, "Xiagangzhi de jiben shenghuofei bixu yao baozhang" (The basic livelihood allowance of laid-off staff must be guaranteed) *ZGLD* (July 1999): 30.

52. Among others Zhang, Zuoji, "Dangqian zaijiuye gongzuo mianlin de wenti yu duice," (The issues facing present reemployment work and measures to handle them) *ZGJY* (June 1998): 5.

53. Interviews, August 26, September 4 and 7, 1999.

54. Interview, September 1, 1999.

55. Luo, Chuanyin, "Xiagang tiaozheng laodong guanxi," (Layoffs readjust labor relations) *ZGLD* (June 1999): 18.

56. Yue, Wei, "Zaijiuye tujing you duotiao," 15.

57. Wang, Baoyu, "Zai jiuye gongcheng renzhong dao yun," 3.

58. Interview, September 1, 4, 6, 1999.

59. Jianghan daxue ketizu (Jianghan University Project Group), "Wuhan shi shishi zaijiuye gongcheng duice yanjiu," (Policy research on Wuhan City's implementation of the reemployment project) (Wuhan, 1998): 61.

60. Wuhanshi fangzhi zaijiuye fuwu zhongxin, "Wuhanshi fangzhi zaijiuye fuwu zhongxin yuncuo qingkuang huibao", 8–9.

61. See Liu, Zhonghua, "Guanyu zaijiuye gongcheng yu laodongli shichang jianshe di sikao," (Thoughts on the Reemployment Project and labor market construction), *LDNC* (February 1998): 41–43.

62. Hubei sheng zonggonghui shenghuo baozhangbu (Hubei province general trade union livelihood guarantee department), "Yunyong zhengce he falu shouduan, quanli tuijin zaijiuye gongcheng xiang zongshen fazhan," (Utilize policy and legal methods, fully promote the reemployment project to develop in depth) *Lilun yuekan* (Theory Monthly) 2 (1990): 19.

63. Interviews, September 7 and 11, 1999.

64. Qiu, Bai, "Zaijiuye youhui zhengce nan zhixing yuanyin qianxi," (A simple analysis of the reasons why the preferential policies are difficult to implement), *LDNC* (July 1998): 37–38.

65. Zhang, Guoxiang, speech at the 29th meeting of the 8th National People Congress's Standing Committee (29 December 1997), in *GYCKZL* (March 1998): 18.

66. Cheng, Changming, "Hubei Fangxian guoyou qiye xiagang zhigong zhuangkuang diaocha fenxi," (Analysis of an investigation of the situation of state firms' laid-off staff and workers in Fangxian, Hubei), *LDNC* (August 1998): 35.

67. Interview, August 28, 1999.

68. Ma, Zhanyuan, "Qiye zaijiuye fuwu zhongxin jianshe di san-er-yi" (The three, two, one of the construction of enterprise reemployment service centers), *ZGLD* (February 1999): 14.

69. Laodong he baozhang xinxi zhongxin, "Dangqian xiagang zhigong zhuangkuang," 18.

70. Yang and Li, "1999 nian wo guo jiuye xingshi," 5.

71. Zhou and Mao, *Shengcun youhuan,* 289.

72. Ibid., 288–292.

73. Wuhanshi fangzhi zaijiuye fuwu zhongxin, "Wuhanshi fangzhi zaijiuye fuwu zhongxin yuncuo qingkuang huibao," 9–10.

74. Xu, Jianxin, "Yinxing jiuye de xianzhuang ji jiejue duice," (The present conditions of hidden employment and measures to solve it), *ZGJY* (March 1999): 34.

75. Other uses include training, medical fees, compensation for the bereaved, pensions, production self-relief, and management fees. See Li, Peilin, "Zouchu," 12.

76. N.a., "1998 laodong he shehui baozhang shiye fazhan niandu tongji gongbao," (Report of annual statistics on the development of the work of 1998's labor and social security) *LDBZTX* (July 1999): 37.

77. N.a., "On Their Own," *CRF* (Spring 1998): 40. Presumably some of those who gave this response were unaware of existing funds.

78. The slogan was heard at a January 1997 State Council National Work Conference on State Enterprise Staff and Workers' Reemployment. See Yang, Yiyong et al., *Shiye chongji bo* (The shock wave of unemployment) (Beijing: Jinri zhongguo chubanshe, 1997): 220.

79. *GRRB*, 6 May 1998.

80. Among others Guo, Peiying, "Zujin zaijiuye shi jiejue xiagang zhigong shenghuo wenti di zhiben zhi lu," (Promoting reemployment is the road for getting to the root of solving laid-off staff and workers' livelihood problems), *ZGGY* (March 1999): 22.

81. A national survey found 43.5 percent were women in 1998 (N.a., "1998 nian," 10); and two surveys in Wuhan found 51.5 percent and 60 percent to be female, respectively (Wang, Baoyu, "Zai jiuye gongcheng renzhong dao yun," 2; and Jianghan daxue ketizu, "Wuhan shi shishi zaijiuye gongcheng duice yanjiu," 56).

82. For one example, interview, September 1, 1999.

83. Interview, September 1, 2, 4, 1999.

84. Cheng, Xi, "Dangqian wo guo de jiuye yali burong hushi," 61.

85. N.a., "1998 nian," 10.

86. Luo, Chuanyin, "Xiagang tiaozheng laodong guanxi," 18.

87. Deng, Baoshan, "Zhengfu, qiye, he xiagang zhigong zai zaijiuye gongcuozhong de cuoyong," 12.

88. Tian and Yuan, "Shanghai xiagang renyuan," 9.

89. Interview, September 1, 1999.

90. See among others Cheng, Xi, "Dangqian wo guo de jiuye yali burong hushi," 60.

91. The *neitui* are retired early. *Tingxin liuzhi* applies to those who have left the firm but retain an indefinite and ongoing tie to it while obtaining income from a new placement elsewhere. *Liangbuzhao* refers to people who have left their firms, and, at the present, neither demand benefits from the firm nor give anything to the firm.

92. N.a., "Guanyu wuhanshi." There are also those on so-called "long holidays" (*fang changjia*) or who have "retired early" (*tiqiantuixiu*).

93. N.a., "On Their Own," *CRF* (Spring 1998): 40.

94. A study cited in Tian and Yuan, "Shanghai xiagang renyuan."

95. Tian and Yuan, "Shanghai xiagang renyuan," 9–10.

96. Jianghan daxue ketizu, "Wuhan shi shishi zaijiuye gongcheng duice yanjiu," 56–57.

97. Interviews, September, 1, 2, 4, 11, 1999.

98. Interviews, August 30, September 1, 2, 4, and 11.

99. Jianghan daxue ketizu, "Wuhan shi shishi zaijiuye gongcheng duice yanjiu," 57, 91.

100. Interview, August 28, 1999. See note 82.

101. Interviews, August 28 and 30, September 4 and 7, 1999.

102. Zhang, Handong, "Dangqian zaijiuye gongcheng de qi da wuqu," 28.

103. Among others Liu, Guanxue, in *Zhongguo laodongbao* (Chinese Workers' News), 2 May 1998, reprinted in *GYCKZL* (March 1998): 19.

104. Interview, September 6, 1999.

105. Laodong he baozhang xinxi zhongxin, "Dangqian xiagang zhigong zhuangkuang ji ying yinqi zhuyi de jige wenti," 18.

106. Job categories are discussed, among others in Wang, Aiqun, "Dangqian jiuye xin tedian," 29.

107. Laodong he baozhang xinxi zhongxin, "Dangqian xiagang zhigong zhuangkuang ji ying yinqi zhuyi de jige wenti," 20.

108. Jianghan daxue ketizu, "Wuhan shi shishi zaijiuye gongcheng duice yanjiu," 57.

109. Table, Jianghan daxue ketizu, "Wuhan shi shishi zaijiuye gongcheng duice yanjiu," no page.

110. *Jingji cankaobao* (Economic Reference News) (24 March 1998), reprinted in *GYCKZL* (April 1998): 16.

111. Visit to the market, September 4, 1999.

112. Guo, Qingsong, "Shichang jingji tiaojianxia zhongguo chengzhen shiye renkou wenti," 51.

113. Among others Yan, Zhicheng, "Jiejue yinxing jiuye wenti jiujing nan zai hechu?" (Where after all is the difficulty in solving the problem of hidden employment?) *ZGJY* (June 1998): 21.
114. Among others Xu, Jianxin, "Yinxing jiuye de xianzhuang ji jiejue duice," 34.
115. Lei, Peng, "Zhigong peixun yu jiuye cuzin—chengshi fupin de zongyao," 29.
116. Jianghan daxue ketizu, "Wuhan shi shishi zaijiuye gongcheng duice yanjiu," 56.
117. Ibid. 79.
118. Among others see ibid., 88.
119. Lei, Peng, "Zhigong peixun yu jiuye cuzin—chengshi fupin de zongyao," 28.
120. Among others see Cheng, Changming, "Hubei Fangxian guoyou qiye xiagang zhigong zhuangkuang diaocha fenxi," 34.
121. Ibid.
122. Tong, Jingchen, "Kunnan-lijie-bangzhu," (Difficulty-understand-help) *ZGJY* (June 1998): 22.
123. Li, Bingliang, and Guan, Zaiyuan, "Zhongshi zhigong xiagang dui qi zinu di fumian yingxiang," (Pay attention to the negative influence on the sons and daughters of the staff and workers' layoffs) *NBCY* 448 (3 February 1999): 14.
124. Lei, Peng, "Zhigong peixun yu jiuye cuzin—chengshi fupin de zongyao," 29.
125. Tian and Yuan, "Shanghai xiagang renyuan," 8.
126. Interview, August 28, 1999. See notes 82 and 120.
127. Interview, September 2, 1999.
128. Interviews, September 1, 2, and 11, 1999.
129. Among others see Yue, Wei, "Zaijiuye tujing you duotiao," 17.

from:

Mengin, Françoise, & Jean-Louis Rocca, ed.
Politics in China (Palgrave, 2002).

CHAPTER THREE

Three Patterns of Working-Class Transitions in China[1]

CHING KWAN LEE

International capital has ventured en masse into China in search of consumer market and cheap labor. The country has become a latest outlet for global capitalism to resolve its crisis by procuring new sources of absolute and relative surplus value.[2] For China, international capital may lend financial and technological leverages for domestic market reform, which aims to rebuild regime legitimacy on the basis of economic performance. Or, as official ideology has it, market reforms can liberate social productive forces at a primary phase of socialism. The intertwined processes of capitalist globalization and market reform have brought about uneven development of "flexible" factory regimes, dislocation of veteran state workers, and new groups of laborers, including a massive army of the unemployed. Not only do systems or institutions undergo transformation, but classes and class relations are made and remade. Modes and terms of labor struggles too change in the process. This chapter outlines three patterns of "working-class transition" in urban China:[3] (1) the making of the global peasant worker; (2) the remaking of the socialist worker; and (3) the unmaking of the redundant worker. Each of these terms denotes a conjuncture of changing political economy, factory regime, and labor culture, all of which shape the diverse modes and terms of labor struggles. Although the empirical data I use in this study are drawn from Guangdong and Liaoning, these patterns are analytical types, not necessarily limited to or rooted in any specific geographical areas. Global capitalism and market reforms are powerful forces capable of recreating boundaries of social exclusion and economic inequalities along their paths, without regard to national or administrative boundaries.[4] Thus, diverse patterns of labor politics may coexist in the same city, province, or region.

Working-Class "Transition"

I use the term class "transition" instead of class "formation" to highlight a less teleological and deterministic but more nuanced and open process of change in labor experiences. Just as societal transition implies a weakening of structures allowing disproportionate opportunities for micro practices to shape the restructuring,[5] class transition in the context of unsettled system transformation also means more fluid politics and experiences. In a seminal volume on working-class formation, Ira Katznelson suggests four connected layers of theory and history for constructing comparative cases of proletarianization in nineteenth-century Europe and the United States: structure of capitalist development, workplace and labor market organization, shared disposition, and collective action. Historical analyses examine class as contingent (but not random) process of connection among these levels.[6] The heuristic framework I adopt here contains similar levels of analysis but I also incorporate insights from some recent reworking of class analyses[7] that emphasize practices of compliance and resistance as elements in the repertoire of collective action. I also look beyond dispositions shared among workers to explore what Gramsci has called contradictory consciousness and what social theorists describe as multiple identities. Insights drawn from these recent social theories[8] can enrich the conventional Marxist concepts of class consciousness and collective action as well as our understanding of contemporary Chinese labor.

The Making of the Migrant Peasant Worker

This group of workers is most distinguishable by its mobility and rural roots. Masses of young workers hailed from China's vast countryside can and do change jobs frequently, going back and forth between factories and fields, and hopping from factories to factories in search of higher wages and less oppressive work conditions. If "flexible accumulation" means extremely degrading and exploitative factory regimes, the "flexibility" of this labor force has also enabled spontaneous outbreaks of work stoppages and strikes. Opportunities for alternative employment can embolden them to resist, while pockets of localistic solidarity and shared experience of subordination inside factories facilitate collective actions, short-lived and sporadic as they may be. Also, as the state pushes for universalization of labor laws and regulations, their repertoire of actions expands to include collective petitions and dispute arbitration in addition to goldbricking, work stoppages, and strikes. By causing disruption in production and by using institutionalized resources, peasant workers advance demands that are mostly economic and work related (wages, compensations for industrial injuries, more humane management treatment, and so on). In and through these actions, they variously invoke and forge collective identities based variously on native place, human dignity, and quasi-citizens rights. But, migrant peasant workers also accommodate to power in order to pursue their respective "careers at work" and mobility projects. Insertion into global capitalism and labor market provides opportunities for improved life chances beyond peasantry.

Many of the estimated 80–100 million migrants in China at one point or another work in labor intensive factories.[9] According to official figures in 1994, 28 percent of migrant workers are employed in industry, 23 percent in construction, 15 percent in food services, and 5 percent in transport.[10] The southern province of Guangdong has always been the most popular destination for migrants. According to a 1997 Public Security Department report on temporary residents, 70 percent of the 10.6 million temporary residents were engaged in industry, artisanal work, construction, and transport. Fifty-two percent of these migrant workers in the province were women.[11] Nonstate factories are the major employers, although state-owned enterprises (SOEs) also hire migrants to take up the most labor intensive, menial, and sometimes hazardous jobs. The proportion of women in the Pearl Delta region with a high concentration of export processing and foreign-invested factories reached as high as 65 percent.[12]

Designated the vanguard province of open policies in the 1980s, Guangdong first saw the emergence of a new labor group known as *dagongzai* and *dagongmei* (men and women working for bosses). Although contract laborers are not new in China as they have been a constant though minority component in SOEs throughout the pre-reform period, employment relation based on private contractual parties and their predominant majority are. These young peasants supply the main source of labor first for the foreign and joint ventures in Special Economic Zones and increasingly since the 1990s also in private enterprises and subcontracted workshops inside state-owned enterprises in cities like Guangzhou, Zhongshan, Dongguan, and so on. The industrial scene of Guangdong is a microcosm of what has been described as "flexible accumulation" on a global scale. "The current conjuncture is characterized by a mix of... Fordist production ... in some sectors ... and regions ... and more traditional production systems resting on 'artisanal,' paternalistic, or patriarchal (familial) labor relations, embodying quite different mechanisms of labor control."[13]

Factory Regime

Ethnographic studies and journalistic reports in the region are suffused with oppressive features of these production systems. The worst abuses are usually found in foreign firms owned and managed by Taiwanese, Korean, and Hong Kong investors (often registered as joint-ventures or out-processing collectives), and also in local private factories. I have described such production regime as "localistic despotism,"[14] and Anita Chan, who has done extensive fieldwork in Guangdong, has called it a "bonded" labor system or "quasi-apartheid" system.[15] The essential features include a highly coercive management that uses elaborate company codes to regulate minute details of the labor process: from workers' hair and attire, length of time for bathroom visits, to physical mobility inside the factory, food supply, and rest time. Extremely long hours of overtime are often mandatory and not dually compensated. Physical abuse and sexual harassment are common.[16] To enhance employers' control over workers, cash deposits are required or wages are docked. In some cases, legal documents like workers' identity cards and temporary residence permits are withheld by the firms so as to deter workers from seeking jobs elsewhere. Employment relations are usually not secured and protected by labor contract, which although required by the Labor Law is only practiced in 36 percent of private and 63 percent of foreign-invested factories.[17] Instead, management power reigns supreme, often making use of preexisting localistic, paternalistic, and patriarchal authorities. My study has detailed how native-place networks mediate the recruitment of workers and thereby transfer male locals' authority over female kin into factory hierarchy. Localism also implies a strategy of divide and rule inside these firms, diluting class opposition between employers and workers by introducing regional division among them. More recent ethnographic evidence indicates that these shop-floor features have persisted.[18] Especially in smaller privately owned factories, paternalistic policies (special leave privileges, better housing and food, special year-end bonus) are selectively showered on the minority of "core" workers whose technical and/or management skills are crucial for production, while their unskilled locals are given inferior treatments.[19]

Two institutional conditions for such despotic factory systems are the collusion of local officials with employers and the powerlessness or total absence of unions. In many out-processing firms, private enterprises and joint-ventures involving township or district governments and foreign investors, local officials have wielded widespread power in negotiating the terms of land lease, water and electricity supply, security, and management services. The last category is a euphemism for local officials' assistance to preempt labor bureau inspection, to evade paying social insurance contributions for employees or setting up unions. In return, local government benefits from tax incomes and donations for school and road construction. It is also common to find officials being offered nominal, consultative posts in these firms, and they are paid lucrative incomes for their services. Street committees within different districts of a city can host a large number of "collective" (but in reality private, foreign, or joint venture) enterprises under its official banner, and for a handsome management fee, can shield these enterprises from many government regulations on industrial safety and labor policies.[20] Intense competition among localities to lure foreign investment always results in "flexible" enforcement of labor regulations. Despite efforts by the Guangdong Province Federation of Trade Unions to attain 100 percent unionization among nonstate enterprises, only 40 percent of these firms have unions.[21] More importantly, many of these are "company unions" operating as appendages of management, staffed by salaried employees and set up to earn the good will of local labor officials.

Labor Resistance and Accommodation

Like workers the world over, shared experience of exploitation at the point of production triggers diverse and ubiquitous forms of collective resistance. In a private knitting mill where the employer refused to specify the piece rate and workers only learned about the rates when they were paid at the end of the month, workers collectively restricted their output. When urgent and tight deadlines had to be met, the employer was then forced to disclose the piece rate for a particular batch of orders in order to spur workers to maximize labor effort.[22]

But migrant workers are also known for their disruptive capacity. Charles Sabel offers a portrait of peasant workers' militancy in Western Europe in the 1960s and 1970s: "At first a group of peasant workers may tolerate what it understands to be breaches of the contract by the employer. But if abuse continues the group reaches an unspoken consensus to suffer no more. The peasant workers are then likely to explode in rage at the slightest additional provocation, belying in an instant their reputation for docility."[23] Chinese workers demonstrate similar traits, as shown in this representative incident of work stoppage reported in *Wailaigong* (Workers), a popular magazine targeting Guangdong's migrant workers.

They [workers in this shoe factory] have been working continuously for thirty-three hours, from eight in the morning of March 3 to five-thirty in the afternoon on March 4. Exhausted and hungry, these women workers have reached the limit of their anger and indignation. What triggered the explosion of their emotions was a Sichuan woman who had her fingers trapped and crushed in a machine ... When workers rushed to her rescue, the shop floor manager appeared and hurried the workers to go back to work. With a wooden stick in her hands, she scolded, "Falling asleep during work. It's your fault to get hurt like this ... What is there to see? Go back to work!" ... But this time, one voice came shouting back from among the workers, "Damn it, we do not want to work!" Then, several hundred workers left the shop floor, gathered around the factory gate. When reporters arrived around eight in the evening, in the midst of crying and swearing crowds, agitated workers rushed forward to complain about maltreatments by managers.[24]

As early as 1986–87, Shenzhen (the first SEZ in China) witnessed at least 21 strikes in foreign-funded enterprises and the local trade union received about 1,000 worker complaints. Although official statistics on work stoppages and strikes are always incomplete underestimations, these figures are indicative of the tip of an iceberg. In Shenzhen alone, 69 strikes and work stoppages were recorded from June 1989 to the end of 1990. The figure increased to 250 in 1992. From mid-1993 to early 1995 a series of strikes were staged by workers in Japanese-owned plants Canon, Mitusmi, Sanmei, and Panasonic in Shenzhen and Zhuhai SEZs. These incidents varied in duration, from a few hours to several days, and involved up to one to two thousand workers in large factories. The *Shenzhen Legal Daily* reported that during a three-year period ending in 1998, peasant migrant workers instigated 131 strikes and riots (*naoshi*), and 2,042 petitions to different levels of government offices. The report also explained the radical and disruptive potentials of peasant workers. "Because outside workers are relatively concentrated, with little education and only low quality, they cannot handle conflicts rationally. They get emotional easily and fall prey to others' instigation to take extreme actions, escalating the original conflicts."[25]

Based on their experience in handling 14 strikes in Xiamen SEZ in Fujian, two labor officials summarized the characteristics of these incidents as short-lived, economically motivated episodes. They also pointed to the importance of native-place ties, noting that eight out of the 14 strikes occurred in factories with an excessive proportion of workers coming from the same locality, forming regional cliques. As relatives or native place locals, they share strong exclusionary sentiments and solidarity that can easily lead to collective rebellion. Oftentimes, collective subjection to humiliating and degrading treatment led raging workers to stop work. In a widely reported case, women workers refused to work after a shop floor manager demanded them to take off their pants for body search in an attempt to resolve a suspected theft. Blatant affronts on workers' dignity, as forcing workers to kneel down for long hours in public, beating them up for making production mistakes, or even locking up workers in a dog's cage, often aroused spontaneous strikes. Striking workers demonstrated a certain level of organizational savvy, as accounts of these incidents mentioned organizers writing open letters and printing leaflets and flyers to mobilize workers. One commonly used tactic was calling up journalists and news agencies, asking them to come to the factories to bear witness and to report their struggles.[26]

Increasing numbers of migrant workers resort to the state apparatus to redress grievances. While a staggering rise in the volume of labor dispute arbitrations is not restricted to those involving peasant workers, official figures indicate that they are among the most contentious in terms of "collective" arbitrations (defined as those disputes involving three or more workers). The same figures of course also reflect perhaps the more blatant violations of Labor Law by employers in the nonstate sector. Nationwide, in 1994, 58.8 percent of workers involved in collective dispute arbitration came from foreign (including Taiwan and Hong Kong) enterprises. In 1996 and 1997, the rates remained at high levels: 58.5 percent and 44.8 percent respectively. Moreover, the average number of participants in these collective arbitrations has risen from 39.1 in 1996 to 51.2 in 1997. The growth rate of case volume has been even more drastic. In 1994, there were 2,974 cases (15.6 percent of total) involving workers in foreign enterprises, an increase of 75.4 percent over 1993. The rates of annual increase for the following years were: 93 percent in 1995, 76 percent in 1996 and 132 percent in 1997.[27] Disputes taking place in nonstate sectors (foreign-owned, joint-ventures, collective, and private) where most peasant workers are employed account for more than half of total volume of disputes since 1994: 51.1 percent in 1994, 56.3 percent in 1995, 62.2 percent in

1996.[28] Most disputes are economic in nature, with wages, welfare, and social insurance payment accounting for some 50 percent of all causes of conflicts. Wage arrears, estimated to amount to 500 million yuan in Guangdong in 1998, was the cause for more than half of the labor disputes in Guangdong, and disputes involving compensations for industrial injuries are particularly pronounced in private and foreign-invested firms.[29] With more promulgation of by-laws and regulations to supplement the 1995 Labor Law, the scope and volume of disputes and arbitration will expand as more of workers' rights fall within the parameter of government regulations. In sum, while the subversive potential and disruptive capacity of migrant workers are evident, they also eagerly fight for their interests through more institutionalized channels.

Contradictory Consciousness

Migrant workers' "careers at work," or "habitus,"[30] are drawn from diverse sources: past experiences with rural labor, present structures of opportunities, and perceptions of future careers inspired by other migrants' experience. Thus, on the one hand, claiming their actions as "demands for justice" (*taogongdao*), and their employers as "lacking conscience" (*wuliang*), migrant workers' worldview retains expectations of moral reciprocity, enlightened despotism, caring albeit unequal power between employer and worker. But notions of law-given rights also have begun to emerge, as the state increasingly imposes a universal, legal framework to regulate class conflicts covering all workers. These labor regulations and policies offer workers a new cognitive and discursive resource to frame their claims in state-approved idioms. In an illustrative episode about migrant workers' struggle to exercise their legal rights, an injured worker refused to sign a settlement memorandum that was sent to him with a 2,000 yuan "humanitarian compensation" by the factory. He insisted on his entitlement to legal, industrial injuries compensation, and began a long battle against harassment from his employer and different departments and levels of the administration. Investigative reports on incidents like this in the local press have demonstration effect on migrant workers.[31]

From the point of view of young peasant workers, despite all the hardship and exploitation in urban factories, participating in the urban labor market opens up new life experiences. Commodification of labor, demeaning as it may be for all groups of workers, frees peasant workers from personalized control of parents, villagers and kin, and village officials.

These peasant workers do not escape the kind of abstract, impersonal social domination nor alienation and exploitation that underlie capitalist social formation everywhere.[32] Yet, they come to encounter these forces with a history of personal dependence, against which commodified labor is interpreted and experienced as providing personal liberation and independence. In my own study of Shenzhen's migrant workers, cash income is highly valued, when compared to unpaid farm labor on the family field, under the watchful eyes of parents. Some married peasant workers who have violated the state's two-children policies in the countryside have found factory employment a relief from harassment and fines of local village cadres. Young women use money they earn to pay their way out of marriage engagement set up by their parents and fellow villagers.[33] For some women, marriage migration has been found to follow the initial cycles of work migration.[34] With further studies, we may come to understand how women workers pursue this strategy of upward mobility.

Personal savings after a long period of waged labor can finance entrepreneurial ventures that become increasingly common. Praised by the official newspapers as "returned pheonix," rural trendsetters, and innovators, returned migrant workers are courted by local officials keen on creating jobs or finding buyers for inefficient state enterprises. In several counties in Jiangxi, for instance, in 1995, 2,000 returned migrant workers have set up a total of 99 "enterprises." In a county in Anhui, 400 returned workers created 340 jobs for local villagers after they set up six enterprises. Migrant women are no less entrepreneurial: a 1996 survey conducted by the Women's Federation in Hunan found that in one city, where 5 percent of the 700,000 migrant workers have returned to set up rural enterprises, more than half of these entrepreneurs were women.[35] Fellow workers' success instills a collective perception that these are realizable projects for the peasant workers looking into the future.[36]

Yet, entrepreneurial inspirations and an emergent sense of legal rights based on industrial citizenship coexist in tension with their identities as transient residents victimized by discrimination. China's hukou policies only allow them temporary residence in the cities, and deny them social services and housing benefits enjoyed by urban workers. Quotas of migrant workers are set on certain categories of jobs to protect urbanites' employment rights. From shop-floor work allocation to harassment in public areas, migrant workers harbor a strong sense of being subjugated as secondary citizens. Moreover, most of Chinese peasant workers do not see as plausible a long-term career in a Fordist mode of industrial organization, where they can steadily pursue a career along a clear and stable hierarchy of jobs linked to different levels of skills and rewards within the firm. China's insertion into the world market relies on low-cost and labor-intensive products, and most of the jobs created in factories are unskilled ones. Management in all types of enterprises put a premium not on skill training but on lowering labor costs and enhancing disciplines. Against the official rhetoric that personal capacity and effort determine who gets rich first, the standpoint of peasant workers grounded in their experiences is that market socialism does not bring equal opportunity for all. It is not as fair and rational as the state would like to have them believe.

The Remaking of the Socialist Worker

"From master to slave" is how many a socialist worker describes his or her fall from grace as China moves toward market socialism. Although official ideology has proclaimed the end of class struggle at the beginning years of reform, and represses the use of class rhetoric in its official discourses, socialist workers in state-owned enterprises have become ever more class conscious. Historical experience of several decades of state socialism mediates their politics of transition from being "state worker" to "contract worker." Beyond sharing with the peasant worker a nascent sense of labor legal rights, the veteran socialist worker encounters "scientific management," piece rate wage and contract with different frames of mind and moral sentiments. Instead of indignity and injustice, the socialist worker's critique of market socialism centers on class exploitation. The Maoist era is the golden days of socialism from which her present life and society have irrevocably regressed. Yet, rising class consciousness occurs simultaneously with decline in class capacity. Lacking competitiveness in the labor market, the majority of veteran workers who still remain in the state sector have become increasingly dependent on their enterprises, which in turn have "modernized" into despotic regimes of production.

The thirty-million-strong workers in state-owned enterprises now account for 60 percent of all manufacturing workers in China. The ratio varies with regions: in Guangdong, state workers are a minority group, accounting for only 33 percent of the manufacturing workforce. But in Liaoning, the corresponding proportion is 56 percent. Nationwide, in the six-year period between 1992 and 1997, manufacturing workforce in the state sector dwindled by 18.6 percent, or a decrease of 6.88 million workers. Women are still a minority in the state sector. Most (54.2 percent) state workers are 36 years of age or older, and most (57 percent) have only junior high education.[37] In vernacular expression, SOEs are filled with the "3860 Army," meaning women and near-retirement men. In the press, they are told to get rid of their "backward" employment mentality of *deng, kao, tao* (waiting for, relying on, and asking from state enterprise). When state-owned enterprises are called the "historical burdens" fettering the country's economic development, workers there are told to transform themselves from "enterprise man" (*qiyeren*) to "society man" (*shehuiren*). In the reform era, they are seldom referred to as the working class (*gongrenjieji*) except in the ACFTU official paper *Workers' Daily* (*Gongren Ribao*). The new term "*gongxinyizhu*," meaning the waged and salaried, emerges to refer to all employees regardless of enterprise ownership type.

Restructuring of SOEs has proceeded under different policy themes for the past two decades. In the 1990s, the key foci have been separation of ownership and management rights, corporatization, multiple-ownership systems including different forms of share-holding systems. "Grasp the big and let go of the small" is the latest motto, allowing many SOEs to be sold, leased, and subcontracted to private and foreign owners, or to merge into giant corporations. To many SOE workers, these volatile changes have only aggravated their sense of insecurity in the midst of massive unemployment. To them, ownership changes or reorganization of firm structures are abstract forces beyond their control or comprehension. Asked who is the director or chair of the enterprise, or which *danwei* they belong to, many responded with disdain that they could not tell or did not care. Despite the plethora of restructuring strategies, the shop floors of SOEs tend toward a production regime I call "disorganized despotism."[38] I have consistently found this configuration of institutional forces at work in varying degrees in both Guangdong and Liaoning, in factories that have been leased to private subcontractors, and in those that have become share-holding cooperatives or have merged into large share-holding corporations.

Factory Regime

Workers' livelihood and status have actually been improved in the first decade of market reform. Studies found paternalism persisting in state factories in the 1980s. Managers were pressured by their workers to retain profits within the work unit for bonus redistribution or collective consumption like building employee housing, instead of channeling them to central government's coffer. Although director's responsibility system has already been implemented, replacing the old system of party leadership, managers lacked the critical power to dismiss workers. Within the enterprise, neo-traditionalism persisted, extracting obedience and tacit consent of workers via organized dependence and patron–client networks.[39] The relative underdevelopment of the private and foreign sectors in the early years of reform also meant monopolistic markets for SOE products.

The downturn for state workers began sometime in the early 1990s. After the clamp-down on the 1989 student protests, the central government tightened credit control and domestic economy went into depression. SOEs encountered problems of triangular debts, stockpiled goods, and competitions from village township enterprises, foreign and joint ventures, and later private enterprises. The mid-1990s also witnessed the implementation of a series of labor and welfare reforms, and the strong push for "modern enterprise" scientific management, all of which dealt a heavy blow to workers' bargaining and market power. First, labor contract that began as experiment in 1986 became universal requirement for all SOEs by the end of 1995. With permanent employment substituted by fix-term contracts, this reform has for the first time since 1949 provided for no-fault dismissal of workers in SOEs. Because of their age, limited education and firm specific skills, these workers have little market capacity to compete with migrant or young workers for jobs in the nonstate sectors. Thus labor contracts result in accentuating managers' power rather than workers' choice and mobility. Second, welfare commodification in the 1990s has eliminated the "cradle to grave" provisions underlying the previous paternalistic regime. Enterprise clinics, nurseries, schools, meals in mess halls charge near market rates for their services. With deteriorating profitability in many SOEs, many have even stopped operating those facilities. Third, the building of a new societal safety net to replace the system of enterprise welfare has suffered from unsuccessful implementation. Evasion of enterprise contributions by state and especially nonstate enterprises to pension funds, unemployment, maternity, and injuries insurance has been so widespread that some of these insurance funds registered deficits. State workers are thus pinched simultaneously by the state's failure to institutionalize a new safety net and the retreat of enterprise paternalism. Finally, just as workers' bargaining power has been weakened by these circumstances of dependence, unions and party apparatus have been marginalized by an increasingly autocratic management. Primacy of production and economic efficiency means that managers always prevail over dissenting opinions of union chair and party secretary. In many cases, concurrent appointment of party and management cadres has preempted the emergence of dissents within the enterprise leadership. Financial difficulties of SOEs also diminish unions' organizational resources and threaten the personal careers of union cadres.[40]

Perry interpreted 1989 as a protest against inflation! (Yes!)

These changes amount to a disintegration of those institutions that have organized the socialist factory in the past. Hence the notion of "disorganized" despotism: the uneven implementation of reform and the lack of coordination among diverse measures provide the institutional context for the managerial despotism. Scientific management on Chinese shop floors results in the adoption of economic means of labor control like piece rates and financial penalties for rejects, as well as elimination of non-production-related welfare responsibilities.[41] Conflicts abound concerning issues of fair piece rates, disciplines, punishments, and workload distribution that directly affects wages. A comparison with migrant peasant workers is instructive. Migrant peasants workers more often tolerate a reward system based on piece rate as long as the employer honors the payment at the end of the month. On the other hand, state enterprise workers' prior experience with an alternative reward system based on time rate informs a different standpoint. They are more cognizant and critical of piece rate's "exploitative" character:

I give you an example: if the daily output quota is 100 and if you only manage to complete 90, which is 90 percent of the quota, he [the contractor] gives you a rate lower than that for 100. Say if the original rate was 20 cents per unit, now you only get a few cents per unit. He uses this method to push us to produce more .... We don't get any wage for waiting time when we are forced to wait for raw materials. Sometimes we come to the shop floor at 7:30 A.M. and do preparatory work until 11 A.M. We don't get paid if there is no output. In the past, we were paid our basic wage rate during waiting hours or when machines broke down.[42]

Embedded in this indictment of reduced wages is not just the amount of pay but also how labor should be valued. Workers accepted as fair a remuneration system based on a notion of labor as "labor power" (labor capacity) inscribed in the past practice of awarding time-rate wage. That is, basic wages plus responsibility wages that reward workers' technical skill level and job position. However, they experience exploitation under piece rates that only reward "embodied labor" (or labor realized as tangible products). Adopting similar logic and using the socialist tradition of position wage as a moral and economic yardstick (where each worker is rewarded on the basis of a job-position category), another worker complains about the now prevalent "flexible" production process. Workers are required to combine work procedures done by different workers in the past. They have become "multi-skilled hands," but are not rewarded for their "extra" skills:

Very often, one person has to take up two positions, like, a dyeing worker is now also responsible for fabric boiling because the boiling worker has quit or has to take up other positions. We work more, work harder, but are also being cheated more. [How?] If there were two people doing two jobs, they have to give us two points, one for each worker. When one person does two jobs, they give only 1.5 points. So we are cheated![43]

Labor Resistance and Accommodation

Diverse modes of everyday shop-floor resistance are rampant in state factories where workers are both disgruntled and dependent. Fearing retaliation by an all-powerful management who can deny them the only employment they can possibility retain, veteran workers challenge managerial authority in the interstices of production routines. Goldbricking, displacement of effort from regular to second jobs, moonlighting craze, unauthorized wage redistribution within work group, refusal to move out of enterprise housing after labor contracts expire, are widespread.[44] Also ubiquitous is deliberate neglect of production, as this worker reports angrily,

We curse at work all the time because all of us are psychologically off-balance (*xinlibupingheng*). Why should we care about quality any more when the director squanders away our money, having a good time with ladies in the nightclubs or making a business trip to the United States? We deliberately cast a blind eye to defective pieces. We said, "let them [defective works] go." This is how we release some of our anger and preserve our health. You know, these days we do not have medical allowances any more.[45]

More disruptive to production are spontaneous work stoppages that can easily be ignited by the high level of repressed resentment shared by workers. The following incident took place in Shenyang's (and China's) leading heavy machinery factory. After a two-and-a-half-month wage arrears, and workers with no money to pay for the school fees of their children, a mechanic recalled that,

> One afternoon, during lunch break, we were very distressed. We were cursing and spilling out our anger while we ate. Then, at the end of the lunch hour, all two hundred of us on the shop floor simply lost any motivation to resume work. We just stopped, spontaneously, no need to organize (*chuanlian*), without any call from any one, without any leader. The shop floor director learnt about this and immediately came down from his office. He began his thought education, explaining the difficulties the enterprise was experiencing. After one hour, we resumed work. A few days later, we got our paychecks.[46]

In another shop floor of the same enterprise, a similar event of collective outburst took place, as another worker recounted,

> In 1998, we did not get paid for months. But on-duty workers dared not join the retired elderly workers to block traffic or sit-in outside the factory gate. We are more vulnerable to retaliation and arrest than the elderly. But workers did get angry several times. Once, several hundred workers took off their uniforms and went to the headquarter office of the enterprise, demanding to see the Number One (*yibashou*). They were marching through the hallway, looking into each office, shouting his name—"Come out, Chen Yang Zhi!" It's very funny because these workers have never seen this director. Just knew his name. Then, someone saw a man rushing out of the building into the director's sedan. It was him! No one has ever seen this guy since we restructured into this share holding company. Cadres have no direct interaction with ordinary workers these days.[47]

Workers in SOEs have also brought their grievances and claims to the labor–arbitration administration, although official figures indicate that they are less active than other groups of workers. For instance, in 1996, there were 16,390 labor dispute cases involving state workers, or 34 percent of the national total. And for collective disputes, they only accounted for 24 percent. The proportion taken up by state workers shows a trend of gradual decline: the ratio for 1995 was 4.5 percent less than that of 1994, the ratio for 1996 was 7.4 percent less than 1995.[48]

However, the absolute volume of disputes shows a continuous rising trend. In Guangzhou for instance, the first three months in 1998 registered 1,136 cases of disputes, a drastic increase of 146 percent in the number of workers filing disputes with the arbitration committee of the city's labor bureau. The main reason was that the year 1998 was the third year after the universal implementation of a labor contract for all SOEs in 1995. Many of workers' complaints involved disputes with their work units when their three-year contracts expired.[49] Such policy-induced increase will likely continue when more labor regulations prescribed by the Labor Law will be implemented. Moreover, free-of-charge legal counsel services are now provided by the Guangzhou Municipal Federation of Trade Unions and are likely to allow more workers to bring their grievances to administrative system.[50]

Strikes and protests statistics, for what they are worth, do not differentiate state workers who are still employed from those who are laid off. But judging from details of press reports and interview data, it seems that more radical struggles like strikes and public protests are more readily staged by laid-off and retired workers, who are not subjected directly and daily to management supervision and power.[51] Moreover, after a decade of SOE decline, those veteran workers who still remain within the state system are those least competitive in the market economy and are therefore most dependent on SOE employment, no matter how undesirable it has become. The threat of unemployment and the reality of massive layoff are poignant enough to discourage them from adopting open and radical means of resistance. As one worker puts it bitterly and helplessly, "What good does it do us if we make troubles and inadvertently bring it (the enterprise) down?"

Besides, market reforms do open up limited opportunities to some veteran workers. I have documented how some core, skilled workers in SOEs are able to upgrade their living standard and income by leading a dual existence: having one foot in a stable state enterprise and another in the private sector. As maintenance chief, electrician, or head of mechanics department, these "technical backbones" of SOEs enjoy an inordinate amount of bargaining power to extract concession from management, allowing them to combine their SOE jobs with their private pursuits, like running a grocery store, an interior decoration team, a small restaurant, or working as part-time consultants for private or township enterprises. In cities like Guangzhou where the market economy is vibrant and demands are high for all kinds of services, workers with skills and connections have second job opportunities to make up for declining wages from state factories. Even in Shenyang, I have found middle-aged workers using their savings to open small neighborhood restaurants or rent a small stall in the open market to provide meager incomes for family members who have been laid off.[52] Uneven access to the market has created a very differentiated pattern and standard of living among workers who used to share similar ways of life under state socialism. It seems that collective challenges against enterprise authority are less likely where the market economy offers viable alternatives to state employment and where market induces more individualist means of accommodating to the changing economy. Working-class family may increasingly act as an economic unit, in both starting a business or making ends meet, but labor solidarity based on enterprise membership seems to be dampened in places where market economy thrives.

Contradictory Consciousness

Overall, veteran socialist workers experience a great deal of ambivalence toward market reforms. On the one hand, market reforms have brought a general rise in living standard, better supply of foodstuffs and consumer goods, more economic opportunities for some workers and most working-class offsprings. Reforms are both needed and wanted, they reasoned. Many also renounced the excessive and bloody turmoils of Maoist political campaigns that permeated down to the shop floors and made life difficult.[53] On the other hand, Maoism is, nevertheless, very much alive as a moral economy and a critical discourse available and shared by this generation of socialist workers. Discourse of exploitation aside, four decades of state propaganda and ideological education have bequeathed a repertoire of Marxist concepts that, rather ironically, only now make cognitive sense to workers with the arrival of a market society, and just as the state finds it politically inconvenient to use the language of class and class struggle. The reasoning of this ex-activist worker is found in many of my interviews where workers may be less articulate but no less critical: "Labor creates value. I don't believe one should earn within one or two days what others have to spend a lifetime to earn, like those star athletes or a stamp that was sold for a million. Can you tell me what kind of value they create?"[54]

If analytical remarks like these are more likely to be obtained from union or party activists and skilled workers, mass nostalgia for Maoism is a widely shared sentiment among ordinary workers. A powerful moral economy strengthened by a persistent personality cult, Maoism as the golden age of socialism was referred to again and again in my interviews. "When the Chairman was still around ..." or "In old Mao's day ..." were the most common preludes to an avalanche of biting and emotional critique against management of the present. The superiority of Maoism includes: a clean management (versus rampant corruption today), emphasis on skill training (versus total neglect of skill training and a single focus on output volume of low-skill products), efficiency of moral incentives (versus a short-term instrumental exchange relation), and basic needs-oriented rather than output-oriented reward system. The strongest indictments are targeted against the factory managers who are regarded as thoroughly corrupt and utterly incapable. Because reform has given them autonomy and authority, the blame for ailing enterprise performance also falls squarely on these managers. They have become workers' concrete and embodied class enemy in local contexts of struggle, as found in those staged by the army of redundant workers. In short, whereas state ideology and propaganda repress the discourses of class and class conflicts, veteran workers' experiences under market socialism made them ever more class-conscious. While the state constructs an image of SOE workers as unproductive, indolent, and psychologically backward-looking, they see more structural and management-induced causes of their predicaments. They are both supportive and critical of the present social order, a contradictory consciousness allowing for both passivity and activism.

The Unmaking of the Redundant Worker

Massive redundancy is no new phenomenon in socialist China. Unemployment population reached several million in 1953, 1961, 1970, and 1978 respectively. Yet, none of these peak periods matched the duration and magnitude of the current spell of redundancy that is still growing. Beginning in the early 1990s, the redundant population mushroomed to an alarming 12 million, or an unemployment rate of 6.77 percent by 1997. If we include those who are officially employed but are not paid or paid below the minimum livelihood levels, the total approaches 16 million. This scale of unemployment is the most serious in the history of the People's Republic, surpassing that of 1961 when 8.73 million were urged to leave their city jobs in the aftermath of the Great Leap, and that of 1980 when 5.4 million sent-down youth waited for urban employment on their return from the countryside.[55] The Ministry of Labor estimated that there would be an additional 8–10 million redundant industrial workers from 1998 to 2000. Most (96.5 percent) of the redundant workforce have been discharged from SOEs (64.3 percent) and urban collectives (32.2 percent). Nationwide, 47.8 percent of all laid-off workers come from manufacturing industries, 52.3 percent are aged between 36–50, and 60–70 percent are women.[56] The following discussion examines the political economy and the role of state policies in Liaoning. In this northeastern province, redundant workers are not only numerous and concentrated, but are also known for their militant insurgency as they respond to the forces that push them down the class ladder, from the rank of socialist workers to become the new urban poor. I shall discuss the features of the local political economy and of the working-class community that facilitate the emergence of this kind of labor politics of transition.

Political Economy of an Old Industrial Base

In the pre-reform era, Liaoning was considered the "eldest son of the nation" or the "emperor's daughter," cherished and glorified because of the natural resource endowment, strategic location, and early development of basic and heavy industries under Japanese colonization since the early 1900s. In the 1950s, Liaoning was a primary target of state investment and Russian financial aids (59 of the 156 priority projects took place in the northeast), so much so that by 1957, the province contributed 71 percent of iron production, 63 percent of steel production, and 58 percent of steel products to the national economy.[57] Shenyang's machine making industry was of central importance for the nation as a whole. Geared toward the need of the planned economy, Liaoning is the site of 10 percent of the nation's large and medium SOEs and the state sector's contribution to the province's industrial output remains at a high of 50.3 percent, employing 67 percent (93.7 percent if one includes urban collectives) of industrial workers in 1997. The industrial structure inherited from socialist planning proves crippling for the province's development under market socialism. The predominance of big, old, and heavy industrial enterprises meant outdated technology, limited range of consumer goods production, and aging workforce with heavy demands for pension and health-care expenses. Local government's control over subsidiary enterprises and internal structure of management are resistant to change. Development of the private and foreign sectors lags behind what is required to create employment for new and old workers. By 1997, 56.4 percent of Liaoning's SOEs were loss-making, 34.8 percent had an asset–debt ratio of over 100 percent and were de facto bankrupt enterprises.[58] Under these conditions, Liaoning becomes infamously the leading province of lay-off workers: its 1.7 million unemployed workers now account for 13.2 percent of the national total in 1998.[59] By some estimates in internal (*neibu*) documents, the de facto rate of workers without job and or pay varies between 19 percent and 41 percent.[60]

Toward the ends of maintaining political stability and social order, the central government devises three major ways to contain the social and economic consequences of massive unemployment. These are: social insurance reform, poor relief policies, and "reemployment projects" (*zaijiuye gongcheng*), all of which call for government and enterprise responsibility at local levels. Although all of these state initiatives suffer from insufficient funds and are therefore ineffective in alleviating the hardship conditions of the redundants, these policies provide legitimate grounds for unemployed workers to put pressure on local government and enterprise management when the latter fail to fulfill their responsibilities. Therefore, inadvertently, regulations imposed by the central authority are instrumental in constituting workers' interests as citizens' legal rights.

In the blueprint of the reformers, insurance funds for pension and unemployment would provide a societal safety net replacing that provided by the enterprise. But as previous discussions of "disorganized despotism" show, contributions have lagged far behind demands. Between 1995 and 2000, collectible contributions to unemployment funds are estimated to be 46 billion yuan, falling far behind the estimated 71.5 billion yuan actually needed for the unemployed.[61] When most SOEs are loss making and in debts, a vicious cycle is set in which fewer enterprises and fewer employees are contributing and more workers have changed from contributors to claimants of these funds. In Shenyang, for instance, in 1998, 27 percent of participating enterprises in pension funds stopped payment, creating a deficit of 240 million yuan. After waves of protests and public demonstrations by retirees in 1998, the local insurance bureau had to borrow 110 million yuan from the municipal finance and labor departments in order to make payments.[62]

The second way to provide for the redundants is an expanded poor-relief program. Traditionally, the Ministry for Civil Affairs offered relief to three types of destitutes: those without labor capacity, without income source, and without legal supporter. Before 1992, only 0.06 percent city dwellers received regular relief. As market reforms intensified in the 1990s, urban pauperism became more visible and externalized from work units. To maintain social stability, more systematic and ubiquitous provision was needed for all in need of the means of subsistence whatever the cause of their destitution. Beginning in 1993, and based on the experiment in Shanghai, a minimum livelihood protection line has been established in 207 major cities (one third of all cities) all over China.[63] These standards are set by local government, adjusted according to local standard of living and inflation. In Liaoning, the range of minimum livelihood standards is set at 120–160 yuan in 1998. However, administrative and financial constraints made it difficult for effective relief to be made available to the massive destitutes. Only 0.6 percent of urbanites receive regular relief. One study shows that one third of all redundant-worker households have income below the official minimum standard in 1997. To make ends meet, each household has to borrow an average of 130 yuan per month.[64] Despite its limited effects, the setting of an official minimum livelihood standard is widely known and would be used by protesting workers to bolster their claims for unpaid and/or underpaid unemployment allowances.

Finally, the third and major effort by the central government to minimize the destabilizing impacts of reform on unemployed workers is to have local governments launching nationwide but locally based reemployment projects. In each local government (town and city), a task force is formed by the relevant government departments to make use of reemployment funds pooled from government grants, unemployment funds contributed by enterprises, and contributions from the working population. Reemployment centers and funds are set up to support training of lay-off workers, to assist the setting up of private small business in street markets and introduction of jobs, and to subsidize enterprises that take on redundant workers. The ultimate goal is to make workers self-supportive in employment (*zimou zhiye*). Grassroots mass organizations have shifted their priority from being political transmission belts to provision of social services and emergency charity (e.g., "offering warmth initiative") for the destitute redundants.[65] Again, the major obstacle is insufficient funds: with such a massive suspension of production and enterprise insolvency, enterprise and employees simply cannot pay their contributions. Reemployment fund in Shenyang is running with a deficit of 120 million yuan. Many reemployment centers are not operating and only 140,000 (or one third) registered redundant workers fall under the management of these centers.[66]

The significance of these state policies lies less in their effectiveness and more in their effect of transferring the responsibility of solving redundants' predicament from the central to the local levels of government. The gap between central government regulations and the failure of local governments to live up to those regulations is the political space in which redundant workers are waging their struggle.

Resistance and Resignation

Redundancy unties workers from enterprise management's economic control, from party apparatus' surveillance, and from the routine of production life. In contrast to on-the-job workers, collective action by the unemployed almost always occurs beyond the confines of their factories, either in front of the local government offices or on the streets and main roads in cities and towns. Confronting the pressing needs of subsistence and the collapse of enterprise bureaucracy, they are unlikely to bring their grievances to the labor dispute arbitration apparatus (which involves a longer process and usually begins with arbitration committee at the enterprise level). Therefore, what usually happens is public demonstrations, rallies, collective petitions, blocking of rail and road traffic, violence against management. Chinese statistics of strikes and protests should only be taken as rough indications of general trends. In this regard, available figures show persistent labor activism caused by wage and pension arrears, plant closure, inadequate employment, and embezzlement of funds by factory managers. For instance, in 1993, a Ministry of Labor source revealed a total of 2,500 sit-ins, destruction of machines, strikes, and detention of cadres. In the first half of 1995, there were some 3,700 meetings, strikes, petitions, and demonstrations in enterprises and mining plants all over the country. Then, from January to September 1996, the corresponding figure was 1,520, and in October 1997 alone, 455 strikes and demonstrations broke out. The situations worsened in 1998, when in January, February, and March, there were respectively 1,151, 975, 1,255 incidents of worker protests.[67] Researchers also note a geographical pattern of labor protests: provinces that experienced the most turmoil were mostly interior or northeastern provinces with a high concentration of strategic and heavy industries. Some of these inland provinces were the recipients of the Third Front industrialization and plant relocation drive in the 1960s and 70s. But these firms have become the most obsolete and unproductive under a market economy.[68]

In Liaoning and elsewhere, unpaid wages and pensions, or what workers called "subsistence rights" (*shengcunquan*) occupied top priorities in the slogans of protesting workers who were outraged and desperate. "We Want to Work," "We Want to Live," "Our Children Want to Go to School" were the most frequently reported, although there were also those steeped in the idioms of class and socialism, e.g., "Long Live the Working Class," "Eradicate the New Bureaucratic Bourgeoisie."[69] But there were also more pragmatic and specific banners that read "We Want to Meet the Mayor," "We Want to Meet the Provincial Governor," or "Return Us the Shopping Mall," and so on. In interviews with workers and leaders in Liaoning who were core members in these protests,[70] some of which lasted for several years, workers deliberately forgo abstract and radical wordings in favor of pragmatic and specific demands, so as to push the government toward pragmatic resolution of their immediate livelihood problems. Every time the central government announced regulations or a decision to guarantee the rights of the redundants and retirees, they would seize those opportunities to intensify their petitions to local, provincial, and central governments. They consciously framed their claims to echo policies of central government, most notably in banners like "Stop the Loss of State Assets" to demand that their factory not be sold, and "We Want to Live" to demand that minimum livelihood standard be guaranteed.

Plant closure, suspended production, and casualization of employment pose formidable obstacles for workers' mobilization. Yet, in Liaoning, thanks to the welfare legacy of the socialist era, workers live in close proximity to each other in enterprise residential compounds. Disseminating information about petitions, meetings, and fund raising (to finance worker representatives' trips to Beijing or to hire lawyers to write petition documents) were accomplished by words of mouth in daily interaction or by hanging banners in public areas in these compounds. Larger and older enterprises usually have their worker communities intact even after production has stopped. Moreover, the pattern of family-based employment also forms the basis of collective mobilization. In the days of planned economy, the central government resorted to enterprises to absorb surplus labor and it was common practice for workers' immediate family to work for the same unit. "Organized dependence" takes on exacerbated forms of organized familial dependence. So today, when workers protest, family members take turns to show up in rallies and petition, while others in the family are preoccupied with earning a family income.

Not all redundant workers have responded to reform by participating in collective actions. Many only joined in when they saw some likelihood of getting unpaid wages or severance compensation. Many also simply "accept" (renle) their bad luck and fate. Demoralized by poverty and joblessness, more than a few workers have attempted suicide or staged desperate acts of laying on railroads, regardless of results or risks. Most are forced to take up petty and extremely low-pay service jobs, peddling steamed buns or vegetables in street markets, or becoming tricycle drivers in small towns. Most of these jobs bring in 2–300 yuan a month, just enough to cover food and basic expenses. The atomizing effects of the market are most obvious among workers in smaller SOEs that had not built workers' residential communities in the past. Laid-off workers reported that they lost contact with either the enterprise management or their coworkers once the enterprise accounting office stopped distributing allowances and they never returned to the factory premise.

Contradictory Consciousness

Like workers still employed in ailing SOEs, redundant workers have developed a sharpened class consciousness as reform imposed devastating dislocation in their lives. For this massive group of workers, the transition is not just one of labor aristocracy to contract worker, but to society's rejects. Cadres' mismanagement and corruption, and their accomplices in local government became the concrete class enemies, because power has been devolved from the center to these local agents. "Cadres have become capitalists" is a popular indictment. The rhetoric of class draws on popular memories of the Maoist era. The nostalgic narratives about Maoism are not only indicative of individuals' critique of the present by way of the past in front of an interviewer. They are excerpts from a community of discourse, told and retold by the working class in their daily lives. These narratives of Maoism are more than just representational of redundant workers' collective consciousness and memories; they are arguably the ontological condition of class, meaning that they constitute experience and mediate social action.[71] This point is driven home most clearly to me when interviewing leaders of worker protests in Liaoning. Mostly in their 40s, they were the generation that has suffered the consequences of state initiatives: the Great Leap deprived them of a healthy childhood, the Cultural Revolution left them little education and sent them to hard labor in the countryside, and then came market reforms making them redundant. When they joined the enterprise in the late 70s after returning from the countryside, the Maoism they now glorified as the heyday of working-class commitment and leadership was already in its waning state and production was in disarray. The communal and familial narratives of what Maoist factories were like recursively constitute their identities, rather than their experiences having given rise to those identities. Theirs is an imagined Maoism, all the more powerful as a source of moral economy because it lacks the ambivalence and contradictions that tainted real life Maoism. Older workers' memories of the socialist past include political turmoil, violence, and poverty that they abhor. Therefore, although class consciousness is evidently on the rise and informs the actions of the unemployed, the logic of class consciousness is more nuanced than it seems.

Also evident from the banners and strategies of protesting workers is the legalistic framing of their claims and interests. In the past few years, out of concern for social stability, central leadership periodically issued documents reiterating their commitment to the reemployment project and to guarantee basic livelihood of the redundant and retired. These moments were seized by worker leaders to mobilize more actions, exploiting the gap between central policies and local failure to put them into practice. In Liaoning, the legal minimum of 120 yuan livelihood standard was repeatedly used by workers in petitions and negotiations with local government officials. In other cases, the Bankruptcy Law, which prescribes procedures for an enterprise to be declared bankrupt, has also been cited to accuse management of illegally bypassing the Workers' Council in the sales of the enterprise. Worker leaders seek legal advice from law students or lawyers who are willing to offer advice. They have also been very attentive to news reports about government regulations and policies. Some of them strategically plan their petitions to make use of the hierarchy of authority between municipal, provincial, and central governments.[72] In one instance, by threatening to bring their case to the provincial government during protests, workers succeeded in forcing the local officials to agree to their terms of severance compensations. In another factory, after two years of continuous petitions and demonstrations outside the mayor's office, workers' leaders brought their case to Beijing where officials dispatched orders to require their provincial and municipal subordinates to examine their complaints.[73] These strategies and action follow the logic of what has been called "rightful resistance" or "policy-based resistance" by peasants against local officials' taxation and corruption.[74] Through these actions, workers develop a sense of legal and welfare entitlements as Chinese urban residents, which the state has accorded them. In short, the politics of transition to redundancy, as the case in Liaoning shows, might involve a politics of class intermingled with a politics of citizenship—struggles to defend class interests via claiming civil (or legal) and social (or welfare) rights endowed by the Chinese state.

Yet disgruntled workers are under enormous pressure to eke out a meager income the best they can. Odd jobs and street peddling are much more labor intensive and insecure than SOE jobs, but these activities are the top priorities in redundant workers' lives now. Pooling human and economic resources among family members is another common survival strategy. Unemployed young couples move in with retired parents to make savings on rents and food. Pensioners who are lucky enough to be paid regularly provide capital for their children to start a small clothing stall in the local market. The immediacy of everyday life, the moral outrage against official and enterprise corruption, and the pervasive critique of the market are hinged together in uneasy balance. The state's persistent concern with workers' "imbalance psychology" is a disguised recognition of a powerful disruptive force lurking beneath a market society.

Conclusion

Leslie Sklair has argued convincingly, with examples from around the world, that although contemporary capitalism increasingly organizes globally, the resistances to global capitalism can be effective where they can disrupt its smooth running (accumulation of private profits) locally.[75] This observation is particularly true in authoritarian societies like China. Where independent labor organizing is ruthlessly repressed, the hope and the strength of labor resistance lies not in any potential organizational prowess of the working class but in its capacity to defy and disrupt locally. In this chapter, I have traced how migrant peasant workers, socialist workers, and the redundant workers fight their own battles in the niches carved out by global capitalism and market reforms. Disruptive collective resistances at the point of production are generated by the exigencies of exploitative shop–floor relations in both "flexible" global factories and "modern, scientific management" in state-owned enterprises. In the case of the redundant workers, public activism was facilitated and necessitated by the dismantling of enterprise control.

Beyond oppression, however, global capitalism and market forces do offer some degree of liberation from state domination and more personal relations of power. As some state workers and their offspring find opportunities of upward mobility, migrant peasant workers also attain unprecedented, albeit temporary, economic and personal independence in the new, market socialist order. Through both accommodation and resistance, workers' collective mentalities are reworked and transformed. Identities and memories of class, nascent conceptions of citizen rights, and more traditional sentiments of native-place localism form the repertoire of solidarity, intertwined and invoked to inform logics of collective actions that defy scientific predictions or theoretical normalization.

Notes

1. I should thank Mark Selden, Liz Perry, Ruth Collier, Tak-Wing Ngo, Delia Davin, Dorothy Solinger, and Jean-Louis Rocca for their comments.
2. David Harvey, *The Condition of Postmodernity* (Oxford: Blackwell, 1989): 186.
3. This chapter deals with manufacturing workers in urban China only, and has thus left out workers in township and village enterprises in rural areas. For the latter cases, see discussions in

Sally Sargeson, *Reworking China's Proletariat* (New York: St. Martin's Press, 1999); and Yang, Minchuan, "Reshaping Peasant Culture and Community," *Modern China* 20, 2 (1994): 157–179.

4. Manuel Castells, *The Rise of the Network Society* (Oxford: Blackwell, 1997).

5. Michael Burawoy, and Katherine Verdery, eds, *Uncertain Transition: Ethnographies of Change in the Postsocialist World* (Lanham: Rowman & Littlefield Publishers, Inc., 1999).

6. Ira Katznelson, "Working Class Formation" in *Working-Class Formation*, eds.Ira Katznelson, and Aristide R. Zolberg (Princeton: Princeton University Press, 1986). See a useful critique in Margaret Somers, "Workers of the World, Compare!" *Contemporary Sociology* 18, 1 (January 1989): 325–329.

7. John R. Hall, ed., *Reworking Class* (Ithaca: Cornell University Press, 1997); Scott G. McNall, et al., eds, *Bringing Class Back In* (Boulder, Co.: Westview, 1991).

8. For instance, Craig Calhoun, *Critical Social Theory* (Oxford: Blackwell, 1995); Craig Calhoun, ed., *Social Theory and the Politics of Identity* (Oxford: Blackwell, 1994); Pierre Bourdieu, *An Outline of a Theory of Practice* (Cambridge: Cambridge University Press, 1977); Charles Sabel, *Work and Politics* (Cambridge: Cambridge University Press, 1982).

9. Total numbers of migrants always vary with the different definitions and samples used in different studies. Eighty–100 million is the most commonly accepted estimate. See discussions in Delia Davin, *Internal Migration in Contemporary China* (New York: St. Martin's Press, 1999); Dorothy Solinger, *Contesting Citizenship in Urban China* (Berkeley: University of California Press, 1999): 15–23.

10. *Far Eastern Economic Review* (4 April 1996).The quoted figures are compiled by the Ministry of Agriculture.

11. Public Security Department, *A Compilation of National Statistics of Temporary Residents, 1997* (Beijing: Zhongguo Renmin Gongandaxue Chubanshe): 82.

12. Tan, Shen, "Gender Differences in the Mobility of Rural Labor," *Shehuixue Yanjiu* (Sociological Research) 1 (1997): 42–47.

13. Harvey, *The Condition of Postmodernity*, 191.

14. Ching Kwan Lee, *Gender and the South China Miracle* (Berkeley: University of California, 1998).

15. Anita Chan, "Labor Standards and Human Rights: Chinese Workers Under Market Socialism," *Human Rights Quarterly* 20, 4 (1998): 886–904.

16. Tang, Shan, "Sexual Harrassment: Migrant Women Workers' Dual Identity and Discrimination," *Shehuixue Yanjiu* 4 (1996). Local press in Guangzhou carries many stories of abuses in foreign-owned enterprises. For some English translations of these reports, see Anita Chan, "The Conditions of Chinese Workers in East-Asian Funded Enterprises," in *Chinese Sociology and Anthropology*, ed. Anita Chan, 30 (Summer 1998).

17. *Nanfang Gongbao* (Southern Business News) (11 August 1999).

18. Pun, Ngai, "Becoming *Dagongmei* (Working Girls): The Politics of Identity and Difference in Reform China," *The China Journal* 42 (July 1999): 1–18. For Zhejiang, see Sargeson, *Reworking China's Proletariat*.

19. In-depth interviews with workers and owners of three private enterprises in Guangzhou in 1996 and 1999. Special favors, like extra year-end bonus, additional sick leave and monetary compensation after industrial injuries, frequent home visits and homemade food for injured workers during the hospitalization period, always succeed in fostering loyalty among the core workers who benefit from these treatments.

20. Fieldwork in private and joint-venture firms in Guangdong between 1996 and 1999.

21. Anita Chan, "Labor Relations in Foreign-Funded Ventures," in *Adjusting to Capitalism*, ed. Greg O'Leary (Armonk, New York: M.E. Sharpe, 1998): 122–149. During an interview in 1998 with a Guangzhou Municipal Federation of Labor Unions, the cadre responsible for organization claimed the unionization rate among actually operating nonstate factories in Guangzhou was 78 percent. He reasoned that the lower rates reported in the press or by academics could have resulted from including in the base number those contracted but not yet actualized investment projects.

22. Interviews with workers in a private knitting factory in Guangzhou in 1996.

23. Charles Sabel, *Work and Politics* (Cambridge: Cambridge University Press, 1982): 133. Of course family resemblance stops there. The absence of leftist political parties or adversarial unions in China removes the institutional bases for sustained labor militance as was found in Western Europe.

24. *Wailaigong* (Foshan, Guangdong) 4 (1999): 6. For other accounts of strikes and work stoppages, see Anita Chan, ed., *Chinese Sociology and Anthropology* 30 (Summer 1998).

25. *Fazhibao* (Legal Daily) (8 December 1998): 6.

26. *Yanchenggongbao* (Guangzhou Business News) (22 April 1999); Anita Chan, ed, *Chinese Sociology and Anthropology* 30 (Summer 1998).

27. *Zhongguolaodong* (China Labor) 8 (1999): 16.

28. Wang, Wen-zeng, *Zouxiang Laodongzhengyi* (Toward Labor Dispute) (Beijing: Jingjikexue Chubanshe, 1998): 8.

29. *Laodong Zhengyi Chuli Yu Yanjiu* (Labor Dispute Handling and Research) 1995, 1996, 1997, various articles; *Nanfang Gongbao* (11 December 1998).

30. Charles Sabel, *Work and Politics,* builds on Bourdieu's notion of "habitus" to argue that workers' "careers at work" shape their political response to class mobilization. While it is beyond the scope of this chapter to engage both concepts, my data suggest that "career at work" is too constrained to work-related identities and aspirations, not allowing for labor's multiple identities that originate outside of skill and work roles.

31. *Yangchengwanbao* (Guangzhou Evening News) 94, 95, 96 (October 15–November 4, 1998).

32. Moishe Postone, *Time, Labor and Social Domination* (Cambridge: University of Cambridge Press, 1993).

33. Ching Kwan Lee, *Gender and the South China Miracle.*

34. Christina Gilmartin, and Tan, Lin, "Where and Why Have All the Women Gone? Women, Marriage, Migration and Social Mobility in China," paper presented at the International Conference on Gender and Development in Asia, November 27–29, 1997, Chinese University of Hong Kong.

35. *Guangdong Laodongbao* (Guangdong Labor News) (29 May 1997); *Far Eastern Economic Review* (4 April 1996): 22. Tan, Shen, "The Relation Between Migrant Women Workers, Foreign Enterprises, Local Government and Society in the Pearl River Delta," unpublished manuscript, 1997.

36. Plans for different kinds of small business ventures in the city and in home villages were frequently mentioned in interviews with migrant workers. Hardship in factories is accepted as a temporary cost to be paid to realize a longer-term ambition.

37. Guangzhou State Statistics Bureau, 1995 Guangzhou Industrial Census.

38. Ching Kwan Lee, "From Organized Dependence to Disorganized Despotism: Changing Factory Regimes in Chinese Factories," *The China Quarterly* 157 (1999): 44–71.

39. Andrew Walder, "Wage Reform and the Web of Factory Interests," *The China Quarterly* 109 (1987): 22–41; "Factory and Manager in an Era of Reform," *The China Quarterly* 118 (1989): 242–264; "Workers, Managers and the State," *The China Quarterly* 127 (1991): 467–492; "The Decline of Communist Power: Elements of a Theory of Institutional Change," *Theory and Society* 23, 2 (1994): 297–323.

40. Ching Kwan Lee, "From Organized Dependence to Disorganized Despotism." In a series of interviews with 20 union cadres in Guangzhou's enterprise, industry, and municipal trade unions in 1998, all reported difficulties in carrying out their union work in the 1990s. One of them sarcastically remarked that union work has become a form of art. Union cadres are challenged to master this art: how to protect workers' rights without being charged by management as obstructing production.

41. See also Zhao, Minghua, and Theo Nichols, "Management Control of Labor in State Owned Enterprises: Cases from the Textile Industry," *The China Journal* 36 (1996): 1–21.

42. Interview in Guangzhou, February 3, 1996.

43. Interview in Guangzhou, March 30, 1996.
44. Ching Kwan Lee, "The Labor Politics of Market Socialism," *Modern China* 24, 1 (1998): 3–33.
45. *Laodong Zhengyi Chuli Yu Yanjiu* 5 (1996): 13–15; 1997, various issues.
46. Interview in Shenyang (Liaoning), May 19, 1999.
47. Interview in Shenyang (Liaoning), May 18, 1999. For other incidents of work stoppages in Guangzhou, see Ching Kwan Lee, "The Labor Politics of Market Socialism."
48. Same as footnote 45.
49. *Guangdong Laodongbao* (21 December 1998).
50. *Guangzhou Ribao* (Guangzhou Daily) (23 December 1998).
51. Worker participation in the 1989 student protests has not gone unnoticed. But, it did seem to be an exception rather than a general trend for "employed" workers to have the time and will to participate or organize in collective protests.
52. Ching Kwan Lee, "The Labor Politics of Market Socialism," "From Organized Dependence to Disorganized Despotism," and fieldwork in Liaoning in 1999.
53. Life history interviews in Guangzhou, 1996–1998.
54. Interview in Guangzhou, February 3, 1996.
55. Li, Peilin, "Unemployment Management in Old Industrial Base," in *China's Economic Opening and Changes in Social Structure,* eds. Hu, Yaosu, and Lu, Xueyi (Beijing: Shehuikexue Wenxian Chubanshe, 1998): 83–105.
56. Hu, Angang, "Zhongguo Chengzhenshiyezhuangkuangfenxi," (An analysis of China's unemployment condition), *Guanli Shijie* (Management World) 4 (1998): 47–63; Chang, Kai, "Gongyouzhi qiye zhong nuzhigong de shiye ji zaizhou ye wenti de diaocha yu yanjiu" (A survey on unemployment and reemployment of female employees in state owned enterprises), *Shehuixue Yanjiu* 3 (1995): 83–93.
57. Margot Schueller, "Liaoning: Struggling with the Burdens of the Past," in *China's Provinces in Reform,* ed. David S.G. Goodman (London: Routledge, 1997): 100; Li, Zhining, *Dagongye yu zhongguo* (Big industry in China) (Nanchang: Jiangxi Renminchubanshe, 1997): 215–229.
58. Xu, Pinghua, et al. *Guoyouqiye Xiagangzhegongzaijiuyeyunzhoushewu* (Practical handbook on the re-employment of SOE laid off workers) (Shenyang: Shenyang Chubanshe, 1998): 261–262.
59. Hu, Angang, "Zhongguo Chengzhenshiyezhuangkuangfenxi"; Liaoning Urban Employment Research Team, "Conditions and Strategies of Liaoning's Urban Population and Employment," *Guanli Shijie* 5 (1998): 69–76. Redundancy here means both registered unemployed and registered off-duty (*xiagang*) workers. The latter is an institutional relic of state socialism, and refers to those who have lost their jobs, but not their labor relation with their enterprise that continues to be responsible for contributing to their pensions, social insurance, and livelihood allowances. There is a third category of redundant workers who are not counted in these figures: those unregistered off-duty workers whose enterprises merely suspend production and refuse to register them as off-duty in order to evade financial responsibility. In this chapter, I use the terms "redundant," "laid-off," and "unemployed" interchangeably as they refer to similar actual conditions of unemployment.
60. Antoine Kernen, and Jean-Louis Rocca, "The Reform of State-owned Enterprises and its Social Consequences in Shenyang and Liaoning," unpublished manuscript (1998): 16.
61. Feng, Tongqing, "Jiejiezhongguodalu xianjieduan chengzhenshiyewentidisilu" (Thoughts on solving China's urban unemployment problems), paper presented at the International Roundtable on Social Security, March 3–5, 1998, Hong Kong.
62. Yang, Yiyong, and Xin, Xiaobai, "A Report on Laid-offs and Re-employment," in *1999: Zhongguoshehuixingshi yu yuce* (1999: Analysis and forecast of social situation in China), eds. Yu, Xin, et al. (Beijing: Shehuikexuewenxian Chubanshe, 1999): 248–249.
63. Tang, Jun, "Zhongguo Chengzhen Jumin Zuitishenghuobaozhang Yanjiubaogao" (A survey report on minimum livelihood security system for Chinese urban residents) in *Zhonggou-shehuifuli yu shehuijingbubaogao* (A report on social welfare and social progress in China), eds. Shi, Zhengxin, and Zhu, Yong (Beijing: Shehuikexuewenxian Chubanshe, 1998).

64. Jiang, Shuge, et al. in *1999: Zhongguoshehuixingshi yu yuce*, eds.Yu, Xin, et al. 315.

65. Antoine Kernen, and Jean-Louis Rocca, "The Reform of State-owned Enterprises and its Social Consequences in Shenyang and Liaoning."

66. Yang, and Xin, "A Report on Laid-offs and Re-employment," 250.

67. Jean-Louis Rocca, "Old Working Class, New Working Class: Reforms, Labor Crisis and the Two Faces of Conflicts in Chinese Urban Areas," unpublished manuscript 1999. These figures are quoted from a Hong Kong based magazine on Chinese affairs, *Zhengming* (Contentions).

68. Alan Liu, *Mass Politics in the People's Republic* (Boulder, Co.: Westview, 1996).

69. Elizabeth Perry, "Crime, Corruption and Contention," in *The Paradox of China's Post-Mao Reforms*, eds. Merle Goldman, and Roderick Macfarquhar (Cambridge: Harvard University Press, 1999): 317–321; Ching Kwan Lee, "Pathways of Labor Insurgency," in *Chinese Society: Change, Conflict and Resistance*, eds. Elizabeth Perry, and Mark Selden (London: Routledge, 2000).

70. Interviews in Shenyang and Tieling in Liaoning, between May and August 1999.

71. Special issue on "Narratives and Social Identities," in *Social Science History* 16, 2 (1992), articles by William Sewell, George Steinmetz, and Margaret Somers.

72. For details on some of these protests, see Ching Kwan Lee, "The Revenge of History: Collective Memories, Unemployment and Worker Protests in Northeastern China," *Ethnography* 1, 2 (2000): 245–265.

73. Fieldwork in May and July 1999. These two cases took place in Tieling, an industrial town in Liaoning.

74. Kevin O'Brien, "Rightful Resistance," *World Politics* 49 (1996): 31–55; Thomas P. Bernstein, "Farmer Discontent and Regime Responses," in *The Paradox of China's Post-Mao Reforms*, eds. Merle Goldman, and Roderick Macfarquhar, 197–219.

75. Leslie Sklair, "Social Movements and Global Capitalisms," in *The Cultures of Globalization*, eds. Frederic Jameson, and Masao Miyoshi (Durham: Duke University Press, 1998): 291–311.

PART II

Wealth: The New Frontier

CHAPTER FOUR

Money, Power, and the Problem of Legitimacy in the Hong Kong Special Administrative Region

TAK-WING NGO

The popularity of the Hong Kong government has been low since the establishment of the Hong Kong Special Administrative Region (SAR) in July 1997. This is rather surprising given the fact of the SAR government's painstaking attempts to uphold the freedom enjoyed by the people, to maintain a good relationship with Beijing, to offer business incentives for investment, and to reform social services for the improvement of community welfare. In fact, a simple checklist of actions taken by the SAR government shows the enormous amount of work done in just two years of its governance.

This chapter looks at this puzzle and argues that the problem derives from the way business and politics are institutionalized in the SAR political system. The government finds itself trapped by contradictory demands inherent in the system. Policy responses to the prevailing government–business relations have evoked criticism from all corners of society, thereby discrediting the popular legitimacy of the government.

From Laissez-Faire to Strategic Planning

Let us begin with a simple survey of what has been done by the SAR government. First and foremost, basic human rights and individual freedom—issues that the Hong Kong people were most worried about—have been more or less preserved. The clearest indication is the continued existence of the Hong Kong Alliance in Support of the Patriotic

Democratic Movement in China, an organization that has been classified by Beijing as a subversive body. It is still functioning and is allowed to launch protest activities against human rights abuse in China. Mass gatherings have continued to be organized in commemoration of the June 4 massacre. Even the Falungong society, which Beijing recently suppressed so forcefully, continues its activities openly in Hong Kong.

While taking great effort to keep "business as usual" after the handover, the chief executive of the Hong Kong SAR, Tung Chee-hwa, has been eager to reform various aspects of the colonial system. Proposals in the areas of housing, education, social welfare, environment, and the civil service have been put forward. An ambitious housing program had been launched, with the target of building 85,000 public and private residential units per year for ten years. The original plan was that 70 percent of the population would own their own homes by the year 2007. In the area of education, more emphasis has been given to civic education and innovative teaching, and the mother tongue is now the endorsed medium of instruction. The SAR government also announced its plan to implement a Mandatory Provident Fund. A plan of this sort had been endlessly debated under the colonial administration for years. With the objectives of providing retirement pension for the aging population and fostering a sense of belonging to the community, the SAR government eventually ironed out the difficulties and implemented the scheme in 2001. Another bold attempt of the Tung administration was to change the long-existing system of civil service employment. The Tung administration proposed to replace permanent employment with a contract system, thus putting an end to the iron-bowl employment. This means new civil servants will be employed on contract basis; and only those who have proven their ability over the years will be offered permanent positions when they are promoted to the managerial rank. In the area of environmental health, a Council for Sustainable Development will be set up to advise the government on environmental matters.

At the same time, the SAR government has also unveiled its proactive stance on the long-term development of Hong Kong. This represents one of the most prominent departures of the SAR government from its colonial predecessor, who typically adopted a laissez-faire attitude toward economic planning. This laissez-faire policy of the colonial authorities represented not only an attempt to maintain a pro-business environment (given by low profit tax, limited social welfare provisions, minimum labor protection), but also a strategy to safeguard the interests of the commercial élite who benefited from free trade and free capital inflow and outflow.[1] State promotion of industrial development that has been typical in other East Asian countries was lacking in colonial Hong Kong. At the same time, the colonial government upheld a principle of nonselective intervention that refused any demand for preferential allocation of resources to particular business sectors or specific enterprises.[2]

Notwithstanding the free market cliché reiterated by the SAR government, the deviation from the laissez-faire approach has been more than obvious. In his first policy speech as the chief executive, Tung Chee-hwa revealed his vision for development planning by setting up a Commission on Strategic Development. The commission was entrusted with the task of reviewing the economy, human resources, education, housing, land supply, environment, and relations with the mainland, with a view to formulate plans for maintaining Hong Kong's competitiveness.[3] This new vision of strategic planning was further developed in Tung's 1998 policy address. He identified seven areas of strategic priority for developing Hong Kong: making it a leading city for information technology, a world center of design and fashion, a regional center of multimedia information and entertainment services, a world center for Chinese medicine, a leading supplier of high value-added products, a regional center for professional talents and services, and the marketplace for technological transfer between China and the world.[4]

A number of concrete plans were set in motion in the months that followed. These included the setting up of a Commission on Innovation and Technology in March 1998. Following its recommendations, a HK$5 billion Innovation and Technology Fund and an Applied Science and Technology Research Institute were set up to support research. A Provisional Hong Kong Science Park Co. Ltd was incorporated in 1998 to plan, develop, and manage the science park on a 22-hectare site at Pak Shek Kok. A new business hub was targeted for location on 38 hectares of reclaimed land off the Central District waterfront. Tung Chee-hwa also announced the development of a world-class teleport at Chung Hom Kok to provide high-quality global satellite links.

In addition to the above-mentioned, there are even more ambitious and controversial plans. A HK$13 billion cyberport project to develop Hong Kong into a world center of computer technology was announced in 1999. A few months later the government concluded a joint venture project with Disney to build a theme park on Lantau Island. The park— meant to be a big boost to the tourist industry—will cost HK$14 billion in total, with the SAR government contributing HK$9 billion in cash and HK$6 billion in loans. The project is expected to create 16,000 jobs, and the first phase is scheduled to be completed in 2005. Furthermore, discussions have been going on between the government and potential investors from Taiwan and the United States to set up a silicon harbor, with investment projects expected to cost more than HK$1 billion for the production of computer chips.

The above checklist of plans and projects is impressive. It unveils the ambition and the vision of the Tung administration. In contrast to its colonial predecessor's reserved attitude toward industrial upgrading, the Tung administration has been keen to take an active role in leading Hong Kong to the high-tech world. It is therefore puzzling that the Tung administration is afflicted with low popularity. What is even more surprising is the distrust showed by both the working class and the business community toward the SAR government. An anti-Tung campaign was mounted by some members of the business community. Business leaders who once supported Tung's running for office have expressed deep dissatisfaction toward the Tung administration. At the same time, numerous demonstrations were staged by labor unions in protest against the poor performance of the SAR government.

Administrative Incompetence of the SAR Government

One of the factors contributing to the low popularity of the SAR government is administrative incompetence. A number of incidents have been mismanaged by the government, unleashing public outcry and criticism. First and foremost is the way the government handled the financial crisis and the subsequent economic recession. The SAR government was slow in responding to the Asian financial crisis and underestimated the severity of the crisis. The severe impact on the banking system, the stock market and the property market was not fully apprehended when the government defended the US dollar peg with high interest rates. Worse still, no action was taken until the stock and property markets plummeted to half of their pre-crisis value. When a nine-point economic rescue package was announced in June 1998, it was deemed too late for "a dying patient."[5]

Other incidents that revealed the administrative incompetence of the SAR government include the handling of the "bird flu" epidemic. The epidemic first appeared in October 1997, but the government ignored its seriousness and took little action. As the flu spread and caused several deaths, the Fishery and Agriculture Department got into a panic and decided to slaughter all chickens in the territory. The operation was poorly conducted and received a lot of negative reports in media coverage. Even the housing program, the education reform, and the civil service reform have been criticized for their administrative bungling. The housing policy was hailed as a top government priority, and strict implementation of the specified targets was promised. However, in the wake of the Asian financial crisis and the subsequent recession, the housing target became unrealistic. Under strong pressure from land developers, the government was compelled to suspend the land sale program and the housing targets. Likewise, the mother tongue policy in schools was fiercely opposed by parents and teachers. The government eventually backed down by allowing selected schools to continue teaching in English. But the selection procedure drew a barrage of complaints. Similarly, the civil service reform was criticized by civil service unions as unfair, because the new contract system applied only to the rank and file, but not the administrative grade staff.

The most blatant demonstration of incompetence came from the new airport. Complete chaos reigned when the airport opened on July 6, 1998. The central computer system broke down and the cargo-handling services collapsed. Facilities, from telephones to toilets, were out of order. Hundreds of passengers and tons of cargo were affected. Losses were estimated at HK$4.6 billion. Later investigations brought to light the appallingly inadequate supervision of the project. Mismanagement turned the multibillion HK$ project into a monument of shame.

The administrative incompetence of the SAR government in handling the economic crisis and the above-mentioned issues certainly has negatively affected the popularity of the government. However, more deep-seated problems in the political institutions of the SAR exist so that, regardless of the financial crisis and unexpected turns of events, the dilemma of popular legitimacy is bound to surface.

The Marginalization of Popular Sector Influence

From the outset, the middle class and the grassroots sector have had good reason to be distrustful of the SAR government ever since they were marginalized in the SAR politics. In fact, such marginalization began during the transition period, when middle-class professionals formed political parties, mobilized popular support by articulating a pro-welfare platform, and won landslide victories in District Board, Municipal Councils, and Legislative Council elections.[6] With popular support and organizational power, they demanded a democratic SAR government that was constituted by universal suffrage and returned by direct election.

Alarmed by the threat of being excluded in a system constituted by popular elections, business interests sought patronage from Beijing.

Beijing's interests against the development of a fully representative government in Hong Kong coincided with that of the business élite. On the one hand, Chinese leaders believed that Hong Kong's capitalist system should be run by the bourgeoisie. On the other hand, Beijing was suspicious that a fully elected government would serve to insulate the SAR government from central government influence, and that it would perpetuate colonial interests by popularly elected pro-British and anti-Chinese politicians.[7]

As a result, the transition turned gradually from a process of pact negotiation into one of political exclusion. The reformists sought a popularly elected system that could exclude pro-business and pro-Beijing interests. Business and pro-Beijing interests sought a system that could exclude anti-business and anti-Beijing candidates, by avoiding popular elections as much as possible. Eventually, business interests won the struggle for domination. Business leaders and pro-Beijing activists were increasingly drawn to the forefront of the political stage. They became the new power interlocutors through their appointment as members of the Basic Law Consultation Committee, Hong Kong Affairs Advisers, District Affairs Advisers, Preliminary Working Committee, and Preparatory Committee. At the same time, middle-class professionals and activists who advocated democratic reform were increasingly marginalized. They became the target of political exclusion.

Eventually, the Basic Law adopted a political system that limits the proportion of direct territory-wide election in the SAR legislature. Half of the seats are reserved for functional constituencies that include mainly economic sectors such as banking, trading, manufacturing, and so on. Franchise in these designated economic sectors is in general limited to the employers only, hence guaranteeing business domination. Another portion of seats is to be returned by an Election Committee whose membership is anything but popularly elected and is therefore subject to manipulation. Furthermore, business interests are also well represented in the selection of the chief executive by the Selection Committee.

Seeing the Basic Law provisions as trying to exclude their participation in SAR politics, the reformists supported the reform introduced by the last governor, Chris Patten. Despite stern warning from Beijing and strong condemnation by the business community, Patten carried out his reform. He expanded the number of electorates in the 1995 Legislative Council election by five times, by extending the eligibility of functional constituency voters to the entire working population, and by abolishing the appointed membership of District Boards and Municipal Councils. Although the reformists won a landslide victory in both direct and functional constituency elections, the Legislative Council was abolished by Beijing after the handover. It was replaced by an appointed Provisional Legislative Council on July 1, 1997.

The politics of exclusion continued after the handover when the SAR government and the Provisional Legislative Council were charged with the responsibility of drawing up a new electoral arrangement to replace the Patten reform.[8] Under the new arrangements, the popular vote for functional constituencies introduced by Patten was replaced by the corporate vote for a new list of functional constituencies. The number of eligible electors was dramatically reduced from 2.5 million to 180,000. The majority of the newly added functional constituencies for the 1998 election belonged to the business sector, including import and export, textile and garment, wholesale and retail, shipping and transport, and insurance. These were added to the existing constituencies such as banking and finance, industry, commerce, real estate and construction, and tourism. Altogether the functional constituencies occupied half of the total 60 seats in the Legislative Council.

The May 1998 election result shows that the functional constituency election had succeeded in ensuring the dominance of business voice in the legislature. One-third of the candidates in the functional constituency election were uncontested, all but two of them were businessmen. Over half of the elected functional constituency councilors were connected to business interests. In terms of party affiliation, the Liberal Party—backed by big business—won the most seats, obtaining nine out of the total 30 seats.

Another area of electoral change endorsed by the Provisional Legislative Council was the composition of the Election Committee. According to the Basic Law, ten seats of the first SAR Legislative Council should be returned by an Election Committee. Under Chris Patten this Election Committee was composed of elected District Board members. The new law replaced it with an 800-member Election Committee coming from four functional groups and returned by consultation and corporate voting. The committee eventually (s)elected 10 pro-Beijing loyalists during the May 1998 election. Among them, one was affiliated to the Liberal Party and three to the Hong Kong Progressive Alliance. The latter represented the interests of small pro-Beijing businessmen.

The arrangement for direct election was even more tricky. According to the Basic Law, 20 seats of the first SAR legislature should be returned by popular votes in geographical constituencies. Past records of direct elections show that the reformists used to win by a great margin. To prevent landslide victories of the reformists in future elections, the Preparatory

Committee abandoned the existing single-seat-single-vote system in 20 geographical constituencies. The system was believed to have benefited the Democratic Party and its allies during the 1995 election.[9] After a long deliberation, the SAR government and the Provisional Legislative Council adopted a proportional representation system in five geographical constituencies. The new system was seen as favoring "minority groups," hence allowing the less organized and less popular parties such as the pro-Beijing Democratic Alliance for the Betterment of Hong Kong (hereafter Democratic Alliance) and the pro-business Liberal Party to obtain seats.

During the May 1998 election, the new electoral system did prevent the reformists—led by the Democratic Party and its allies—from gaining an overwhelming victory, although they still won 14 out of the total 20 directly elected seats. Despite the victory in the direct election, the reformists were still in a minority position in the Legislative Council. This is essentially what the Basic Law and the electoral law intended to achieve.

The advantage enjoyed by pro-business parties in elections is not the end of the story. The Basic Law provides strict safeguards against popular sector pressure within the Legislative Council. In the first place, Legislative Council members can introduce private bills related to public expenditure, political structure, or government operation, only with the written consent of the chief executive. Furthermore, for private bills to pass through the legislature, a majority vote is needed in each of the two groups: the group comprising functional constituency members and the group comprising geographical constituency members (elected by direct elections and by the Election Committee). As critics rightly observe, these requirements not only restrict the influence of popularly elected parties, but also allow the functional group members to veto political demands put forward by directly elected members.[10] And since the pro-business parties, the Liberal Party and the Hong Kong Progressive Alliance, already hold half of the seats from the functional constituencies, business can exercise de facto veto over popular sector demands. One example is the veto over a motion demanding the public utilities to lower their rates. The motion, debated on November 11, 1998, received 22 votes in favor, one against, and five abstentions in the direct election/Election Committee group, but received 11 votes in favor and 11 against in the functional group and was vetoed. The motion failed despite the fact that it received a total of 33 votes for compared to 12 against among the 60 members.

Elsewhere I argue that the above arrangements prevent any possibility of creating a "contingent consent" in SAR governance.[11] Under such a consent, the political élite agree among themselves to compete in such a way that those who win electoral support can exercise political authority and make binding decisions until the next round of contest.[12] In contrast to this procedural consent that produces contingent policy outcomes, the SAR political system guarantees that the popular sector will not capture political authority even if it wins electoral support and that pro-labor policies will have very a limited chance of passing through the legislature.

Popular Resentment toward Business Domination

Popular resentment toward business domination and the marginalization of grassroots influence in the SAR political system has become increasingly noticeable. From the onset, the general public is skeptical about the integrity of businessmen, and believes that business interests have excessive political influence in Hong Kong. Opinion surveys have long revealed popular distrust toward business interests.[13] Viewing business leaders as being dishonest and undependable, public opinion reflects a low regard for and confidence in the political leadership of business interests. In such circumstances, as one observer points out, it becomes more difficult to take up public positions on issues without being accused of acting in bad faith or pursuing private gain.[14]

Perhaps the most indicative sign of this distrust toward businessmen-cum-politicians is the result of the May 1998 election. None of the 12 Liberal Party members who contested the 30 directly elected seats was elected. The losers included Lee Peng-fei, leader of the party who had been a legislator for 20 years. Out of the total 1.48 million votes cast in the five geographical constituencies, the Liberal Party received only 50,335 votes. However, such a decisive vote of no-confidence by the general public does not reduce the influence of business in the SAR legislature. Business interests still control over half of the seats from the functional constituencies, thus allowing them to veto any policy proposals initiated by pro-labor parties.

A number of incidents have helped to fuel suspicion toward the business-dominated political system and the executive authorities led by a shipping magnate-turned chief executive. During the Basic Law drafting process, labor unions suggested that the right of Hong Kong labor in collective bargaining and industrial strike should be stated in the Basic

Law. This was rejected by the business-dominated Basic Law Drafting Committee, even though the suggestion was strongly upheld by the pro-Beijing Federation of Trade Unions. Shortly before the handover, the Legislative Council passed seven ordinances that enhanced labor rights, welfare benefits, and environmental protection. Their promulgation was a result of the electoral success of the middle and working classes in the 1995 election. After the handover, the Executive Council made no delay in asking the Provisional Legislative Council to freeze these ordinances immediately by passing three readings in one day. At the end, four of the ordinances (on collective bargaining, relaxing the restriction on labor unions, barring discrimination against labor unions, and broadening the scope of the Bill of Rights) were successfully suspended.

There was an outpouring of skepticism when Tung Chee-hwa appointed Executive Council member Leung Chun-ying to look into the housing policy. Leung was in charge of studying and making policy recommendations concerning the provision of residential units, with a view to finding a solution to overspeculation in the real estate market that has deprived many people, including even high-income professionals, from owning a residential flat. The appointment was widely criticized as inappropriate because of the conflicts of interests between Leung's public responsibility and his private business. Leung is the owner of a surveying firm in the property market, and has strong ties with property developers.

Another public uproar occurred when Secretary of Justice Leung Oi-see decided not to prosecute the owner of the English newspaper *Hong Kong Standard*, Aw Sian. Aw was investigated by the Independent Commission Against Corruption for her involvement in corruption and fraud connected with forging the circulation of the newspaper. The secretary of justice decided to prosecute Aw's subordinates but not Aw herself. Leung Oi-see insisted initially that Aw's exemption from prosecution was in accordance with "public interest," and not because of Aw's personal friendship with Tung Chee-hwa and her connection with Beijing. Tung was a former board member of Sing Tao Holdings, which controlled *Hong Kong Standard*. Under strong public pressure for a fuller explanation, Leung Oi-see eventually gave the reason that since Aw operated a huge enterprise, her prosecution might affect the livelihood of many workers. Such an explanation invited even more criticism, since it implied that wealthy businessmen with hundreds of staff in their employ were above the law. The welding of money to power has never been so apparent.

Popular skepticism toward government–business collusion intensified during a period of deteriorating labor relations in the wake of the economic recession caused by the Asian financial crisis. A striking example is the salary-cut row of the Hong Kong Telecom. Angry workers launched industrial actions and condemned the "shameless bourgeoisie" when the company announced a salary cut of 10 percent despite an outstanding profit of HK$17 billion. Such a high profit derived partly from the company's monopolistic rights over local and long-distance calls. Before the salary-cut proposal, the company had already launched a massive layoff. The salary cut set an example for other companies in the wake of the recession. Labor activists demanded that the legislation on collective bargaining—abolished by the business-dominated Provisional Legislative Council—should be revived.[15] Union leaders also criticized the Tung administration for failing to tackle unemployment problems, address the grievances of the working class, and remind employers about their social responsibility. The numerous projects initiated by the Tung administration were seen as creating a favorable business environment for investors while ignoring the immediate difficulty of the laboring class.[16]

Business Discontent with SAR Politics

In view of the above, observers have been quick to point out that the business community has maintained its influence and position as the central force in SAR politics.[17] Other skeptics put it more bluntly: it is a continuation/reproduction of the "colonial pact" that allowed business people to rule Hong Kong.[18] The interesting question is: if the political arrangements of the Hong Kong SAR represent a continuation/reproduction of the "colonial pact," why was there no strong public outcry against government–business collusion during the colonial era? Generations of political scientists have noted "an unholy alliance of businessmen and bureaucrats" under cooptive politics of the colonial regime.[19] British merchant houses such as Hong Kong and Shanghai Banking Corporation, Jardine, Swire, and so on, had been sitting in the Executive and Legislative Councils making decisions on financial, land, or labor policies. Yet no similar uproar in public opinion arose such as that against Leung Chun-ying's appointment.

Before examining why there was no strong public accusation of government–business collusion during the colonial period, let us look at a further puzzle in SAR politics. Notwithstanding the powerful business influence in SAR governance, the business community is increasingly discontented with the political environment and is distrustful of the

Tung administration. Business leaders blamed the overpoliticization of Hong Kong society and the increasing interference of politics in commercial activities. They gave the example of the housing market. When housing prices escalated sharply in 1997, Democratic Party member Li Wing-tat blamed speculators for pushing up housing prices. But when the housing market collapsed in 1998, another Democratic Party member Chan Wai-yip organized street demonstrations demanding the cancellation of purchase agreements as a result of the price drop.[20]

The business élite is annoyed by the fact that the continuation of business domination is now under severe attack despite the fact that the Basic Law promises business as usual for 50 years. The view of the Liberal Party chairman Tien Pei-chun is illustrative in this regard. Tien blamed the last colonial administration under Chris Patten for introducing political reforms that brought in "populist politicians who entice voters with free lunches and welfare promises." Tien anticipated that after the handover, "with economics taking precedence over politics, we will return to a more orderly and productive environment which we had during the time when our GDP growth was double what it is today."[21] However, the political reality after the handover disappointed him. In Tien's opinion, populist politics still dominate the SAR. In his view, the Democratic Party, Front Line, and the Democratic Alliance are in essence labor parties. "They keep criticizing employers as unconscientious all the time," he complained. As he sees it, the 20 directly elected politicians are behaving in the same way: they are only concerned about increasing labor welfare.[22] Representing the Hong Kong General Chamber of Commerce in the Legislative Council, Tien has been strongly against increasing labor welfare while supporting wage cuts during the recession.

Other business leaders like Tien are worried about losing their dominance in the political system if the pace of direct election speeds up. Since the Basic Law only lays down the composition of the Legislative Council and its voting procedures up to the year 2007, further democratization may take place. Some business leaders have thus begun to lobby the government not to reduce the number of seats elected by functional constituencies after 2007 so as to preserve the influence of business.[23] The success of the first SAR legislature election in 1998 added to the anxiety of the business community. With the record-high voting rate of 53.29 percent, even the pro-Beijing Democratic Alliance has suggested that the Legislative Council can already be fully directly elected in 2004, instead of waiting for the review in 2007.

Of all these business grumbles, the biggest bombshell came from Li Ka-shing. Li is a close friend of Tung Chee-hwa and is commonly seen as the number one tycoon in Hong Kong. The public was shocked when Li announced an investment strike on December 22, 1998. He stated that he decided to give up a HK$10 billion investment project because of the deteriorating political environment of Hong Kong. Li's statement aroused panic in the government. Both the chief executive and the chief secretary reacted swiftly. Tung emphasized that they took Li's view very seriously; while the chief secretary, Anson Chan, held discussions with Li directly to clear the air that Li was not lashing out at government performance.

Li's discontent with the so-called deteriorating "political environment" was echoed by other members of the business community.[24] The incident reminds us of the investment strike declared in 1989 by Wang Yung-ching, the Formosa Plastics Group magnate in Taiwan. In response to the growing criticism, brought about by democratization, that the government–big business nexus was dominating the economy and exploiting the workers, Wang threatened to stage a capital flight to flex his political muscles.[25] Behaving in the same way as Wang, Li Ka-shing expressed his discontent toward SAR politics and pressed the government to improve the investment environment.

The anxious response of the Tung administration to Li Ka-shing's discontent reminds us of Lindblom's seminal work on *Politics and Markets*.[26] In a market-oriented system, not only does the government have to collaborate with business, but it must also often defer to business leadership to make the system work. In the case of the Hong Kong SAR, this collaboration goes even further. The chief executive is "elected" by a Selection Committee comprising business tycoons and vested interests in the territory. Unlike the colonial governor who was appointed directly from London and therefore need not count on the patronage of the British *taipans*, the chief executive of the SAR relies heavily on the business constituency for his political career. In such circumstances, the anxious response of the Tung administration toward Li's statement, as critics observed, only adds to popular sector skepticism about the collusion between money and power.[27]

Government–Business Collusion and Rent Seeking

Business discontent is not confined to the deteriorating political environment as a result of increasing pressure from the popular sector. There is a growing distrust toward the Tung administration. This is the reason why Tung Chee-hwa was so alarmed by Li Ka-shing's discontent. Earlier on an anti-Tung campaign was mounted by some members of the business community together with some former members of the business-dominated Preparatory Committee.[28] Even Lee Peng-fei, the former Liberal Party chairman who represents major business interests and who once supported Tung's running for office, expressed deep dissatisfaction with the performance of the government, and accused the government of failing to live up to its responsibility.[29]

The business community is skeptical about the impartiality of the Tung administration in arbitrating conflicting economic interests. Longstreth[30] reminds us that businessmen meet as "hostile brothers" in the political system. Although they are capable of joining forces to meet an external threat to "bourgeois class relations," they are more characteristically divided among themselves by their market position, policy goals, ideological orientations, and so on. While they do not dispute the fundamentals, that is, the creation of wealth, they dispute over an ever-shifting category of secondary issues—such as trade policy, tax rates, and regulation and promotion of business. The ability to arbitrate the conflicting interests of these hostile brothers in an impartial manner therefore hinges on the credibility of the government. In the Hong Kong case, this has been put in serious doubt.

A prominent example is the unusual confrontation staged by the largest property developers against government decisions over the cyberport project. During the budget speech of March 1999, the government announced its decision to build a multibillion HK$ cyberport on a 26-hectare site of prime land. The project comprises the construction of an ultramodern office and residential complex that provides high-capacity telecommunication links, research laboratories, and multimedia facilities. In addition to providing 4.3 million square feet of residential areas, the project will provide space for 30 medium-to-large enterprises and 100 small enterprises, creating 16,000 job opportunities. The first phase of the project is set for completion in 2002, while the whole project is expected to be finished in 2007.

What was surprising for the business tycoons, who all have a stake in property development, was that such a huge project was decided without any public planning sessions, open land auctions, or invitations for tender. The development of the cyberport was entrusted to the Pacific Century Group, a company set up in 1993. The company is owned by Richard Li, the 32-year-old son of Li Ka-shing. According to the government's calculations, the cyberport project will cost HK$13 billion, with the Pacific Century Group investing HK$7 billion while the Hong Kong government provides the land at an estimated cost of HK$6 billion.

The government's granting of private treaty to Li Ka-shing's son to develop the lucrative project invited condemnation from other developers who viewed it as cronyism. Senior officials denied the accusation and insisted that Pacific Century was chosen for its technological expertise, good connections, and willingness to take risk.[31] However, subsequent news reports reveal that senior officials were skeptical of the project, and only Tung Chee-hwa showed his firm support right from the beginning when Richard Li proposed it to the government.[32]

In an unprecedented move, the territory's ten largest land developers—with the exception of Li Ka-shing's company—through a legal adviser issued a joint statement to the government challenging the whole project. They offered to buy the residential land for HK$8 billion, and promised to pay the government an additional HK$3 billion to be derived from the sale of the residential units.[33] During the exchanges between the government and the land developers, widespread concern was expressed about the fear that the cyberport project would be nothing more than a land development project dressed up in technological garb. Over 75 percent of the construction was destined for residential units. Pacific Century would earn 54 percent of the sales profit. In other words, the deal grants Pacific Century the rights to furnish 4.3 million square feet with residential units through an investment of HK$7 billion. One report estimated that if the residential land was sold by open auction, the return would be close to HK$10 billion.[34]

Furthermore, according to the deal, the commercial units will be rented between HK$6 to HK$7 per square foot, compared to the current prevailing rates of HK$20–40 in prime districts. As a result, a number of high-profile companies, including Hewlett-Packard, IBM, Yahoo!, Oracle, and Softbank, have already registered their tenancy agreement. This was also one of the factors that worried other land developers. They feared that the cyberport would attract their existing tenants to the new site. One of the land developers that is likely to be most affected by the cyberport is the Kowloon Wharf Group, which accommodates many high-tech companies in its rental office complexes.

The case of the cyberport reflects not only the conflicts among big businesses in Hong Kong, but also the attempt of rival business interests to capture the economic rent created by government intervention and to undermine rivals by means of market protection and closure to competition. Market closure guarantees monopolized advantages by invoking the authority of the government to set up barriers—say, by legislation or by offering private tender—to restrain competitors and newcomers.[35] By designating certain areas development priorities, the government helps to divert societal resources into particular sectors. And by awarding specific companies the exclusive rights to develop prioritized projects, the government allows these companies to capture the monopolistic rent. In this regard, the various ambitious projects and development initiatives proposed and/or undertaken by the Tung administration exemplify instances of rent creation, while the cyberport case provides an example of rent seeking.

Other businessmen, especially land developers, have jumped on the bandwagon and forwarded similar proposals for subsidized land in the name of high-tech project development. Proposals such as a communication hub, bio-tech center, Chinese medicine center, and so on have been submitted. Of these, the Cheung Kong Group owned by Li Ka-shing has successfully obtained a government land grant to develop a shipping terminal in North Point. Cheung Kong owns a number of land sites near the North Point waterfront. The land grant allows the group to convert the individual sites into one large area for the construction of a shipping terminal-cum-hotel complex.[36] Incidentally, the project was also strongly opposed by Kowloon Wharf, which operates the existing Ocean Terminal in Tsim Sha Tsui. Kowloon Wharf is owned by the Pao Yue-kong family. The Pao family runs a shipping and real estate empire that is the main business rival of Oriental Overseas owned by the Tung family. Pao's son-in-law, Peter Woo, who heads the Kowloon Wharf, had been a major contender, along with Tung Chee-hwa, for the first chief executive position.

Besides the above incidents, the issue of the SAR government's impartiality is further aggravated by the fact that some Hong Kong tycoons have intricate business relations with the mainland government. The majority of the business conglomerates in Hong Kong—including those owned by the Tung family, the Li family, and the Aw family—have established joint ventures with various levels of government, party, or even military authorities and enterprises on the mainland. Many mainland enterprises, including direct subsidiary companies of central and provincial governments, are also operating and cooperating with local businesses in Hong Kong.[37] Doubts have been raised over whether the government can prevent rent seeking by the powerful who want preferential treatment in exchange for political support.

The situation represents a dilemma when money and power weld together. On the one hand, the domination of business interests in the political system ensures the enactment of pro-business policies and resistance against populist demands. On the other hand, uneven influence within the business community allows some people to gain personal advantage at the expense of their competitors. In other words, the business community as a whole may profit, but some members profit a lot more than the others. A few businessmen do realize the contradictions embodied in the existing political system and they therefore support political reforms. They believe that democracy can guarantee free competition in the market, and warn that there will be monopolies without democratic control.[38] Others simply direct their anger at Tung Chee-hwa. They hope that a different chief executive will extend preferential treatment to them instead of their rivals.

For the Tung administration, the situation also presents a dilemma, if not an impasse, in governance. In the first place, the government has to favor selectively the interests of the business élite to gain their support. At the same time, it has to assume the role of an arbiter of sectional interests within the ruling élite when policy conflicts arise. Worse still, it has to convince the wider public that it is a watchdog against rent seeking, in order to avoid widespread discontent over the unfair political system.

The Breakdown of Substantive Consent

Let us recapitulate what has been discussed so far. We began by asking why the SAR government under Tung Chee-hwa has become so unpopular despite the fact that it has been trying to do a lot for the community. We contend that putting the blame on the administrative incompetence of the SAR government hardly scratches the surface of the matter. A deeper reason is to be found in the institutional artifact of the SAR political system. Popular resentment derives from the marginalization of working-class participation in SAR governance and the collusion between money and power in undermining labor interests. Discontent also exists among the business élite over the constant attack from the marginalized popular sector against government–business collusion. Furthermore, there is growing distrust among some members of the business community with regard to the impartiality of the Tung administration in arbitrating conflicting business interests.

All in all, criticisms from all sides are levied against government–business collusion in the Tung administration. In the eyes of the laboring class, the priority given to the development of technology—which Tung hails as a big push to Hong Kong's economic future—represents the government's preoccupation with creating investment opportunities for business while ignoring the immediate problem of unemployment for workers. For the business community, many of the technology projects are nothing more than land development projects that generate huge profits for a privileged few.

We can now turn back to the puzzle mentioned earlier about the absence of strong public criticism against government–business collusion under British rule. It should be noted that until the 1980s, members of the Legislative and Executive Councils as well as other advisory committees were all appointed by the governor. The entire colonial system relied on the support of the coopted business élite and the popular acquiescence of those excluded from participation. The Basic Law can be seen as a failed attempt to preserve such a political order for the SAR.

Again, the failure of the SAR to reproduce the "colonial pact" has a more deep-seated reason than what is commonly assumed. In the first place, acquiescence toward political exclusion during the colonial era cannot be attributed, as some studies did, to the political apathy of the Hong Kong Chinese owing to their refugee mentality or inward-looking familial ethos.[39] Nor is it because the colonial government spared itself from societal pressures by disengaging itself from social affairs through a policy of laissez-faire.[40] Recent studies have highlighted that, contrary to the idea of political aloofness, conflicts among social actors had been profound during the colonial period, while the "reach of the colonial state" had been penetrating in manipulating and managing social conflicts.[41]

In the second place, government–business relations under colonial rule were never simply a matter of business capture or government–business collusion. Rather, the colonial system was maintained by the painstaking upholding of a delicate policy consent among the ruling élite. Like the SAR government, the colonial administration was torn between the contradictory tasks of offering privileges to business in exchange for political support, assuming an arbiter role among competing business interests, and acting as a watchdog against rent seeking to prevent widespread discontent.

The colonial government tackled the above dilemma by forging a "substantive consent" among the ruling élite.[42] It set a limit on both the bureaucratic and the business élite about their privilege and relative power. In contrast to the "contingent consent" mentioned earlier, the consent is "substantive" because it was not based on electoral or procedural arrangements, but by policy outcomes. This substantive consent involved the inseparable components of allowing business domination in the power oligarchy and yet upholding a policy against preferential treatment for selected business interests. Under this consent, besides the privilege of sharing policy-making power, the oligarchic interests were guaranteed that their vital interest of profit making would be protected and facilitated by the government. This was realized by a range of pro-business policy measures, including low profits tax, limited social welfare provisions, minimal labor protection, free enterprise, and free capital inflow and outflow. All of them worked to facilitate profit maximization, a policy goal that was proudly admitted by the colonial government.

At the same time, the ruling élite agreed to constrain its privileges by accepting a policy of nonselective intervention. This means that the colonial government refrained from using public resources to assist or protect individual business sectors and enterprises. This avoided rent seeking by individual élite groups, ensuring that policy outcomes were acceptable to the less powerful and the wider population of players. It represented the solution offered by Wildavsky to Lindblom's problem about business capture of the government: reducing the abuse of public power by business through reducing government intervention.[43]

This policy of nonselective intervention, together with the above-mentioned policy of low taxation, limited welfare, minimal labor protection, free enterprises, and so on, was commonly labeled as constituting a policy of laissez-faire. Hong Kong has been well-known for being the only existing modern economy that came closest to the laissez-faire ideal, when in fact the nineteenth-century economic doctrine was ingeniously appropriated and articulated here to serve as a political mechanism for consensus building.[44]

With a few exceptions, the government adhered strictly to this principle with "an almost religious fervor."[45] Demands for preferential allocation of resources—including land grants or loans for high-tech projects—were all rejected. Whenever conflicts arose over the deployment of resources, it was settled with reference to the principle of nonselective intervention. As a result, market monopoly and ruthless rent seeking were constrained within limits. Substantive consent thus formed the basis of political acquiescence even though the majority of the population was deprived of any chance in sharing ruling power.

We can see why a similar kind of substantive consent has not been achieved after the handover. To do so requires the power interlocutors to restrain their privileges, and the peripheral players to believe that they will not be intolerably disadvantaged in view of such volunteered restraints. Such a consent, however, proves to be difficult because of changing government–business relations.

From the outset, the functional constituency election encourages rather than discourages rent seeking. When legislative power is divided into the hands of economic and social groupings, different interests fight hard to be included in a functional constituency. Representatives of the functional constituencies, most of whom being businessmen-cum-politicians, are meant to protect the interests of their own sectors rather than to constrain the pursuit of sectoral interests. Elected councilors run the risk of losing their electoral support in the next election if they are not seen as advancing the interests of their functional constituencies. In essence, interest conflicts are institutionalized in the legislative system, making any general policy consent difficult.[46] Similar logic holds for the Selection Committee responsible for choosing the chief executive. The committee comprises vested interests with whom the candidates have to make deals in order to win their votes. It is therefore no surprise that the impartiality of the chief executive is viewed with skepticism when policy decisions involving business conflicts are taken.

In such circumstances, the various proactive development projects initiated by the Tung administration represent the most obvious deviation from any substantive consent. Setting aside many critics' suggestion that these projects violate the macroeconomic principle of free market or non-interventionism, such development projects provide opportunities for the granting of selective privileges, and can thus be used to reward supporters and punish enemies. But in doing so, it undermines the role of the government as an impartial gatekeeper and damages the popular legitimacy of the system.

Conclusion

Any modern state in a capitalist economy is confronted with contradictory tasks. On the one hand, it must act to support wealth creation and to selectively favor those groups whose acquiescence and support are crucial to the existing order. At the same time, it must conceal such interventions, in order to maintain its image as being fair and just. When such concealment fails, state intervention generates conflicts by inviting more demands for favorable treatment. And when conflicting demands cannot be fulfilled, mass loyalty is threatened, precipitating a legitimation crisis.[47]

In this regard, the colonial administration and the Tung administration faced the same contradictory tasks. However, they differed in the way they dealt with the contradiction. During the colonial era, a delicate balance had been sought to give oligarchic business interests more voice in running the territory on the one hand and yet keep their power in check on the other hand, thus avoiding widespread discontent among the powerless. Put differently, government–business relations in the colonial era had been prevented from degenerating into rent-seeking exchanges by a unique institutional safeguard—what I term "substantive consent" among the ruling élite in this chapter. By refraining from granting special economic privileges to selected business interests through the principle of nonselective intervention, substantive consent kept business power in check, avoiding the emergence of a rent-seeking society as described in Krueger's[48] seminal study. It gave rise to what some writers called a "collaborative advantage" in government–business relations that characterized the East Asian developmental states.[49]

In contrast, the SAR political system charted out by the Basic Law preserves the domination of business without institutionalizing a mechanism to check business power. In our terminology, the Basic Law provisions break up the substantive consent without replacing it with a contingent consent. Not only can business interests veto pro-labor policies and marginalize popular sector influence, they can also exchange political support with personal gains. The tendency to slip into government–business collusion creates skepticism and distrust, not only among the workers and the middle class, but also among members of the business community. Being fully aware of its limited popular legitimacy, the Tung administration tried hard to prove itself by staging high-profile projects. However, before seeing any developmental results, many of these interventionist projects have already degenerated into activities for rent seeking, thereby further undermining the legitimacy of the SAR government.

The subtle changes in government–business relations after the handover escape the attention of many observers. As one critic puts it: one cannot but wonder why the SAR government fared so badly, given its continuity with the efficient and well-respected colonial civil service that preceded it.[50] In such circumstances, Tung Chee-hwa automatically became a scapegoat of the problem, being held personally responsible for his incompetent leadership. While administrative incompetence certainly accounted for part of the problem, a great deal of the legitimacy dilemma came from the institutional artifact laid down by the Basic Law. Changing the chief executive will only bring about a shift in power interlocutors, but the contradictory tasks still cannot be reconciled unless money and power are institutionalized in a different way.

Notes

1. Tak-Wing Ngo, "Industrial History and the Artifice of Laissez-Faire Colonialism," in *Hong Kong's History: State and Society under Colonial Rule,* ed. Tak-Wing Ngo (London: Routledge, 1999): 133.

2. Tak-Wing Ngo, "Social Values and Consensual Politics in Colonial Hong Kong," in *The Cultural Construction of Politics in Asia,* ed. Hans Antlöv, and Tak-Wing Ngo (Surrey: Curzon Press, 2000): 144–145.

3. Hong Kong Government, "Building Hong Kong for a New Era," Address by the Chief Executive the Honourable Tung Chee Hwa at the Provisional Legislative Council Meeting on October 8, 1997.

4. Hong Kong Government, "From Adversity to Opportunity," Address by the Chief Executive the Honourable Tung Chee-Hwa at the Legislative Council Meeting on October 7, 1998.

5. *Yazhou Zhoukan* (Asia Weekly) (29 June–5 July 1998): 30.

6. Alvin Y. So, "Hong Kong's Embattled Democracy: Perspectives from East Asian NIEs," *Issues and Studies* 33, 8 (1997): 63–80.

7. Xu, Jiatun, *Xu Jiatun's Memoir of Hong Kong* [in Chinese] (Hong Kong: United Press, 1993): ch. 6.

8. Tak-Wing Ngo, "Hongkong onder Chinees Bestuur: Het Dilemma van Verandering en Continuïteit," (Hong Kong under Chinese Rule: The Dilemma of Change and Continuity) *Internationale Spectator* 51, 5 (May 1997): 274–278.

9. Choy, Chi-keung, *Insight into the Hong Kong Electoral System* [in Chinese] (Hong Kong: Ming Pao Publishing Co., 1998): 20–34.

10. Ma, Ngok, and Choy, Chi-keung, "The Evolution of the Electoral System and Party Politics in Hong Kong," *Issues & Studies* 35, 1 (January/February 1999): 191.

11. Tak-Wing Ngo, "Changing Government–Business Relations and the Governance of Hong Kong," in *Hong Kong in Transition: The Handover Years,* ed. Robert Ash, Peter Ferdinand, Brian Hook, and Robin Porter (London: Macmillan, 2000).

12. Guillermo O'Donnell, and Philippe C. Schmitter, *Transition from Authoritarian Rule: Tentative Conclusions about Uncertain Democracies* (Baltimore: Johns Hopkins University Press, 1986): 59.

13. Lau, Siu-kai, and Kuan, Hsin-chi, "Public Attitude Toward Laissez Faire in Hong Kong," *Asian Survey* 30, 8 (1990): 773; Lau, Siu-kai, Kuan, Hsin-chi, and Wan, Po-san, "Political Attitudes," in *Indicators of Social Development: Hong Kong 1988,* ed. Lau, Siu-kai, Lee, Ming-kwan, Wan, Po-san, and Wong, Siu-lun (Hong Kong: Hong Kong Institute of Asia-Pacific Studies, Chinese University of Hong Kong, 1991): 202; Thomas W. P. Wong, and Tai-lok Lui, "From One Brand of Politics to One Brand of Political Culture," Hong Kong Institute of Asia-Pacific Studies Occasional Paper No. 10 (Hong Kong: Chinese University of Hong Kong, 1992): 28–30; Wong, Siu-lun, "Business and Politics in Hong Kong During the Transition," in *25 Years of Social and Economic Development in Hong Kong,* ed. Benjamin K.P. Leung and Teresa Y.C. Wong (Hong Kong: University of Hong Kong, 1994): 230–232.

14. Michael Yahuda, *Hong Kong: China's Challenge* (London: Routledge, 1996): 107.

15. *Yazhou Zhoukan* (28 September–4 October 1998): 18–19.

16. *Yazhou Zhoukan* (12–18 October 1998): 26–31.

17. James T.H. Tang, "Business as Usual: the Dynamics of Government-Business Relations in the Hong Kong Special Administrative Region," *Journal of Contemporary China* 8, 21 (1999): 294.

18. Jean-Philippe Béja, "Hong Kong Two Months Before the Handover: One Territory, Two Systems?" *China News Analysis* 15 (April 1997): 6.

19. Peter Harris, *Hong Kong: A Study in Bureaucracy and Politics* (Hong Kong: Macmillan, 1988): 57; also John Rear, "One Brand of Politics," in *Hong Kong: The Industrial Colony,* ed. Keith Hopkins (Hong Kong: Oxford University Press, 1971); Stephen N.G. Davies, "One Brand of Politics Rekindled," *Hong Kong Law Journal* 7, 1 (1977): 44–84; Benjamin K.P. Leung, "Power and Politics: A Critical Analysis," in *Social Issues in Hong Kong,* ed. Benjamin K.P. Leung (Hong Kong: Oxford University Press, 1990).

20. *Yazhou Zhoukan* (1–7 June 1998): 27.

21. *South China Morning Post* (29 June 1997).

22. *Yazhou Zhoukan* (30 November–6 December 1998): 26.

23. *Yazhou Zhoukan* (4–10 January 1999): 47.
24. *South China Morning Post* (12 and 24 December 1998); *Yazhou Zhoukan* (4–10 January 1999).
25. Tak-Wing Ngo, "Business Encirclement of Politics: Government-Business Relations across the Taiwan Strait," *China Information* 10, 2 (Autumn 1995): 7–8.
26. Charles E. Lindblom, *Politics and Markets: The World's Political-Economic Systems* (New York: Basic Books, 1977).
27. *Yazhou Zhoukan* (4–10 January 1999): 46.
28. Kuan, Hsin-chi, "Hong Kong under 'One Country, Two Systems'," *China News Analysis* (1–15 August 1998): 11.
29. *Yazhou Zhoukan* (6–12 July 1998): 44.
30. Frank Longstreth, "The City, Industry and the State," in *State and Economy in Contemporary Capitalism*, ed. Colin Crouch (London: Croom Helm, 1979): 160.
31. *Far Eastern Economic Review* (1 April 1999): 51.
32. *Yazhou Zhoukan* (5–11 April 1999): 22; *Next Magazine* (12 March 1999).
33. *Yazhou Zhoukan* (3–9 May 1999): 42.
34. *Next Magazine* (12 March 1999).
35. Alan Cawson, Kevin Morgan, Douglas Webber, Peter Holmes, and Anne Stevens, *Hostile Brothers: Competition and Closure in the European Electronics Industry* (Oxford: Clarendon Press, 1990): 22–24.
36. *Next Magazine* (28 May 1999).
37. See Tak-Wing Ngo, "Business Strategy, State Intervention and Regionalization in East Asia," in *The Dialectics of Globalization*, ed. Menno Vellinga (Boulder, Co.: Westview Press, 2000).
38. *Yazhou Zhoukan* (4–10 January 1999): 48.
39. See Lau, Siu-kai, "Utilitarianistic Familism: An Inquiry into the Basis of Political Stability in Hong Kong," Social Research Centre occasional paper (Hong Kong: Chinese University of Hong Kong, 1977).
40. See Lau, Siu-kai, *Society and Politics in Hong Kong* (Hong Kong: Chinese University Press, 1982).
41. Tak-Wing Ngo, "Colonialism in Hong Kong Revisited," in *Hong Kong's History: State and Society under Colonial Rule*, ed. Tak-Wing Ngo (London: Routledge, 1999).
42. Ngo, "Social Values and Consensual Politics in Colonial Hong Kong".
43. Aaron Wildavsky, "Changing Forward Versus Changing Back," *Yale Law Journal* 88 (1978): 227.
44. Tak-Wing Ngo, "Economic Intervention and Non-Intervention: The Ruling Strategies of Hong Kong and Taiwan Compared," [in Chinese] *Hong Kong Journal of Social Sciences* 12 (Autumn 1998): 1–16.
45. Peter Harris, *Hong Kong: A Study in Bureaucracy and Politics*, 159.
46. Ngo, "Changing Government–Business Relations and the Governance of Hong Kong."
47. Cf. Fernando Henrique Cardoso, and Enzo Faletto, *Dependency and Development in Latin America* (Berkeley: University of California Press, 1979): 209; Guillermo O'Donnell, "Tensions in the Bureaucratic-Authoritarian State and the Question of Democracy," in *The New Authoritarianism in Latin America*, ed. David Collier (Princeton: Princeton University Press, 1979): 290; and David Held, and Joel Krieger, "Accumulation, Legitimation and the State," in *States and Societies*, ed. David Held et al. (Oxford: Martin Robertson, 1983): 493.
48. Anne O. Krueger, "The Political Economy of Rent-Seeking Society," *American Economic Review* 64 (June 1974): 291–303.
49. Ben Ross Schneider, and Sylvia Maxfield, "Business, the State, and Economic Performance in Developing Countries," in *Business and the State in Developing Countries*, eds Sylvia Maxfield, and Ben Ross Schneider (Ithaca: Cornell University Press, 1997).
50. Kuan, Hsin-chi, "Hong Kong under 'One Country, Two Systems'," 11.

CHAPTER FIVE

The Making of China's Rentier Entrepreneurs Élite: State, Clientelism, and Power Conversion, 1978–1995

DAVID L. WANK

Studies of economic liberalization in Africa, Asia, and the Middle East show how emerging markets create rent-seeking opportunities, stimulating the rise of a private entrepreneurial class that profits through connections to officialdom.[1] Similarly, studies of the post-socialist market economies of China and Europe highlight an entrepreneurial élite operating in clientelist ties with party-state agents to access politically controlled resources.[2] This chapter considers this process of economic élite formation in post-socialist orders from the perspective of a local situation in China.

This chapter organizing concept is power conversion. This refers to the process in clientelist ties whereby entrepreneurs' economic wealth is converted into officials' discretionary control over resources, legal or otherwise, and then back again into entrepreneurs' economic wealth. The central premise is that successive policies of economic liberalization, by affecting the state monopoly context in which rent-seeking occurs, stimulates new strategies and movements of power conversion. This conversion is a dynamic process that evolves along with the expansion of the market economy. Examining this evolution in the context of successive state policies from the late 1970s until the mid-1990s illustrates how a class of persons emerges who are not agents of the party-state but are able to accumulate wealth. This is a major transformation from the previous "high" communist order in which material well-being was a function of direct position in the party-state bureaucracy.[3] However, administrative control is still crucial for wealth accumulation, and the new private entrepreneurs obtain it through power conversion.

The insights of this chapter are grounded in fieldwork on private business conducted in China 1988–90 and briefly in 1995, primarily in the port city of Xiamen, a special economic zone in Fujian province on the southeast coast. The core data consists of repeat interviews with 107 operators of private firms engaged in the wholesale trade (*maoyi gongsi*),[4] as well as intense socializing with some of the sample members and limited participant observation in private firms.[5] In the following section I will review extant arguments on private entrepreneurship and power conversion in late and post-socialist orders while subsequent sections will describe processes of power conversion.

Power Conversion in Post-socialist Market Economy

Various accounts of business operators in China's market economy emphasize the conversion of state power over resources into private wealth accumulations by entrepreneurs pursuing capitalist business strategies. In one earlier account new market policies are said to create new opportunities for entrepreneurs to forge relations with state agents for access to officially brokered resources.[6] The focus is firstly on how non-official projects influence the state structure and secondly on the new converging interests of private citizens who are both entrepreneurs and local state agents. Dorothy Solinger describes this power conversion as "symbiotic":

> The onset of reform has begun to erode this singularity of the path to power, just as it has seemingly freed nonstate actors, by opening opportunities for new occupational alternatives for the members of the long-isolated society. Nonetheless, the differentiation of social forces that is accompanying the reform is quite a partial one, so that categories that were previously discrete and unrelated have instead become in some senses symbiotic ... For the Chinese urban entrepreneur who operates on a scale of some size, the state and its institutions remain the principal source of start-up capital; in addition, entree to the state's means of production and guidance through its regulatory and informational labyrinth has been the sine qua non for business activity ... The new "bourgeoisie," such as it is, then, is one whose members usually lack their own means of production, independent capital, material supplies, and modes of operation.[7]

Another earlier account focuses on how current officials use their position of office to directly allocate resources for their private gain.[8] The focus here is how current state agents manipulate their position of office for private gain. Jadwiga Stanizskis terms this "political capitalism":

The ... linkage of power and capital (including various forms of turning power over goods in short supply into capital with a definite market value—used as "entry" capital to a private firm) can be given the common name "political capitalism." ... Its basic features are: first, the power in industry and the state administration is linked with activities on one's own account in a private company. Second, the main customer of these companies is not the consumer market but state industry (e.g., defense industry). This form also serves to maintain the consumption of the nomenklatura as a social group on a relatively high level. Third, profits are derived from the exclusive access to attractive market, information and supply (such access is made possible by the dual status of the nomenklatura owners).[9]

These accounts of power conversions raise several questions. First, each illuminates only a single societal movement in what I argue is a broader process of class formation. On the one hand the symbiosis account focuses on how societal actors become entrepreneurs but not on how officials become entrepreneurs. On the other hand the political capitalism account only considers how nonstate agents pursue capitalist business. This chapter considers these diverse societal movements as a dynamic of class formation.

The static character of these accounts also raises the problem of how the situation evolves. The conversion of power is portrayed as a relatively enduring structure, akin to rent seeking in standard political economy,[10] in which the scarcities created by state monopoly control become the locus of profit for business. However, this raises the question of what happens in later stages and what distinguishes the different stages. Stanizskis' account suggests an evolution in policy initiatives by the state to close rent-seeking opportunities, but there is no account of the efficacy of these policies in terms of the corresponding actions of entrepreneurs.[11] In this chapter I depict the interaction of the shifting opportunities in resources under state monopoly control created by successive state policies to promote private markets and the corresponding entrepreneurial strategies to exploit these new opportunities.

The final problem is that, while the foregoing accounts recognize the importance of particularistic ties—social capital—in the state structure for private business, the ties themselves are not explained. Instead the process of class formation is treated as a relatively monolithic process of persons from broadly similar backgrounds, nonofficials or state agents, rising up to take advantage of the new opportunities in the state's economic and administrative monopoly created by marketization.[12] In other words, the issue of how persons actually acquire the ties necessary to pursue capitalist business is not considered. In this chapter I problematize the issue of how entrepreneurs acquire social capital.

An Evolutionary Perspective

My starting point is the concept of power conversion in late communism propounded by Akos Róna-tas[13] who draws attention to the evolutionary interaction of state policies of market liberalization and entrepreneurs' clientelist networks. He argues that expanding opportunities for private business in Hungary over time from household farming to noncorporate petty business to corporate capitalist business, gives rise to entrepreneurs' successively greater business needs in the state structure. This is because, given the lack of a national market, the state remains the only integrative structure in the realm and the state bureaucracy is the key source of information on supply and demand between market segments. Any business beyond petty craft and retail in small locales requires brokerage in the bureaucracy. In short Róna-tas suggests a dynamic link between state policies, new rent opportunities, and clientelist social capital: as state policies expanding opportunities for private business also raise social capital barriers for acquiring state resources, it is successively higher-ranking officials who can readily overcome barriers.

The argument that subsequent policies legalizing corporate private business serve to raise social capital barriers to entry relative to earlier policies raises further questions in regard to China. First, the expansion of opportunities for private entrepreneurship from noncorporate family business to corporate business has proceeded over four policy initiatives from 1978 to 1994: the Individual Business Household policy that legalized petty private business beginning in the late 1970s; policies institutionalizing privately-run cooperatives in the collective sector in the mid-1980s, the Private Enterprise Interim Regulations of the late 1980s that legalized limited liability companies, and the Company Law of the mid-1990s that legalized corporations and the corporatization of state assets. Extending the logic of Róna-tas's view to China suggests that each policy initiative simultaneously expands the scope of private entrepreneurship while raising social capital barriers to entry.

The second question raised by Róna-tas's view is how entrepreneurs are able to avail themselves of new opportunities. This view that petty firms permitted under earlier policies are run by persons who were never officials, while larger corporate firms that are subsequently legalized are run by former state agents, does not explain how the former group who started business earlier acquire the necessary social capital over time to develop sizable enterprises under subsequent policies. For among China's successful private entrepreneurs are persons who were not former cadres but rather societal actors who began business early in the reform era as petty shop owners and accumulated the necessary social capital to pursue opportunities under subsequent policies. Also, as one cannot rely on one's previous connections for ever, this raises the question of how all entrepreneurs, both former and nonofficials alike, continue to develop new social capital in the state structure once they embark on entrepreneurship.

Rethinking Power Conversion

The foregoing discussion suggests that power conversion can be conceived as two distinct processes that I will term "structural power conversion" and "practical power conversion." Structural power conversion refers to the kinds of social capital that a person brings to bear on entrepreneurship by prior position. This is mostly the advantages of prior public employment, be it as a worker, cadre, or technician before the onset of entrepreneurship, which are then carried over to private entrepreneurs. Such a process is indicated by such popular idioms as "leaping into the sea" (*xia hai*) and "carrying over personal ties" (*ba guanxi laguolai*), which refer to movement of persons and resources from public employment to private entrepreneurship.

Practical power conversion refers to the forging and maintaining of social capital through strategic invoking of cultural techniques.[14] Knowledge of these techniques, such as gift-giving and expressing compliance, are widely diffused in society and can be strategically used by entrepreneurs to cultivate social capital with state agents. Practical power conversion is indicated by such idioms as "investing in personal ties" (*guanxi touzi*), which refers to the creation of new kinds of social relations, and "walking on the edge of the policy" (*zou zai zhengce de bianshang*), which refers to the need for social capital to engage in ambiguous activities not necessarily permitted by a policy. One of my informants likened it to swimming in the sea after one has leaped into it.

Both processes of power conversion are constrained by the shifting state monopoly and ongoing entrepreneurial perceptions of the utility of access to its resources. Under central planning before the late 1970s, practically all economic activity was controlled by the state through the private and collective sectors and the private sector was practically nonexistent. Since the late 1970s, successive policies have expanded the scope of private business, thereby shrinking the scope of the state monopoly. The expanding scope of private business can be seen in the successive policies permitting private firms to employ more persons, use complex production methods, and form partnerships. The shrinking state monopoly can be seen in the decline of the number of commodities subject to direct allocation and dual pricing, reduced state participation in wholesale trade and foreign trade, and the increase in state enterprise trade with private firms.

However, even as successive policies shrink the state monopoly, the remaining resources under state control (i.e., the residual) becomes more highly valued. This is partly because the growth of the market economy makes the resources remaining under state control increasingly valuable. Thus, for example, the growth of the market economy has increased the value of land, which remains under state ownership, because increasing business competition has made location of the business site an increasingly important business consideration. This has helped push up urban land prices and increased the cost of discretionary access to land.[15] Also, the growth of the market economy has increased the value of protection by state agents. The ongoing perception among entrepreneurs that the legal court system is simply an administrative tool of the state rather than a source of impartial justice fuels ongoing entrepreneurial demand for supporters in the bureaucracy to intervene when necessary to provide timely information on policy changes, ward off predation from other agencies, and, if necessary, seek to influence the outcome of court cases. The production of clientelist ties with officialdom through the processes of structural and practical power conversion enables entrepreneurs to pursue these opportunities.

Structural Power Conversion: Leaping into the Sea

The process of structural power conversion proceeds through successive cohorts of entrepreneurs, each departing from higher-ranking positions vis-a-vis the state structure than preceding ones. The entrepreneurs in each cohort have the necessary social capital through prior public employment to overcome the social capital barriers to entry for exploiting the new opportunities in private business created by later state policies of market liberalization. I have termed the cohorts, respectively, the "speculator," "worker," "functionary," and "cadre cohorts."

From Speculator to Entrepreneur

This first entrepreneurial cohort consists of former speculators— formally unemployed persons who were conducting unlicensed trade prior to taking out a business license. I have termed these entrepreneurs the "speculator cohort," reflecting the state's labeling at the time of such trade as speculation *(toujidaoba)*. They are the only cohort whose members had no formal position in the state agencies or enterprises prior to obtaining a business license after 1978.

The emergence of the speculator cohort stems from the Individual Business Family policy promulgated from 1979 that permitted persons to set up small retail, service, and artisanal businesses employing up to seven persons. Amendments in 1982 removed restrictions on the use of mechanized production and transport, and permitted capital pooling. However, key restrictions remained in place such as the seven employee limit, restrictions on access to bank loans, and a ¥100 ceiling on the amount of receipts. These restrictions served to keep these private businesses small and unable to conduct more lucrative trade with the state sector.

Members of this cohort come from several backgrounds. Some are from pre-revolutionary bourgeoisie families who, due to their subsequent bad class label, had been pushed out of their public units to fend for themselves. Others are persons who had been petty traders in the 1950s, were collectivized in the late 1950s, and reemerged again during the brief policy liberalization in the early 1960s, where they then remained on the fringes of society as private traders. Finally, there are young men who were school dropouts and ineligible for public job assignments so they joined gangs for support and protection. All these persons had been conducting furtive trade for a livelihood before the introduction of the Individual Business Family policy. The policy legitimated their business activities and brought them above ground.

When they began licensed business, their ties with officialdom were mostly with street-level officials who routinely interact with citizens during the course of governance. Their early underground trade was known to these officials who adopted a "live and let live" attitude. Their trade was often the sole income for their families and, as long as they did not appear to become wealthy, officials tolerated it. Over time the officials and entrepreneurs came to know each other and trust developed between them. As one businessperson told me, the head of his residence committee (*juwehui*) in 1989 was the same person who had headed it in the mid-1950s. Over decades of political vicissitudes they have come to understand (*huxiang liaojie*) each other despite occasionally opposite positions of enforcer and quarry during state-initiated campaigns.

From the onset of their licensed business in the late 1970s and early 1980s, these entrepreneurs were supported in various ways by the street-level officials. However, as these officials have little authority over productive resources, this support has been mostly in such administrative matters as favorable licensing procedures and insider information on tax evasion, anti-corruption, and economic rectification campaigns. One key form of support was simply to notify speculators of the new Individual Business Family policy and guide them through the licensing procedure. This was crucial because former speculators, burdened with memories of harsh anti-business campaigns in the 1950s and crackdowns on youth gangs from the 1970s, feared state agencies and were wary of licensing their activities. Officials they knew encouraged them to obtain licenses and, due to the lack of significant competition at this early phase of market reform, they rapidly accumulated wealth.

The business activities and networks of these entrepreneurs reflects their connection to street-level officials who provide few economic resources.[16] For start-up capital they have relied on income generated from prior speculative trade, sources that are independent of ties with officialdom. Such trade consisted of selling ration coupons and smuggled watches and shoes from Taiwan. It also consisted of obtaining goods from other places for resale in Xiamen: for example several speculators frequently traveled to Shanghai in the 1970s to purchase toiletry items unavailable in Xiamen, which they resold upon return to Xiamen. Former speculators also relied on small amounts of money borrowed from friends and family members. Their trade in such widely available consumer commodities as textiles and foodstuffs also reflects their weak social capital with officialdom. Many of these commodities are produced by private factories in southern Fujian and Guangdong provinces and sold to other private businesses. Such trade networks are primarily intra-regional, usually in southern Fujian province or extending into the adjacent Chaozhou and Pearl River Delta regions of neighboring Guangdong province to the south and the Wenzhou district of neighboring Zhejiang province to the north.

From Worker to Entrepreneur

The next entrepreneurial cohort to emerge consisted largely of former workers in collective manufacturing enterprises. Their emergence was stimulated by the authorizing of privately-run collectives, first through local urban government policies as early as 1982 and then codified in national policy in 1984.[17] Such collectives are attached to city government agencies and public units, mostly at the district level and lower. They require a minimum of four partners who are unemployed, and provide the economic start-up capital. These firms operate independently of their government sponsors except for the payment of monthly management fees. Although regulations require that after-tax profits be divided among a public accumulation fund, a welfare fund, wages, and dividends, the partners decide the proportions, the only stipulation being that dividends not exceed 15 percent of the share's values and that shares not be publicly traded.

I found that the original partnerships of these cooperatives usually brought together persons with different capitals; some provided economic capital, others had human capital, usually in the form of such artisanal skills as carpentry, metalworking, welding, and electrical repair, and at least one was the offspring of a fairly high-ranking cadre and therefore invested significant social capital into the enterprise. However, these partnerships tend to break down fairly quickly due to conflicts with the most capable partner, usually a former worker with artisanal skills, buying all the shares. By then the departure of the well-connected cadre offspring did not matter because her or his social capital had already been invested in the firm.

Before embarking on entrepreneurship, these capable persons were mostly working in collective manufacturing enterprises at the district level or lower and moonlighting outside their jobs. This was not difficult, as overstaffing at the public firms gave them plenty of free time while their artisanal and technical skills were much in demand in the booming urban construction sector. Moonlighting let them realize the market value of their labor as their monthly earnings were often at least ten times greater than their public wages. This prompted them to see great opportunity in a business career. Still private entrepreneurship was a risky undertaking and many of these entrepreneurs took extended unpaid leaves of absence (*tingxin liuzhi*) from their firms rather than resign outright.

The social background and prior occupations of these entrepreneurs are reflected in their networks. Many have extensive ties with their former public enterprises, as well as other enterprises in the same industry, and with supervisory administrative agencies in the industrial sector. Also, as many are high-school graduates, their classmates were assigned state-sector jobs upon graduation and so they have networks of former classmates scattered through the local government as workers and managers in state enterprises and as administrative officials in city government agencies. These officials, particularly those in district governments, often control significant commodities as well. Finally, as urban high-school graduates, older members of this cohort had been sent to rural village during the Cultural Revolution. Their long periods of rustication, often in the nearby suburbs, have given them useful connections to rural governments to get land for factories.

The most oft-mentioned source of start-up funds for the worker cohort is income from moonlighting prior to obtaining a business license. As already mentioned, they used their skills acquired in the course of their public employment to earn large incomes. The second largest source of start-up capital involves unlicensed trade. This trade involved larger lots of such commodities as cable and wire, steel rods, wood, bricks, and power tools that were stolen from their public factories. The social background of entrepreneurs in this cohort also constrains the business that they conduct. Many trade in car parts, hardware, and construction materials, areas of trade that originated in a combination of the artisanal skills and social capital of the partners of the cooperatives.[18] Also quite a few have ventured into such production and service oriented ventures as printing and packaging operations, vehicle repair, and shipping and transportation.

From Functionary to Entrepreneur

The next cohort of entrepreneurs worked as functionary cadres and entered business with the promulgation of the 1988 Private Enterprise Interim Regulations. This policy permitted legally private firms with no restriction on number of employees, fewer restrictions on business lines than the Individual Business Household policy, sophisticated forms of ownership in sole proprietorship, partnerships, and limited liability, easier access to loans from state banks, the setting up of subsidiary firms, unrestricted trade with public sector enterprises, and no ceilings on the value of receipts.[19]

These entrepreneurs had been previously employed in state-sector public units at the city government level. Most had worked in such distributional bureaus as the Commerce Bureau and the Grain Bureau or as purchasing agents in industrial enterprises. Practically all were high-school graduates, many having graduated from Xiamen's élite Number 1 and Double Ten high schools where they numbered cadres' offspring among their classmates. Finally, many are descendants of pre-revolutionary business families and have relatives in Taiwan, Hong Kong, and southeast

Asia. Reflecting the higher status of private business by the late 1980s, many simply resigned outright when they embarked on licensed business rather than take a leave of absence.

The social networks through which they conduct business reflects their social backgrounds. Many have networks that extend well beyond the southeast coastal region. This is especially true of former purchasing agents whose networks reach to such industrial centers as Wuhan, Shanghai, and Shenyang. They previously plied these routes to procure inputs for their public units and then use them in private business. They also have many former classmates in regulatory agencies who work in the Xiamen City government and in state foreign trade corporations in Fujian province. Finally, through their family backgrounds, they have many overseas relatives who operate their own trading companies outside the People's Republic of China.

These social networks have shaped their business activities. In regard to start-up financial capital, by far the largest source is overseas kin.[20] Although the funds are derived through channels independent of officialdom, they can be used by entrepreneurs to enter officially brokered business lines and foreign trade. The second most cited source of start-up capital for this cohort is income generated by private trade on the side while working as purchasing agents. Indeed when many of these persons obtained business licenses, they simply continued to trade in commodities they were already dealing. Also there is the greater tendency of this cohort to have financial start-up funds from such sources as leasing firms and bank loans that require large investments of social capital with officialdom.[21]

Finally, the networks also constrain the business lines of these entrepreneurs. Many trade commodities only available from public enterprises such as chemicals and, in one case, coal. Because these commodities were still controlled by the state monopoly in the late 1980s and early 1990s, they were underpriced relative to world prices. Therefore this cohort also engages much more heavily in import–export trade than the previous cohorts.[22] But, as private firms were not authorized then to directly conduct foreign trade, they had to seek a state foreign trade corporation to sponsor the trade. Obtaining this sponsorship on favorable terms also required ties with officials in the corporations.

From Cadre to Entrepreneur

The Company Law of 1994 permitted the establishment of limited liability corporate firms that could raise capital through public issues of shares on stock exchanges. There are two ways to establish a corporation. One is the corporatization of state enterprises: persons and corporations could receive control of the enterprise after compensating the state for the market value of its assets. The other is for successful private firms to make a public stock offering. This law therefore entailed a further expansion of the operating scale of private business. In my sample, all cadre entrepreneurs who founded corporations did so through the first way.

The Company Law attracted people from higher posts in state units at the city and provincial governments and from the People's Liberation Army and the Communist party.[23] Also, most of these entrepreneurs from my sample were not from Xiamen. In this they differed from the other entrepreneurs who were all from Xiamen and viewed Xiamen as their operational base. Cadre entrepreneurs had come to Xiamen because it offered certain economic advantages, such as ease of foreign trade, but they had significant operations elsewhere in China.

These entrepreneurs draw on high-level networks in the state in their business activities. This can be seen in their sources of start-up capital. A primary source of start-up funds has been bank loans. Most were obtained through partnerships with public units. Some former cadres established private companies when they resigned from their public jobs and then set up joint capital (*hezi*) enterprises with state enterprises. The bank loans were made to the joint ventures with the state partner serving as guarantor. Former military officers obtained bank loans by tapping networks of former comrade-in-arms who had returned to their rural villages as leading officials. These friends let cadre entrepreneurs use village land as collateral for bank loans. Another source of start-up funds was unlicensed trade prior to establishing their corporation. One lucrative opportunity in the mid-1990s was created by the triangular debt situation.[24] This occurred when state banks were ordered by the central state to stop lending money to unprofitable state enterprises, causing a liquidity crises, and making state enterprises unable to pay other state enterprises for commodities they had purchased. To generate cash, enterprises consigned the commodities they produced to well-connected persons to sell them. These persons then remitted profits to the state enterprises after taking a hefty cut for themselves. Other opportunities for unlicensed trade were linked to insider information on upcoming policy changes. For example one city government cadre read a new policy document prohibiting state enterprises from giving cash bonuses to employees at Spring Festival. Spotting an opportunity, he promptly purchased large amounts of watches and home appliances that he then sold to public enterprises as Spring Festival presents for employees, thereby enabling the state enterprises to circumvent this new regulation. Also, many entrepreneurs received another benefit when, during the corporatization process, they used ties with high officials to ensure that the compensation value of state assets was below market value.

The business activities of this cohort also reflect their connections to the highest levels of state power. They tend to trade in coal and construction materials, commodities that, as already noted, require connections with officialdom in the mid-1990s. These commodities were produced in northern China and shipped to Xiamen for sale in the booming southern construction industry and for export to southeast Asian countries. Obtaining foreign trade permits for such large commodity exports also requires excellent connections with officials in the state trade corporations.

The foregoing discussion of structural conversion has described how each new policy that expands opportunities for private entrepreneurs induces people from more highly-ranked positions in the party-state bureaucracy to "leap into the sea" of business. Later entrants tend to possess the necessary social capital to take advantage of newer opportunities. This is because much business advantage does not consist of economic capital accumulation rather of social capital accumulations with officialdom. However, with each new policy initiative some entrepreneurs from earlier cohorts also pursue the new opportunities, raising the question of persons from less advantageous positions obtain the necessary social capital.

Practical Power Conversion: Swimming in the Sea

The social capital of an entrepreneur is not only a preset function of the structural position from which one "leaps into the sea" of the market economy, but is also created through cultural techniques while swimming in the sea. These cultural techniques constitute practical power conversion. Social capital must be cultivated to prevent the stagnation of existing ties and encourage the formation of new ones. Examining these techniques sheds light on how all entrepreneurs maintain their earlier social capital and on how some entrepreneurs overcome social capital handicaps stemming from the low structural position at which they started business and cultivate the ties necessary to pursue opportunities in subsequent policies.

Techniques of Cultivating Social Capital

Several common techniques of practical power conversion are described here that I have termed "associational," "compliance," "gift-giving," and "marriage." Associational techniques refers to the cultivation of social capital through participation in various types of state-sponsored business and societal organizations (*shetuan*). Some entrepreneurs actively assume positions as officers in these organizations, enabling them to work closely with the supervising officials, thereby generating some affect between them that can be converted into administrative favors useful to their business or into introductions to even more highly placed officials. Some entrepreneurs also deploy associational techniques to enhance their reputation in ways that are useful in personal interaction by assuming political positions in the party-state. Entrepreneurs have become local representatives of the Chinese People's Political Consultative Committee and National People's Congress while a few were seeking Communist party membership. Participation in these activities is more desired by members of earlier cohorts whose original social capital was quite low: this is because participation can confer business-enhancing ties with officials but also requires significant time commitments, and therefore entrepreneurs with sufficient social capital eschew this. A second strategy is compliance with activities of various government agencies in order to deepen relations between its agents and an entrepreneur. Toward this end, an entrepreneur visibly demonstrates conformity with the demands of an agency. For example, some entrepreneurs have been commended by the Tax Bureau as "tax-paying activists" (*nashui jijifenzi*) and their deeds are publicized and they are given banners and placards to display. Conferral of such symbols deepens understandings between the designated entrepreneurs and bureau officials. Awards tend to be particularistically allocated and visibly signify an entrepreneur's favor by the designating bureau, forestalling administrative harassment by other bureaus.[25] Such displays of active conformity are closely linked to the associational strategies just described, as entrepreneurs deemed more compliant are more likely to be tapped for leadership positions in associations.

Compliance also occurs through providing liturgies. Some of these are at the behest of local government, such as funds to repair and decorate government offices and subsidize local school activities. The agencies and their agents come to feel some obligation to support entrepreneurs who give funds. Other entrepreneurs devise their own philanthropic activities, such as providing new clothes to the elderly in the neighborhood or paying for musical instruments for local school bands: the ensuing publicity for their deeds provides them with a measure of prestige and goodwill that is useful in subsequent interactions with officialdom.

Gift-giving is another technique of creating social capital. This consists of transactions commingling popular perceptions of instrumentality and affect with the specific mix linked to the explicitness of expectations and timing of reciprocity.[26] Such practices as banqueting are deemed less instrumental (or in popular parlance are not considered corruption) because no cash is exchanged. Furthermore, there might also be no explicit request by an entrepreneur. Indeed, part of the strategy is to build up feelings of obligation that can be tapped to deal with future uncertainties. At the other extreme is cash, which is considered more instrumental, and it also accords with state definitions of corruption. Expectations are more explicit and communicated during the transaction. Of course many transactions are actually more ambiguous then these two examples indicate. Cash can be given to officials in ways that are not popularly viewed as corruption. For example cash can be given in a red envelope (*hong bao*) at Spring Festival to an official under the guise of an offering for her or his children's education without any explicit requests for reciprocity. Likewise company shares can be proffered or expensive commodities such as televisions and air-conditioners given as gifts without explicit demands being proffered.

Finally, marriage is another technique. Marriage can be used by entrepreneurs who are not officials or from lowly backgrounds to create strong personal bonds with officials in bureaus. It can also be used by entrepreneurs who are officials to amplify the advantages of their social backgrounds. The strategic use of this by entrepreneurs can involve marrying off female offspring to men working in strategic bureaus. For officials this promises a comfortable financial future, an important consideration given the low salaries of officials and the relatively high rates of inflation. For entrepreneurs this promises insider information on policies and expeditious treatment in matters considered by the bureau, and channels of communication to other bureaus.

A Case Study of Clientelist Social Capital Production

Let me provide a case study of how some of these techniques constitute enterprise development. I will focus on the case of a Xiamen entrepreneur who, within ten years from the onset of market reform, had become a famous entrepreneur operating on a national scale. His story illustrates how entrepreneurs who emerged during an earlier policy initiative forge the necessary social capital to ride the waves of successive policy initiatives.

The Ever Wealthy Company was started by Chen Youfu, a former unemployed youth who worked sporadically on the Xiamen docks as a stevedore. In 1979 he began to collect used bottles for resale and saved enough money to start a small grocery shop licensed under the Individual Business Family policy. He also assumed a leadership position in the Self-Employed Laborers Association, in which membership was mandatory for business licensed under the Individual Business Family policy. This position let him develop close ties with the officials in the district level Industry and Commerce bureau that managed the organization. In the mid-1980s these officials selected him to be one of the first persons in Xiamen to be licensed to operate a privately-run cooperative under new policies in the mid-1980s. Chen switched his business line to imported car parts, an increasingly lucrative business as foreign cars began pouring into the market. At this time, state policies also authorized the establishment of cooperative banks at the urban district level. Chen's supporters in officialdom helped him get a large loan from a state bank to buy controlling shares in a district-level cooperative. Using loans obtained from this cooperative, Chen arranged for a car-parts sales exhibition and sent out notices all over China. Through liberal use of kickbacks he then landed orders with public purchasing agents from all over the country.

His firm's explosive growth caught the eye of officials in the city-level government, who then supported his bid to become a national youth model entrepreneur. During the subsequent awards ceremony in Beijing he met state factory managers who sold him cable and other products in scarce supply in the building boom along the southern coast. In 1988 he was arrested on charges of economic crimes during a major economic rectification campaign and, after a lengthy struggle by his patrons to prevent his case from coming to trial, was reputedly sentenced to several years in prison in a secret trial. Upon his release he went back into business. His company had survived and, by selling off its real-estate holdings it rebuilt its financial capital. He also invited high-ranking officials to lavish parties in a public display of his connections. Chen then went into the real-estate business in Xiamen. In 1994 with the implementation of the Company Law, Chen's firm became one of the first privately-run cooperatives to be authorized to make a public stock offering and become a corporation. This public offering generated further cash, enabling Chen to engage in real estate development as far-flung as office towers in Shanghai's booming Pudong district and public infrastructure projects such as a bridge over the Xiang River in Hunan province's capital of Changsha.

In examining the rise of Chen Youfu it is apparent that his business success owes little to any ability to spot new market opportunities but rather to his ability to manipulate associational, compliance, and gift-giving practices to forge support among officialdom. Indeed, Chen's choice of business at each stage of his firm's development showed little entrepreneurial talent in spotting new business opportunities. To the contrary, each new business line he entered was simply following contemporary business trends: groceries in the early 1980s, car parts and construction supplies in the mid- and latter 1980s, and real estate in the 1990s. Instead his entrepreneurial talent lay in developing the necessary ties to pursue new opportunities in successive policies.

Riding the Policy Waves

Each phase of the development of Chen's firm is linked with its reformulation by a new policy, from family shop, to privately-run cooperative, to corporation.[27] What is the role of these reformulations in converting state power into his firm's wealth? First, the reformulations enabled him to obtain access to resources that were contained in the shrinking but increasingly valuable state monopoly. For example the shift from private family shop to privately-run cooperative in the mid-1980s enabled him to expand from retail to wholesale trade and facilitated his access to imported automotive parts. Also, as both the wholesale trade and import–export trade were proscribed for private trade, his firm's redefinition as a cooperative enabled him to circumvent this restriction.

Much of Chen's efforts in redefining his firm under each policy initiative was to be included in the "preparatory committee" (*choubei hui*) that precedes widespread implementation of a policy. As the first step in local implementation of a policy, the Industry and Commerce Bureau selects entrepreneurs considered reliable by bureau officials. Such entrepreneurs are the first group of persons to be licensed under a new policy. This gives them a crucial business advantage because the new enterprise form is not yet widespread and so there are few competitors to take advantage of the new opportunities while regulatory bureaus are still unaware of its loopholes and rent-seeking opportunities. Thus, Chen consistently used his firm's position in a given policy context to invest in more highly placed social capital with officialdom in order to be included in the preparatory committee for the next policy initiative that, in turn, enabled him to reformulate his enterprise into the new type of firm legalized under the new policy and reap windfall economic profits owing to the initial lack of competition. Also, the new ties that Chen cultivated gave him access to the kind of rent-seeking opportunities lying in the allocation of commodities and contracts remaining within each policy initiative. This can be seen in his operation of a privately-run cooperative that subsequently enabled him to forge new relations and obtain access to import licenses and bank loans. It can also be seen in his elevation to a national model of a young entrepreneur with the support of city government officials, which enabled him to meet the director of northeast state enterprises who sold him scarce commodities.

Chen's activities also illustrate the risks of a business strategy that relies so thoroughly on practical power conversion. Its techniques more readily fit state definitions of corruption, and entrepreneurs who rely heavily on such practices are more susceptible to being charged with economic crimes during economic rectification campaigns. This is precisely what happened to Chen in the late 1980s. His downfall was rumored to stem from charges of corruption lodged by officials who were not on his payroll. In other words, his process of entrepreneurship, which relied heavily on buying officials in order to pave the way to the advantages of a new policy, also created jealousies and conflicts among the local officialdom that eventually derailed him, at least temporarily.

While all entrepreneurs rely on practical power conversion techniques to varying in degrees, it enables entrepreneurs from lower social structural positions to compensate for their low levels of social capital by forging more efficacious ties. However such a business strategy is especially risky.

The Making of an Economic Élite

This chapter has described the formation of China's new rentier entrepreneurial élite as a dynamic process of power conversion. One constraint on this process is successive state policies of market liberalization that shift the opportunities for rent-seeking and the kinds of necessary clientelist ties. These policies have shrunk the overall scope of the monopoly even while creating a higher valuation for resources remaining under state control. By the 1990s, these resources consisted largely of access to bank capital, land, administrative protection, and foreign trade. Also, reflecting ongoing lack of faith in the legal system, entrepreneurs still perceive ties with officialdom as useful in protecting their wealth in legal disputes with other business concerns and from predation by state agencies and officials. This situation stimulates ongoing entrepreneurial perceptions of the desirability of administratively controlled resources and the need for clientelist ties.

Another constraint is the social capital resources available to an entrepreneur to access politically controlled opportunities. This constraint is constituted by the ties among officialdom that an entrepreneur possesses through prior occupation. Occupations among entrepreneurs vary by bureaucratic rank which, in turn, constrains the social capital each possesses when leaping into the sea. Another constraint is the need to swim in the sea by replenishing social capital and forging new clientelist ties to obtain new opportunities. This is achieved trough facility in cultural techniques to produce obligation and trust in relationships. Those leaping from lower bureaucratic heights have to swim harder to stay afloat by engaging in a wider range of riskier relationship building techniques.

To what extent are this chapter's findings applicable to China's capitalist business class in general? The prominence of power conversion as a route into the economic élite might be less pronounced among other elements of the business class. For example, there may be variation by business line. The wholesale trading companies described in this chapter may rely on official brokerage more than other business activities. This is because the wholesale trade information on commodities is forthcoming through exchanges in contrast to other business lines, such as manufacturing, where information is also of a technical sort and constituted by knowledge of the production process. Therefore, industrial entrepreneurship might require less clientelist ties and entail less power conversion than trading entrepreneurship. There might also be variation by age cohort and educational level. Older persons were socialized in the planned economy when ties with officials were routine for enhancing consumption and careers while younger persons socialized in the market economy might be less familiar with the cultural techniques of gift-giving. Also, younger entrepreneurs in business lines linked to higher levels of education and more foreign contacts might be more likely to view ties with officials as corrupt and illegitimate. They might be more familiar with the discourse of legal rights and less willing to defer to officials' demands.

What of the future of the rentier entrepreneur élite? Its formation rests on the persistence of state monopoly over land ownership and such basic commodities as energy resources and raw materials, administrative restrictions on bank loans and foreign trade and, inconsistent enforcement of laws. Changing state policies that permit new forms of private enterprise but maintain these monopolies reproduce the perception among entrepreneurs of the need for ties with officials. In this context power conversion is an institutionalized route into the capitalist business class. It is conceivable that the state monopoly will eventually disappear and that power conversion would no longer be a basis for expansive business. Yet the wealth accumulations of rentier entrepreneurs achieved through prior power conversions would no doubt ensure the prominence of this group within any newly reconstituted bourgeoisie for sometime.

Notes

1. Catherine Boone, "The Making of a Rentier Class: Wealth Accumulation and Political Control in Senegal," *Journal of Development Studies* 26,3 (1990): 425–429; Kiren Aziz Chaudry, "Economic Liberalization and the Lineages of the Rentier State," *Comparative Politics* 27,1 (1994): 1–25; Paul D. Hutchcroft, "Obstructive Corruption: The Politics of Privilege in the Philippines," *Rents, Rent-seeking, and Economic Development: Theory and Evidence in Asia,* ed. Mushtaq H. Khan, and K.S. Jomo (New York: Cambridge University Press, 2000): 207–247.

2. Choi, Eun Kyong, and Zhou, Kate Xiao, "Entrepreneurs and Politics in the Chinese Transitional Economy: Political Connections and Rent-Seeking," *The China Review* 1,1 (2001): 111–135; Akos Róna-tas, "The First Shall Be Last?: Entrepreneurs and Communist Cadres in the Transition from Socialism," *American Journal of Sociology* 100, 1 (1994): 40–69.

3. Ezra Vogel, "From Revolutionary to Semi-Bureaucrat: The 'Regularization' of Cadres," *The China Quarterly* 29 (January–March 1967): 36–60; Andrew G. Walder, *Communist Neo-Traditionalism: Work and Authority in Chinese Industry* (Berkeley: University of California Press, 1986).

4. Due to the blurring of legal property rights in China's market economy, I use the term "private" in a nonlegal sense to refer to entrepreneurs who are private individuals in that they are not formally employed as agents of the partystate. "Private" firms refers to the concerns operated by private entrepreneurs.

5. One hundred private firm operators were interviewed in 1988–90 and constitute the first three cohorts (speculator, worker, and functionary) described in this chapter. The other seven were interviewed in 1995 and constitute the cadre cohort. The sample and fieldwork are discussed at length in David L. Wank, *Commodifying Communism: Business, Trust, and Politics in a Chinese City* (New York: Cambridge University Press, 1999): 12–22; 244–251.

6. Liu, Yia-ling, "The Reform from Below: The Private Economy and the Local Politics in the Rural Industrialization of Wenzhou," *The China Quarterly* 130 (June 1992): 293–316; Dorothy J. Solinger, "Urban Entrepreneurs and the State: The Merger of State and Society," in *Reform and Reaction in Post-Mao China: The Road to Tiananmen,* ed. Richard Baum (New York: Routledge, 1992): 104–123.

7. Solinger, "Urban Entrepreneurs and the State: The Merger of State and Society," 123.

8. Jadwiga Staniszkis, " 'Political Capitalism' in Poland," *East European Politics and Society* 5, 1 (1991): 127–141.

9. Ibid., 136–137.

10. Robert Bates, *Markets and States in Tropical Africa: The Political Basis of Agricultural Policies* (Berkeley: University of California Press, 1981); Anne O. Krueger, "The Political Economy of the Rent-Seeking Society," *American Economic Review* 64, 93 (1974): 291–303.

11. Staniszkis, " 'Political Capitalism' in Poland," 139–140.

12. The fact that the persons possess these ties is assumed by either their background as officials or the functional need for connections to the state by societal actors.

13. Róna-tas, "The First Shall Be Last?"

14. Yang, Mayfair Mei-hui, *Gifts, Favors, and Banquets: The Art of Social Relationships in China* (Ithaca, New York: Cornell University Press, 1994).

15. For example, early on in the reform era, the state permitted the private trade and production in textiles, and now these commodities circulate entirely according to market forces of supply and demand. However, ownership of real estate is still a state monopoly. In the early 1980s, rents for real estate were quite low but the increasing wealth of private business has helped to bid up the price of real-estate for choice business sites and real-estate development. By the late 1990s, real-estate ownership had become one of the few remaining monopolies of the Communist party, and the rental value of real estate has skyrocketed. Now prices are extremely high, with real estate in China's major coastal cities comparable to that of international cities such as London, New York, and Tokyo. The high prices also reflect the relative scarcity of choice in real estate, and insider information and influence are essential to procuring this commodity.

16. The key resource is business sites, as many local collectives control property while the local branches of the Industry and Commerce Bureau control the allocation of stalls in many marketplaces.

17. This policy was partly induced by problems stemming from the Individual Business Family policy because the myriad restrictions on business imposed by this policy led to the consumption rather than reinvestment of profits. As the legalization of unrestricted private enterprises was still ideologically problematic at the time, the privately run collective policy was an innovation that permitted a drastically increased scale of private capital without appreciably expanding the formal private sector.

18. The car-parts trade is a case in point. Persons who had skills in metalworking, spray-painting, and welding set up car body repair shops in the early 1980s. Owing to the large number of Japanese-made cars and trucks that had been imported, there was much demand for this service. However, as most vehicles then belonged to public units, obtaining business required official brokerage; therefore the successful garages relied on their well-connected partners for this. As economic accumulation increased, these firms branched into the more profitable trade of car parts. This required extensive use of kickbacks with the purchasing agents from public units.

19. This policy was intended in part to end the administrative confusion generated by the proliferation of cooperatives. The ambiguous status of cooperatives as privately-operated but publicly-owned firms caused confusion in such administrative matters as taxation. The new regulation established a clear policy of private ownership for larger scale business firms.

20. These amounts are much larger than the amounts that former speculators received from kin and friends in China.

21. Leasing involves district level wholesale companies. Although leases are tendered in auction, bid-rigging is widespread to favor those with ties to the officials of the wholesale firms' parent public units. The assets of the firms are undervalued to reduce leasing fees in exchange for under-the-table payments to the officials. This gave to lessees at low cost firms for three to five years with much profit-generating potential: see David L. Wank, "Producing Property Rights: Strategies, Networks, and Efficiency in Urban China's Nonstate Firms," in *Property Rights and Economic Reform in China,* ed. Jean C. Oi, and Andrew G. Walder (Stanford: Stanford University Press, 1999): 257–258, 261–264. Bank loans are also officially brokered. They require a public unit to serve as the guarantor, and so ties with officialdom are necessary.

22. In many cases relatives abroad in trade are the purchasers of the commodities and then resell them elsewhere in southeast Asia.

23. In the earlier cohorts there were only two Communist party members out of the 100 entrepreneurs. By contrast all seven members of the cadre cohort that I interviewed were Communist party members.

24. The unlicensed trade of persons in this cohort was much larger than the unlicensed trade within previous cohorts.

25. Also, once a bureau bestows such legitimacy on an entrepreneur, it has a vested interest in assuring his continued legitimacy. For example, the Tax Bureau is unlikely to charge a designated tax-paying activist with tax evasion, as the charge would question the judgment of tax officials for bestowing the honor in the first place.

26. The building of obligated personal ties through gift-giving is a key element of what is termed *guanxi* practice (Yang, *Gifts, Favors, and Banquets*).

27. The only enterprise form lacking in this sequence is as a private company under the 1988 Private Enterprise Interim Regulations. Although Chen's firm was beginning the process of changing its legal status from a cooperative to a private company in 1988, the first in Xiamen to do so, his arrest in the middle of the year halted this.

PART III

New Patterns of Social Networks

CHAPTER SIX

Country Maids in the City: Domestic Service as an Agent of Modernity in China

DELIA DAVIN

Introduction

Many observers have commented that rural to urban migration is one of the most striking social and economic phenomena in China today, with hugely important implications for the development of the cities and the newly-industrializing areas to which migrants go, and for the rural and often poor areas of the hinterland, which they leave. Migration is a major concern within China as official statements at national and local government levels on labor, public security, birth planning, education, and housing frequently show. The Chinese media offer considerable, largely hostile coverage of migration,[1] and a growing scholarly literature explores the reasons for the increase in migration, provides estimates of migrant numbers, and evaluates their impact on the sending and destination areas.[2]

Much of the growing literature on internal migration insists on the newness of the phenomenon. Population movement is indeed now taking place on an unprecedented scale. Rapid industrialization has given rise to demands for cheap labor, decollectivization has revealed great labor surpluses in the rural areas, and the relaxation of the strict household registration system that tied the peasants to the villages in the Maoist years has allowed rural people to seek a better life in the towns and cities of China. However the insistence on newness can mask the fact that today's migrations are often influenced by the past. Some migration continued in China, even in the period when restrictions were at their most severe.[3] Connections between, for example, sending areas in Shandong and destination areas in China's northeast were never severed. Some important migrations are built on old foundations. Zhejiang village is the area of Beijing settled by migrants from Zhejiang province. These people who now make and deal in clothing for markets in China and abroad come from communities with a long tradition of leaving their villages to work as itinerant traders.[4] One would not have to rewrite reports of conditions in the industrial dormitories of Shanghai in the 1920s very heavily to make them fit conditions in the factory dormitories of the Chinese Special Economic Zones in the 1990s.[5]

In this chapter I want to look at a particular group of migrants in contemporary China that I think is interesting, the women who leave their villages to go to do domestic work in the homes of urban families. I discuss why their numbers have increased so much since the economic reforms, where they come from, and how they are recruited. I describe their lives in the cities, the conditions in which they work, and the impact that their sojourn has on them and their native places.

The image usually conjured up by the words "female migrant" in contemporary China is perhaps that of an assembly-line or garment-trade worker, a trader, a waitress, or a prostitute. All these occupations are associated with post-reform economic modernity. I argue that the maid is also typical of female migrants and that despite the traditional nature of domestic service as an occupation for women, in contemporary China it can be a force for modernity with the potential to transform the lives of individuals and their communities. Indeed, because they are unique among migrants for their close contact with urban people during their sojourns in the cities, maids may do more to bring new ideas on lifestyles, family life, and consumption to the villages than other returned migrants who have had less contact with urban people.

Domestic service is of course an ancient profession and one found in many societies. In imperial China it provided women with one of the few ways they could earn a living outside the family. In twentieth-century Europe the number of servants and the numbers of households employing servants has declined dramatically. Perhaps for this reason, domestic service is often perceived in Europe only as a traditional occupation and is not easily associated with modernization. Yet both in England and in France, the numbers of domestic servants peaked in the 1880s and 1890s, well after the Industrial Revolution.[6] In this period, in England, one in every six women was a servant. In both countries more women were employed in domestic service than in any other occupation well into the twentieth century. Servants were used to support the comfortable leisured lifestyles of the prospering middle classes and to relieve middle-class women of the drudgery then associated with child-rearing, feeding the family, and caring for an elaborately furnished house without the benefit of labor-saving machinery. Domestic service acted as a bridge for young women between the rural world of their childhood, where they had no economic future, and the cities. The involvement in domestic service of rural women in nineteenth-century Europe is seen by historians as having contributed to the modernization of their outlooks, expectations, and lifestyles and to have contributed to the development of urbanization.[7]

Domestic Service in China since 1949

Well-off families in urban China normally employed maids before 1949 and continued to do so after the establishment of the People's Republic. Communist officials soon imitated the habits of the urban middle classes if they could afford to. It has been claimed that the connection between the Communist New Fourth Army and Anhui was a factor in the development of the migration of young women to Beijing to work as maids. New Fourth veterans assigned to jobs in the capital after 1949 were sent back to the villages of Anhui when they needed a maid.[8] At this stage there was no political problem about employing a maid; indeed, the practice was specifically legitimized for high-ranking cadres under the cadre stipend system. In the early 1950s, cadres were paid in kind with a small allowance to cover cash expenses. Women cadres over a certain rank were given money to allow them to keep a servant so that they could carry out their responsibilities without domestic worries.[9]

From the 1950s in China, almost all educated urban women worked after marriage and motherhood, yet taking care of a family was extremely laborious. Few homes had hot water, many still lacked tap water, and most cooking had to be done on a coal stove. The uncertainty of supplies and the lack of domestic refrigeration meant that much time had to be devoted to shopping. The provision of child care through a system of crèches and nurseries eased the problems of child-rearing, but housework, laundry, and the preparation of meals remained burdensome. Those who could afford to employ a maid gained real improvements in lifestyle. They no longer had to rush out from work to shop in the lunch hour, or to stand in line in the canteen waiting to buy hot food to take home for the evening meal. Parents had the reassurance of knowing that someone was at home with the children when they had to attend evening meetings or political study. There was more time for enjoyment on Sundays, a day that less fortunate families had to spent doing the laundry and cleaning. Of course only a small minority of urban families could afford a maid. As a maid's wage was equivalent to about half that of a skilled worker, most families simply had to struggle to get everything done for themselves. But the numbers of maids in Beijing were significant enough that in 1964 street committees were instructed to organize political study groups for them. It is clear from memoir literature that it was quite normal for the children of both the new and the old elite to grow up in families with a maid.[10]

Discussions of the wages and hours of maids in the press in the 1950s tended to be sympathetic toward the needs of employers. An article in the official magazine for women[11] advised that maids could be expected to work more than the eight-hour industrial day as their work was not intensive. However it did make one concession toward the rights of maids by commending the practice of giving them one day off a fortnight. Cadres were urged to treat their maids as equals but not to turn a blind eye to their faults or to try to win their loyalty by paying more than the average wage. Such behavior would upset the stability of the labor market. Maids were urged to remember the revolutionary content of their work that, although not directly productive, allowed others to take their place on the productive front.[12]

The Cultural Revolution saw a change in the political line on employing servants. The practice was now condemned as bourgeois. Senior women cadres began to talk of learning to cook, or buying all their meals from the canteen and sending their maids away. Some acted on this and discharged their maids. However, some maids remained. Indeed, there were élite households, in which the maid kept the home together and took care of children too young to be involved with the Cultural Revolution when parents and other family members were away at meetings, sent to the countryside or detained.[13]

Domestic service in the 1950s and 1960s was usually an occupation for women who had no other way to earn money. Some maids came from the countryside when they were young. Until the 1960s it appears to have been easier for a young woman without urban registration to enter the cities to become a maid than for any other reason. As time went on and the restriction on migration into the cities took effect however, young maids became rare. Young urban women had come to scorn a job with such low status, long hours, and low pay, and rural women were no longer allowed to enter the cities to take it up. Most maids in this period were middle-aged, illiterate, and unskilled. Many, especially in the north, still had bound feet, for the practice of footbinding had lingered on longest among the poor. Their clothes tended to be traditional and little influenced by the new styles that came in after 1949. Their physical appearances thus confirmed their backward, old-fashioned image. Although some might have originated from the countryside, they had made their lives in the cities and usually acquired urban residential status when restrictions on movement between the cities and the rural areas were introduced in the 1950s. Some resided in their employers' homes but many others had homes and families in the neighborhood to which they returned at night. Those who planned to retire to their villages in old age might send remittances to relatives, but visits home were quite rare.[14] The influence that such migrants had on their areas of origin was correspondingly slight.

Domestic Service after the Economic Reforms

There has been a large increase in the number of families employing domestic help since the economic reforms. Many factors have contributed to an increase in the demand for maids: urban prosperity, the emergence of well-to-do dual-career families, the disappearance of the political taboo on employing maids, and the development of a culture of domestic comfort. Even population policy has played its part. Lowered fertility means that more can be spent on the precious only child. Young parents anxious to safeguard the health of these infants shun crèches. They fear infections and believe that very young children will thrive better at home. Women employed in state industries, government service, or education are entitled to six months paid maternity leave if they undertake to limit themselves to a single child. Women in nonstate employment may have less long. When this leave is finished, mothers face the problem of finding someone to care for their babies. Most favor a grandmother or the help of another family member, but when no relative is available they search for live-in help. If the family is well-to-do, live-in help may be recruited even in addition to a female relative, so that one woman can devote most of her time to the baby.

On the supply side the most important factor in the increase in domestic labor has been the relaxation in the restrictions on rural people entering the cities to seek work. The recent development of domestic service reflects the pull that the cities can exert on poor rural areas.

Maids in the cities are now almost exclusively recruited from the countryside. Urban employers complain at the amount they have to pay their maids, yet a maid's wages and prospects would not tempt any urban family to regard domestic work as a good opening for a daughter. The hours are too long, the opportunities for advancement too few, and the job is considered demeaning. Young women from the poorer areas of China's countryside, however, see domestic service in the city as offering all sorts of possibilities: the experience of city life, the chance to help their parents with money or to save for a dowry, and the opportunity to buy pretty fashionable clothes. Domestic service is easy to enter. It does not require large sums of capital or an extensive network of urban contacts. It draws on skills that most rural girls have acquired some grounding of in their own homes. Moreover, the rural parents of a female migrant may feel that she is safer in domestic employment that provides accommodation and a quasi-familial situation than searching for other types of employment.

Employer/maid relations in contemporary China are influenced both by traditional patterns and by the market. As in the past, in contemporary urban society most migrant maids live with their employers. Some people still recruit maids from villages with which they have some connection or from the families of their rural relatives. Most, however, find their maids through the recommendation of friends or relatives who ask their own maids to introduce a suitable person. A maid who leaves her employers on good terms usually introduces a successor. Most big cities also have domestic employment agencies, often run by the Women's Federation, through which maids and employers may make contact.[15]

A maid may be treated more like a junior member of the family. She is expected to show respect and obedience to her employers. They frequently attempt to exercise a rather paternalistic control over her life, what she wears, where she goes on her day off, and whom she sees. One woman I interviewed told me that she bought clothes for her maid holding back a part of her wages to compensate.[16] This was necessary, she explained, because the girl did not know what was appropriate for a maid to wear and might otherwise be tempted by outrageous fashions. The same woman complained of the "naughty" behavior of Anhui maids who went off to parks together on Sundays, compared notes on their wages, and came home to press for more if they were not among the highest paid. Yet maids may also be treated with real concern and affection. Some employers try to help their maids with reading and writing or show them how to run a bank account. All will try to train them to cook better according to the tastes of the family, and to use modern cleaning methods and whatever domestic appliances are available. If the maid is entrusted with child care the family will also talk to her about nutrition, hygiene, and the right way to bring up a child. It is significant that the preferred term for a maid in contemporary China is *aiyi* (auntie) and maids often use kinship terms to address their employers.

To some extent maids share the family's living standards, eating better and staying warmer than other migrants from the countryside. Many enjoy exclusive daytime access to the family television. But being a live-in maid obviously has disadvantages. Some employers are anxious to control their maid's behavior but take no responsibility for her welfare or happiness. Living space is very short, even in prosperous urban homes. Maids rarely have any privacy. They may share a room or even a bed with the child they care for, or may sleep in a curtained-off area that is used as family space during the day. Living with the family they are constantly "on call" except during their time off, which is usually one day a week but can be as little as a half day a fortnight. Nursemaids who are left alone with a young child by employers out at work all day may live very lonely lives. This problem is especially severe in the high-rise blocks that now ring many Chinese cities. The isolated domestic life of city apartments is in sharp contrast to social life in village courtyards where many young maids grew up. Employers often fail to appreciate the huge culture gap that a girl from village China must traverse when she comes to live in a high-rise in an urban area, or the isolation that she must experience alone all day in an apartment.[17]

The women who work in domestic service differ in important ways from their predecessors in the 1950s and 1960s. They are young women who come to the city in their late teens and stay for a few years. A few marry and settle, or become so attached to their employers or to city life and its amenities that they seek to remain, but most carry out their plan to return to the villages. For the present at least, the barriers on long term settlement for rural migrants usually ensure that their stay is temporary and the great majority return to their home areas to get married.

After new arrivals from the countryside began to dominate domestic service from the late 1970s, the prefix of *xiao*—little or young—was almost always used with *baomu* or *aiyi,* emphasizing the youth of these new recruits. When maids leave an employer, they usually introduce a relative or friend to take their places. Thus each cohort from the countryside is replaced by a slightly younger one from the same area. This circulatory form of migration ensures that it has the maximum impact on the sending areas. The migration of maids to Beijing and some other major cities is dominated by chains from specific places. The best-known, of course, is the migration of young women from Wuwei county and the surrounding area in Anhui Province, the so-called Anhui *xiao aiyi*.

Married women from the villages do sometimes seek jobs as maids in the cities, but tend to do so only in exceptional circumstances, such as extreme financial difficulty, marital disharmony, or widowhood. Single women are in the majority among live-in maids because the life is not seen as appropriate for a married woman. When married women do become migrants, their husbands or their husbands' families may claim some right over their earnings. I interviewed one woman from Anhui who came to Beijing to flee a violent husband in Anhui. Unfortunately he had traced her there and demanded the repayment of her brideprice before he would agree to a divorce. This took up six months of her wages.[18]

The young single women who make up the majority of the domestic workforce are not entirely passive or unable to look after themselves. There is plenty of evidence that they have been able to push their wages up, and conditions have certainly improved since the 1950s. A day off, usually Sunday, is now expected and most *baomu* would be reluctant to work more than an eight-hour day. The old assumption that a maid must simply work the hours that the employer requires is disappearing. Hours now have to be negotiated. Maids often refuse to clear the evening meal because it would keep them at work too late, or they insist that their employers eat early if they are expected to wash up.

In recent years, another model of domestic service has emerged in the large cities. Female migrants have begun to hire themselves out on an hourly or daily rate to cook or do domestic work. Some live with their own families in the migrant settlements in and around the cities, others are on their own in the city and rent a space to stay, usually in a peasant household in the peri-urban area. This system of employment is preferred by slightly older women as it allows them to work clearly defined hours, and to enjoy some personal or family life. By working for several different families during the week they can usually earn considerably more than they would in a live-in position. This arrangement also allows them to search for other types of employment offering higher pay, more interest, or better status while allowing them to fall back on domestic work if things go wrong. Some women do domestic work as a second job in order to be able to save or remit more.[19]

Employers seem to have mixed feelings about hourly paid maids. They are uneasy about the changed power relationship in this system of employment. They complain that the women feel free to leave whenever they find better paid work, are more likely to negotiate about jobs they will and will not do, are unwilling to stay late in the evening and are likely to pilfer food to take back to their own homes. They also fear that the maid may connect with criminals or thieves and help them to steal from the apartment. On the other hand, many employers are glad of the privacy they gain when a maid lives out. Most urban families, even when well-to-do, are short of living space. The availability of a maid who does not need accommodation may therefore be welcome. Moreover, the possibility of employing a part-time maid enables more families to afford domestic help.

Maids who rent their own homes and hire themselves out to clean or cook at an hourly rate are challenging not only the custom that servants should live in and work full-time for one family but the whole relationship of authority that went with the old system. Living independently, they pay for their own food and accommodation but earn more than they would if working for a single family and enjoy greater personal freedom. The arrangement encourages a sharper distinction between work and leisure. The hourly worker may work more intensively, but she can decide the hours she will work and her free time is more truly free. Her employers lose the paternalistic power to supervise her life and may not even know exactly where she lives.

We see therefore that domestic service has undergone considerable change in the 50 years of the People's Republic. The institution of domestic service was little questioned in the 1950s when many elite communist families employed maids in order to enable their women to work. It came under challenge and was often condemned during the Cultural Revolution. The economic reforms, the relaxation of the political climate, the growing number of prosperous dual career families, the single-child family policy, and the easing of restrictions on rural to urban migration all contributed to a considerable increase in domestic service. But maids in post-reform China differ in significant ways from their predecessors. They are young, mobile, and ready to change jobs in order to obtain better conditions. They expect to return one day to their home village and are thus anxious to maximize the benefits of their temporary migration.

Domestic Service and the Sending Areas

Boserup[20] observed that generally women are heavily involved in rural–urban migration where there is little for them to do in the villages. The Chinese case would appear to fit this view. Most migrants are male, but the numbers of female migrants appear to be increasing. Women migrate in large numbers from areas in Anhui and Sichuan where there is a huge surplus of rural labor, and unless there has been large-scale male migration, women play little part in agriculture. In Wuwei county, Anhui for example, there is so little land per capita that women ceased to work on the land because there was not enough agricultural work to keep all the members of peasant families busy.[21] Female hotel workers in Chengdu told the same story in interviews.[22] Their labor was not needed on the small plots their families farmed. Their parents did not expect them to remit money home. They were grateful merely to be relieved of the burden of feeding them.

Migration thus turns previously dependent young women who have been worth little in economic terms into earners who may greatly improve family living standards. Whether they are maids, factory workers, or service workers, through migration young women are enabled to make a material difference in the lives of relatives back home and in the lives they will live upon their return. Although in poor areas some of the money that migrants remit may be used for subsistence, much of it is set aside for house construction, wedding finance, and investment in setting up small enterprises. Wan reports that in Wuwei, Anhui, most households with migrant maids occupy conspicuously new and better houses than those without migrants. In 1988 a brick and cement house in Anhui cost 5–7000 yuan, far more than could be saved from the income from the land.[23] In the sending areas of Sichuan also, new homes mark out the villages and indeed the households from which migrants have left.

The earnings of migrants are also used to cover the increasing expenses of rural marriages. Marriage costs are a major expense for peasants in contemporary China. They were the second most important use of remittances after house building in Anhui, where at the beginning of the 1990s brideprice cost 3–4000 yuan and dowry ranged from a few hundred to 2000 yuan.[24] The man's family bears the greater share of the costs of marriage. Unmarried male migrants may save for their own weddings, but the earnings of unmarried women often go to help with their brother's marriage costs. Young women may also save the costs of their own dowries, thus relieving their families of a significant expense.[25]

When the young couple sets up a new household in the rural areas, much of the brideprice and the dowry go to finance the purchase of household goods. The earnings of migrants make it possible to increase both dowry and brideprice. Remittances sent back by migrants are also spent directly on consumer durables. The families of migrants are therefore more likely than other villagers to own bicycles, sewing machines, cassette recorders, televisions, and even videos.

When migrants return with money and skills they may often be able to turn these to their advantage. Many businesses in the sending areas are owned by returned migrants or by the families of migrant workers. Returned women workers in Sichuan have set up small dress-making concerns catering to local demand. Exceptional returned migrants may even be able to mobilize contacts in the destination area to set up more ambitious enterprises supplying or processing for plants there.[26] Capital, entrepreneurial know-how, and contacts outside the immediate area are all in short supply in the rural areas and migrants are likely to be at an advantage in obtaining them.

However, the impact of the movement of population backward and forward between the rural and urban areas is not limited to standards of living and consumption. Attitudinal change is another important consequence of population mobility and one in which maids are probably especially important. Caldwell has written, "Circular forms of movement, far more than permanent migration, have the potential of spreading new ideas, attitudes and knowledge to rural areas and contributing greatly to processes of social change."[27] Returning migrants hasten attitudinal change in the villages because they themselves have acquired new ideas and attitudes in the cities. But the influences received and the degree to which they are absorbed differ because individual experiences of migration are so different.

The strongest urban influences are surely absorbed by the young rural women who work as maids. Living within an urban family they become aware even of the most intimate details of their employers' lives. Their work is focused on care of the home, and often of children so that domestic arrangements, home furnishings, and consumer durables are all things of importance in their lives. They become accustomed to living with electricity, running water, and sanitation. They see a different model of marriage and family interaction, and a family setting in which low fertility is felt to be desirable. They observe urban life from the streets, from magazines, and from television and films, but also in their daily interactions.

The urban popular culture to which migrants are exposed through television, films, and popular magazines tends to cater to fantasies and to promote consumerism. It features people who are well-dressed and live in homes of far higher quality than ordinary Chinese, even in the urban areas, could realistically hope for. Fashion is dominant in magazines for women that also contain features on grooming, makeup, and hairstyles. Articles on film focus on appearance and romance. Where allusions are made to sex it is in the context of moral codes, happy marriages, or romance.

When young migrants return to the rural areas they have to readjust to life in a very different environment. The urban influences they have received may make the process difficult. They will push for changes that may be impossible to bring about. They reenter a household whose age-based hierarchy will mean for most of them the loss of the autonomy and independence that they had when they were away from home. If they were successful as migrants their earnings fall on their return. But the reintegration of these more fortunate migrants may be eased by the esteem accorded to them for the contributions they have made to family income and their knowledge of the outside world.

For many the most difficult adjustments are connected with the urban influences they have absorbed. The ideas they take back from the cities, whether about love or more companionate marriage, or about home comforts, consumer goods, and luxuries involve them in conflict and perhaps disappointment when they return to their rural lives. One of the most likely areas for conflict is marriage. In peasant society marriage is a family affair and marriage finance is supplied by the family. A bride is seen as a new daughter-in-law and a new member of the family just as much as she is a wife. Her health, character, and abilities, the contacts she will give her husband's kin, the brideprice her family require and the dowry she will bring are all matters of concern to her husband's family. Where young migrants have been influenced by an urban popular culture that promotes ideals of courtship, mutual attraction, and love matches, there may be conflicts over the arrangement of marriages.

The older generation may also disapprove of the extravagance of the young when returnees seek to furnish and equip their houses or dress themselves and their children according to their new tastes. Many returnees experience considerable difficulty in resettling in the countryside and deep frustration at the things they cannot change. Return migrants speak of their unhappiness at being criticized for their clothes and show a nostalgic longing for news about the cities. Wan Shanping noted the dislike felt by young women who had lived in the cities for rural latrines.[28] They found it hard to reaccustom themselves to these and other hardships that in their childhood they had taken for granted.

Young people who have worked in the city can often be distinguished from other villagers by their appearance. This is especially the case with the young women who wear brightly colored, more fashionable clothes, more expensive and less practical shoes, and sport modern hairstyles. Their appearance often seems to deny their current environment. In defiance of Chinese tradition they may sacrifice warmth and comfort for appearance. I recall seeing a young returned migrant in a village outside

Chengdu. She was sitting in her doorway knitting. It had been raining heavily and none of the roads in the village were made up. All around her was a sea of mud, yet she was wearing white high-heeled shoes made of thin leather. The distinctive appearance of the returnees makes them attractive as models for other young women.[29] In Anhui the desire to buy clothes was found to be an important motive for female migration.[30] The return of one cohort to the village reinforces the desire of the next to experience urban life and the movement of population is thus self-perpetuating.[31]

Conclusion

I have argued that domestic servants are an especially interesting migrant group in contemporary China, unique for the close contacts they have with the privileged urban population. Early in this chapter I recalled the numbers engaged in domestic service in Europe a century ago and the modernizing influence historians think they ultimately had on their communities. Domestic service in contemporary China does not compare in scale with Europe in that period. Maids make up only a very small proportion of the tens of millions of rural migrants who have left their village homes to seek work elsewhere in the past 20 years. But their numbers are not insubstantial and because they are drawn almost exclusively from a few limited areas, they can be expected to have a considerable influence on their home villages. This is a field that awaits thorough research. We may expect that because the particular conditions of the migration of maids brings them into close contact with urban lifestyles, values and family relationships, their expectations and hopes may have been changed in even more profound ways than those of other migrants to the cities. This will be expressed in the way they try to live when they return to their villages.

Notes

1. Delia Davin, "Delinquent, Ignorant and Stupid. Migrants in the Chinese Press," *China Perspectives* 9 (January/February 1997): 6–11; Dorothy Solinger, *Contesting Citizenship in Urban China: Peasant Migrants, the State and the Logic of the Market* (Berkeley: University of California Press, 1999).
2. Hein Mallee, "In Defence of Migration: Recent Chinese Studies of Rural Population Mobility," *China Information* X, 3–4 (Winter 1995–Spring 1996).
3. Diana Lary, "Hidden Migrations: Movement of Shandong People, 1949–1978," *Chinese Environment and Development* 7,1 and 2 (Spring-Summer 1996): 56–72; T. Scharping, "Urbanization in China since 1949: A Comment," *The China Quarterly* 109 (March 1987).

4. Xiang, Biao, "ZhejiangVillage in Beijing: Creating aVisible Non-state Space through Migration and Marketized Networks," in *Internal and International Migration: Chinese Perspectives,* eds Frank N. Pieke, and Hein Mallee (Richmond, Surrey: Curzon Press, 1999).

5. Jean Chesneaux, *The Chinese Labor Movement* (Stanford: Stanford University Press, 1968); E. Honig, *Sisters and Strangers: Women in the Shanghai Cotton Mills, 1919–1949* (Stanford: Stanford University Press, 1986); A. Knox, *Southern China: Migrant Workers and Economic Transformation* (London: Catholic Institute for International Relations, 1997).

6. Theresa MacBride, *The Domestic Revolution: The Modernization of Household Service in England and France 1820–1920* (London: Croom Helm, 1976): 14–15.

7. Abel Chatelain, "Migrations et domesticité féminine urbaine en France XIIIème-XXème siècles," (Migrations and woman's domestic service in the city in France XIIIth–XXth centuries) *Revue historique économique et sociale* 4 (1969); MacBride, *The Domestic Revolution.*

8. Wan, Shanping, *From Country to Capital: A Study of a Female Migrant Group in China,* unpublished M.Phil. thesis, Oxford Brookes University, 1992. In fact this migration chain seems to be much older than the New Fourth Army connection (Wan, *From Country to Capital*; Solinger, *Contesting Citizenship in Urban China,* 223).

9. Delia Davin, *Womanwork: Women and the Party in Revolutionary China* (Oxford: Oxford University Press, 1976): 184.

10. Chow, Ching-li, *Le Palanquin des larmes* (The palanquin of tears) (Paris: Opera Mundi, 1975); Cheo, EstherYing, *Black Country Girl to Red China* (London: Hutchinson, 1980); Cheng, Nien, *Life and Death in Shanghai* (London: Grafton, 1986); Chang, Jung, *Wild Swans Three Daughters of China* (London: Harper Collins, 1991);Yang, Rui, *Spider Eaters, A Memoir* (Berkeley: University of California Press, 1998).

11. *Zhongguo Funu* (Women of China) (1 September 1956).

12. Davin, *Womanwork.*

13. Fieldwork, Beijing, 1987.

14. Fieldwork, Beijing, 1987.

15. Heather Zhang, "Making a Difference in their Own Lives: Rural Women in the Urban Labor Market in North China," *Leeds. East Asian Papers* 50 (1997).

16. Fieldwork notes, Beijing, 1984.

17. Fieldwork, Beijing, 1987, 1994, 1995.

18. Fieldwork, 1987.

19. Fieldwork, Beijing, 1994.

20. Ester Boserup, *Women in Economic Development* (London: St Martin's Press, 1970).

21. Wan, *From Country to Capital:* 89–90.

22. Fieldwork interviews, 1994.

23. Wan, *From Country to Capital:* 95–96.

24. Wan, *From Country to Capital:* 97.

25. Wan, *From Country to Capital;* and fieldnotes, 1994.

26. Wan, *From Country to Capital:* 99–100.

27. J. C. Caldwell, *African Rural–Urban Migration: The Movement to Ghana's Towns* (Canberra: ANU Press, 1969): 45.

28. Wan, *From Country to Capital:* 106.

29. Fieldwork, 1994.

30. Wan, *From Country to Capital:* 58.

31. Young women in Jiangsu in the 1930s were similarly drawn to work in factories in the cities because they longed for the sort of clothes they saw women migrants wearing on their visits home. See, Zhang, Xinxin and Sang, Ye, *Chinese Lives: An Oral History of Contemporary China,* translated, edited and introduced by W.J.F. Jenner and Delia Davin (New York: Pantheon, and London: Macmillan, 1988). Chinese original published as *Beijing Ren* (Shanghai: Cultural Publishing House, 1986): 261.

CHAPTER SEVEN

Power beyond Instituted Power: Forms of Mediation Spaces in the Chinese Countryside

ISABELLE THIREAU AND HUA LINSHAN

Since the political and economic reforms carried out in the countryside, the nature of the relations established between grassroots levels of government and local inhabitants has been a core issue in many debates. The main concept usually mobilized to analyze such relationships is that of power, most studies trying to assess if the power detained by local cadres has declined or increased during the recent decades, or if its nature has changed.[1] Such a concept seems to be implicitly used in its Weberian acceptation. In other words, what is discussed is political power considered as the domination exercised by some men upon others and based on the use of legitimate violence, the concept of economic power being sometimes mentioned and coupled with that of political power. As a consequence, the analysis usually relies on an opposition or at least a dichotomy between local officials and the rest of the population. Moreover, the formal organs of power at the village level, namely the Party Branch and the Village Committee, appear to be the main relevant units of analysis, a focus also supported by the rising interest in village elections.[2]

A somehow different but complementary picture of power issues emerges when one tries to observe the political life at the village level, that is to look at how decisions regarding village affairs are taken and local rules elaborated. Fieldwork done in four villages (three located in Guangdong province and one in Anhui province) reveals first of all the diversity of possible answers to this question: all four villages exhibit quite different patterns regarding the number and the nature of the spaces where village common affairs are discussed, as well as the way the Village Committee and the Party Branch effectively perform their institutional roles according to the particular economic, political, and social context they are embedded in. Moreover, the observations made show that local issues are often discussed successively in a plurality of spaces more or less formally structured, including but not restricted to the formal organs of power. Within such spaces individuals mobilize their resources to judge the situation at stake and eventually influence the adoption of a given solution: they can indeed criticize past decisions, offer new arguments, clarify common references by comparing the legitimacy of the diverse principles claimed to be appropriate to solve a particular local issue, or organize further action. In other words, if power is rather understood as the capacity to participate in and influence local decisions regarding common affairs— a capacity of course unequally distributed—then new actors and new spaces, outside the formal organs of power, may become relevant units of analysis. At least, their presence and their impact in the four localities observed seems to call for a systematic questioning of their potential local relevance.

Such an approach emphasizes how formal decisions at the village level are increasingly the result of a process of negotiation, justification, or argumentation by villagers, a process that is supported by two main factors. First of all, the major political changes introduced at the end of the seventies, and which allow us to consider present Chinese society as belonging to a post-revolutionary stage, are characterized by the renouncement of the official claim that all transformations are possible and that irresistible historical forces exist. Such renouncement means as a consequence the possibility but also the necessity for social actors—whether they possess an official authority or not—to publicly exercise their capacity of judgment in order to evaluate situations, find relevant arguments to justify their decisions, legitimate their actions by identifying and mobilizing normative principles considered by others—at least to a certain extent—to be shared and acceptable. It was indeed the domination of exclusive ideological and normative concepts such as that of class struggle that legitimated officials to interfere in all aspects of social and economic life and support the public identification of given actions as right or wrong. Their dismissal has launched the need for a debate among members of the society—despite the constraints still prevailing—regarding what are reasonable, acceptable, or unacceptable words and actions, and leads to denying local officials any specific legitimacy in this realm.

Secondly, the diverse economic reforms introduced have encouraged a growing differentiation of interests and social positions, inside and

(tension w/ Solinger?)

outside the group of local cadres, involving the necessity to devise new rules, develop new practices, and create new institutions to coordinate complex social and economic exchanges and regulate local divergent interests. At the village level, such processes are usually carried out through a succession of face-to-face interactions and discussions, leading to confrontations, but also eventually to some form of common understanding of the situation. Moreover, in various localities, an increasing interdependence between cadres and other inhabitants, which is not fully captured by a classification according to economic criteria such as local enterprises ownership system, supports the need for some form of local negotiation.

It is not our aim to depict political life in the four villages observed as characterized by communal consensus, nor to posit that each local inhabitant has equal capacity to participate in local discussions and influence final decisions. Resorting to violence by local officials to protect their interests and positions, but also inertia or paralysis of local political life, has often been reported. However, it seems that another possible outcome of the present stage of post-revolutionary stabilization in Chinese villages is the multiplication of local mediation spaces where different ways to identify and manage common issues can be mobilized, confronted, and eventually combined, diverse links being established between the spaces coexisting in a single locality.

Without being able to discuss here in a rather systematic and detailed way the situation in each of the villages observed, we would like simply to introduce some of the spaces where various social groups, including local cadres, express their views, discuss the legitimacy of official decisions, develop alternatives—that is those spaces involving activities that in various ways complement but also influence those performed within the formal organs of power. To prevent any misunderstanding, it should be clearly stated that the analysis of these formal organs, their composition, the sources of their legitimacy as well as the content of their actions and decisions are obviously fundamental elements to understand political life at the village level. However, as stated before, the growing complexity and stratification of the rural society have supported the emergence of new social oppositions and alliances in which officials are deeply embedded. The growing autonomy of local inhabitants if compared with the pre-reform era has also increased their willingness to evaluate village leaders' actions while it created new patterns of mutual dependence. As a consequence, official decisions are more or less directly influenced by the advice and comments expressed outside the formal committees, as well as reflecting a variety of institutional constraints but also normative expectations, social obligations, and economic interests.

The social practices chosen here for discussion are far from being exhaustive. Moreover, their influence varies a lot according to localities. Five forms through which local policies may be elaborated, revised, or criticized are nonetheless distinguished in this chapter: the discussions held within all kinds of committees backed by official provisions; the gathering of punctual and somehow extraordinary village assemblies or meetings; the emergence of forms of organizations often acknowledged by local cadres but not supported by official policies; the consultation process of specific social actors developed under various circumstances by the leading organs of power; and finally the informal circulation of comments and advice regarding the legitimacy of the decisions taken and the way common affairs should be managed.

The Growing Number of Organizations
Backed by Official Provisions

With the transformation of administrative boundaries and the new autonomy assigned to the village unit, the number of official organizations that can exist in a village has enlarged. Part of these organizations are inherited from the previous collectivist system, while others are rather linked to the new policy launched after the reforms as well as to the new problems arising from it. To be sure, it is sometimes a simplification to put the organizations we are going to mention in the same category. As a matter of fact, we include here all kinds of committees or organizations that are supported by legal documents or official provisions. However, some of them are compulsory while others are not. Some may be created by officials while others have emerged out of some form of collective or concerted action from the part of villagers. Moreover, the local situation is often rather complex and requires one to make distinctions between organizations that bear the same name in various localities but are actually of a different nature: a rather traditional form of organization, such as a kinship, can for instance borrow the terminology of an official committee. One should therefore not only look at the name of these organizations but also at the main principles guiding their functioning to assign them a specific place in the local political scene.

We can first of all mention as examples of organizations backed by official provisions those listed by Yu Keping in the paper he wrote about Dongsheng village in Fujian province.[3] Among the 16 organizations (called in the paper *minjian zuzhi*) found by the author in this administrative village, 13 can be considered to be supported by some kind of official documents or incitement: the Village Committee (*cunmin weiyuanhui*); the Elders' Association (*laonian xiehui*); the Birth Control Association (*jihua shengyu xiehui*); the Youth League Branch (*tuan zhibu*); the Women Representatives' Committee (*nüdaihui*); the Committee for Security and Protection (*zhibaohui*); the Mediation Committee (*tiaojiehui*); the Economic Cooperative (*jingji hezuoshe*); the Research Committee on cereals and sugarcane and the Research Committee on fruit-trees (*liangzheyanjiuhui* and *guoshuyanjiuhui*); the Villagers' Militia (*cunmin bingying*); and three groups formally constituted but that gather only occasionally: the Villagers' Representatives (*cunmindaibiao*); the Group for the Public and Democratic Management of Village Affairs (*cunwu gongkai minzhu guanli gongzuo xiaozu*); and finally the Group for Financial Management (*cunmin licai xiaozu*). According to Yu Keping, although the Elders' Association is often in Fujian province an association based on kinship ties and representing different descent groups, the situation is different in Dongsheng where such a body is mainly involved in organizing cultural activities for women over 55 and men over 60 years old. The above list is of course far from being exhaustive. Other researchers have indeed noticed the development of organizations such as Committees for Diminishing Villagers' Burden (*jianfuhui*) or of Small Groups Against Corruption (*fanfubai xiaozu*), which are clearly the outcome of a local mobilization.[4] But the enumeration provided by Yu Keping, which concerns a single community, is nonetheless telling of the growing number of official organizations that may exist.

Such bodies supported by official provisions are often neglected or dismissed as playing a very limited part in today's local political life. The way they may directly or indirectly participate in debates and decision-making processes regarding village affairs is usually considered a rather irrelevant issue. It is not our claim to suggest that all these organizations do offer a venue for some kind of public discussion of local affairs. Many of them are mainly executive bodies or organizations controlled by local cadres. Yu Keping in his article mentions for instance that most of the committees described are headed by the 42 Party members of Dongsheng. However, such assemblies may sometimes be recognized as the leading role in the management of village affairs. This is the case for instance in Beiwang village (Hebei province), a locality studied by Susan Lawrence[5] where the Villagers' Representatives Assembly rather than the Village Committee constitutes the highest authority. This assembly meets once every month and has been assigned five defined functions: to make decisions affecting all households, to supervise the Village Committee, to remove if necessary some of its members, to oppose wrong decisions taken by this committee, and finally to write the codes of conduct. It may also be the case that one of these official organizations is involved in devising and heading some form of collective action. For instance, in August 2001, the Villagers' Representatives of Tan village in Shunde county (Guangdong province) organized the sitting of some 2,000 residents at the entrance of the village in order to publicize two main requests: they wanted to be allowed to supervise village accounts, and they asked for genuine village elections to be held.[6]

However, even when these official organizations do not play a leading role, their multiplication means a multiplication of the spaces where discussions are held regarding village affairs, and further actions may be elaborated. It means also that a growing segment of the population is formally assigned the possibility to participate to such discussions.

Let us consider for instance Mulan, one of the four natural villages observed. Mulan, located in Panyu county, is considered since Guangdong province adopted the national appellation an "administrative village," which had in 2000 a population of 1,361 persons. The 281 households are dominated by the members of three surname groups: Li, Luo, and Jia. Three Party secretaries only have run Mulan since 1959: the first one was in charge of local affairs from 1959 to 1986, the second one remained in this position from 1986 until 1992, while the third one was nominated in 1992 just in time to supervise the dramatic changes implied by the land expropriation carried out in 1993 in order to establish a new economic development zone. A compensation of 12,000 yuan was paid for each *mu* of land expropriated, plus another compensation fee for the former private plots. About 50 percent of the total amount of compensation fees were redistributed to the households, the remaining sum of about 14 million yuan being managed by village officials to support local economic development. The Village Committee and the Party Branch are in Mulan one and the same body. Party members elect five members for the Party Branch, the positions within the Party Branch and the Village Committee being then distributed among the five elected individuals. It should be added that although since 1993 both the village head named Li and the Party secretary named Jia have been trying to take initiatives and promote the village economic development, both of them have failed due partly to their attempts to privilege their own kin in these economic endeavors. The two men, both Party members, indeed fought for the position of Party secretary, each supported by different groups at the upper level. If the Party secretary named Jia maintained his dominant position after the recent elections, both men still run local affairs although they seldom address each other. Each of their attempts in the economic field has nonetheless been met by the fierce opposition of the rival, who was generally able to make the whole project collapse. Such hostility culminated during the summer of 1998 when the new Party Branch was to be elected, as the Party secretary was criticized by his enemy for having promoted 13 of his kinsmen as new Party members during the previous years.

Besides this leading organ of power combining both the Party Branch and the Village Committee and within which competition is fierce, six official organizations do exist in Mulan: the Villagers' Representatives Assembly, the Committee for Security and Protection, the Committee for Economic Development, the Group for Financial Management, the Mediation Committee, and finally the Committee of Women's Representatives, each of these two last organizations constituted in 2001 by a single person. Some of these bodies play a rather limited formal part in local affairs but are quite active informally. The Villagers' Representatives for instance (as well as the old Party members actually) resent the fact that they are very rarely convened by village leaders to discuss local affairs. The strategy often mobilized by village leaders confronted with the growing number of organizations supposed to supervise their work is indeed to try to prevent their members from launching formal discussions. However, some Villagers' Representatives in Mulan participate in many of the informal debates carried out in the village. They help identify and formulate the problems and requests of the "masses," problems and requests that they will then transmit to local officials, repeated pressures being made on these officials to solve the issue at stake.

Other spaces play a formal and important part in the local political life. Some questions are for instance debated successively within the Village Committee and the Committee for Economic Development. Although the Party secretary is officially assigned a leading role in both bodies, the heads of the second organization include non-Party members such as individuals who enjoy economic and social resources enabling them to eventually attract investors. Some of these persons are rather highly considered for their success by villagers who, on the other hand, resent the Party secretary actions. In other words, they are partly supported by a segment of the population that does not overlap with the Party secretary followers. During discussions held within the Committee for Economic Development, such successful Mulan inhabitants clearly consider their own economic interests but cannot neglect those of their supporters. In other words, although they do not act as official representatives of other residents, they introduce within the discussions the interests and positions of local inhabitants that the Party secretary, acting alone, would eventually neglect. However, after land was expropriated, the Party secretary became quite dependent upon these successful private entrepreneurs to find the needed resources to meet collective expenses and cannot therefore completely ignore their suggestions.

But the organization that has clearly gained authority among most villagers is the Group for Financial Management. As mentioned earlier, when land was expropriated, village officials kept 50 percent of the compensation fees to develop collective economy. Three companies were created with outside investors but all of them failed. The right to operate four stone-pits in the village was assigned to outsiders also in exchange for the payment of part of the benefits. However, such payments have been rather low. Moreover, four years after the expropriation took place the amount of the compensation fees kept by village officials to promote local economy had vanished.

> In 1998, we had enough. How could it be that each company had failed? How could it be that each year each of the four stone-pits made almost no benefits? There was a lot of talk going on in the village, a lot of discontent. … Actually, people often come to me in Mulan to express their discontent. … I knew something had to be done. I had read about Groups for Financial Management in other places so we decided to create such a group. We first considered a few persons that could join the group and then told the Villagers' Committee about the willingness of the masses to create such a group. We talked about the support of the Government for such committees … Finally, they had to call a village assembly and the group was formed … .[7]

It should be added that the primary-school teacher speaking above and other inhabitants of Mulan had already been quite active during the compensation movement, organizing collective actions to express their claims for higher compensation as well as for a more balanced distribution of the compensation fees between households and the village as a unit. Besides this teacher, two persons were chosen to join the group: a retired doctor and a villager about 40 years old, having finished secondary school when he was young.

Although the Group for Financial Management cannot really supervise village accounts, it creates some pressure on the leading organ of power. Moreover, its members are highly considered by many local inhabitants who will often turn to them to express their discontent and discuss alternative ways to meet village expenses. While the group is restricted to three people, its presence supports and therefore influences many of the informal debates going on among a much wider group of people in all kinds of informal places in Mulan. Moreover, the authority gained by this group has forced since 1998 village cadres to "give face" to its members by consulting them formally over important local issues.

In Ping'an village, located in Taishan county (Guangdong province), another official organization is actually playing an important part: the Elders' Association. Ping' an is a single-surname village comprised of about 63 households in 2001, which formed under the people's commune two production teams.[8] As was the case in many localities of Guangdong until 1998, the former brigade was called an "administrative district" (*guanli qu*) and Ping'an was just considered a village, actually headed by a Village Committee. Since 1998, Ping'an is officially considered a "peasants' small group" (*cunmin xiaozu*), but it actually preserved the rather extended independence from the former brigade that natural villages developed in Guangdong after the reforms. One seven *mu* pond rented by auction forms the main collective resource of the village, most of the village expenses actually being met by the contributions sent by overseas relatives. Besides the Village Committee, three other official organizations exist in Ping'an: the Elders' Association, the Cultural Association, and the Security Team. The Elders' Association—as well as the Cultural Association—is located in one of the village ancestors' temples, which became a place for village meetings after the temple was deemed to be collective property. Most members of the Elders' Association are men playing mah-jong together in the afternoon. While playing, they often discuss village affairs, evaluate past decisions, debate about what could be done to improve the village environment or economic activities. They also tell each other what other residents have been saying in other settings about the issue at stake. Through repeated discussions, they eventually reach some form of agreement on certain matters, which will then be reported to the village head: "We, the old people, support you on this issue ..."; "We, the old people, believe that ... ."[9] The support or criticisms expressed by such body are clearly taken into account by the village head as well as by other local organizations.

Official organizations outside the formal organs of power are often, it is true, firmly controlled by local cadres and by various types of local élites using such channels to protect their mutual interests. However, this should not encourage observers to automatically dismiss the relevance of the debates and negotiations held within such organizations. As a matter of fact, in villages characterized by absence of collective economic resources to be controlled by local cadres like Ping'an or, on the contrary, in villages where local élites are highly diversified like Mulan, influential discussions and decisions may eventually be carried out within such spaces. More pointedly, the transformations brought about by the reforms imply a transformation of the part played by these official organizations: faced with the absence of clear guidelines from above constraining the management of village affairs, faced with the variety of arguments that can be now mobilized to identify what is right under certain circumstances, faced with the diversity of interests developing within one single community, many of these organizations cannot be only executive bodies: they are also spaces where discussions are held, contradictory positions are confronted, and as such they may influence to a certain degree the decision-making process in a village. Moreover, members of these leading organs of power usually know that important local issues will also be discussed by villagers within other existing spaces, more or less formally structured. Therefore, they often try to anticipate the outcome of such debates when having to reach a decision.

The Gathering of Village Assemblies and Meetings

Another venue for public debate consists of the assemblies and meetings convened under certain circumstances to discuss village affairs. If such spaces exist by definition on temporary grounds and are not formally structured, they may offer an opportunity for most villagers to express their viewpoints, since all inhabitants or one representative by household are usually invited to participate. Here also, as was the case for official organizations, one cannot identify general rules that would be valid for all localities. Our aim is only to point out the fact that village assemblies can play an important part in the local political life. This at least is what we witnessed in the village of Honglong during a few months running from September 1996 to June 1997. Honglong village is located in Nanhai county (Guangdong province). Composed of 52 households in 2001, it formed one single production team under the people's commune.[10] The main collective resource of the village is composed of its 85 ponds, which are rented by auction to Honglong inhabitants every five years, an annual rent being paid by the families operating a pond to the Village Committee. In 2001, four enterprises run by outsiders also paid a rent to the village for the land occupied. The situation in Honglong has been particularly complex as far as leading organs of power are concerned. Since the reforms, the village has indeed been headed by what was locally called until 1998 a Village Committee composed of three people: the head of the committee, an accountant, and a villager in charge of women and social affairs. Beginning in 1994, a reform was launched in Nanhai county: shareholding companies were to be created at the level of the former brigade in order to run all collective property. Such companies would be responsible for renting villages' land, managing the amounts of money thus gathered and, more generally speaking, coordinating local development. Part of the benefits would be redistributed to the villages to meet specific needs as well as to local inhabitants, each inhabitant being a shareholder in the company. In order to prepare such reform, a "board of administrators" (*dongshihui*) formed of six people was elected in Honglong in June 1994. These were the first genuine elections carried out in Honglong. The villager who received the most votes and who was as a consequence labeled "head of the board" was someone considered by the villagers to enjoy a rather high level of culture, to possess good technical skills regarding fish-breeding, and to be daring: he was detained for a few years in 1962 for involvement in petty capitalism activities. The village accountant was also elected to this board, but the village head was not. During more than two years, the situation in Honglong remained plagued with uncertainties: the village head was no longer called to participate in meetings at the upper administrative level but he still possessed the village seals and other documents necessary to run local affairs. In May 1996, the Village Committee was officially dismissed and the board of administrators appointed as leading organ of power in Honglong. Its duties were nonetheless to begin only in February 1997, once the reform would begin to be enforced and the village ponds would be redistributed.

To explain the reform to Honglong villagers, a first village assembly was convened by the former brigade and headed by two of its leaders. This assembly paved the way to a succession of meetings that deeply influenced the management of local affairs. If village public discussions are often feared by local officials, it is indeed because such gatherings may give rise to a process of denunciation of what are considered to be officials' wrongdoings. This is exactly what happened in Honglong on September 8, 1996. During the meeting, villagers expressed their refusal to consider the reform at stake if past unsolved issues were not settled. Moreover, they denied the legitimacy of the *guanliqu* officials to head such a reform on various grounds: these officials had for instance never considered Honglong truly part of the district, a discrimination illustrated by the fact that the village was the only one to have no running water; they had taken past economic initiatives that had all failed; they had often selected irrelevant criteria to collect fees, such as asking villages to contribute to the building of a new primary school according to the surface of land cultivated by the villages and not to their population while, as one inhabitant argued, "individuals and not fields go to school."[11] Whatever the context and the particular arguments mobilized, formal assemblies often witness such public evaluation of the way power has been exercised by local officials. All kinds of unfulfilled normative expectations and unachieved objectives are thus expressed that, once clearly and publicly stated, affect in various ways how local authorities will run local affairs as well as how local inhabitants will cooperate with them.

But such assemblies are not only a place to voice one's anger: they can eventually influence the decisions of upper administrative levels. As far as Honglong is concerned, the two meetings successively organized to explain the reform to local inhabitants met with such fierce opposition (and the same happened in all the villages of the former brigade) that the township government decided to postpone the reform. It should be noted that villagers did not contest during the meetings the reform itself, but rather expressed their lack of confidence in the capacity of the brigade officials to run such a company, and they also criticized one particular aspect of the reform. The reform project as described by the officials implied that households, besides paying an annual rent for the ponds, would remit just after the auctions 20 percent of the annual rent for each pond operated to the shareholding company, an amount of money that would be paid back to them five years later, that is during the next redistribution process. Villagers asked to be paid the interest stemming from such banking deposits.

Village meetings can also end up modifying the composition of official organs of power. Thanks to the assemblies held in Honglong and to the informal exchanges within the village that followed, most of the villagers found out that they were also dissatisfied with the head of the board of administrators and developed the needed cohesion to express their criticisms. Eventually, a new assembly ended up with the resignation of the head of the board of administrators. On November 25, 1996, a village meeting aimed at determining a minimum bid for each pond was gathered. While the head of board had just mentioned the name of a first pond and was waiting for villagers' opinion regarding an acceptable minimum bid, a villager rose to his feet and shouted "40,000 yuan!" This was obviously not a serious proposal. The bidding process stopped immediately, which was the aim of such an intervention, while another resident added: "Past issues have not been settled; what was to be done has not been done, how can we just go on distributing the ponds?" The head of the board of administrators to whom these words were addressed rose to his feet, took the wooden box containing the name of the ponds and threw it into the nearest pond. A few minutes later, he was back with a long firecracker. Having lit it, he walked away without a word. Everyone understood his message: he had just resigned from his position. Most of the villagers stayed in the building where the meeting had been convened and began to voice their grievances against him. Among them was the fact that two main issues had not been solved since 1994: the installation of running water and the recovery of a main road belonging to the village but occupied by a few households coming from outside and collecting used plastic items.

Finally, it should be added that such assemblies can eventually replace local organs of power in making decisions regarding local affairs. Let us mention here another meeting observed in Honglong. One day in 1995, the heads of a few households coming from Guangxi province who had recently moved to the villages asked the villager in charge of women's affairs if their children could attend the village nursery. As a matter of course, this would allow the children's mothers to participate more quietly in all kinds of economic activities. Since the Village Committee had to find an appropriate answer to such a request, its members began to talk about it informally with village inhabitants. The reactions gathered were nonetheless so passionate and antagonistic that an assembly of household representatives was convened to reach a consensus on the issue. The debates carried out during the meeting were very intense. Not only did they allow the expression by various individuals of a diversity of arguments concerning the important issues of village membership and distribution of collective rights, but they ended up by reaching an agreement that the village leaders acknowledged and applied: migrants' children could be accepted at the nursery on the grounds that "everyone is a human being," but their parents would be required to pay higher monthly fees to the village than Honglong inhabitants, increasing as a consequence the village collective fund and the well-being of its members.[12] The interests of the village as a community were therefore safeguarded, an argument that proved very useful to convince those who opposed attendance of migrants' children to the local nursery. This is one among many examples illustrating the fact that such assemblies are sometimes a space where village inhabitants exercise their capacity to engage in a public discussion and make decisions affecting the material and nonmaterial environment in which they coexist.

Of course, as shown in the examples above, as soon as such assemblies are convened, they tend to become spaces where the validity and legitimacy of the decisions taken by village or higher authorities are questioned. This is why local officials are often reluctant to call them. Fieldwork observations reveal indeed that in many localities tensions do exist between village leaders who do not wish such meetings to take place and those inhabitants who contest officials' actions and decisions and want opportunities for public discussions. As a consequence, village assemblies are very rare in these localities. However the absence of such assemblies does not always reflect a kind of political passivity. The efforts displayed by officials to prevent any type of public discussion as well as those displayed by villagers by means of all kinds of provocations to launch such a debate may indeed be quite intense. They actually reveal the potential impact of the words expressed and the actions performed under these circumstances. One should add that the risks involved in the gathering of such assemblies are actually considered so great that they are explicitly mobilized by some local governments to explain the absence of elections of Village Committees. Leaders in one county of Hebei province mentioned, for instance, the contradictions that existed according to them between the policy of village elections and the other official requirement regarding local stability.[13] As a matter of fact, the work of the leading officials at the provincial level is mainly evaluated according to the results obtained in two areas: birth control and what is called "global governance," or *zonghe zhili*, which, broadly put, means the capacity to maintain social order. Negative achievements in these two fields can lead to officials' dismissal.[14] The main criteria used to judge the level of social order achieved is the absence of major demonstrations, collective complaints, or any kind of important social unrest. Officials at county and township levels are also evaluated according to these two criteria, to which are added the collection of taxes, the building of the Party, and the degree to which financial capital has been attracted to the locality. As a result, a special interpretation of the Organic Law prevails in that particular county: to preserve social order, elections of Village Committees are held only when villagers' anger regarding their cadres is so great that all other means to solve the situation have failed. If the situation is not that tense, the township authorities nominate, after a consultation process including various individuals and groups, the main village officials. In order to avoid using the word "nomination," or *renming*, such authorities speak of a simple "adjustment" (*tiaozheng yi xia*). As a matter of fact, to organize village elections appears for many officials as a threat to social order: angry villagers who have not been given other opportunities to express their discontent may use the needed meetings to prepare the elections to voice their anger regarding not only village officials but also upper-level cadres.

As a result, in the villages where the relationships between local leadership and at least part of the inhabitants are strained, cadres may develop a strategy of avoidance of village residents or accept compromises because they want to prevent public meetings being held. In other words, they are encouraged to engage in some form of cooperation with villagers in order to prevent a particular controversial issue from escalating into an articulated conflict and from offering an opportunity for a public discussion. There is no need therefore for a meeting to be effectively held to have some influence on the way power is exercised: the potential threat inherent to the calling of such assemblies is clearly understood both by those who hold official positions and by the other inhabitants, and as such it bares some impact on their relationship as well as on the influence they can mutually exercise.

The Emergence of Village Organizations
Not Backed by Official Provisions

The third type of space discussed here is not prevalent in all villages, but fieldwork shows that it exists in many more localities than usually thought. It includes all kinds of village organizations, unofficial as far as state authorities are concerned but very formal from local inhabitants and local cadres' perspectives. These bodies are often anchored in religious, kinship, or economic spheres. Some of them may be called traditional in the sense that the source of their legitimacy lies in practices or institutions linked to the pre-1949 period. However, they are not traditional if such expression is supposed to mean that they are similar to organizations that existed in the past. As a matter of fact, they do not represent mere forms inherited from the past but rather the mobilization on present terms—that is bearing the influence of the Maoist period as well as that of post-reform transformations—of past arrangements and principles.

Yu Keping lists in his article on Dongsheng village two organizations of this type: the Fund for endowment (*jijinhui*), which actually lends money to local inhabitants, and the Temple Association or *miaohui*. Among many studies describing this kind of organization, one can also mention the observations made by Liu Xiaojing[15] who has shown the importance of kinship organizations in Hebei province. Such organizations (which gather in multi-surname villages only part of the village population) hold regular meetings to solve internal disputes as well as conflicts between kinship groups. Depending on the issue at stake, a smaller body can be constituted that includes the main leaders of these kinship organizations, but also local

cadres members of these kinship groups, as well as other village residents
related for one reason or another to the problem being discussed. Such
bodies, which will meet until the issue is solved, actually borrow a rather
bureaucratic appellation since they are called "bureaus." The same issue
can therefore be successively discussed, or discussed back and forth,
within the Party Branch and within these kinship organizations (either
during bureaus or wider assemblies). Although some individuals participate in both gatherings, their respective positions are not identical within
both spaces, nor is it identical the hierarchy of arguments considered to
be valid and appropriate.

Three out of the four villages observed possess such forms of organization: a Temple Association has been created recently in Mulan, a
Committee for the Dragon-Boat Festival plays an important part in
Honglong, while Ping'an has seen the emergence of a Committee for the
Village Embellishment. However, the distribution of power between the
formal organs of power and such organizations differs widely among
the villages considered.

In Mulan, the Temple Association was created in 1997. It was preceded
by a succession of incidents and failures of private economic initiatives
that appeared to be progressively interpreted by residents as the consequence of the absence of any temple in the village. This issue was discussed in various settings. Finally, the Village Committee (and Party
Branch) agreed to the request made by a segment of the population to
build a new temple where the former one used to stand. The Party secretary actually played a major part in convincing the village resident whose
land had to be taken away to build the temple to agree to this project, and
in finding an appropriate compensation for him (only 80 percent of the
village land had been expropriated in 1992, and households still enjoy the
right to use some land for domestic purposes around the house or to grow
vegetables). However, although the Temple Association is recognized and
somehow supported by local organs of power, such a body composed of
a few old people is mainly in charge of religious activities.

In Honglong, the Committee for the Dragon-Boat Festival, which was
under the same name as the leading body of the village before 1949, has
resumed its activities during the eighties. If it has not recovered its former
position, it cooperates to a certain extent with the Village Committee to
run local affairs. For instance, officially speaking, the Committee for the
Dragon-Boat Festival is only in charge of organizing the festival, which
is now held on October 1 and is performed with three other neighboring villages.[16] However, it can also support local expenses such as restor-
ing village roads and bridges when the collective fund is not sufficient,

a support that implies some form of discussion and agreement between the members of both committees. It should be added that coordination between these two bodies was facilitated during the nineties by the fact that the head of the village was also a member of the Committee for the Dragon-Boat Festival. Generally speaking, it can be said that although this last organization does not rely on specific traditional principles (actually, its present leader used to be the vice-head of the production team and often mobilizes normative principles anchored in the Maoist period), it represents a space where the actions engaged are characterized by a willingness to support horizontal links within the community, as well as to preserve it from state or upper administrative levels' interference. In other words, the discussions held and the decisions taken within this space participate in the tentative delineation of a private sphere at the local level. For instance, part of the village's collective land has been somehow "privatized" and assigned to the Committee for the Dragon-Boat Festival. As a matter of fact, in 1986 the heads of this organization obtained the right from the Village Committee to be remitted the annual benefits stemming from the renting of the two ponds and the few *mu* of land that formed the village common property before 1949. To justify their claim, they explained that it appeared reasonable to use "the benefits stemming from collective property for this common activity." The decision finally adopted did not deny the collective property rights over these ponds and parcels of land but recognized the present right of usage held by this specific committee on a past common property. It is easy to argue that in the absence of this unofficial organization, such a claim would not have been made, such a debate would not have been held, and such a new norm governing village assets would not have emerged.

Moreover, when the reform previously described regarding the creation of a shareholding company was mentioned in the area, some Honglong residents argued that they would not let the former brigade manage the few ponds that used to be common property before 1949 because "these ponds belong to Honglong village and not to Honglong production team." The words "village" and "production team" actually designate the same social unit, but in this sentence the village as a local community is opposed to the production team as the lowest unit of the vertical administrative system established under collectivization.

That the Committee for the Dragon-Boat Festival is the place where horizontal links between local inhabitants but also between neighboring villages is assessed and protected can also be observed by listening to the main criticism actually raised against the head of the board of administrators and tending to his resignation. One day in September 1996, two months before his resignation, he was asked by some residents from a neighboring village to explain the preparations done in Honglong for the coming festival; the head of the board had replied that this was none of his business. Moreover he had been absent during the whole festival. One villager explained just after he resigned: "We are not asking him to head the festival, to be in charge of it, but this is one of the most important common issues in the village, how can he act as if all this had nothing to do with him and still decide about village affairs?"

Another one was even more explicit: "The festival, it is linked to the village temple, to the village as a group if you want. How can you defend our interests above if you don't care about village affairs?"[17]

In Ping'an, a Committee for the Village Embellishment (*cunrong weiyuanhui*) was created at the beginning of the nineties. Its composition reflects a fundamental concern for kinship ties: each of the four lineage segments existing in the village are represented by one or two individuals. As was the case before 1949, the village leadership emerges therefore out of a process bringing together the main leaders of each segment. However, it would be misleading to believe that such an organization functions the way former lineage councils operated. As a matter of fact, the committee members have not been chosen out of their support for the lineage as an institution but for their capacity, demonstrated in the past, to act in defence of the villagers' interests. For instance, they include today the person in charge of Ping'an during the collectivization process. Moreover, the decisions taken by the committee are often the outcome of a combination of principles and rules, anchored in different periods of Chinese history but also in different realms: national provisions, social norms, and local practices are indeed mobilized to run village affairs. Such a committee has nonetheless become the leading organ of power in Ping'an. The so-called Village Committee, although associated with many discussions, often acts as a mere executive body. More pointedly, a decision of the Village Committee that would not enjoy the support of the Committee for the Village Embellishment would be rather difficult to enforce.

The existence of these organizations illustrates once again the multiplication of the mediation spaces that characterizes some Chinese villages nowadays, a phenomenon that cannot but influence power relationships. Within such spaces, village affairs are indeed given another opportunity to be evaluated by other segments of the population. Negotiations parallel to those existing within more official bodies are led, compensation mechanisms are found, alliances or divisions are reinforced. Moreover, the debates carried out mobilize arguments eventually different from the official ones and illustrate the recognition of other forms of authority than those stemming from the occupation of an official position.

The Consultation Process Initiated by Village Leaders

We are dealing here with a practice that is not linked to any clearly delineated space and that is often characterized by a lack of publicity and visibility. It concerns indeed the growing tendency of some village leaders to take the advice of given individuals or groups before making a decision while no official rule or policy requires them to do so.

Such form of consultation process was actually well-established before 1949; village or lineage leaders but also heads of specialized institutions such as Chambers of Commerce often required the opinion of individuals within or outside the group who might help them solve a particular issue by providing their advice, information, or expert knowledge.[18] Moreover, it was not abandoned after 1949. Many village leaders under the collectivist era would indeed solicit former cadres and rely on their experience to help them appreciate the situation and make relevant decisions.[19] This kind of consultation process seems nonetheless to have become increasingly frequent in many localities after the economic reforms. Although it can lead to the formation of a new body appointed by village cadres whose opinion will be requested on important issues concerning the village development, such as the Committee of Talented Men mentioned by Yu Keping in his article, it is usually carried out on informal terms.

The advice of given residents may be sought out by official leaders for a variety of reasons. Such a gesture can indeed be done in order to increase the legitimacy of the decisions taken by official bodies. In Honglong for instance, three members of the Village Committee during the nineties used to invite two former village cadres to their meetings when important issues were discussed. They did so explicitly to add more "representativeness" (*daibiaoxing*) to the debate as well as to the decision taken. The meetings were usually held in the shop run by the woman in charge of social affairs and any villager could actually join the discussions.[20]

The same process has been observed in Mulan. When elections were held during the summer of 1998 to choose the new Party Branch, it was decided at the township level that in order to increase the "representativeness" of the new branch (and therefore of the new Village Committee), residents besides the Party members should be consulted over the list of preferred candidates. While during the previous elections of the Party Branch the list of such candidates had been established after a discussion involving only officials at the township level and village Party members,[21] several meetings this time were held under the direction of a township official. The various groups successively met by those heading the elections in Mulan were the old Party members, the young Party members, the Group for Financial Management, the private entrepreneurs of the village (whether their enterprises were located within or outside the village), and the residents who had contracted some collective property. It should be added that, as already stated, to promote economic development and achieve given collective tasks, village and township leaders often need the material and nonmaterial support of successful local economic actors. One way to achieve this purpose is to make residents a party to the decision-making process about local affairs. Such a process of consultation is usually informal as seen above, but it can also take the form of the constitution of a formal body like the Committee for Economic Development in Mulan. In other words, the dependent position of some village leaders upon given individuals or groups may encourage the first ones to "give face" to the second ones by requiring their opinion on different matters. Another mechanism stemming from the same logic but departing nonetheless from the various forms that consultation processes may assume is to integrate these residents to the leading organs of power.

Such an informal procedure of consultation—as well as the formal integration of successful residents to leading organs of power—may of course end up encouraging some form of collusion between village cadres and local economic élites. In Dongtu administrative village (Hebei province), whose population amounted in 1997 to 861 individuals, there were in the same year 48 enterprises employing a minimum of four persons and a maximum of 200 persons. Some of these enterprises are private while others have been contracted to local inhabitants. As in Mulan, the Party Branch and the Village Committee are one and the same body and new Party members are mainly chosen among entrepreneurs on the explicit but contradictory grounds that they "represent the masses" (*daibiao qunzhong*) and "can lead the villagers to prosperity" (*daidong cunmin zhifu*). As a consequence, entrepreneurs and officials clearly exercise a monopoly on village official positions in order to prevent other individuals who might not share their interests to decide about local affairs.[22] However, consultation mechanisms of local residents on economic or other local issues do not systematically hide such situations. In villages such as Ping'an and Honglong, the individuals whose advice is required often enjoy limited economic success but are considered to have an expertise and knowledge in various fields, or are simply recognized as smarter than others. More importantly, such residents are supported within the village by a group of persons who have progressively acknowledged their capacities. They can therefore, if they agree on a given issue with formal leaders, arouse somehow automatically the support of a much wider segment of the village population to the leader's decision.

As a matter of fact, the diversity witnessed today in Chinese villages concerning the normative principles and rules deemed to be appropriate and reasonable under certain circumstances, as well as the diversity of social positions and economic interests, imply new uncertainties concerning the identification and management of common affairs. It implies also that various individuals outside the formal organs of power may enjoy some form of authority upon at least given segments of the population thanks to their specific social or economic resources. Local cadres can therefore choose to seek the approval of those residents regarding the adoption of a specific rule or measure that will then have a chance to be supported by various groups within the village.

Consultation processes may thus be carried out to increase the legitimacy of village cadres' decision, to consider other arguments and identify a more valid perspective, to get the material but also nonmaterial support of locally influential individuals, and to get the adhesion of local inhabitants to the decision adopted, and so on. Such a mechanism can also be adopted when village leaders want to be sure that villagers encourage, or at least do not disavow, one of their initiatives in a situation where gathering a village meeting may be difficult. For instance, in Honglong village, the head of the Village Committee launched a consultation process during the first weeks of 1995 with various members of the village—former cadres, specialized households in fish-breeding, residents having privileged links with upper authorities—to ascertain whether he should join other villages' leaders in their public denunciation of local Party members who did not pay the needed annual rents for the ponds they operated. The outcome of the various discussions and consultations held actually was positive.[23]

For a variety of reasons—some of them stated above—village leaders often choose therefore to contact specific residents and require their opinions on given issues, or at least make sure that they will not oppose a particular official decision. Fieldwork reveals that the time thus spent to seek the advice of different individuals may actually be quite important. As mentioned earlier, this kind of consultation process may be considered as the opposite of a common space of discussion. Its initiative lies indeed in local cadres and all individuals concerned do not have equal access to it. Such a process often tends to reproduce and consolidate the new social stratification existing within the village. Moreover, although it takes various forms, from private and rather confidential discussions to semi-public gatherings in a township restaurant, for instance, where the discussions will be held under the scrutiny of all kinds of witnesses and commentators, the whole process is usually characterized by a low degree of publicity and visibility. If it is true that this form of consultation may cover the exchange of goods and services between some village leaders and given individuals or groups and, as a consequence, protect first of all both parties' interests, it would be misleading to interpret this type of practice only from such a perspective. It should be remembered indeed that villages represent a social space characterized by mutual knowledge of all members of the group, as well as by a history of support or conflict between households over generations. Residents' preferences and expectations are therefore expressed in different ways in different settings. More pointedly, disagreements with other village residents over specific issues may not always be easy to express in rather formal and public settings, as shown by Liu Shiding.[24] As a result, one possible way to grasp the variety of opinions held on a given matter and to establish a form of consensus may be to engage in a consultation process involving successively various individuals.

To capture the form and intensity of local consultation practices is therefore an important means to apprehend effective power relationships, as well as to observe how final decisions emerge out of a specific process of argumentation and negotiation. A continuum can indeed be established between, on the one hand, places where village officials such as Party secretaries decide alone in a rather authoritarian way about village affairs and those, on the other hand, where such officials instead transmit decisions eventually taken or at least largely influenced by others. From the institutional point of view, both officials enjoy the same power. But as far as the effective power relationships and the decision-making process regarding village affairs are concerned, these two situations are very different.

The Informal Circulation of Comments and Alternative Proposals

This fifth and last issue concerns the influence on local discussions and decisions of the variety of opinions and criticisms raised informally within the village. Within small territorial units such as villages, comments and evaluations are indeed made about officials' actions in all kinds of spaces ranging from private spaces like houses to public spaces such as restaurants or shops. One cannot actually spend a few days in a given locality without witnessing discussions evaluating and often criticizing officials' actions. More or less reliable information is often simultaneously spread and alternatives to the official choices are expressed. It is not rare to see villagers on such occasions raising rather than lowering their voices, as if they wanted to be sure that their words would be heard and reported. These are obviously very general comments and once more situations vary a lot in this realm: one should look at specific contexts to measure the role eventually played by such informal, indirect moments of contestation.

It should be noted, however, that in all four villages under study such informal spaces of discussion play a rather important part in local political life. Moreover, in Lijiacun, the village located in Anhui province where fieldwork has been done, which has not been mentioned until now, debates and discussions are not carried out in official or nonofficial organizations that simply do not exist besides the formal organs of power, but on such premises. Concerted action of local residents is also devised through a succession of informal talks taking place in various parts of the village.

Informal talks and discussions are important channels to publicize and more pointedly to make known to village cadres local opinions about specific issues. For instance, in early January 1997, a village assembly was called in Honglong to discuss the coming redistribution process of local ponds. It had been the practice in past years not to allow a family who had already won the right to operate one of the village ponds to make a bid on a second pond while other households had no pond. In other words, each household should have acquired the right to operate one pond before candidates could express their wishes regarding the remaining ponds. However, the population growth in Jiujiang township had modified the ratio previously existing between the number of households and that of ponds. In most villages, there were now fewer ponds than households. The previous practice was therefore declared unsatisfactory by local authorities and a new rule was announced: households could make bids whenever they wanted. Honglong, a small village with a large surface of land, was in the opposite situation: it had at that time some 85 ponds to be distributed among some 44 households. The residents thus expressed their wish to keep the old practice. However, local authorities disagreed, arguing that a single rule had to be adopted in all the former production brigade. The village then split into two groups: the households specialized in fry-breeding that therefore needed as many ponds as possible, and the other residents. Both began to launch informal discussions in all kinds of settings to make their positions known and to justify them: members of the first group claimed that the new procedure was more fair since each household was given equal opportunity to make a bid on each pond, while those of the second group focused on the system of collective property of the ponds at stake and on the need for such property to meet the basic needs of all households. There were no real confrontations between members of both groups during such debates, but the position of the residents was quickly known and spread around the village. Moreover, through that channel, a pressure was made on the board of administrators by those wishing to launch a new discussion with upper authorities on this issue.

Besides this general informative role, informal comments that threaten to damage officials' reputation can eventually force them to make a move. More broadly speaking, cadres' power is more uncertain than it was before the economic reforms. Local inhabitants have become less dependant upon officials, and they are therefore much more open and articulated in their criticisms. As a result, the informal circulation of criticisms regarding the legitimacy of cadres' actions and the description of alternatives to the official choices can affect the local political scene in many ways, lead- ing sometimes to the transformation of village rules and practices. Threatening local cadres' reputation is indeed explicitly acknowledged today by some villagers as an efficient tool to force some cooperation. A Mulan resident stated for instance: "Since the reforms officials care about their reputation, they care about what people say about them. This is a great reform. And when they don't care about villagers' opinions, they care about what others outside the village will think about them. This is why it is sometimes so efficient to write to the media ... But as a cadre, if you do not listen to villagers' opinion, how can you be sure they will not turn to the media? That is why cadres tend to listen to villagers a little bit more nowadays and this is why to comment about officials and to super- vise them is quite linked today."[25]

During the spring of 1999, problems arose within the administrative village of Lanwan in the outskirts of Guangzhou.[26] This is one of those villages whose inhabitants have become quite wealthy by renting almost all land for economic and urban development. Collective benefits are redistributed on a regular basis to the various members of the village and they are enough to make quite a comfortable living. As a consequence, the practice of taking a secondary wife (*bao er nai*) quickly developed. During the spring of 1999, village wives began to criticize the existing situation. They did so in places as varied as houses, streets, and shops, claiming that the large benefits stemming from collective property were actually harming local families. Through a succession of informal discussions and debates, they came up with the following idea: husbands who would engage in such an immoral behavior should be deprived of their annual share of collective benefits. Such shares should instead be given to their wives. Having reached a certain consensus on this issue, they went to see the Party secretary and asked him to introduce such a reform. Confronted with his repeated refusal to adopt such a policy, the representative chosen by the group of women told him that they had no choice but to "sing about him" wherever they could. In other words, they would damage his reputation by saying everywhere that he was a person of bad morality since he supported the immoral behavior of most male village inhabitants. They launched such a movement of informal criticism that after a few months the Party secretary adopted the proposed reform. The circulation by some village women through informal means of a negative opinion regarding their Party secretary was therefore on that occasion efficient enough to introduce some changes within the village. The reasons why this village official yielded to the women's pressure is difficult to assess in the absence of more information regarding the local context. However, in Honglong as well as in Mulan, cadres tried on a few occasions to protect their own reputations and to prevent a broader movement of criticism by paying attention to the opinions circulating within the village.

Another important consequence of this type of unofficial circulation of information and argument is to eventually pave the way for a common action of local inhabitants. Through this type of very informal exchange, a form of consensus can indeed emerge among local residents regarding the necessity to launch a given joint action. In Honglong, such an informal process supported the formation of a local agreement regarding the way an official procedure should be effectively implemented. As a matter of fact, after the debates and discussions mentioned above, the bidding process for the village ponds was held one day in January 1997. The upper administrative levels had required the new rule to be applied: each household could make a bid on each pond, not withstanding the number of ponds it had already acquired the right to operate. However, as the first bids were expressed, an informal rule quickly emerged, being somehow adopted in the same process that it emerged, and which had been anticipated by no formal meeting: households that had already been assigned a pond refrained from overbidding when a family with no ponds showed an interest for one of the village ponds. In other words, local residents rejected the right formally assigned to them by the new official rule.

They interpreted and applied the new rule according to the old one. Even the specialized households whose interests were nonetheless to operate as many ponds as possible followed the trend in the fear, if they did otherwise, of arising the hostility of most local families. Although the result achieved still reflected the new social stratification within the village, some households concentrating most of the ponds in their hands, it was nonetheless generally considered more reasonable than the one that would have been achieved if the new official rule had been strictly applied. A common normative framework has thus been elaborated out of a process involving on the one hand formal meetings during which the new rule was contested as well as various normative expectations expressed and, on the other hand, an intense process of informal discussions in all kinds of settings within the village.

If such informal spaces do play an important part in Mulan, Honglong, and Ping'an, it is obviously in Lijiacun that they are most important since the other forms of space mentioned above are just nonexistent. Lijiacun, located in Nanling county (Anhui province), is a natural village that used to form a production team. Labeled today a "small peasant group," it belongs to an "administrative village" headed by a Village Committee and a Party Branch. No other form of organization, backed or not by official provisions, can be observed in Lijiacun or at the upper level. No village assemblies are ever called. Besides the land, the few collective assets of the former brigade have somehow been privatized by officials of the "administrative village" and no form of redistribution is done to the "small peasant group." The relationships are so strained that Lijiacun villagers just ignore the officials of the "administrative village" when they pass by them. Three persons have been chosen by Lijiacun residents as heads of their administrative unit. Although they enjoy some consideration, they are not expected to supervise or influence the decisions made above. Apparently, any form of political life is therefore absent in Lijiacun. Actually, one can say that informal discussions are carried on almost on a daily basis in order to discuss all kinds of local issues and make common decisions regarding the various topics that are not dealt with by the former brigade, for instance religious, agricultural, or migration problems. A few households—one in particular that belongs to a villager who enjoyed a formal position for a few years under the collectivist system and whose six sons still live in Lijiacun—are the places where many discussions are held, usually after work. In such occasions, local inhabitants voice their criticisms regarding upper officials, eventually express some threats regarding what might happen to them one day, but also devise concerted action to improve the village's situation and eventually distribute tasks in order to achieve specific purposes. In other words, they may not be engaged in some form of collective action or of constitution of formal bodies that one could easily label as reflecting some form of political consciousness. Nonetheless, through repeated informal debates and negotiations, they are trying to achieve some common understanding of their situation, as well as trying to modify through common action, and despite their helplessness in many realms, the environment they are embedded in.

Among the five types of practices discussed as having the capacity to affect the way power is exercised, this is the one most specific to villages considered as territorial units characterized by the particular links and the face-to-face interactions existing between members of the group. It is indeed difficult to understand power issues and the decisions taken by local leaders without considering this capacity of villagers to express themselves and act in a concerted manner without having to hold a formal meeting. Such a capacity illustrates nonetheless the necessity to clearly distinguish between natural villages (whether they form today a "peasant small group" or an "administrative village") and these specific units formally labeled an "administrative village," but which are actually composed of a group of natural villages or hamlets. In this last case, such processes of informal diffusion of opinions and references for common action will be much more difficult to observe.

Conclusion

The list of five forms of mediation spaces mentioned in this chapter is far from being exhaustive. Collective action such as those analyzed by Kevin O'Brien and Li Lianjiang[27] could have been mentioned also. Moreover, to understand the part played or not by these various spaces in different villages, one really needs to describe much more systematically the local context, as far as economic, but also social and cultural, issues are concerned. One needs also to follow the way a specific issue affecting all households in the village will be successively discussed in a variety of spaces, and observe how such discussions eventually influence the decision reached.

However, the aim of this chapter is mainly to stress that one possible response to the present post-revolutionary experience in Chinese villages is the widening process of residents' participation in local affairs, a participation that may express itself through denunciations of officials' decisions and actions but also through the influence exercised, more or less directly, on the formal decisions adopted. This widening participation is illustrated by the increasing number of mediation spaces allowing individuals, outside the formal organs of power, to exercise their capacity of judgment and offer references for common action. This seems to hold true despite the attacks launched, often successfully, by village officials in many localities to prevent such participation.

Within such spaces, which have not been analyzed here from a normative perspective, some form of power is indeed mobilized whose links with instituted powers vary a lot, ranging from confrontation to cooperation. Such power can be described as the power to provide others with given interpretations of the situation at stake, to identify the rules and norms that should be mobilized, to convince others of their validity and legitimacy, to devise actions in conformity with such rules and norms. However, this is done from a variety of perspectives regarding the identification process and management of what residents in a given locality believe to have in common. More pointedly, within such spaces, the hierarchy of positions, of relevant normative principles as well as that of interests may vary. For instance, the Party secretary's position within the Party Branch and within the kinship organization he belongs to are not the same; the normative principles and the interests considered in both places are not the same either. In this sense, the possibility for a specific issue to be discussed in more than one space, and the mutual influence exercised by such discussions, offer an opportunity to develop a local consensus—even temporary—at the village level regarding the degree of legitimacy of given positions, norms, and interests. It provides also an opportunity to make publicly known on what issues differences really stand. It should be stressed that the mediation spaces mentioned above are even more important politically speaking, despite their small size and their local anchorage, and that they participate in the assessment of a complex and often contradictory heritage regarding the way village affairs should be run, as well as being arenas where local usages, social norms but also national policies are discussed, confronted, interpreted, and applied.

By observing whose voice is repressed and whose opinion is required, and by questioning the multiple venues where debates are held and where principles or arguments are confronted and legitimized, one can capture the social alliances and oppositions effectively existing within villages and try to make sense of the relationship established between officials and other villagers as a dynamic process changing with the rise of new opportunities and new forms of interdependence.

Notes

1. Jean Oi, "Fiscal Reform and the Economic Foundations of Local State Corporatism in China," *World Politics* 45, 1 (1992); *Rural China Takes Off. Institutional Foundations of Economic Reform* (Berkeley: University of California Press, 1999); Victor Nee, and Su, Sijin, "Institutions, Social Ties and Commitment in China's Corporatist Transformation," in *Reforming Asian Socialism: The Growth of Market Institutions,* eds John McMillan, and Barry Naughton (Ann Arbor: University of Michigan Press, 1996).

2. Melanie Manion, "The Electoral Connection in the Chinese Countryside," *American Political Science Review* 90,4 (1996): 736–748; Jude Howell, "Prospects for Village Self-governance in China," *The Journal of Peasant Studies* 25, 3 (1998): 87–111; Daniel Kelliher, "The Chinese Debate over Village Self-Governance in China," *China Journal* 37 (1997): 63–90; Kevin O'Brien, "Implementing Political Reforms in China's Villages," *Australian Journal of Chinese Affairs* 32 (1994): 33–59; Shi, Tianjian, "Village Committee Elections in China: Institutionalist Tactics for Democracy," *World Politics* 51 (1999): 389.

3. Yu, Keping, "Zhongguo nongcun de minjian zuzhi yu zhili," (Local organizations in Chinese villages and their administration) *Zhongguo shehui kexue* (Social Sciences in China) 30 (2000): 85–96, and 31 (2000): 99–106.

4. Zhao, Shukai, "Shehui chongtu yu xinxing quanli guanxi," (Local conflicts and the new balance of power) *Zhongguo nongcun guancha* (Observing Chinese villages) 2 (1999): 38–46.

5. Susan V. Lawrence, "Village Representatives Assemblies. Democracy, Chinese Style," *The Australian Journal of Chinese Affairs* 32 (1994): 61–68.

6. *Oriental Daily News* (5 August 2001).

7. Interview, Mulan, February 3, 1998.

8. For a better understanding of the traditional social organization in Ping'an, see Isabelle Thireau, and Hua, Linshan, *Enquête sociologique sur la Chine, 1911–1949* (Sociological study of China, 1911–1949) (Paris: Presses Universitaires de France, 1996).

9. Fieldwork observations, Ping'an, May 1996, January 1997, July 2000.

10. For a better understanding of the transformations carried out in Honglong after the economic reforms, see Isabelle Thireau, "Recent Change in a Guangdong Village," *The Australian Journal of Chinese Affairs* 19/20 (1988): 289–310.

11. Interview, Honglong, September 30th, 1996.

12. For a description of the type of arguments exchanged as well as the agreements eventually reached during such assemblies, see Isabelle Thireau and Hua, Linshan, "Une analyse des disputes dans les villages chinois. Aspects historiques et culturels des accords concernant les actions justes et raisonnables," (An analysis of disputes in Chinese villages. Historical and cultural aspects of just and reasonable actions) *Revue française de sociologie* XXXIX, 3 (1998): 535–563.

13. Interviews, Zuo County, August 1998.

14. The importance assigned to the second objective encouraged for instance the development of new forms of coordination between police and legal institutions at the various levels of the provincial administration or the designation of one representative for ten households in some villages to report all kinds of security problems or troubles.

15. Liu, Xiaojing, "L'art de desserrer les nœuds. Logique et procédés employés pour élaborer un accord et prévenir un affrontement entre deux clans," (The art of loosening knots. Logics and procedures mobilized to establish an agreement and prevent an inter-lineage feud) in *Disputes au village chinois. Formes du juste et recompositions locales des espaces normatifs* (Disputes in Chinese Villages. Forms of justice and local recompositions of normative spaces), eds Isabelle Thireau, and Wang, Hansheng (Paris: Editions de la Maison des Sciences de l'Homme, 2001).

16. Honglong residents had already established privileged ties with the members of these three villages before 1949.

17. Observations, Honglong, November 1996.
18. Thireau, and Hua, *Enquête sociologique sur la Chine, 1911–1949*.
19. Interviews, Ping'an, March 11, 12, and 13, 1999; interviews in Boston with former Honglong officials, August 10, 2000.
20. Observations, Honglong.
21. Observation and interviews, Mulan, July and August 1998.
22. Interviews, Dongtu, August 1998.
23. Observations, Honglong, January and February 1995.
24. Liu Shiding, "De la préférence individuelle au choix collectif. Un cas de redistribution des terres en Chine rurale," (From Individual Preference to Collective Choice: A Case of Land Redistribution in Rural China) in *Disputes au village chinois,* eds Isabelle Thireau, and Wang, Hansheng.
25. Interviews, Mulan, March 5, 2000.
26. Interviews with a Lanwan official and his wife, Guangzhou, June 1999.
27. Kevin O'Brien, and Li, Lianjiang, "Villagers and Popular Resistance in Contemporary China," *Australian Journal of Chinese Affairs* 32 (July 1994): 33–60.

CHAPTER EIGHT

Enterprises, Entrepreneurs, and Social Networks in Taiwan

GILLES GUIHEUX

Taiwan's "economic miracle" has long been credited to the Guomindang state and to the strategies of foreign multinational corporations looking in the 1960s for cheap labor. The most recent research challenges this assertion and questions the efficiency of the state's policy. That the Taiwan state is fundamentally at the source of economic development is questioned. Private entrepreneurs, rather than the state, are now credited for economic development. In fact, the state has played a much more minor role in Taiwan than in Japan or Korea. The Taiwan experience tends to contradict the developmentalist[1] or interventionist school. At best, the intervention of the state contributes to explain a less unequal distribution of revenues in Taiwan than in Korea—notably because it has constrained the development of big enterprises and conglomerates.[2]

Whereas the first type of analyses were, for the most, macroeconomic, recent researches mobilize more sociological and anthropologic approaches. Authors underline how Taiwan's economic prosperity is based on small-scale, family-centered, export-oriented satellite factories in local neighborhoods. What is considered the real miracle in Taiwan's economic success story is how industrial production spread as far as almost every village of the country in a relatively short time. In fact, between 1956 and 1966, the rate of growth in the manufacturing industry was 7.2 percent in rural areas, as opposed to 5.3 percent in urban areas, with rural areas absorbing 46 percent of all new manufacturing jobs. Their share of the country's total manufacturing employment increased from 37 to 41 percent. Most of this

employment was concentrated in five industries: food, textiles and clothing, metal products, chemicals, and machinery and equipment.[4]

I do not intend to get into the debate over the role of the state vs. the
initiatives of private entrepreneurs. We do acknowledge the contribution
of private small entrepreneurs to Taiwan's economic development. What
I mean to do is look upon the social basis of Taiwan's development, to
analyze the social environment in which entrepreneurs are "embedded"
and to look at society as a force in the country's economic success. The
concept of "embeddedness" was developed by Granovetter[5] to express
the fact that economic transactions in pre-market as well as in capitalist
societies exist within social structures that give them their shape and
influence their outcomes. Social structures consist of a set of social relations in which economic actors act to fulfil expectations. The argument
that Taiwanese entrepreneurs have available to them resources inherent
in social relations of the community, offers an example of the impact that
embeddedness can have on individual economic action.

My argumentation will be based on several recent research projects. I
intend here to integrate my own fieldwork focusing on Taiwan's big
businesses into a broader perspective, referring to sociological and
anthropological field surveys of Taiwan's small- and medium-sized enterprises. In 1992, G. S. Shieh[6] inaugurated the publication of a series of
works on this topic. Based on field research conducted in 1988 and 1989
in two different Taipei's suburbs, Sanzhong and Xinzhuang, the author
argues that the export-oriented industrialization in Taiwan is sustained
through network labor processes (i.e., the subcontracting systems) and a
micro-entrepreneurial mechanism that is unfolded in network labor
processes. The subcontracting system consists of a variety of small- to
medium-sized units of production at its different layers, which require
little, if any, capital to carry out some steps, not all, of the labor-intensive
production. Shieh's work is a pioneer work in underlining the importance of subcontracting as the basis for Taiwan's economic development.
Some other research was conducted on specific activities. In 1992, Ka
Chih-Ming conducted fieldwork in a Taipei suburb, Wufenpu, meeting
more than 300 families manufacturing ready-to-wear garments for local
consumption—the final production being sold in small shops or night
markets.[7] In 1989–1990, Ian A. Skoggard conducted field research in
Caotun, 20 kilometers south of Taizhong—Taiwan's third biggest
town—on shoe industry producing for the international market.[8]
During the same years 1989 and 1990, Hsiung Ping-Chun did fieldwork
on factories located in the central part of Taiwan, manufacturing
wooden jewelry boxes for exports.[9] We will also refer to field research

conducted by Chen Jieying in 1995–1996 on Taizhong's mechanical industry.[10] These works, which pay attention to very different types of production regarding the level of technology, the markets (local and global), or the location (central and northern parts of the island) may be used to give a relatively complete image of Taiwan's small enterprises' social frame.

In the first part, we will underline that one of the reasons for the success of Taiwan's capitalism is that it fitted into preexisting social structures. In the second part, we will illustrate how social networks were used to mobilize different types of resources, capital and human resources, among others. Thirdly, we will question the historical feature of this mode of production. Is Taiwan's family capitalism outdated? Our answer will refer to other studies conducted on Taiwan's high-tech industry and on big enterprises. Our ambition here is to consistently introduce recent sociological research on Taiwan's economy and society to those who pay attention to the evolutions taking place in the People's Republic of China.

The Societal Basis of Petty Capitalism in Taiwan[11]

Taiwan's present economy is made of a large number of small- and medium-sized enterprises. In 1997, there were 1,020,435 small- and medium-sized enterprises in Taiwan, representing 97.81 percent of the total number of all enterprises.[12] These enterprises employ 7,198,000 people, that is to say 78.43 percent of the country's total manpower. The total number of wage-earning employees in small- and medium-sized enterprises amounted to 4.449 million, corresponding to 69.27 percent of Taiwan's wage-earning labor force.[13] In terms of turnover, small- and medium-sized enterprises amounted to 32.11 percent of the total turnover of Taiwan's enterprises. On the national market, they represented 33.10 percent of total sales.[14]

Three main factors contribute to explaining the importance of small- and medium-sized enterprises in Taiwan's economy. First, the Taiwan state has been reluctant to promote big private enterprises or conglomerates that could have challenged its authority. This especially depicts the Guomindang's attitude from the 1950s to the 1970s. As it was exclusively controlled by Mainlanders,[15] the state feared that big enterprises owned by Taiwanese entrepreneurs might threaten its autonomy.[16]

A second factor that contributes to explaining the importance of small- and medium-sized enterprises in Taiwan's economy is their suitability for the constraints of the global market. Until the early 1960s, Taiwan's inner economy was dominated by big public enterprises and private enterprises. When the bureaucracy decided to adopt an export-oriented strategy,[17] it led to the increase of small- and medium-sized enterprises selling their products not on the national market, controlled by big enterprises, public or private, but to foreign clients, multinational corporations settled either on the island or in the United States, Japan, or Europe. They were taking advantage of local, cheap, and relatively qualified labor to produce labor-intensive and low-technology items for international markets. Besides, the instability of these markets—orders put to one subcontracting firm could easily be cancelled or transferred to a competitor—discouraged entrepreneurs from making heavy investments. The high degree of dependency upon foreign multinational firms, the type of products—labor-intensive—the instability of global markets, all contributed to limit the size of Taiwanese firms working for global markets. Besides, small Taiwanese firms are not only subcontractors for foreign multinational companies, but are themselves embedded in a network of subcontracting relations. And that's one of the key reasons for their flexibility: at the peak season, they pass on excess orders to subcontractors whereas, at the low season, they still make use of their total production capacity. That's how Taiwan was able to conquer large shares of international markets for such products as textiles, shoes, or plastic products. These complex networks of production, between foreign firms and small Taiwanese firms and among local firms themselves, are responsible for Taiwan's enterprises' competitive edge on the global market.

These networks of production among Taiwanese firms are the consequences of the various pathways taken by rural industrialization. Shieh identifies three different pathways of rural industrialization, which differed fundamentally according to the size of capital investment. In some cases, urban workers who have been accumulating capital, know-how, and commercial connections go back to their native villages in the countryside. Friends and families who would contribute capital, land, or know-how were brought in as partners. This is the most common pattern of rural industrialization in terms of the number of workshops and factories found in the countryside. In some other cases, urban enterprises looking for cheap labor force choose to open a factory in rural areas. Although these urban capitalists are fewer in number than the small-scale entrepreneurs, they represent by far the largest proportion of capital investment in the countryside. Finally, there are employees of rural factories who decide to set up their own businesses. The initiative for this process comes from high-level managers who find little room for advancement at the top of small companies and strike out to set up their own factories or workshops. The new firms, or "daughter-factories," maintain good relations with the older factories, which provide them with orders.

The owners of Caotun's shoe workshops and factories had prior work experience at various levels in the shoe industry. Some have worked in larger shoe factories, either as workers or managers, in workshops or in trading companies. This experience is important, for it enables future entrepreneurs to acquire the business and technical expertise necessary to run a small factory and to establish the vital personal relationships on which the subcontracting system is based.[18]

Thirdly, and this is the point we would like to emphasize, the rapid development of this form of capitalism in Taiwan was made possible by preexisting social structures. The transfer of technology in Taiwan was made possible by the presence of appropriate social relations for capitalism to take root and grow.

In the case of the shoe industry, its origin lies in the workmanship of hats, a craft industry mainly relying on women working at home until the 1960s.[19] Hatmaking began in Taiwan at the end of the nineteenth century. In the 1950s, the development of a petrochemical industry made possible the use of synthetic fibers in the making process. Some hatmakers started to use these fibers, then progressively weaved with synthetic fibers the upper parts of shoes. The technology of shoe manufacturing itself was fitting traditional social groups. It consists of three main steps: the cutting of the raw material, the tying up of upper parts together, the tying of these pieces to the sole. These three steps are seldom made in the same plant. The second step, that is the more labor-intensive, is often made at home by women. The third step of the manufacturing process is the only one that needs expensive machinery. It is also a process that cannot be interrupted (the gluing in particular). So, the third step that requires a continuous process and expensive machinery is the most centralized and capitalized part of shoe production and is made in large plants. The two previous steps can be made in a small-sized factory or put out to women working at home. Thus, the technology of shoe manufacturing allowed for the possibility of decentralized production. This industry flourished in Taiwan because "its manufacturing process could be pulled apart into its component parts to accommodate more traditional patterns of ownership found in local society."[20] The history of Taiwan's shoe industry shows how modern production processes have poured into the preexisting household-based hatmaking industry.

This example shows not only that technology does not, by itself, determine the degree of decentralization, but that in return social relations found at the local level influence the industry's pattern of ownership and organization. The technology of shoe manufacturing lent itself to dismemberment of traditional social groups, resulting in a fragmented pattern of ownership and production. The fragmented ownership found in the shoe industry, together with a largely female work force, are evidence that social relations outside those determined by technology itself have shaped the production process.

This type of organization proved to be particularly efficient. In the 1970s, Taiwan substituted itself for Japan as the first provider of plastic shoes on the global market. In 1973, Taiwan got ahead of Japan as the first exporter of shoes to the American market. During the ten following years, production increased at a rapid rate of 50 percent a year. In 1980, the shoe industry was the third sector contributing to Taiwan's exports after textile and electronics, its share in the country's total export going from 1.8 percent in 1968 to 5.2 percent in 1972 and 7.45 percent in 1986.[21]

What the example of the shoe industry shows is that Taiwan's small entrepreneurs have been skillful in organizing manufacturing processes to produce for the world market on the basis of preexisting social relations, especially in rural communities. We are now going to show how social means have been used to mobilize all sorts of resources, especially capital and labor. In fact, capitalist relations in Taiwan's small industry appear to be concealed behind traditional social relations, such as relations based on kinship or common local origin.

Social Networks and the Mobilization of Resources

Preferring to use recent macroeconomic data and fieldwork on specific regions or industries, we would like now to give concrete illustrations of how capitalism in Taiwan poured into traditional social relations. We will show how individual entrepreneurs have been able to mobilize resources because of their membership in networks of community, a capacity that James Coleman has named "social capital."[22] Resources acquired by Taiwanese entrepreneurs through social capital are often less expensive (or even free) and often carry with them the expectation of reciprocity.

Mobilization of Capital

Social networks are first mobilized for raising the necessary capital resources. Table 8.1, based on a survey conducted in 1997, gives a complete

Table 8.1 Financial resources of the manufacturing sector (in percent)

	Total	Large enterprises	Medium-sized enterprises	Small-sized enterprises
Loans from Taiwanese banks	80.32	82.71	83.75	78.92
Own resources (liquid funds)	52.19	64.88	62.81	46.09
Retained profit	36.39	50.38	47.81	29.67
Loans from friends or parents	21.16	1.2	6.88	30.4
Rotating credit associations	16.5	0.3	1.56	24.55
Other forms of loan	9.67	25.11	16.56	3.21
Loans from foreign banks	7.24	17.89	9.69	3.16
Loans from cooperatives	5.01	0.6	1.56	7.09
Issuing bonds and securities	3.77	11.58	3.75	1.09
Others	4.46	4.21	3.75	4.66

Note: Large enterprises: more than 200 employees; Small enterprises: less than 100 employees; Medium-sized enterprises: between 100 and 200 employees. Each enterprise could give several answers.

Source: Zhongxiao qiye baipishu (White book on small- and medium-sized enterprises) (Taipei: Jingjibu [Ministry of Economic Affairs], 1998): statistical annex, p. 23.

picture of the different types of financial resources according to the size of enterprises. Small-sized enterprises appear to be specific regarding financial resources, for almost one-third get financial resources from friends and parents, and one fourth from rotating credit associations. These associations, based on the principles of reciprocity—each member being able, at his turn, to borrow from the others—and of confidence between members, can be considered a group of people personally acquainted to each other. To put it in other words, one would not take part in a rotating credit association—as either borrower or lender— if one's involvement was not "guaranteed" by some kind of specific relation—the *social* relationship attesting that the individual does not represent an *economic* risk for other members.

Parents and friends, rotating credit associations can be considered two *social* channels to mobilize capital. The importance of these figures is confirmed by other micro-level analyses. In Wufenpu, 20 percent of the entrepreneurs were given initial capital by their parents, 21 percent got a loan from parents or friends, 15 percent borrowed from a rotating credit association (Table 8.2).

As one informant puts it: "To do that kind of business [ready-to-wear garments workshop], you don't need to have a great amount of money. You only need a good social network and a good reputation [*xinyong chedekai*]. You can start with only 50 or 60,000 yuans."[23]

In Taizhong mechanical industry (Table 8.3), initial capital is mostly raised through social networks. Only 18 percent of the informants asked

Table 8.2   Origin of capital at the time of the foundation of the enterprise in Wufenpu garment workshops

Personal capital, of which:	84	61.8 percent
Personal savings	56	41.2
Capital given by parents	28	20.6
Loans from parents and friends	29	21.3
Rotating credit associations	20	14.7
Loans from banks	3	2.2
Total	136	100 percent

Source: Ka, Chih-Ming, *Market, Social Network, and the Production Organization of Small-Scale Industry in Taiwan. The Garment Industries in Wufenpu* [in Chinese] (Taipei: Institute of Ethnology, Academia Sinica, 1993): 48.

Table 8.3   Origin of the initial capital at the time of the foundation of the enterprise in Taizhong mechanical industry

	Number of cases	Share (in percent)
Entrepreneur himself	260	67
Financial aid from his parents (mother/father)	94	24
Financial contribution of brothers or sisters★	38	10
Financial contribution of friends★	37	10
Rotating credit associations	126	32
Loans from financial institutions	70	18
Loans from friends	15	4

★ Who therefore become partners in the capital of the enterprise.
Note: Informants could give several answers.
Source: Chen Jieying, *Taizhong dongguangyuan lu daxing jieguo zhongxiaoqiye yanjiuhua* (Taizhong: Tunghai University, 1996): 4–2.

financial institutions for a loan. One-fourth got financial aid from their mothers or fathers, one-fifth got contributions either from brothers and sisters, or from friends.

If entrepreneurs are reluctant to apply for loans from banks, it is sometimes by choice, it is also because they cannot apply. It is especially the case for Wufenpu workshops, many of which are part of the underground economy. One informant tells: "If I have never dealt with a bank, it is because my enterprise is not registered with the administration. Without a certificate from the administration, I can not apply for a loan. To get this certificate, we are facing a lot of problems, because our factory … we have built it without care. […] Residential buildings cannot be used as factories. I am at the head of a small enterprise, and it is very difficult to get the certificate. I have to find other ways. Without certificate, no aid, no support from the government. If I had a certificate, things would be easier. Without one, risks are numerous. That's why I have to find private persons to support me. The cost [of a loan from a private person] is completely different from the cost of a public bank."[24]

The appeal to parents or friends to finance the enterprise leads to a fragmentation of the capital. As Table 8.3 shows, one fifth of Taizhong mechanical enterprises surveyed are co owned by colaterals (brothers or sisters) or friends of the entrepreneur. In the case of the shoe industry, nearly a third of Caotun's factories (31.9 percent) are limited partnerships (*gufen youxian gongsi*), which means that ownership is distributed among more than one person. Partnerships can include family members, friends, or both.[25] The main reasons for forming partnerships are to pool capital, spread risk, and secure trust. Most families do not have sufficient capital to start a workshop and therefore need to pool their capital with relatives and friends.

Mobilization of Labor Force

According to Table 8.4, the entrepreneur's family is a non–negligible resource of labor for its enterprise. According to the macro survey conducted in 1997, 10 percent of the labor force in firms of less than 100 employees are members of the boss's family and do not receive any salary for their work.

Field research confirms this evaluation. In Wufenpu workshops (Table 8.5), almost 5 percent of the labor force is made of members of the boss's family who do not receive any salary for their work. Eighteen percent of the workforce is made of members of the boss's family who

Table 8.4 Status of labor force in small- and medium-sized enterprises

Wage-earning employees	61.5 percent
Individual entrepreneurs	21.23 percent
Non-wage-earning employees (members of the boss' family)	10.25 percent
Employers	7.02 percent

Source: *Zhongxiao qiye baipishu*, 1998, p. 3-2. These figures are based on a survey of enterprises of less than 100 employees conducted in 1997.

Table 8.5   The different types of workers in Wufenpu workshops

	Number of persons	in percent
Non-wage-earning members of the boss's family	20	4.44
Wage-earning employees (members of the boss's family)	84	18.67
Employees sharing a same local origin with the boss	93	20.67
Piece-work wage-earning employees		
native of Wufenpu	211	46.89
native of some other place	42	9.33
Total	450	100

Source: Ka, Market, Social Network, and the Production Organization of Small-Scale Industry in Taiwan, p. 82.

receive a salary, and another 20 percent is made of wage-earning employees who share with the boss a same local origin. In total, approximately one half of the workforce is related to the boss either by kinship or by local origin relationship. This figure might even be higher if we accept the hypothesis that the number of employees who are kin of the workshop's boss are probably underevaluated by the interviewees.

This situation can be explained by the hiring process in Wufenpu. Familial labor force mainly consists of young women, daughters or sisters, who work in the workshop until their marriages. When they get married, they continue to work, but then they move to their husband's workshop. As an informant puts it: "I have sewn for two years at my older brother's ... after my marriage, my husband has opened a ready-to-wear workshop and I went to work with him. I have stopped working for my elder brother."[26] Often, these young women do not receive a salary, but only "pocket money," and they live at the house of their boss.

The wage-earning labor force often consists of young adults who have left their native countryside to come to work in Taipei. Whenever entrepreneurs need some extra employees, they make trips to their native village mostly to hire young women (to do the weaving part of the manufacturing process that is also the most labor-intensive), who happen to be daughters of acquaintances and extended family members. The relationships between employees and the entrepreneur are not strictly contractual. They are often linked to their boss by kin or friends. Their boss provides for their food and accommodation (they usually live with their boss's family), and takes care of their well-being (in Chinese: *zhaogu shenghuo*). The boss is held morally responsible for his employees by the girls' parents. The relationship between the boss and his employees is much more than a simple employer-to-employees relationship.[27]

Production of Consent among Workers

The particularistic relationship between the boss and his employees has a certain number of advantages compared to a pure contractual relationship. Hiring employees through social networks proves to be very efficient in producing consent among workers and efficiency at work. For instance, employees who have more than contractual relationships with their bosses stay longer than others in the same workshop do. Employees who have come to work through particularistic relationships with their bosses leave the workshops for noneconomic reasons (the first reason for leaving is marriage, the second a disagreement), whereas employees who do not have particular relationships with their bosses—and do not receive a salary but are piecework-paid—leave for economic reasons (insufficient wage).[28] Personal ties with the owners make young women hesitate to find out how they might otherwise have been paid and treated in the current job market.

Manufacturing garments is very labor-intensive and requires constant adaptation to seasonal fashion. Thus, a relatively small profit margin is maximized through tight labor control. To stay competitive, social mechanism ensures personal loyalty, reduces labor turnover, and increases productivity. These young girls, according to one owner's description are "diligent, docile, willing to take orders and work overtime."[29]

In Caotun, in the shoe industry as well, workers are recruited among members of the family, friends, neighbors. Workers are brought in by friends who work at the factory or by friends of the factory owner and managers. Even if labor is not drawn on the basis of a familiar social tie—for enterprises also advertise for workers by posting signs outside the factory and along roadsides—it will assume the nature of personal relationship over time, and not remain strictly a contractual relationship.[30]

If maintaining friendly and neighborly relationships is a social practice that existed prior to the arrival of capitalism, maintaining friendly relations with workers takes on new meaning in an industry where there is the need to develop and maintain a pool of potential workers that can be drawn from on an irregular basis. As orders vary in size, so does a workshop's demand for labor. Personalized labor relations not only help to maintain the labor pool but are also important in maintaining discipline and production quality in the subcontracting system. If a worker is introduced to a factory owner through a third person, that worker is obliged to maintain good relations with the factory boss, so as not to embarrass the mutual friend and cause him or her to lose face. Also, the establishment of close personal ties helps bosses to teach workers the new tasks required by each new order and shoe style.[31]

Shieh adds another feature of the system that explains how it generates consent among workers. Indeed, "the basic process is to manufacture consent by manufacturing 'bosses.' "[32] Indeed, many wageworkers want to become their own "bosses," and opportunities are numerous because starting as a subcontractor requires little capital and skill. And most of the resources for spin-off (such as capital, labor, source of work, skill) are raised with the help of the former boss. Thus, opportunities for setting up their own workshops may calm down workers who would prefer to "exit" to become their own bosses rather than to "voice" out as wageworkers. In so doing, the system produces workers' loyalty.

This process of spreading family capitalism is confirmed by other field research. In Wufenpu, new immigrants coming from the countryside are first employees of those who have come earlier: women work in the sewing part of the manufacturing processes, men work in other activities. After a few years of apprenticeship, women get married whereas men set up their own businesses as subcontractors of their previous employers. In Taizhong, the owner of a mechanical workshop tells: "People coming from my own village in the same business, they are numerous! People who have been working in my workshop before setting on their own, they too are numerous."[33]

Summing up, Shieh identifies three main advantages of family members as the primary source of labor of small workshops—and it can be extended to any worker related to the boss by personal relationship—elasticity, flexibility, and low labor cost.[34] First, family members are willing to work for long hours and work overtime to meet deadlines when the hired workers refuse to lengthen their working time. As one informant puts it, "When the deadline was urgent and the hired workers refused to work overtime, we family members had to work overnight to meet the deadline." Second, this labor force is much more flexible than the formal procedure of recruiting workers to adapt to the cycle of the activity. Shieh mentions the case of a small electronic workshop that needs extra workers in order to meet a deadline. The partner of the workshop replies that since he and his wife cannot come the next day, he would ask his sister-in-law to come to help. After a batch of work is finished and the deadline is met, the family workers would go back to their normal employment in other units of production, without compensation from the subcontracted workshop. Thirdly, it is cost-saving as family members—like spouses or children—often do not receive pay for their work in the workshop. At most, the children may receive pocket money. "We children did not receive a wage from father. But he would give us some pocket money when we finished, say, one thousand pairs of shoes."

Thus, family as a surplus labor squeeze enables the family workshop to be a shock absorber and an initiator of a downward price spiral. But family workers in the workshop may also serve the functions of pace setting and monitoring when the family workshop expands to recruit some wageworkers. When a shoe-sole workshop started to recruit neighbors as wageworkers, the sons and daughters worked hard to serve as the "model workers," whereby the work pace was set by them, and other hired workers had to follow.[35] In so doing, family workers play a control function.

In the labor system of Taiwanese family capitalism, we should add that women stand in a specific position. Most analyses assume "that individual family members have equal access to resources, equal opportunity to pursue personal interests, and equal power in decision making,"[36] whereas any family is in fact the result of a construction and may gather contrasted interests, notably from a gender point of view. That is the most interesting part of Hsiung's contribution to the analysis of Taiwan's petty capitalism; she analyses the gender dimension of a productive system that has heavily exploited gender inequality to its own advantage. Focusing her study on the employment experiences and the family lives of married women, Hsiung shows that gender inequality is manifested in its most familiar forms: female workers earn a lot less than male workers, are assigned to more labor-intensive tasks, and have fewer chances to be promoted. She concludes that the capitalist logic of subcontracting interlocks with patriarchal practices.

Mobilization of Other Resources

Social networks, notably kinship or neighborhood relationships, are mobilized by entrepreneurs to provide capital, employees, as well as many other resources: raw materials, technology, information on markets. Questioned as to the reason why entrepreneurs in the garment industry chose to settle in Wufenpu (Table 8.6), almost half of the informants did not mention the economic advantage of the localization (such as easy access to raw materials, markets, or subcontractors), but mentioned the social benefit of being among parents and friends.

Table 8.6   The choice to locate in Wufenpu

Patronage of friends and parents*	102	47.4 percent
Closeness to the market (Taipei city)	78	36.3
Already settled in Wufenpu	9	4.2
Low land cost	8	3.7
Easy access to raw materials	6	3
Easiness to put outwork	4	1.9
Others	8	3.7
Total	215	100

* In Chinese: *qinyou keyi huxiang zhaogu.*

Source: Ka, *Market, Social Network, and the Production Organization of Small-Scale Industry in Taiwan,* p. 43.

And in fact, among Wufenpu garment entrepreneurs, 76 percent have kin working in the same sector.[37] In Taizhong, in the mechanical industry, half of the informants have close parents (colaterals, or father/mother) in the same sector.[38] Indeed, kin are requested to gain access to all kind of resources: raw materials, technology, markets.

To conclude, let us quote the example of one family group who settled progressively in Wufenpu (Figure 8.1).[39] W's family is settled in Zhanghua, Fangyuan xiang in the center of the west coast of the island. They are farmers. The husband of W's maternal aunt (W1) is the first of the family to come and settle in Wufenpu at the beginning of the 1970s. In 1974, encouraged by W1, W's father (W2) comes to work in Wufenpu together with his two elder sons—who are not yet of age—and his two elder daughters. With some money (30,000 NT$) raised by his sons W3 and W6—who have been working in cements—and a check from his brother W1 (50,000 NT$), W2 rents a workshop and buys secondhand machines. W2, his wife, and their two daughters start to manufacture ready-made garments. To increase his labor force, W2 goes back to Fangyuan where he hires young women. Six years later, W2 has bought two houses in Wufenpu. Because the building sector is going through a crisis, W's two brother, W3 and W6, give up their job in cements, and come to work in the clothing industry in Wufenpu. Some cousins of W come and settle in Wufenpu as well. First, a son of a paternal uncle (W11), working before as a tailor in the south of Taiwan, comes to work with his uncle (W's father, W2). Then his brothers W9, W10, and W12 come to work in Wufenpu as subcontractors for other workshops. In 1986, W's father gives their share of inheritance to his sons. The two

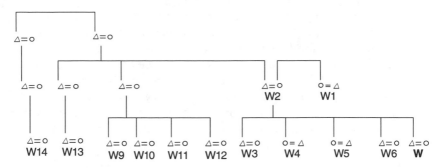

Figure 8.1   W's family network

Source: Adapted from Ka, *Market, Social Network, and the Production Organization of Small-Scale Industry in Taiwan*, p. 53.

older sons inherit their father's workshop. Other sons set up their own workshops. The daughters, W4 and W5, after their marriage, leave the family house and work in their husbands' workshops. In 1985, the individual W sets up in business for himself; in his workshop, he employs two sisters of his wife and six young girls from Fangyuan. One year later, W asks another cousin (W13) to leave his job in construction to come and work with him. Another cousin (W14) leaves his previous job for medical reasons, and comes to work in Wufenpu, first as an employee of W, and then he sets up his own business.

The progressive settlement of W's family in Wufenpu in the garment sector makes clear how many different types of resources may pass through a kin network: capital, investment opportunities, employment opportunities, orders through subcontracting or know-how.

Cooperative Competition

Close social relationships lead to the practice of cooperative competition among small enterprises. In fact, cooperation through networks on one side and competition on the other side should not be considered two antithetic social versus economic experiences.

Cooperation and competition simultaneously coexist among small enterprises. In the jewelry-box manufacturing, for instance, assembly factories compete with one another on price, number of work orders, and quantity of each work order when they do business with trading companies. There is also a fierce competition when they contract work out. So factories of the same type compete with one another. But, at the same time, because of the importance of subcontracting and the dependency of one firm upon the others, factory owners need to maintain reasonably friendly relationships with others in the system. So as to be able to receive overflow work orders or to sell its own excess work orders at a good price, each factory is compelled to maintain good relationships with other factories in the same category. "Factory owners make endless efforts to manoeuvre between competition and cooperation. The skills and practices of granting or requesting favors, and saving face, on one hand, and cultivating connections, on the other, are crucial to success" concludes Hsiung.[40]

About technological cooperation among enterprises, one entrepreneur from Taizhong mechanical industry tells: "Small- and medium-sized enterprises work in a competitive environment. How to upgrade our technology? You import a product from abroad, you try to manufacture it, you try to overcome the problems you get into. Suppose I don't know how to manufacture this product. All the enterprises know each other, so I am going to discuss this technological problem with others. So, if small- and medium-sized enterprises are competitors regarding production and prices, for the technology, we help each other. Our present technological capability, that's how we have reached it.... Research and development, for a small enterprise, is impossible because we lack capital and human resources. On the contrary, we improve a lot discussing together. If I don't know how to do something, I will ask someone else who will help me to overcome this problem."[41] According to this informant, competition takes place on the quality product level, or on the price level, but entrepreneurs at the head of small enterprises are bound to cooperate with each other to upgrade their technological ability, and they exchange their know-how. An informant in Wufenpu tells: "That members of a same family help each other is part of life ... but business deals are rare, especially if you manufacture the same item. Then, relations are very sensitive, there are no exchanges, things are rather secret."[42] Cooperation goes by itself among members of the same community, but it has some limits so that the economic interests of each member are never jeopardized.

Sectorial industrial organizations play a great role at the same time organizing cooperation and exchanging information within the community on one side, and mediating competition on the other side. In the case of the shoe industry, the Taiwan Footwear Manufacturers' Association was set up in 1967. Its main role has been to reduce competition among manufacturers, a competition that might bring down profits and slow down the development of the industry. For instance, at the end of 1969, all the manufacturers signed an agreement (with the support of the government) that set a minimum price for shoes sold on foreign markets. This cooperative competition enabled the sector to develop itself at a rapid pace. Between 1968 and 1973, as the number of manufacturers multiplied by 300, the quantity of exports increased by 900 percent (from 20 million pairs—US$20 million—in 1969 to 200 million pairs—US$186 million—in 1973).[43] Trade and industrial associations help moderate competition and exchange information and mutual aid.

The predominance of small firms in the manufacturing, as well as the wide spreading of subcontracting networks, the prevalence of the ideal and practice of spin-off, or cooperative competition, are not exclusive to Taiwan, and can also be found for instance in Hong Kong.[44] The mechanisms of reproducing the Taiwanese capitalism are not unique. What is specific to the reproduction of the Taiwanese capitalism may not be the mere existence of the subcontracting network. Rather, it is the peculiar form that the Taiwanese subcontracting network takes: it penetrates deeply into households, it activates mobilization of labor force, and it creates numerous tiny units of production, which offer abundant opportunities for spin-off. All these ensure the supply of cheap and flexible labor power and the manufacturing of consent among workers.

A General Pattern of Business Operation

Several factors and recent evolutions may lead one to think that the system described in the previous section is outdated, as if it were characteristic of one historical step in the process of Taiwan capitalism development, a feature of mainly the 1960s and 1970s. Familial capitalism, in Taiwan as in most capitalist countries, would be bound to disappear in the face of an emerging managerial capitalism. We will first review the different elements that might confirm that hypothesis: the moving out of Taiwan of the most labor-intensive industries and the upgrading of local industry. Even so, the analysis of two other economic realities in Taiwan—the emergence of a transnational community across the Pacific in high-technology industries, the modes of control and development of Taiwan conglomerates—will lead us to conclude that other types of social networks still pervade the economy. We will end with a theoretical revision of the concept of "network."

Family Capitalism: A Historical Mode of Production?

Since the middle of the 1980s, the appreciation of the New Taiwan dollar, the increase of labor and land costs have forced small enterprises producing labor-intensive products to move out of the country, mainly to Southeast Asia and Mainland China. The evolution of the proportion of exports to be credited to small- and medium-sized enterprises is one macroeconomic indicator of the fact; this figure has been continuously declining, from 57.29 percent of Taiwan total exports in 1993, it has gotten to 48.77 percent in 1997.[45] In the case of the shoe industry, whereas United States buyers began to subcontract production to other countries in the 1980s, Taiwan's trading companies encouraged manufacturers to set up overseas plants in China, Indonesia, the Philippines, or Thailand. According to a Taiwan Footwear Manufacturers' Association survey, in 1989, only 55 percent of Taiwan's shoe factories were still in production, 41 percent had stopped production in Taiwan but had kept the manufacturing of dies and lasts on the island, and 4 percent had closed down.[46]

As far as the Taiwanese factories established in China or in Southeast-Asian countries are concerned, the question from then on is to what extent Taiwanese entrepreneurs can duplicate their pattern of business development outside the island, how they set up in local communities, how they convert local labor force to capitalist production. Without answering that question, let us mention for instance the fact that numerous factories, notably those set up in Special Economic Zones in China, employ a great number of young women coming from the countryside, just as it was the case in Taiwan's early stages of economic development. The open question of the possible duplication of the Taiwan pattern is all the more relevant in Mainland China as Taiwanese entrepreneurs operate under specific conditions. Because of the lack of political recognition between the two shores of the strait, entrepreneurs carry out their projects on the mainland in particularly risky conditions on the aspect of legal guarantees. The weakness of the administrative and legal frame in China might lead them to resort to other means of securing their activities.

Another indicator of the changing situation of Taiwan's economy is the continuous decline of non-wage-earning employees in small- and medium-sized enterprises. Most of them, mainly kin, were working in labor-intensive tasks that are declining. At the macro level, a relative diminution of the non-wage-earning employees can be observed: they represented 10.72 percent of the total labor force of small- and medium-sized enterprises in 1996, 10.25 percent in 1997.[47]

In fact, the critical issue is the upgrading of Taiwan's industry to a high-tech level. As the Taiwanese struggle to transform their economy from one based on labor-intensive manufacturing for export to one dominated by high technology and trading, the system of satellite factories, small units firmly embedded in local communities may be nearing its end. In the garment industry for instance, Ka observes that since the 1980s, competition is more acute than ever and the reliance on social networks—kin and friends—is declining; they are mainly mobilized at the time of the foundation of the workshop, and in case of serious economic crisis. "At the very beginning, you rely on kin, but afterwards, you rely mainly on yourself," an informant tells.[48]

So, recent evolutions could lead to conclude that Taiwan's petty capitalism is outdated, because it is associated with a step of the development of capitalism on the island that was coming to an end in the 1980s: at the same time rapid urbanization and rural industrialization, production of low quality labor-intensive commodities and a certain type of linkage to the global market (Taiwan manufacturing under foreign brands). Does that mean that Taiwan's economy is converging toward a rational model of economy exemplified by big Western managerial firms?

The question cannot yet be answered and there is not one but several paths that Taiwan's economy might take. Are small- and medium-sized enterprises doomed to disappear because of their inability to invest in Research and Development? As the case of the information industry attests, not all high-tech industries require large-scale investments and huge factories. If owners of small- and medium-sized enterprises cannot heavily invest in Research and Development, they can and they do invest in their children's education. Young entrepreneurs, trained in scientific universities, either in Taiwan or overseas, may apply their new scientific knowledge in industries that can be started with little capital. So one possibility is that the new generation of small entrepreneurs may be grassroots venture capitalists in new scientific industries. If it is the case, Taiwan's small enterprises might be compared to Third Italy, which consists of units at the same time small and producing of high-quality products.

In fact, at this point, we would like to demonstrate that the pattern of development that had been forged in local communities, either rural or urban, pervades other parts of Taiwan's economy, taking two examples: first one sector, the information industry that is highly connected with its Californian counterpart, and second another type of enterprise, big conglomerates. In these two cases, economic activity does not rely only on rational objective criteria, but also on personalistic relationships between individuals.

The Construction of a Transnational Community in High-technological Industry[49]

The prosperity of Taiwan's information industry notably relies on intense linkages with the United States, and Chinese communities settled there. Chinese immigrants, as well as many other ethnic communities, build social networks in the country where they settle. Taiwanese engineers who graduated from American universities and who decided in the 1970s and 1980s to stay in the United States, notably in the Silicon Valley region, were no exceptions. These networks can be considered "ethnic resources" in the sense that they support professional success; through them, information on jobs, investment, and technological opportunities circulate, in part because immigrants lack access to the mainstream markets (especially financial markets). But, at the same time that Silicon Valley's Taiwanese immigrants constructed social networks tying themselves together within the region, they were also building bridges back to Asia. These transnational networks give the region's Chinese immigrants an important advantage if compared to competitors who lack the language skills, cultural know-how, and contacts to succeed in Asia. Chinese immigrant engineers typically maintained informal ties to Asia even after settling in the United States. It was quite common in the 1980s for entrepreneurs to raise capital from friends and family in Asia to start businesses. Others informally sought customers, suppliers, and business contacts among former classmates. These informal connections typically built on and reinforced preexisting social networks such as college or even high-school alumni relationships, already tying Taiwanese together across the Pacific Ocean.

The connections between Silicon Valley and Taiwan were formalized with the formation of the Monte Jade Science and Technology Association. It was started in 1989 by a group of senior Taiwanese engineers with the explicit intention of bringing together Chinese technologists in the region and in Taiwan and to promote business cooperation and investment between executives and companies in the two regions. The organization sponsors all kinds of events, such as an annual meeting, monthly dinners, special occasional seminars. It promotes social interaction and business collaborations between engineers from both sides of the Pacific and enhances entrepreneurial opportunities in both places. The creation of a "transnational community" was further strengthened by the return of some Taiwanese engineers from the United States to their native country, notably to settle in Xinzhu Industrial Park.[50] What was once a one-way flow of technology and skill from the United States to Taiwanese has now become a two-way thoroughfare as these two regions build complementary strengths. Silicon Valley remains the leader in innovation, new product definition, and technology development, while Taiwanese enterprises in turn offer high-quality, low-cost volume production capabilities, product design and improvement, and efficient integration and commercialization.

We should add that the Taiwan State played a key role in the construction of this "transnational community": it has had a regular policy of inviting Sino-American engineers to give lectures in Taiwan, it was also the initiator of the Xinzhu Industrial Park that was to accommodate many enterprises set up by so-called "returnees," American-trained Taiwanese engineers. What the case suggests is that "communities" or "collective identities" that may be mobilized in the frame of economic activity are not necessarily given by preexisting social links (kinship, friendship) or geographical situation (neighborhood) but may be the result of an active process of construction. What we can learn from the history of Taiwan's big businesses will lead United States to the same conclusion.

Taiwan's Big Businesses and Networking

In Taiwan's big business groups (*guanxi qiye* in Chinese), personal networks play a key role in the control of the enterprise's member of the same group. The unity of the business group is not built through a series of crossed capital interests between enterprises or through the central role played by a bank as in Japan or Korea. It mainly relies on the participation of the very same people in key positions on boards of trustees and at the effective direction of the enterprises. In these groups, there is no formal command structures as in Western firms; instead, one finds a highly flexible management structure that rests on networks generated by personal relationships. It is the personal relationships based on reciprocal trust and loyalty that connect enterprises together.[51]

The history of the development of the *Tainang bang*[52] is a good example of this reality. The group was started in the 1950s; at that time, it associated several entrepreneurs native to the same village near the city of Tainan, who decided to invest in the textile industry. Then, they progressively diversified their activities to cement, food industries, and more recently in the 1990s banking. At each step of the development, the same core of individuals—around whom new partners were invited—take part either as investors or managers. The group was originally based on a social network based on a common native place, but the network was enlarged and diversified as the economic activities grew, and it now includes people sharing no "objective" link—such as common native place relationship or kinship—to the core individuals. The importance of personal relationships is such that the yearbook of Taiwanese business groups,[53] next to a chart of the enterprises of each group, makes public the links (kinships or simple partnerships) between the core individuals controlling the group.

Personal networks connect not only entrepreneurs together, but also entrepreneurs to the Taiwan State. It is even argued that, compared to what have taken place in Japan or in Korea, personal connections have been characteristic of the relationships between big businesses and the State in Taiwan, whereas formal and institutionalized channels for the negotiation of economical goals and policies have lacked.[54] During the 1950s up to the 1980s, a concrete set of connections has linked the State to the biggest private individual entrepreneurs. Of course, since the democratization of the regime, big businesses have found new means of influence in the political arena.[55]

A Definition of Networks

The above remarks on a transnational community across the Pacific in high-tech industries and on Taiwanese big business groups lead us to precisely what we mean by "network". Networks considered in the case of small- and medium-sized enterprises are mostly based on an objective shared attribute: kinship, a common native place, neighborhood. What we learn from the two other cases is not only that attributes can change and are flexible, but that they can also be the result of a process of construction. One individual may belong simultaneously to different social groups based on a shared common identity, depending on its own different identities: kinship, common native place—that can mean the village, the county, the province, or even the nation—membership of an alumni association, and so on. But social ties that are instrumentally mobilized in economic activities are not limited to those based on objective criteria; they can be constructed. Social links, or *guanxi*, are open and have a borderless nature.[56] There are no limits to the networks at the basis of Taiwanese big businesses or of the success of Taiwan's high-technology industry.

What these two cases help us to demonstrate is first that networks have no explicit boundaries and the absence of clear boundaries allows a person to extend his or her network ties to another person with whom they have no preset relationship. So, social ties are contractible and extendable. Second, these two cases help us to answer the question of the outdated social features of small- and medium-sized Taiwanese enterprises. Social networking appears not to be limited to one kind of enterprise, in terms of size, type of technology, or geographical localization.

Entrepreneurs at the head of big businesses or in high-technology industries also appeal to social resources to succeed.

Conclusion

Taiwan's economic development has offered United States an opportunity to see how social capital works. Big firms as well as small firms,
single firms as well as business groups, firms producing labor-intensive or
high-tech products, all operate in the same institutional environment
and are subject to the same framework of rules and relationships. "Family
firms"—"family" used here as a metaphor to define any group of people closely associated—exist throughout the entire economy. Family
firm is an organizational pattern, instead of simply being a type of
business.

We acknowledge that small- and medium-sized enterprises intensively tied to a precise district do not mobilize the same networks as
those that are internationalized and for which their localization is almost
unimportant. As there are different patterns of operation for Western and
Asian firms, there are variations between Taiwanese firms as well. But we
want to underline that, in Taiwan, entrepreneurship has largely depended
upon social resources available from networks, i.e., social capital, for its
development. The self-help network of supportive kinship and community subgroups has provided many resources critical to the development
of entrepreneurship, and still does: financial support, sources of labor,
training, business contacts and advice, as well as attitudes, values, or role
models. These bonds are not simply emotional, characterized by sentiment; they are instrumental in what the bonds allow an individual to
accomplish. Connections between entrepreneurs, between entrepreneurs and the government, are basically pragmatic. These bonds can be
considered a means to heighten the calculability of situations that in
other respects might be quite risky.

Such an embeddedness of economic activity in social relationships has
proven to be capable of producing its own sources of allocative efficiency. These business practices certainly differ from Western practices
but are no less capable of producing profits and economic control. The
"family" firm is not a type of organization doomed to be replaced by
more modern organizational types. In the Chinese context, participants
use close relational bonds as organizational principles to create and
manage large and modern firms. The case of Silicon Valley's Taiwanese
entrepreneurs even suggests that the social structures connecting localities in the global economy may be as important as the more commonly

recognized actors in accounts of globalization, states, and multinational corporations. From a historical point of view, Taiwanese enterprises, small-, medium-sized, as well as big businesses, are more and more exposed to the outside world, expanding their activities overseas, in China, Southeast Asia, and capitalist economies. My assumption is that this evolution does not mean that the "motor" of Taiwan's prosperity is changing. If original networks were highly embedded in a specific social or geographical territory, new networks still function, expandable and transnationalized.

Notes

1. The notion of developmental state was first set out by Chalmers Johnson, *MITI and the Japanese Miracle* (Stanford: Stanford University Press, 1982).
2. The debate on the efficiency of the Taiwan state has been explicitly opened by Dollar Aberbach, and Sokoloff, *The Role of the State in Taiwan's development* (New York: M. E. Sharpe, 1994).
3. Ian A. Skoggard, *The Indigenous Dynamic in Taiwan's Postwar Development: The Religious and Historical Roots of Entrepreneurship* (New York: M. E. Sharpe, 1996): 53.
4. Samuel P. S. Ho, *Economic Development of Taiwan, 1860–1970* (New Haven, Conn.: Yale University Press, 1978): 83.
5. Mark Granovetter, "Economic Action and Social Structure: The Problem of Embeddedness," *American Journal of Sociology* 91 (1985): 481–510.
6. G. S. Shieh, *"Boss" Island, The Subcontracting Network and Micro-entrepreneurship in Taiwan's Development* (New York: Peter Lang, 1992).
7. Ka, Chih-Ming, *Market, Social Networks, and the Production Organization of Small-Scale Industry in Taiwan. The Garment Industries in Wufenpu* (Taipei: Institute of Ethnology, Academia Sinica, 1993) [in Chinese].
8. Skoggard, *The Indigenous Dynamic in Taiwan's Postwar Development.*
9. Hsiung, Ping-Chun, *Living Rooms as Factories, Class, Gender and the Satellite Factory System in Taiwan* (Philadelphia: Temple University Press, 1996).

10. Chen, Jieying, *Taizhong Dongguangyuan lu Daxing jieguo zhongxiaoqiye yanjiuhua* (Research on small-sized enterprises of Dongguangyuan lu—Daxing jieguo in Taizhong) (Taizhong: Tunghai University, 1996). This research is one example of the sociological work conducted on small- and medium-sized businesses under the supervision of Professor Cheng-shu Kao, founder of the Institute of East Asian Societies and Economies (IEASE) at Tunghai University in Taizhong.
11. We use the term "petty capitalists" in the sense of entrepreneurs producing for the market but through firms organized on a system based mainly on kinship and personalistic social ties. See Hill Gates, *China's Motor: A Thousand Years of Petty Capitalism* (Ithaca: Cornell University Press, 1996).
12. *Zhongxiao qiye baipishu* (White book on small- and medium-sized entreprises) (Taipei: Jingjibu [Ministry of Economic Affairs], 1998): 2-2.
13. *Zhongxiao qiye baipishu*, 2–3.
14. *Zhongxiao qiye baipishu*, 2–5.
15. Mainlanders who had followed Chiang Kai-shek to Taiwan after the defeat in 1949, in contrast to Taiwanese settled on the island for several generations.
16. The Statute for the Encouragement of Investment adopted in 1960 gave enterprises few incentives to merge or increase their scale of production.

17. In 1958–1959.
18. Skoggard, *The Indigenous Dynamic in Taiwan's Postwar Development*, 115–116.
19. On the history of the shoe industry, see ibid., 53–66.
20. Ibid., 94.
21. Ibid., 56.
22. James Coleman, *Foundations of Social Theory* (Cambridge: Harvard University Press, 1990).
23. Ka, *Market, Social Networks*, 48.
24. Chen, *Taizhong*, 4–4.
25. Skoggard, *The Indigenous Dynamic in Taiwan's Postwar Development*, 118.
26. Ka, *Market, Social Networks*, 83.
27. Ka, *Market, Social Networks*, 84.
28. Ka, *Market, Social Networks*, 89–90.
29. Ka, *Market, Social Networks*, 87.
30. Skoggard, *The Indigenous Dynamic in Taiwan's Postwar Development*, 124–125.
31. Skoggard, *The Indigenous Dynamic in Taiwan's Postwar Development*, 125–126.
32. That is one of the main conclusion of G. S. Shieh.
33. Chen, *Taizhong*, 5–12.
34. Shieh, *"Boss" Island*, 139–140.
35. Shieh, *"Boss" Island*, 141.
36. Hsiung, *Living Rooms as Factories*, 19.
37. Ka, *Market, Social Networks*, 44.
38. Chen, *Taizhong*, 5–13.
39. Ka, *Market, Social Networks*, 51–55.
40. Hsiung, *Living Rooms as Factories*, 72.
41. Chen, *Taizhong*, 4–11.
42. Ka, *Market, Social Networks*, 56.
43. Skoggard, *The Indigenous Dynamic in Taiwan's Postwar Development*, 54.
44. See for instance Tony Fu-Lai Yu, *Entrepreneurship and Economic Development in Hong Kong* (London: Routledge, 1997).
45. *Zhongxiao qiye baipishu*, 2–6.
46. Skoggard, *The Indigenous Dynamic in Taiwan's Postwar Development*, 65.
47. *Zhongxiao qiye baipishu*, 3–2.
48. Ka, *Market, Social Networks*, 56.
49. The following analysis is to be credited to Anna Lee Saxenian, "Silicon Valley's New Immigrant Entrepreneurs and Their Asian Networks," paper presented for International Conference on Business Transformation and Social Change in East Asia, Tunghai University, May 1998.
50. The Xinzhu Industrial Park was opened in 1981.
51. Gilles Guiheux, "Les conglomérats taiwanais," *Economie Internationale* 61 (1995): 159–172.
52. Ichiro Numazaki, "Tainanbang: The Rise and Growth of a Banana-Bunch-Shaped Business Group in Taiwan," *"The Developing Economies* XXXI, 4 (1993): 465–484; Gilles Guiheux, "Le *Tainan bang*: logiques économiques et logiques sociales dans l'histoire d'un conglomérat taiwanais," (The *Tainan bang*: Economic and social logics in the history of a Taiwanese conglomerate) *Entreprises et Histoire* 12 (1996): 101–111.
53. The China Credit Information Service publishes the *Business Groups in Taiwan* yearbook.
54. Peter Evans, *Embedded Autonomy* (Princeton: Princeton University Press, 1995).
55. See the contribution of Françoise Mengin in this volume.
56. On this topic, see Ambrose Yeo-chi King, "Kuan-hsi and Network Building. A Sociological Interpretation," *Daedalus*, 120, 2 (1991): 63–84; Ichiro Numazaki, "The Laoban-led Development of Business Enterprises in Taiwan: An Analysis of the Chinese Entrepreneurship," *The Developing Economies* XXXV, 4 (1997): 440–457.

PART IV

Negotiating Territorial Borders

CHAPTER NINE

The Southern Chinese Borders: Still a Frontier

GRANT EVANS

The southern borderlands of China have over this century moved from being an ill-defined frontier to being a carefully demarcated border. This shift, in fact, was initiated by the French in Vietnam and Laos,[1] and by the British in Burma, who brought with them the cartography of the modern (colonial) state. It was, however, only after 1949 that the Chinese state brought a similar insistence on policing its vast territory up to the last "sacred" inch. Yet, its attitude to the border seemed to be that it was potentially porous in one direction, south. Thus, during the Vietnam War in the 1960s it began building a road south from the Chinese border into Laos to support the Pathet Lao.[2] There were border tensions with Burma in the 1960s and China supported the Burmese Communist party there. A bitter border war was fought with formerly fraternal Vietnam in 1979, whereupon, in a remarkable appropriation of Western Cold War rhetoric, the latter interpreted the building of the road in Laos (previously seen as comradely help to the Lao revolutionaries), as part of a preplanned Chinese drive south to Cambodia, and beyond. Besides military hardware and personnel, however, little else moved. The combination of communist economic policies and the policing of the border meant that commerce was scarce. Change only came with the opening up of China under the policies of Deng Xiaoping in the 1980s.

But how should we conceptualize these borders, which from the point of view of the center seem so "sacred"? How do they look and what do they mean to the people who live along them? Indeed, a large number of the people living along the southern border are not Han

Chinese, something that is more clearly so along the Lao and Burmese section of the border. In what sense is the border "Chinese" to them? Given that ecology, ethnicity, and geography do not respect borderlines and play their part in constituting micro-worlds that do not conform to lines drawn on maps or fantasies of sacred territory held by the center, how do they contribute to the dynamics of borders? These local complexities, among others, mean that borders, however fixed they seem, are always involved in broader social and economic processes that constitute these borders over time.[3]

The fluidity of border relations can be seen if we simply consider the opening up of the land borders between China and the mainland Southeast Asian states in the past two decades. For example, we have shifts in the ethnic composition of the border. In some cases it has seen the reestablishment of a previous status quo, such as the return of ethnic Chinese (Hoa) traders to the northern borders of Vietnam. During the conflict with China along the border in the late 1970s and early 1980s the Hoa were compelled to move away from the border for "security" reasons, and many fled Vietnam as refugees. Today, they have moved back in strength, and border towns like Mong Cai and Lang Son once again have large and thriving Hoa population.

By comparison, the towns inside Laos along its border with China have always been small, and the volume of trade low. The ethnic Lao are in a minority in the provinces of Phong Saly, Oudomsay, and Luang Nam Tha, all of which have ethnically very mixed populations of Khmu, Lue, Hmong, Koh (Akha), Phu Noi, Haw (Yunnanese Chinese), and others. While Haw have always played an important trading role and tended to base themselves in the towns, the boundary between ethnic Chinese towns and ethnic "other" rural areas has been blurred. For example, Haw (who are sometimes thought of as a "hilltribe") also engage in slash-and-burn upland cultivation. Many Chinese left Laos after the 1975 communist takeover, and the population dropped from 100,000 to 10,000. This included a significant number of Haw from the north, and the subsequent conflict with China in the late 1970s caused more to leave, although they were not compelled to do so, as they were in Vietnam. One interesting consequence of this, according to Andrew Walker,[4] was that not only was it ethnic Lao who took their place, but ethnic Lao women who atypically began to engage in long-distance trade throughout the northern region of Laos and into southern Yunnan.

The main centers of Chinese activity in Laos have been in the south and are oriented toward the Overseas Chinese in Bangkok. In the north, Rossetti[5] writes in her important survey of the Chinese in Laos, "the number of Chinese ... has long fluctuated according to the strategic ambitions of the country's 'powerful neighbor,' as it is an area that China considers as its own sphere of influence." Not all the Chinese fled, and those that remained provided a core for the return of Chinese to the border, including Chinese who have never lived there before. For example, a Lao-Chinese from Pakse in the south of Laos, who had studied Chinese in China, moved to Luang Nam Tha with his wife from Hebei to act as an interpreter in Lao-Chinese trade, at the same time setting up a small coffee shop in the main street. Luang Nam Tha, nevertheless, remains an ethnically mixed town, with many Lao, Black Tai, Lue, and others living there. The town of Phong Saly has always had a predominantly Haw and Phu Noi population, and this remains true today. Rossetti claims that here "two families of Yunnanese origin control the town's economy. These families serve as go-betweens not only for private businessmen from Xishuangbanna prospecting for markets in the region, but also for visiting Chinese officials."[6] Oudomxay is quite simply ethnically mixed, although there is a growing Chinese trade presence. A survey by Khampheng Thipmuntali of the Lao Institute of Cultural Research and myself of the Oudomxay market in mid-1995 found that about one-third of the traders were Haw, one-third Phu Noi, and one-third were Hmong. In the long term, however, we may see the Chinese move into a position of clear dominance in such markets through their ability to manipulate ethnically based regional trade networks. "All in all," Rossetti argues, "in the space of a few years, the urban areas of Namtha and Oudomxay have begun to look like Chinese cities, where Chinese characters are posted on shop front ... the economy in the north is becoming very 'Chinese', with a massive influx of capital, technology and workers."[7]

The Deng reforms in China set in motion tens of millions of Chinese migrants who are no longer tied to their localities and workplaces. Developments in transportation in China also made them much more mobile than ever before. As documented in a major new study of internal and international migration[8] they naturally headed for the main cities along the coast of China, but many also headed for less populated minority border regions, and to the countries over the border and beyond, to the "Golden Mountain" of America or Europe. As one writer in this study comments:

Another alternative is to leave China from Yunnan in the Southwest, going first to Thailand or Mianmar and from there to Ukraine or Moscow. Three ways of illegal exit are known. Small groups travel from Kunming in Yunnan on foot, riding bicycles, or with the help of border officials to northern Thailand. This journey takes about twenty-four days. Far away from the main roads, large groups of up to 200 people are smuggled through the jungle to Mianmar and from there to Thailand. The third alternative is by boat down the Mekong river through Mianmar and from there on to Thailand.[9]

Standing on the Lao side of the border one can almost feel the sheer weight and size of these people in motion. By comparison with China the Lao population is miniscule, barely 4.5 million people, comparable to that of a minor city in the PRC. The Lao have attempted to control the flow of Chinese into the country, and in this they may have been aided by the fact that Chinese migrants have their eyes on richer countries beyond Laos. Nevertheless, one can find Chinese itinerant traders way down in the south of Laos, and in mid-1999 I was surprised to find a small dumpling restaurant in the capital Vientiane that had just been opened by people from Liaoning in the far northwest of China. They couldn't speak anything other than Mandarin.

In the towns along the Burmese side of the border we find a much greater proportion of trade with China. "In 1996, Yunnan's trade with Burma (excluding smuggling) totaled $362 million.... Trade with Vietnam, Thailand and Laos totaled $85 million."[10] Unofficial estimates of this trade are over $800 million. This makes the stakes along this border high and drives Chinese migration into Burma, something the government has less control over than in Laos. Bertil Lintner writes: "In Mandalay, in northern Burma, Yunnanese are buying up shops, restaurants, hotels and karaoke bars—even citizenship. 'When a person dies in Mandalay, his identity card is sold to a broker across the border in Ruili, who resells it. The picture is then changed and the new owner has become a Burmese citizen who can settle and buy property in Burma,' explains a Chinese in Ruili who is involved in the business."[11]

The Chinese migrants are also, of course, headed for Thailand. Lintner quotes a Chiang Mai resident saying: "As a Thai, I feel overwhelmed. Of course, Chinese have been moving southwards for centuries. But we have never seen as many new businessmen, and settlers, as now."[12] But Thailand is for many simply a staging point for travel to other parts of the world through human smuggling rackets controlled by notorious "snakeheads." Andrew Forbes comments on the changing nature of the current wave of migrants: "They're much more patriotic and loyal to the motherland. The new-wave Chinese are very different from those who migrated in the past. They have grown up in a country that has been far more unified than before. There's now a different sense ... of being Chinese.\[13] Affluence in China has also meant a rapid rise in tourists to Thailand, 432,995 in 1998, thus making them more visible in every way in the region.

The rapid growth of the Chinese economy and the rising incomes there have also had an unexpected ecological impact on its southern neighbors. The new rich in China, and there are many of them, have raised demand for wild animals and plant species both for the table and for medicinal purposes.[14] The natural habitats of these species are in the northern forests of Vietnam, Laos, and Burma and they are smuggled across the borderline. Once again the sheer size of China's population means that even if only a relatively small percentage of the country gets rich it presents a major threat to the flora and fauna in the border regions. Besides this, there has been massive logging of the forests in Burma by Chinese companies who have denuded whole mountain ranges. Cease-fires engineered by Rangoon with various rebel groups has also meant, according to one informant, that "the rebels have become timber companies. They've still got their guns, but their struggle for autonomy or whatever is over."[15] They too sell the timber to China. A perhaps more benign ecological impact can be seen, however, just outside of Luang Namtha where a rubber plantation has been established. One is normally struck by the sharp ecological shift between Laos and southern Yunnan because of the large-scale presence of such plantations in the latter (see below). The plantation in Namtha was being worked by ethnic Hmong who had fled to China during the tense years of 1979–85, and during their sojourn there had been put to work on a Chinese plantation. Now repatriated to Laos they formed the workforce of the new plantation, the produce of which is contracted to a Chinese company. Thus does a Chinese landscape march south.

Of course, a boom in the drug trade has also been an outcome of the opening up of the Chinese borders to the south, and Chinese on both sides of the border have been quick to cash in on it. Indeed, at the town of Pingyuan on Yunnan's border with Vietnam, traffickers had taken complete control until in August 1992 they were overwhelmed after an 80-day battle with security forces. Criminal networks, however, spread across the region and include many state officials. Not only are drugs flowing across the borders into China, but China itself is fast becoming a large drug-producing and drug-consuming country with, according to Yang,[16] 27 out of its 30 provinces cultivating some illegal opium. While officially the number of addicts is said to number around 300,000, it is believed that the numbers are much higher, and those concerned with the spread of AIDS in China are, of course, increasingly alarmed.

The above issues are some of the broad transformations taking place along and beyond the borders of southern China. But now let us turn to take a closer look at transformations just inside the southern border of Yunnan.

Sip Song Pan Na/Xishuangbanna

Across from Laos lies the Dai (Tai Lue) Autonomous Region of Xishuangbanna (or what is known in Tai as the Sip Song Pan Na[17]), established by the PRC in 1953. Its capital is Jinghong, which is also the name of one of the three counties of the region. The other two are Menghai and Mengla, the former leading into Burma, the latter into Laos. The population of the region is under one million, of which one-third are Han; one-third Dai; and one-third other ethnic groups, the largest being Hani, with approximately 153,496 persons, other groups having less than 50,000 such as Bulang, Jino, Yao, Lahu, Miao, and so on. In the 1950s the Han made up only 2.3 percent of the population, the Dai 47.3 percent, and the other groups 50.4 percent.[18]

For several hundred years this region had a variable tributary relationship with the Chinese empire in which the latter increasingly exercised its power through a *tusi* system (i.e., a form of indirect rule described in detail Wiens's book[19]). In the twentieth century with the gradual formation of a modern Chinese state obsessed with borderlines and total control over every inch of claimed territory, so we have seen a growing Han political presence in what became designated "minority regions" by the modern state. Definitive Han colonization of Xishuangbanna only began after the communist revolution in 1949,[20] despite the establishment of "autonomous regions" for minorities, a historical peculiarity of Marxist–Leninist "nationalities" policy implying no lessening of Han political control of these regions, only some concessions to some local customs.[21] Han political control was exercised from the cities and towns, while the rural areas remained exclusively populated by Dai and other groups. This pattern began to change in the late 1950s with the creation of state farms for growing tea, and in the 1960s, state rubber plantations, all of which were overwhelmingly staffed by Han immigrants.[22] Thus from a Han population of 5,708 in the 1950s we see a rapid growth to 229,083 in the 1970s. Yet, during this time of communist austerity and "self-sufficiency," these large state farms were like small towns—separate and distinct Han nodes in the countryside.

Jinghong by the early 1980s had become a city of approximately 30,000 people, most of whom were Han administrators, shopkeepers, transport workers, soldiers, and the like. At the time of his fieldwork in the late 1980s Hsieh Shih-chung observed that the "Dai who live in town are usually civil servants. A majority of them are former aristocrats and their relatives and descendants,"[23] and claimed most of these seemed determined to assimilate into the dominant Han culture and to shake off their "stigmatized" Dai ethnicity.

The Golden Quadrangle

From 1949 up until 1978 there was almost no foreign trade with Yunnan, which lived up to its reputation as a "mysterious land beyond the clouds." Following Deng Xiaoping's declaration that China must modernize, this situation began to change rapidly. Initially it was the coastal provinces that opened up to the outside world, but then in the 1980s the slogan "gateway into Southeast Asia" marked Yunnan for development in the region. In 1985 the provincial government released the "Yunnan Province Temporary Provisions on Border Trade," and trade growth along its southern border has accelerated ever since. Matt Forney's description of a briefing given by a senior Yunnan economist in 1997 captures the mood well:

> Che Zhimin whacks his pointer onto a wall-size map of Asia and drags it noisily from Hong Kong to New Delhi. After a contemplative pause, he repeats the operation from Rangoon to Moscow. Then he glares at his guests, exasperated, as if only an idiot could still miss his point. "Look where the lines cross!" he yells. "Yunnan! ... It will make the Strait of Malacca obsolete. It will be like uniting Canada and Mexico!"[24]

Xishuangbanna is Yunnan's border "doorstep," and Jinghong its natural frontier development headquarters. It provides the Chinese anchor for the so-called "economic quadrangle" incorporating China, Laos, Burma, and Thailand, the southern Thai anchor of which is Chiang Rai. Plans for this region include massive transport infrastructure projects of roads and river transport, with Jinghong developing into a major port on the Mekong River as well as a center-point for road transport to Kunming, the capital of the province. In 1991 an international airport was opened at Jinghong, which will be a crucial hub in interregional air transport.

In the mid-1990s, as a further step in this direction, Yunnan Airlines acquired a 60 percent stake in Lao Airways.[25] Promoters of the concept speak brashly of being able to drive all the way from Singapore to Kunming, and in response to this, local entrepreneurs are preparing snares along the way for the modern Asian businessman.

Tourism is planned to be one of Yunnan's biggest money earners, playing on the province's reputation in China as being full of natural forests and populated by colorful minorities, of which there are claimed to be 24. And Xishuangbanna, it could be said, has become the jewel in the ethnic-tourism crown of the province.

All of these developments have caused a building boom in Jinghong for office space and for large, modern hotels, and, of course, for housing for the growth in governmental administrators, businesspeople, and ordinary workers. The multi-storied Banna Mansion Hotel loomed up into the skyline in the early 1990s, a huge clockface at its pinnacle seeming to announce, "Jinghong, your time has come!" Other large international hotels have since sprung up. In the past ten years the population of Jinghong has quadrupled, from 30,000 people to 130,000 in 1996, and there are projections that it will reach 230,000 by the year 2006. In what was already a Han-dominated city, almost all of this growth is accounted for by Han immigrants from other provinces. Thus one consequence of the opening of the borders has been the definitive Hanification of Jinghong City.

Han Tourism

Ironically, or perhaps predictably, along with this irrevocable Hanification of Jinghong has gone its embellishment with "ethnic characteristics" to make it attractive to tourists. This is most apparent in the ubiquitous use of yellow to mark something as Dai-yellow roofs on buildings that may also try imitate the roof of a temple, yellow walls, and so on. This style has been repeated throughout Xishuangbanna.[26] When tourists first look out of their aircraft windows at Jinghong airport they are greeted by its expansive and striking yellow roof, and they know they have reached another, "wondrous" part of China. But, as Hsieh has remarked, the Dai themselves "feel nothing toward the yellow symbolism of Jing Hong, because it is based on a Han image of Dai culture."[27] Another key symbol that is promoted is that of palm trees. These are planted along the roads even as the foundations of new buildings are being set. They suggest the "tropical paradise" promised in the tourist brochures.

Since the opening up of China foreign tourism has skyrocketed from 1.88 million tourists in 1978 to 43 million in 1994, and it is still increasing. Less noticed, and much more spectacular, has been the massive growth in Chinese domestic tourism over the same period, and especially since the early 1990s following the government's implementation of a nationwide holiday system granting each employee 7–15 days annual leave. This, combined with rapidly rising incomes especially in the coastal provinces, has led to a "travel craze," according to *Beijing Review*.[28] In the main cities of China (as already in Hong Kong and Taiwan) culture has taken a modernist turn. Far-off places are no longer associated with banishment or viewed with fear and trepidation, and many Chinese tour companies promote their tours with the slogans: "go to the boundary areas!", "Frontier Tours," and "Minority Nationality Tours." According to Zheng and Wang, "Chinese tourists mainly focus on sightseeing, and the richness and uniqueness of natural resources ... In general, the frontier cities have much richer resources for nature tourism, more unique and spectacular than inner regions."[29]But they also argue: "The essence of tourism is the pursuit of cultural difference and similarity."[30] Domestic and Overseas Chinese tourists travel, say, to the Confucian temple, and this will reinforce their sense of cultural "similarity" to Han; when they travel to minority areas it is to experience cultural difference. All of this fits very neatly with Gladney's argument about modern Chinese nationalism, and the creation of a unified Han ethnicity this century by the Chinese state.[31] Minorities, as he has argued, receive an inordinate amount of publicity in the PRC. Why? Because by looking at minorities (however their image is actually constructed) "Han" people can say, "that is not us." Tourism, therefore, helps to consolidate the idea of a unified Han ethnicity in modern China.[32] Thus travel does not take one further away from home, but paradoxically consolidates one's identity with home. In this sense one can perhaps talk about the "domestication of the frontier" in contemporary China, or about how traveling to the frontier helps consolidate the center.

Figures provided by tourist officials in Jinghong show that in 1994 the region received 10,000 foreign tourists, and 1.2 million domestic tourists and in 1995, 30,000 foreign tourists and 1.5 million domestic tourists. Most of the foreigners were from Southeast Asia, probably Thailand. These officials said that for a short time, over 1992–93, there were many Japanese tourists, and this appears to have been associated with speculation about the origins of the Japanese people.[33]

The main attractions for tourists in Xishuangbanna are tropical rainforest sights and products from the rainforest, especially medicines (whether they be herbal or from endangered animal species), and Dai culture. While one attraction of internal tourism for Chinese is the lack of problems with language and with travel documentation, a trip to the frontier in Xishuangbanna also allows a brief, visa-free, one-day international excursion into Burma, mainly to buy jade. When late morning comes down in Da Lou, for example, the place is suddenly choked with minibuses that have traveled from Muang Hai or Jinghong to carry Chinese tourists across the border into Burma for shopping.

The image of the Dai promoted among the Chinese is that they are "safe," nonviolent, and not "primitive," signaled by the fact that they have their own writing system and an institutionalized Buddhist religion. But perhaps the dominant image peddled is that of illusive, beautiful Dai women in their long colorful dresses. The sexualization of Dai women in the Han imagination can be seen in the ubiquitous imagery of Dai women bathing half-naked in the rivers. Originally promoted by the so-called Yunnan school of painting, this image is reproduced photographically in all tourist promotion, and on billboards (see Figure 9.1). The viewing of Dai women bathing has become a tourist treat for Han, and when we were in Muang Han in the middle of 1996 we saw a banner stretched across the road saying: "See women bathing down by the river after 5 P.M.!" We enquired from the local Dai about this and they claimed that it was Hani women hired by tourist promoters. These Hani women would pretend to be Dai and allegedly did not mind exposing their breasts, in contrast to the modest Dai.[34] Because of voyeuristic Han tourists many Dai women around main tourist centers have had to find new bathing locations.

This sexualization of Dai women is consonant with a sense of "lawlessness" on the frontier that is, in imaginary terms, at the edge of cultural constraints. Hence the Han have fantasies of sexual freedom and license among minorities, and among the Dai in particular. Such fantasies also grow out of a Confucian society's incomprehension of the status of women in non-Confucian societies, where relative female freedom in mate choice is mistaken for sexual libertarianism. When Han, men in particular, travel to this frontier, they move to the edge of their own cultural constraints and seek sexual adventure among these allegedly "sexually wild" women.[35] A recent sexual "adventure" that has been added to the frontier has been the promotion of transvestite cabarets just over the border from Da Lou in Mong La, Burma, which are put on by "girls" from Thailand. Thus one aspect of tourism to Xishuangbanna is the development of a variety of sex tourism such as we have seen in other parts of Asia, the growth of prostitution there, and

Figure 9.1 *"Come into our Spa"*

the attendant problems of sexually-transmitted diseases. It is estimated that Jinghong has around 500 prostitutes, most of them Han immigrants, some of whom pretend to be Dai, and a small number of Dai and other minority women. For a time the authorities blamed the spread of AIDS on the "sexually irresponsible" Dai, but recently it has been shown that there are more Han AIDS cases in Jinghong than Dai.[36]

Dai and Han

Many of the Dai both in and around Jinghong are reasonably financially secure at the moment, certainly compared with the poor Chinese immigrants from elsewhere who do the laboring jobs and other menial jobs in the city and the countryside. But a little probing among them quickly reveals foreboding about the future, especially among parents for the future of their children.

To compete in a Chinese world these children require a knowledge of spoken and written Chinese. Most young Dai, however, are not good at written and spoken Chinese, while their spoken Dai is simply the language of the household. For the urban Dai and those who have been absorbed by the expansion of places like Jinghong the problem is increasingly acute, as they have to compete directly with Han Chinese. The problem is partly one of the structure of the labor market. Dai women who function as tourist icons can often find work in the tourist industry as waitresses or hostesses, whereas there are fewer openings for men. For Dai who remain farmers this problem is not acute and they are less affected by feelings of inferiority.

The Thai or the Lao, whatever feelings they may have vis-à-vis the economic success of the Chinese in their countries, at least know that the latter must publicly defer to Thai or Lao culture, because it is the former who control the state. But Han are under few such constraints in Xishuangbanna, and many of them believe they have brought "advanced Chinese culture" to these "backward" peoples. Yet, an interesting recent study by Mette Halskov Hansen suggests that Han attitudes are perhaps more nuanced. She points to the important differences between the Han who were sent to the minority areas by Mao in the 1950s and 1960s to establish the state farms who believed they were doing it for the good of the nation, and to bring "civilization" to the border minorities. Today they differentiate themselves from the new wave of migrants who come for "selfish" motives only and look down on the latter. These first settlers, however, came from "civilized" areas. Their children, on the other hand, have been born in Xishuangbanna, and as much as their parents have tried to make them identify with their own native villages in Hunan or Sichuan the children feel that they are somehow "local" (*bendi ren*) and not "outsiders." As Hansen observes, these children do not have a "homeland" like their parents, but nor have they fully acquired a new one:

> Because in spite of the fact that the Han to a large extent control the policy and economy in Panna, the area remains a so-called Tai Autonomous Prefecture and the Han are still faced with resentment (often expressed very subtly) by the Tai (the local numerical majority) and, to a lesser extent, some of the other ethnic minorities. The government has to be headed by a Tai and the majority of government cadres have to be Tai as well. [Hansen notes that the head of the CP, however, is always Han.][37]

These advantages in government employment are resented by these Han who, since 1993, are no longer guaranteed jobs on the state farms. Furthermore, these people are now in direct competition with the new Han migrants. But interestingly these locally born Han have come to accept Tai criticisms of these "poor and dirty" Han from the outside and wish to be identified as insiders, and claim like their parents higher motives for their attachment to the region.

Dai may also take some heart from Thailand's economic success to counter Han claims that they are culturally backward and cannot achieve success in the modern world, and the touristic promotion of "Dai culture" generates some residual pride; but this seems hardly sufficient to generate the sense of confidence required to counter the relentless pressure of Han civilization—which has intensified with the opening of the border.

Buddhist and Cultural Revival

The Cultural Revolution was experienced by the minorities in China as an orgy of Han chauvinism.[38] The Dai, like others, stood by and witnessed the destruction of their pagodas and sacred texts, and had to conform to the Han strictures that no longer allowed young Dai men to join the monkhood. With the reforms of Deng they set about rebuilding their culture and its central organizing feature, Theravada Buddhism. However, they lacked trained monks and Buddhist texts and so they quickly turned to older networks that carried them across the borders into Burma and Thailand to seek help. As Heather Peters[39] writes: "In some instances, monks simply walked from Burma or northern Thailand, using the centuries old routes, to offer their services in the newly established *vat*. In 1985 I observed Shan monks from Burma at village *vat* around Jinghong." Subsequently I and other observers who have interviewed young monks in temples in Sip Song Pan Na have been surprised by their resourcefulness as so many of them have traveled down to Thailand, the north, the northeast, and even to Bangkok, to pursue their temple education. The continuing importance of a temple education for the Dai is documented by Hansen[40] in her study of the impact of the Chinese educational system on the younger generation. This movement in pursuit of a Buddhist education back and forth across the border has also led to cross-border participation in Tai Lue religious festivals in, for example, Muang Sing in Laos.[41] Buddha images to replace the ones destroyed during the Cultural Revolution have been imported from Thailand. Moreover, cross-border kinship contacts have been consolidated, and subsequently economic ones as well. As Peters remarks: "All of these things obviously reinforce a sense of Pan-Tai ethnicity which is manifested through Buddhism."[42]

Border Flux and Flows

The opening of the southern Yunnan border has meant different things to different groups of people. For Chinese entrepreneurs and state enterprises it has opened up a vista of economic opportunities, articulated

most strongly in the "economic quadrangle" concept. They have moved
to Jinghong and begun the economic and architectural transformation
of the city. In their wake has followed a stream of poor migrants from
Sichuan or Hunan who in the eyes of the locals are prepared to do "*anything*" to earn a buck, and they are both feared and looked down on
because of it. In and around Jinghong these are the laborers, the peddy
cab drivers, the prostitutes, and drug addicts. Some of them are intent on
traveling beyond the border to Burma, Laos, or Thailand, where they
find similar work. The richer among them are intent on migrating to
Europe or America, or anywhere. The presence of these outsiders has
presented special problems of identity for the second or third generation
Han who have been born in the autonomous region, and as Hansen
documents it has caused them to more firmly root their identity there.
For yet other Han who have been released from the suffocating shack-
les of Maoism the region is a tourist fantasyland, and plans are afoot to
connect Jinghong to Chiang Mai and Luang Prabang in Laos as a
"tourist triangle" to compliment the "economic quadrangle." But for all
of these Han, movement down to the border has one way or another
had the paradoxical effect of consolidating the Han "center."

As for the Dai living in the immediate vicinity of Jinghong, their lives
have been radically changed by the above developments and their future
economic status is precarious. But they and Dai generally have embarked
on a cultural revival that has also been made more possible by the opening of the border and their ability to draw on the cultural resources of
Burma, Thailand, and to a lesser extent, Laos. So, the opening of the border has fortified their resistance to Han social and cultural penetration of
the region—which from the Han point of view arrests them in "backwardness." Some Dai have acted as intermediaries for Han in this cross-
border interchange. Thus, in Muang Sing, Laos, I have seen young Dai
women acting as interpreters for Han tradesmen or itinerant traders. But
it is only a part role.

Gaubatz[43] argues that "China has not yet witnessed the 'end of the
frontier' ... The frontier regions are still inhabited by non-Han Chinese
peoples who have maintained their distinct identities. Massive settlement
of the frontiers by Han Chinese, including agrarian settlement as well as
urban migration, and fuller integration of these regions into the political,
economic, and social orbit of "China Proper," are not likely to extinguish
these ethnic frontiers ... "The fact that the frontier remains open means
that we will continue to see Han flow into these areas. But in contrast
to the past, opposition or compliance to this movement of Han is not
phrased in terms of tributary relations but in terms of ethnicity and even

nationalism (in Tibet, for example). In this interaction the ethnic groups are increasingly drawing on modern ideas of identity, and in the case of the Dai have access to cultural ideas about who they are from beyond the Chinese border, a relationship unknown in the past. Increased inter-action between them and Thailand through the opening of economic relations that facilitate travel and contact will no doubt sustain this sense of ethnic distinctiveness into the foreseeable future.

Underlying all of these developments are the economic plans for the Greater Mekong Region and the "economic quadrangle." While the 1997 Asian economic crisis suddenly arrested many of the more grandiose schemes for the region, the long term determination of governments, the Asian Development bank, chambers of commerce, and businessmen to develop the area remain on track.[44] Furthermore, the Mekong River, which has always ignored state-imposed boundaries, is now demanding transnational management and the Mekong Committee has been reactivated in recent years.[45] Thus from the micro-movements of an ethnic minority, to the macro-movements of the Mekong, the southern borders of China remain in a state of flux.

Notes

1. P. B. Lafont (ed.), *Les Frontières du Vietnam* (The Vietnam borders) (Paris: L'Harmattan, 1989).
2. McMurtie G. Godley, and Junny St Goar, "The Chinese Road in Northwest Laos, 1961–73: An American Perspective," *Laos: Beyond the Revolution* (London: MacMillan, 1991).
3. For a discussion of these issues see Thomas A. Wilson, and Hastings Donnan, "Nation, State and Identity at International Borders," Chapter 1, *Border Identities: Nations and State at International Frontiers*, eds. Thomas A. Wilson and Hastings Donnan (Cambridge: Cambridge University Press, 1998).
4. Andrew Walker, *Legend of the Golden Boat: Regulation, Trade and Traders in the Borderlands of Laos, Thailand, China and Burma* (London: Curzon Press, 1999): 154–155.
5. Florence Rossetti, "The Chinese in Laos," *China Perspectives* 13 (September/October 1997): 28.
6. Ibid., 29.
7. Ibid., 29.
8. Frank N. Pieke, and Hein Mallee (eds), *Internal and International Migration: Chinese Perspectives* (Richmond, Surrey: Curzon Press, 1999).
9. Karsten Giese, "Patterns of Migration from Zhejiang to Germany," in *Internal and International Migration*, eds. Pieke, and Mallee, 204–205.
10. Matt Forney, "Yunnan Rising," *Far Eastern Economic Review* (11 September 1997): 55.
11. Bertil Lintner, "Reaching Out," *Far Eastern Economic Review* (11 September 1997): 58.
12. Bertil Lintner, "Migration: The Third Wave", *Far Eastern Economic Review* (24 June 1999).
13. Cited by Lintner, "Migration: The Third Wave".
14. See, for example, "Can We Tame Wild Medicine?" by Rob Parry-Jones, and Amanda Vincent, *The New Scientist* (3 January 1998).
15. Quoted by Bertil Lintner, "River of Dreams", *Far Eastern Economic Review* (22 December 1994).

16. Dali L. Yang, "Illegal Drugs, Policy Change, and State Power: The case of Contemporary China," *The Journal of Contemporary China* 4 (1992).

17. "Sip Song Pan Na" can be translated as the 12 Tai principalities (*muang*). It should not be mistaken with the Sip Song Chu Tai of Vietnam. In the drawing of the borderline by the French, British, and Chinese earlier this century one of the principalities centered on Kengtung fell to Burma, while two others partly fell to Laos, one centered on Muang Sing in Luang Nam Tha, the other in Phong Saly.

18. Hsieh, Shih-chung, *Ethno-political Adaptation and Ethnic Changes in Sipsong Panna Dai: An Ethnohistorical Analysis*, unpublished Ph.D. dissertation (University of Washington, 1989): 61.

19. Harold J. Wiens, *China's March Toward the Tropics* (Hamden, Conn.: The Shoe String Press, 1954).

20. Wiens writes: "Aside from the officials, a few soldiers, and individual tradesmen, and aside from a few villages of Han—Chinese mountain farmers [Haw] who paid tribute to the T'ai rulers, there were no Han Chinese in the land in 1943." Ibid., 314.

21. The fragility of these structures was shown by their abolition during the Cultural Revolution, experienced in minority areas as a radical outburst of Han chauvinism. The Xishuangbanna Autonomous Region was abolished in 1966 and reestablished in 1984.

22. See Ann Maxwell Hill, "Chinese Dominance of the Xishuangbanna Tea Trade: An Interregional Perspective," *Modern China* 15, 3 (1989); Bernard Henin, and Mark Flaherty, "Ethnicity, Culture, and Natural Resource Use: Forces of Change on Dai Society, Xishuangbanna, Southwest China," *Journal of Development Studies* X (1995): 219–235. The ecological effects of this were equally dramatic. Over this period virgin forest decreased from 66 percent to 26 percent of the region according to Hsieh citing a mainland source (*Ethno-political Adaptation and Ethnic Changes*, 220).

23. Hsieh, *Ethno-political Adaptation and Ethnic Changes*, 275.

24. Forney, "Yunnan Rising," 54.

25. This deal, which was partly made for political reasons between now "fraternal" countries, was an economic disaster and has since come apart. Lao Aviation's fleet is in such a state of disrepair that the UNDP in Laos and other international organizations have warned their officials against flying with them, and foreign travel agents are doing the same.

26. Hsieh speculates that the idea of yellow was struck upon because of its association with the colour of Dai Buddhist monks' robes (*Ethno-political Adaptation and Ethnic Changes*, 249). Theravada Buddhism is one clear cultural feature that marks Dai off from the Han. Gaubatz in his study of urban transformation on the Chinese frontier writes about how this has become a feature of the post-Mao era. "This emphasis is part of a general rejection by contemporary urban planners of the attempts to standardize the form and appearance of Chinese cities that marked the Mao era. The stress today is on creating unique images for the cities that reflect the culturally diverse nature of the regions they occupy ... The application of local styles is sometimes contrived and not necessarily a true representation or preservation of local culture." Piper Rae Gaubatz, *Beyond the Great Wall: Urban Form and Transformation on the Chinese Frontiers*, (Stanford: Stanford University Press, 1996): 316.

27. Hsieh, *Ethno-political Adaptation and Ethnic Changes*, 251.

28. 17–23 October 1994.

29. Zheng, Hongfang, and Wang, Hongxiao, "Establishing Tourism as a Precursor Industry and Developing Frontier Cities," *Minority Research* 3 (1996) [In Chinese]: 29.

30. Ibid.

31. Dru Gladney, "Representing Nationality in China: Refiguring Majority/Minority Identities," *The Journal of Asian Studies* 53, 1 (1994).

32. Gladney (ibid.) presents an argument for the modern construction of Han ethnic consciousness.

33. Emiko Ohnuki-Tierney in her book *Rice as Self: Japanese Identities Through Time* (Princeton, New Jersey: Princeton University Press, 1993) talks of how some Japanese folklorists, after hearing about Dai rituals for the rice goddess, speculated that Japanese may have had their origins

among the Dai. Some of this speculation may have filtered through to the tourist trade, which then sponsored tours to Xishuangbanna. However, this bizarre episode in "roots" tourism seems to have petered out rather quickly.

34. In Hani villages exposed breasts are a common sight and are not sexually problematic.

35. For a discussion of similar issues in a Miao area in China see Louisa Schein, "Gender and Internal Orientalism," *Modern China* 23, 1 (1997).

36. For some of this information I would like to thank Sandra Hyde, a medical anthropologist who has been working in Xishuangbanna.

37. Mette Halskov Hansen, "The Call of Mao or Money? Han Chinese Settlers on China's Southwestern Borders," *The China Quarterly*, 158 (June1999): 410.

38. For a detailed discussion of the impact of the Cultural Revolution in Sip Song Pan Na see Hsieh, *Ethno-political Adaptation and Ethnic Changes*; and Heather Peters, "Buddhism and Ethnicity Among the Tai Lue in the Sipsonpanna," *Proceedings of the 4th International Conference on Thai Studies*, 3 (11–13 May 1990) Institute of Southeast Asian Studies, Kunming, China.

39. Peters, "Buddhism and Ethnicity," 349.

40. Mette Halskov Hansen, "Teaching Backwardness or Equality: Chinese State Education among the Tai in Sipsong Panna," in *China's National Minority Education*, ed. Gerard A. Postiglione (New York and London: Falmer Press, 1999).

41. Khampheng Thipmuntali, "The Lue of Muang Sing," in *Laos: Culture and Society*, ed. Grant Evans (Chiang Mai: Silkworm Press, 1999).

42. Peters, "Buddhism and Ethnicity," 349.

43. Gaubatz, *Beyond the Great Wall*, 316–317.

44. See, for example, Woranuj Maneerungsee, and Somporn Thapanachai, "Greater Mekong Subregion: Thailand, China to Help Laos," *Bangkok Post* (23 January 2000).

45. Peter Hinton, "Is It Possible To Manage A River? Reflections from the Mekong," in *Development Dilemmas in the Mekong Sub-region*, ed. Bob Stensholt (Monash Asia Institute, Monash University, Melbourne, 1996).

CHAPTER TEN

Taiwanese Politics and the Chinese Market: Business's Part in the Formation of a State, or the Border as a Stake of Negotiations

FRANÇOISE MENGIN

The part played by business in the Beijing-Taipei dispute has already been analyzed.[1] Tak-Wing Ngo, in particular, has aptly highlighted the relation between business and politics, and confirmed, in the case of Sino-Taiwanese relations, Lindblom's suggestion[2] that the influence of business is based on its control over investment decisions.[3] Taiwanese investors on the Mainland are not passive as political players; quite the contrary, they have been actively exercising their bargaining power—i.e., the fact that they can withhold investments—and have increased their political influence in doing so. This chapter would like to add further elements.

Because of Beijing's irredentist policy, and if one leaves aside the hypothesis of the PRC taking over Taiwan by force, growing exchanges between the two sides of the Taiwan Straits raise the issue of the strength, even the autonomy, of the state in Taiwan. Consequently, from the point of view of an internationalist, there is a twofold questioning: one is related to international relations theory, and partakes in the debate over the state-centric paradigm; the other is about China's partition, that is the securing of an autonomous political entity on Taiwan, and the nature of the Sino-Taiwanese border. As a matter of fact, this chapter relies on the presupposition that the unresolved sovereignty dispute does not impede one from considering Taiwan as a state, in the Weberian sense; moreover, it will leave aside the identity issue (are people in Taiwan Taiwanese, Chinese, or Taiwanese and Chinese?), as it does not introduce conclusive elements into the general questioning.

Stateness at the Time of Globalization
Cross-straits Relations as an Apposite Case of Transnational Links

Since the opening of legal indirect trade in 1987, and of legal indirect investment in 1991,[4] cross-straits economic exchanges expanded at high speed. At the beginning of 1999, at the time the research for this chapter was carried out, the number of Taiwan-invested companies in China was already 40,608, and real investment totaled US$208.7 billion, according to Mainland statistics.[5] Besides, the value of the island's exports to China accounted for 16 percent of its total exports. Beyond overall figures, Taiwan's dependence upon China also results from the structure of bilateral trade that is investment-driven. Most Taiwanese exports to Mainland China are meant for Taiwanese enterprises, and are, in large part, composed of manufactured and semi-manufactured products, as well as of machinery and equipment.[6]

The importance of the business's leverage—that of the big business above all—on Taipei's Mainland policy can also be assessed by the swiftness with which some large groups have straightaway after they entered the Chinese market brought to the fore crucial issues in terms of national security, such as the opening of direct links.[7] It was not until 1993 that the Chang Rong group (Evergreen), mostly operating in the transportation field, made public plans to invest on the Mainland. But a few months later, it was putting pressure on the government to allow direct sea and air links, while obtaining the permission for building a container warehouse in Shanghai, an investment worth US$6 million. Moreover, the forming of this "Greater China market" (*Da Zhonghua shichang*) has not been triggered by any intergovernmental regulatory action. Quite the contrary, only unilateral measures inspired by security concerns have been taken to slow down this "society-led" investment flow.

The capacity of the state in Taiwan to regulate the growing relocation tide on Mainland China is called into question as firms are freeing themselves from state regulations. This process is all the more significant as the sovereignty dispute between the two sides has not been settled. Quite the contrary, tensions have risen in the Taiwan Straits since the budding negotiation process was more or less suspended in 1995. In short, the Taipei government is facing a constant dilemma: giving priority to national security at the risk of slowing down economic growth, or enhancing the latter at the expense of the former. The solutions of "off-shore shipping centers" (*jingwai hangyun zhongxin*),[8] as well as that of the opening of the so-called three small links—direct exchanges with the Mainland are limited to the offshore islands of the Taiwan area[9]—are significant in this respect. They are compromises between the overall national interest and the interests of the individual enterprises, but also expedients in order to postpone the opening of direct links.

There are different ways of assessing Taipei's Mainland policy. Any normative approach close to the strong-state paradigm must conclude to a complete failure. In the short run, some initiatives—the opening of the offshore shipping centers for instance—can be presented as calculated responses to strategic problems. Yet, in the long run, Taipei's policy appears as a residual regulation of the general banning that prevailed for about 40 years on cross-straits exchanges; more, it appears as an ex post legalization of the breaches opened by firms: from 1993 to 2001, Taiwanese investment projects in China that did not call into question national security and domestic economic development were authorized as long as they were conducted in an indirect way.[10] The special wording Taipei's Mainland policy has been subject to from 1996 to 2001— "patience over haste" (*jieji yongren*)—bears witness to the many efforts to slow down large-sized-firm projects in China.[11]

In fact, the government's regulation lagged far behind the current situation. More than 60 percent of cross-straits trade was conducted directly.[12] Even in the field of infrastructure and high-tech industries, firms were often escaping from restrictive regulations as most of them were already internationalized and could resort to their subsidiaries located in third countries to conduct such projects on the Mainland. As to the requirement of indirect trade, there were many infringements of the rule: trade through Hong Kong covered in fact a whole range of situations[13] that made the Sino-Taiwanese border all the more blurred.

Cross-straits relations can be referred to as transnational relations, a term that has been precisely defined, among others, by Robert O. Keohane and Joseph S. Nye as "the movement of tangible or intangible items across state boundaries when at least one actor is not an agent of a government or an intergovernmental organization."[14] As to the sociology of international relations, Sino-Taiwanese links would be an apposite case of those territorial divisions—termed "Natural Economic Territories" by Robert A. Scalapino,[15] or "Region-State" by Omae Kenechi[16]—that transcend contending interstate relations, due to the rapid development of transnational relations. The forming of these economic zones would testify to the primacy of economic interests over national identification. In other words, the nation-state would be gradually undermined by a progressive remapping of the world that, in the context of growing globalization, is based on functional criteria. Saskia Sassen analyses a "new geography of power,"[17] while for the so-called new French geographers, areas suited to human activities should be defined according to existing interactions whatever the boundaries of the already defined societies.[18]

The Formation of the State versus the Building of the State

Thinking the change in international relations is all the more difficult as "our rationalization of the international is itself constitutive of that practice," as Steve Smith rightly puts it.[19] Is globalization merging nation-state into one single economy, a borderless world? Are there a retreat of the state and a diffusion of state authority, as well as emerging spatial powers that are not dependent upon nation-states' governments?

In this field, one cannot but refer to Susan Strange[20] who has shown that there is no distinction between domestic politics within the state, and international politics between one state and others: national economies cannot be analyzed in isolation from the world economy, and international politics cannot be defined as a study different from other kinds of politics. So, the major hypothesis of her latter works is that the progressive integration of the world economy has shifted the balance of power away from states and toward world markets. Some authors are forecasting the rise of a "global civil society."[21] As Andrew Hurrell aptly puts it when analyzing arguments attacking the state-centerdness of traditional international political theory, this set of arguments is based on the presupposition that "the increased level of economic globalization provides the "infrastructure" for increased social communication—the role of communications technologies in facilitating the flow of values, knowledge and ideas and in allowing like-minded groups to organize across national boundaries."[22]

Parallel to the flow of writings nourishing the thesis of the retreat of the state, and worse its demise—and partly as a response to it—some authors insist on the central part played by the state.[23] Others strive to bridge the gap between the two opposed stances and come to more qualified conclusions. For Peter Evans economic globalization does restrict state power, but it is likely to put public institutions on the defensive, and a "leaner, meaner" state is the likely outcome.[24] For his part, Thomas Risse-Kappen indirectly reassesses the part of the state when he examines how the interstate world interacts with the society of transnational relations. For him, the main question to be asked is "under what domestic and international circumstances do transnational coalitions and actors who attempt to change policy outcomes in a specific issue-area succeed or fail to achieve their goals?"[25]

Beyond opposed paradigms and different questionings, these works share a common presupposition, a state-society dichotomy, a separation between economics and politics, between private and public spheres. Yet, if one considers that spheres are above all overlapping, the issue at stake, when forecasting an undermining of the nation-state by transnational actors, is whether or not there is a dichotomy between the state and a private sphere, the latter being constituted by transnational links.

The hypothesis put forward in this chapter is that transnational activities are no exception in social activities at large: crossing nation-state borders should not be understood as stepping out of one nation-state territory, but as still participating in its making. Rather than focusing on the forming of a transnational society, one should analyze the various processes that alter individual (transnational) strategies into collective ones, on the one hand, and on the embedding of the latter in power relations, on the other hand. The issue at stake is not so much whether the nation-state is undermined by growing transnational relations, but how it is reshaped by the latter; more precisely, how growing transnational ties can go hand in hand with a state-building process. In so doing, there is no question of supporting the state-centric perspective of the realist theory that assumes that states are the only relevant actors in international relations.[26] The point is only to stress the interweaving of transnational factors and governmental action.

Hence, the distinction—already extensively used by some Africanists,[27] but also by some scholars focusing on China[28]—drawn by John Lonsdale between *state-building* and *state-formation* should be transposed into the realm of international relations. In Lonsdale's words:

> [There is] a key distinction between *state-building,* as a conscious effort at creating an apparatus of control, and *state-formation,* as an historical process whose outcome is a largely unconscious and contradictory process of conflicts, negotiations and compromises between diverse groups whose self-serving actions and trade-offs constitute the "vulgarization" of power.[29]

Such a distinction would allow one to understand how a nation-state—in this case Taiwan—does not build itself against the transnational but, on the contrary, how a cultural and economic spatialization can contribute to political territorialization. This would result from overbidding processes generated by the intrinsic contradiction existing between economics and politics within a context of contending sovereignties. About Kenya, John Lonsdale has shown how "State-formation—the vulgarization of power, and state-building—its cultivation, were contradictory processes that complemented each other."[30] Further he states: "If conquest shapes societies, even conquered peoples can force changes in the forms that states take, so leading, to some extent, their captors captive."[31] Lonsdale's words should be related to those of Anthony Giddens who posits civil, political, and economic rights as "arenas of *contestations* or *conflicts,* each linked to a distinctive type of surveillance, where that surveillance is both necessary to the power of subordinate groups and an axis for the operation of the dialectic of control."[32]

This chapter is focusing on Taiwanese politics and the Chinese market. Hence, I shall hardly investigate whether or not Taiwanese firms are managing their business outside central state control in Mainland China.[33] Besides, some distinctive questionings are close to my problematic: that of the privatization of the state, among others.[34] Finally, this chapter fits within broader research works that include cultural logics, that of the anthropologist Aihwa Ong in particular.[35]

Negotiating the Borders: Controlling Wealth
The Transnational Community as a Market of Political Resource

Because of contending necessities, any holistic approach of the transnational realm brings inevitably to the fore an analysis in terms of an alternative, i.e., the transnational or the state, even the transnational versus the state. The first step is therefore to describe the morphology of the Sino-Taiwanese transnational community. There are many cleavages within this community. Usually, they are not set in a conflicting mode. But they imply very diversified interests. The main one opposes large-sized firms to small- and medium-sized ones: they invested on the Mainland at different times, for different motives, and with different location strategies. The latter are the great majority of those 30,000 Taiwanese firms that relocated their production on the Mainland around 1986, even slightly before. On the contrary, large-sized enterprises gained a foothold on the Chinese market from 1992 onward, that is after a twofold governmental initiative had been taken. On the PRC's side, the "open policy" (*kaifang zhengce*) was reactivated, in particular after Deng Xiaoping's southern trip at the beginning of 1992; on Taiwan's side, the government initiated a de facto recognition of the PRC, as well as an *aggiornamento* of its Mainland policy in 1991. But the arrival of Taiwan's large conglomerates on the Chinese market, though late, has not been less massive. In September 1992, among the 50 top private conglomerates, 26 had already invested or were planning to invest on the Mainland.[36] While the average amount invested was US$430,000 prior to 1995, it reached US$2.3 million for that year.[37] When relocating some production units on the Mainland, small and medium-sized firms have, above all, striven to free themselves from growing constraints, while still being export-oriented. For large-sized firms, on the contrary, investing on the Mainland was both a question of capturing a large part of the Chinese market and, for some of them such as the Hexin Group,[38] of seeking after a global strategy, even if it is, for the time being, limited to Asia. Finally, the cleavage between small- and medium-sized enterprises, on the one hand, and large-sized ones, on the other, also covers the localization of the investments. Those of the former have been concentrated on the Southern cost of China—mainly in Guangdong and Fujian provinces—while big Taiwanese groups have straightaway adopted a settling strategy that has encompassed the entire Chinese territory. For those manufacturers, the question was not to produce with lower costs in order to reexport only, but also to sell on the Chinese market. The farm-produce industry President Enterprises Co. (Tongyi) has thus invested as far as the Xinjiang, and the financial group Hualong as far as the Heilongjiang.[39] The map of Taiwanese investments in China has rapidly modified: ranking fifth in 1991–1992, Shanghai's region was second as from 1993.[40]

Besides, as the small- and medium-sized firms, large-sized ones have (re)activated person-to-person relations (*guanxi*). But in this case, *guanxi* have been set at the top of the Chinese political hierarchy, including, in some cases, Deng Xiaoping, Li Peng, or Jiang Zemin. The example of President Enterprises Co. (Tongyi) is significant in this respect. Its investment on the Mainland is the largest one ever made by a Taiwanese firm. It is not until 1992 that Tongyi has invested on the Mainland:[41] but that very year a snapshot has immortalized a meeting between Jiang Zemin, and Kao Ching-yuan, head of the group, as well as a close friend to Lee Teng-hui and a member of the central standing committee of the Guomindang.[42] More, the way the political élite and the economic one are replicated both in China and in Taiwan brings alongside the second and the third generations as from their very childhood.[43]

Parallel to the differentiation of Taiwanese investors on the Mainland, there is that of Chinese actors of the Sino-Taiwanese transnational economy. In this field, the main cleavage brings together central authorities and local bureaucrats. More precisely, and given some of Yves Chevrier's works,[44] and those of Jean-Louis Rocca[45] which have underlined the interweaving between the bureaucratic and the trading spheres, between what is legal and what is not, one must articulate the transnational economy around two main poles: particularistic interests certainly, but also the central power, as it plays a key role in the distribution of the privileges— economic ones mainly—and in the economic and social stabilization. Thus, in order to limit the power of local bureaucrats, the Chinese central government attempted in 1990 to unify the various incentives given to Taiwanese investors.[46] Besides, any holistic approach of the local bureaucracy may also be misleading in as much as Taiwanese investments are unevenly scattered among the provinces. More, Special Economic Zones have, within the provinces, a high degree of autonomy in order to make legislation, and thus to determine the legal framework of foreign investments.

Not only is the transnational community plural, but the fact that strategies are strongly atomized does not impede the forming of collective actors, which, as such, can transform into interest groups articulating policy demands. Certainly small- and medium-sized firms in Southern China constitute a spatialized community and are integrated in various networks. However, they did not try to gather, at first, as their main aim was to make the most of the differential concealed in the mere existence of the border. In other words, their early strategy has not been to strive to obtain alterations of the Chinese and of the Taiwanese laws, but only individual compensations.[47]

However, the Chinese authorities have anticipated the formation of pressure groups, probably because they were fearing it, and have taken the initiative in institutionalizing this community in order to better supervise it. In March 1989, an Association of Taiwan Invested Businesses (*Taizi qiye xiehui*) was established in Beijing, and in June of the same year, an Association of Taiwan Merchants (*Taishang xiehui*) in Shenzhen. During the following years, about 20 of such bodies came into being in the major cities where Taiwan firms had invested. Although this network is highly decentralized—in particular the Beijing association does not interfere in the running of the "local" associations—this network is closely controlled: its administration is staffed by members of the United Front as well as by members of the various local Taiwan Affairs Offices, while members of the party are appointed on an honorary basis.

But it is at the very moment when they were constituted as an organized actor by the PRC's authorities that Taiwanese small- and medium-sized firms have been led to expand their strategy, no longer against the state—that is by calling into question the nation-state framework—but within the state. On the Mainland, the forming of this collective actor has at once strengthened the local bureaucracy to the detriment of the central power, at least as long as Taiwanese investments are concerned. In short, the Taiwanese investors' associations have succeeded in uniting with the local bureaucrats against the central power, in particular so as to postpone the implementation of the labor law.[48]

Yet, at the same time, the Taiwanese investors' associations have offered a specific socialization network to those transnational small- and medium-sized firms. Due to the Chinese initiative, these firms have kept on organizing meetings on the island—at the time of the Chinese New Year or the Tomb Sweeping Holiday (*Qingming jie*) or the Mid-Autumn one (*Zhongqiu jie*)—and these meetings have been joined by representatives of the government, even members of the Legislative Yuan (both from the Guomindang and from the Minjindang).[49] From then on, some bodies (though informal) were being established through which negotiations could be carried on between investors and the government. In other words, in Taiwan, the small- and medium-sized firms have become, due to the very fact that they were no longer atomized actors, an electoral stake. This, in turn, has led them to be associated to the drafting of the Mainland policy of the ruling party, as well as that of the opposition party: in doing so their strategy is "national," and no longer transnational.

And it is a state initiative—that of the PRC government—which has allowed the state (the one in Taiwan) to "regain" this transnational actor. As a matter of fact, the setting of the Chinese network of Taiwanese investors' associations had at once prompted a counter-proposition from the Taipei government. The Chinese National Federation of Industry and Commerce—the Taiwanese employers' organization that was closely supervised by the Guomindang—has established a parallel network of associations: the Taiwan Investors Associations (TIA or *Dalu Taishang xiehui*).[50] But, these associations have been, in a large measure, boycotted by the small- and medium-sized firms, which have considered the move of their government, both too late and too dominated by the large-sized firms.

The latter on the other hand have responded favorably to the setting of the TIA network and the Taipei government has actively developed socialization activities within this network. Large meetings of *Taishang* are periodically organized in Taiwan, such as the annual "TIA Dragon-Boat Festival Friendship Symposium" (*Dalu Taishang xiehui fuzeren duanwujie lianyi zuotanhui*), an event generally co-chaired by officials from the government, and from the Chinese National Federation of Industries.

During such symposiums, participants are generally offering proposals to related government agencies. The issue at stake is not so much the outcome of these proposals, but the "national" commitment it fosters among *Taishang*. The sponsoring of golf tournaments is an apposite example of how the state can instrumentalize transnational networks to recover, on a national basis, transnational actors. Initially, these tournaments were taking place on the Mainland within the framework of the various Taiwanese investors associations set up by the Chinese authorities.[51] But in June 1999, a first edition of a "Taiwan investors golf championship" (*Taishangbei gaoerfuqiu sai*) was organized on the island by the SEF and the Republic of China Golf Association. Preliminary competitions had been held by local Taiwanese investors' associations around Mainland China to select the participants.[52] In addition to an individual competition, there was a team competition, each of the ten teams representing different locations in China. But even in the individual competition, the Mainland "origin" of each participant was recalled (in the overall placing for instance). The "national" dimension of the event was also enhanced by the attendance of members of the government,[53] while President Lee Teng-hui delivered a speech and hosted the prize-giving ceremony.

Although exploiting the differential the border represents initially implies atomized strategies within the transnational space, a whole play of negotiations and of cross-interests is set that progressively turn individual strategy into power relations within each national space (i.e., Chinese and Taiwanese). And this very play of negotiations and of cross-interests progressively alters individual strategies into collective ones. In other words, because of the many cleavages that are being formed within the transnational community, the latter constitutes a "market" of political resources.

Therefore, according to outbidding tactics of rival political entities, on the one hand, and to the tactics of transnational actors on the other hand, the mere existence of this market allows, if not a control of the transnational level by the state—the transnational would be reinstated within the state—at least a recomposition, though partial, of the state by the transnational. The latter then spreads out within the national space— and no longer within the transnational one. Both governments have been able to play a critical part in the forming of these interests groups, within the Sino-Taiwanese transnational community. Whether these initiatives partake in residual or persisting state-corporatism will not be addressed in this chapter. I shall only survey how transnational actors are closely associated with the elaboration of Taiwan's Mainland policy. In so doing, and because this participation is not free from contending stances that require negotiation and compromise, the transnational actor actively participates in the forming of power relations.

A Politicization of Economics

Democratization has resulted in a remodeling of the state-business relationship: it went hand in hand with growing interactions between business and politics.[54] This chapter is limited to the main channels through which the compromise outcomes of Taipei's Mainland policy have been elaborated, and through which actors of the transnational realm have participated in the setting of power relations. It thus leaves aside many features of business-politics interaction in Taiwan, in particular the business associations,[55] or relations between big businesses and the Guomindang-owned firms.[56] Likewise, it does not assess the degree to which interest groups in general are asserting themselves vis-à-vis the state in Taiwan.[57]

As far as cross-straits relations are concerned, transnational economics-domestic politics interaction has operated on a twofold basis: individual commitments of *Taishang* to domestic politics, on the one hand, institutional conflicts, on the other hand. But before surveying *Taishang*'s individual part, it is necessary to place businessmen's activities within a broader scope. If one accepts, what some authors such as Mark Granovetter have clearly shown,[58] that the motivating forces of economics are not confined to merchant interests rationally determined, economics does not stand apart from other social activities, politics in particular.[59] As to Taiwanese big businessmen, Gilles Guiheux's work demonstrates that the employers' legitimacy is not based exclusively on the profession of individual values, but also on that of collective ones.[60] The question here is not whether such a representation may, or may not, reinforce the employers' power within the firm, or whether it is, or is not, based on a posteriori rebuilding. Because of its mere existence, such a representation can be mobilized in order to legitimate the growing involvement of big firms in politics. This mobilization is all the more strong as there exists some collective authorities within which big business is closely associated to the decision-making process.

The participation of businessmen in domestic politics hinges on two different—even opposed—features. The first one partakes of Taiwan's remarkable statute, that is the nonrecognition of the Republic of China as a sovereign state on the interstate arena, while the second one results from the progressive implementation of popular sovereignty that, as far as economics are concerned, has deprived the technocratic élite from a monopoly in the decision-making process.

Since the Republic of China has been excluded from the interstate community during the 1970s, some big managers have been chosen in order to represent—although unofficially—their country abroad, both at the bilateral and at the multilateral level. While normalizing their relations with Beijing, most states have recognized, in an explicit way usually, but also in an implicit one sometimes, the sovereignty of the PRC over Taiwan. Hence, in as much as the Republic of China is still a de facto independent state, a whole range of substitutes for the diplomatic and consular institutions and procedures have been devised on a private basis: there has been a privatization, yet fictitious, of Taiwan's diplomacy.[61] Both for the setting of this network of relations, and for its running, Taiwanese businessmen have played a key role. In particular, not only were members of the government prohibited from travelling abroad in their official capacity, but, up to the end of the 1980s, they were not even hosted, even on a private basis, by their foreign counterparts. Therefore, businessmen have been put in charge of negotiating abroad on behalf of the Taipei government, regarding key contracts as well as import quotas. Some of them became true nonofficial ministers of their country abroad, in particular Koo Chen-fu from the Hexin Group, and his nephew Jeffrey L.S. Koo.[62]

As Taipei's new Mainland policy was closely following the scheme of Taiwan's external relations, it was logical that handling matters of a technical nature arising from cross-straits exchanges be managed by the private sector, acting on behalf of the government. To this end, a private, nonprofit organization, the Straits Exchange Foundation (SEF, *Haixia liangan jiaolu jijinhui*) was established in 1990. But, in fact, as SEF is closely associated with various governmental institutions,[63] it also acts as a spokesman, within the government, for *Taishang*'s interests. As a matter of fact, the very nature of the SEF—public or private—is difficult to assess. On the one hand, 80 percent of its funding is of governmental origin, and SEF functions as a front for Taipei's Mainland policy. Were the relations between Beijing and Taipei to be normalized, the SEF would not have the competence it currently has; it might not even exist. But, on the other hand, the SEF's board of directors is overwhelmingly representing private interests.[64] Besides, the SEF is chaired, since its establishment in 1991, by Koo Chen-fu: born from a Taiwanese family that grew rich during the Japanese colonization, Koo Chen-fu has headed the Hexin Group that mainly operates in the cement industry (Taiwan Cement), on the one hand, and, on the other hand, in the banking and the insurance business. For long, Koo has chaired the Chinese National Federation of Industry and Commerce (a position he has held since 1953). He is also a member of the central standing committee of the Guomindang, and, since 1989, advisor to the President Lee Teng-hui.[65] Above all, he was three times—in 1995, 1996, and 1997—the representative of President Lee at the APEC annual summits. Indeed, the PRC's leadership has been stubbornly opposed to Taiwan being represented, within this forum, by its head of state, or even by its prime minister.

Parallel to this partial devolution to the private sector of a kingly function (a top-to-bottom process), there are the multiple opportunities that democratization has offered to businessmen wishing to weigh on the elaboration of policies (a bottom-to-top process). Though elections were regularly held at the local level since the1950s, it is not before the 1990s that mandates at the central (zhongyang) level have been subject to renewal, those of the Legislative Yuan (Lifa yuan) in particular. Hence, the political legitimization of the Republic of China on Taiwan has resulted, among other things, in growing interaction between political and business interests at the legislative level: in short, electoral campaigns rely heavily on business donations,[66] while firms can now put pressure on legislators to protect their interests. Within this trend, firms investing in China are no exception. Beyond indirect participation, direct participation in electoral politics is increasing as some big businessmen have been elected at the Legislative Yuan.[67]

As far as the deliberation field is concerned, one should also mention the entry of businessmen in the Guomindang's Central Standing Committee: in 1994, four of them have been elected, all coming from leading Taiwanese groups—Koo Chen-fu (Hexin), Kao Ching-yen (Tongyi), Wang Yu-tseng (China Rebar), and Chen Tien-mao (from the powerful Kaohsiung's Chen family that runs, among others, Taiwan Coca Cola). Kao Ching-yen is an apposite example of the various political guanxi a prominent Taiwanese businessman develops. Parallel to his close connections with top PRC's leaders,[68] there are those he has developed in Taiwan with top political leaders, including President Lee Teng-hui, and two of the candidates running for the 2000 presidential elections, Lien Chian and James Soong.[69] And if one comes back to the paradiplomatic level, Kao Ching-yen has also been indirectly associated with the SEF decision-making process, as chairman of the Chinese National Federation of Industries, which is one of the trustee of the SEF. Examples could be multiplied.

Besides, businessmen's participation in the decision-making process has also resulted from their involvement, upstream, in the scholar field through the various foundations and research institutes they have established. During the first years of the democratization process, several foundations were set by big firms, of which some head research institutes that enable the employers to keep up with the reforms, as well as to influence their course. As from 1966, the Hexin Group run by Koo Chen-fu founded the Taiwan Institute for Economic Research (*Taiwan jingji yanjiu yuan*). One of the most significant cases is that of Chang Yung-fa who owns the first Taiwanese conglomerate in the transportation field (Chang Rong Group or Evergreen), and who finances, through the Chang Yung-fa Foundation, the Institute for National Policy Research (*Guojia zhengce yanjiu zhongxin*), which is close to the presidency and, without doubt, one of the most important think tanks on the island. Established in 1989, the year after Lee Teng-hui succeeded Chiang Ching-kuo as head of the state and of the Guomindang, this institute was chaired by Tien Hung-mao, a well-known scholar who has written extensively on Taiwan's political transition.[70] He was appointed Minister of Foreign Affairs from 2000 to 2001. But one can also refer to the Foundation for Democracy, or to The 21st Century Foundation, respectively established by the financial group Hualong and by Formosa Plastics and Xinguang Life Insurance.

Thus, both as to the elaboration and to the implementation of the Mainland policy, parallel to an advisor role or to a go-between part any big businessman can play on an individual ground, there is its taking part in collective authorities, whether they operate in the deliberation field—such as the Legislative Yuan or the Guomindang's central standing committee— upstream in the scholar one—the research institutes for instance—or downstream in the paradiplomatic one—the SEF. And the more the businessman is close to the top of the power—to the president in particular— the more he will have an important part in those various bodies.

Finally, the contribution of transnational economic forces to the setting of power relations results from various institutional cleavages produced by contending logics. As a matter of fact, the development of cross-straits exchanges, which has gone hand in hand with a scattering of specialized bodies that operate according to different necessities, has progressively nurtured important institutional cleavages. At first, the picture appears rather simple: the market-state opposition draws the fault lines, both within the government—the main cleavage opposes the Ministry of Economic Affairs, on the one hand, and the president and the cabinet, on the other hand—and among ad hoc institutions, basically the MAC (Mainland Affairs Council, *Dalu weiyuanhui*) versus the SEF. The MAC was established in 1990 (a few months before the SEF) to formulate and implement the Mainland policy. It is a formal administrative agency under the Executive Yuan (*Xingzhengyuan*), and is on a level with other government ministries and councils. MAC-SEF conflicts have been numerous.[71] Though personal matters as well as community origin (Mainlander versus islander) were involved, these conflicts have set, in an institutional framework, the market versus state dispute. But, at the same time, because Taiwanese investors necessities are represented by a "national" institution, it could progressively be overcome by the state ... at the expense of course of altering its policy, i.e., "forming" the state in Lonsdale sense. From a study of the MAC–SEF conflicts between 1991 and 1993, Leng Tse-kang shows how these confrontations illustrate the split in the political élite and the greater importance of patron–client relationship in Mainland affairs' administration.[72]

But the picture is further complicated in as much as the private sector's participation is not limited to SEF proper. For example, the Ministry of Economic Affairs has set, in 1993, a special committee to handle the department's policy toward China (the Mainland Affairs Committee), which, in fact, is closely linked to the private sector as it includes secretaries-general of Taiwan's important business associations (the Chinese National Federation of Industries, the General Chamber of Commerce of the Republic of China, the Textile Association). Certainly, if the Ministry pushes too far in favor of business interests, the final arbitration will result in a more security-oriented outcome. But, at the end, if one considers the whole decision-making process, the diffuse influence of the business sector is far from being negligible. SEF is also involved in the top arbitrary instance. As far as Taipei's Mainland policy is concerned, the final arbitration belongs to the president who works in close relationship with the Mainland Affairs Planning Group, set in 1993. The Group operates under the Executive Yuan (the cabinet), and brings together, among its 12 members, the chairman and one vice chairman of the MAC, but also the secretary-general of the SEF. Not only has this body played a major part upstream from the SEF when cross-straits negotiations are involved,[73] but it has also arbitrated institutional conflicts, those concerning the liberalization of cross-straits relations in particular. At the end of 1993, for instance, the Group put a (temporary) end to the pressure put by the Ministry of Economic Affairs for implementing the three direct links.[74]

In sum, there is a twofold interpenetration of economics and politics. First, because policies are the outcomes of conflicting interest groups; next, because the issue of defining—and securing—the borders of the state always stands in the picture. Far from shifting the balance of power away from politics and toward private interests—ending hypothetically in a demise of the state—cross-straits relations are politicizing the whole realm of economics. Certainly, the process at work is quite the opposite of that of the so-called strong state, insofar as decisions are not those of a coherent bureaucratic élite. It may even appear that economic policies are less politicized than they were in the authoritarian period in the sense that it is no longer the Guomindang that is dominating the whole decision-making process.[75] But, at the same time, because of growing cross-straits relations, no decision is free from national security concern.

As to the issue at stake in this chapter, it appears that the resilience of a democratic state should not be assessed in relation to the paradigmatic strong state's unitary élite, but, on the contrary, in relation to the existence of various institutional frameworks that can both voice contending issues and fit them into power relations. The question is not so much whether Taipei's cross-straits regulation is a residual one, as whether transnational necessities participate, within Taiwan, in articulating power with society.

Negotiated Borders: Producing Wealth

Taiwan's Competitive Edge

Growing international exchanges do not necessarily forecast the fading of borders; quite the contrary, exchanges bear witness to a differential constitutive of the border. In a context of contending sovereignties, governmental regulations will strive to enhance the national economy's competitive edge, a process that partakes in "state building." But, at the same time, transnational actors also take part in fostering the differential, through overbidding tactics or criminal activities, all these contingent actions being so many "state formation" processes.

Today, Taipei's Mainland policy aims less at restricting cross-straits relations, than at enhancing Taiwan's competitive edge.[76] The government's rhetoric is significant in this respect: officials often speak of the necessity to build an "economic defense line" (*jingji fangxian*).[77] The main tool in this field is the regulations concerning investments on the Mainland, which are authorized if they meet four criteria:[78] they do not compete with Taiwan's domestic industries in the international market; they are labor-intensive; they use raw material produced in China; the line of business would be noncompetitive if continued in Taiwan. Above all, some projects, though not prohibited, belong to the "special case" category: these investments are required to be balanced by investment projects in Taiwan; in particular, the total annual amount of investments on the Mainland[79] by listed companies should not exceed their domestic investments for the same year.

The APROC (Asia-Pacific Regional Operation Center—*Yatai yingyun zhongxin*) project launched by the government in 1995, and renamed in 2000 as the Finance and Legal Coordination Service Center (*Caijing fazhi xietiao fuwu zhongxin*), partakes of the same tactic that aims at counterbalancing the internationalization of Taiwan firms, in particular the relocation tide on the Mainland. The project has a twofold objective: to turn Taiwan into a gateway for American and European firms targeting the Asian market, on the one hand, and to foster domestic high-tech investments on the island, on the other hand. Such a project implies of course a further liberalization of the economy, a process that is late in regard of what was initially scheduled. But, whatever the slowness of the administration, and as regards the argument developed in this chapter, internationalization of firms are considered, in this project, as a tool to foster a nation-states' border.[80]

The enhancement of Taiwan's competitive edge is also the result of individual initiatives on the side of transnational actors. For instance, the bargaining over the huge investment Formosa Plastics Group (Taiwan's largest private employer and biggest exporter) planned at the beginning of the 1990s on Haicang Island, near Xiamen, on the Fujian cost (a US$5 billion petrochemical complex) is significant in this respect.[81] After about two years of negotiations, the Taipei government authorized Wang Yung-ch'ing to go ahead with the building of a US$2.2 billion naphta cracker in Mailiao (Taiwan), a project that had initially been stalled because of environment lobbies' pressure. Moreover, after the Chinese government had risen the deal—offering Wang new preferential terms for the Haicang project—the Taipei government made new concessions, and, on March 29, 1993, the final proposal was US$9.5 billion (an investment that some government economists estimate would add one percentage point to Taiwan's annual GNP growth).[82] This investment is to put Formosa Plastics among the leaders in world petrochemical markets.

In this episode, overbidding tactics, trade-offs, as well as the use of *guanxi* have played a major part at each stage of the bargaining. Chinese authorities have risen the deal by offering important facilities, while top-ranking Chinese officials have been personally involved in the Haicang project: when Wang Yung-ch'ing visited the Mainland to explore the investment opportunities, he was received by Deng Xiaoping, Li Peng, and Jiang Zemin.[83]

At the other end of the spectrum, another example consists of criminal activities that flourish due to the differential the border represents, while fostering this differential by the counter-regulations they bring about. There would be between 30,000 and 40,000 illegal Chinese immigrants in Taiwan, according to SEF estimations. Likewise, organized crime is developing in the Taiwan Straits, often using investment fronts to favor illegal immigration, kidnap, or smuggle counterfeit, drugs, or firearms. Conversely, and in a context of contending sovereignties, criminal activities can be used as a front for interstate politics, military maneuvers in particular. Important fleets of Chinese fishing boats are often crossing the centerline of the Taiwan Straits, and bad weather conditions can be the pretext to board the island: some of the vessels not only carry stowaways sustaining crime gangs, but alleged illegal immigrants are in fact retired PLA soldiers.[84] Yet, at the same time, the internationalization of cross-straits crime contributes to raise security concerns and, hence, to reveal the very existence of a border.

Democratization in Taiwan and the Chinese Market

Certainly the resumption of exchanges between Taiwan and the Mainland, after nearly fifty years of banning, can be perceived as the first step toward a future reunification of China—whatever its form—or, at least, as calling into question the island's de facto independence. However, this is only one side of the picture. The progressive liberalization of cross-straits relations is closely intertwined with the setting of democratic institutions and the building of a Taiwanese nation-state. Notwithstanding the sovereignty dispute and growing tensions in the Taiwan Straits, the current sequence would be that of a "normalization" of Taiwan's external relations. These relations are becoming commonplace, for they are no longer dependent on the principle—and the fiction—of China's unity. Putting an end to the ban on cross-straits relations was essential to democratization, both for legal and symbolic reasons, in as much as it opened the way to an overall replacement of the assemblies elected on the Mainland.[85] It was also necessary in order to give credit to Taipei's new flexible diplomacy that aims at reinstating the Republic of China in the interstate community alongside (and no longer in place of) the PRC. Finally, from a sociological point of view, the relocation tide on the Mainland favored a shift of power from the minority Mainlander group (*waishengren*) to the majority islander one (*benshengren* or "Taiwanese"). Paradoxically, though the former had nurtured the myth of China's unity, the latter has been the main beneficiary of cross-straits liberalization. For historical reasons, people from the *benshengren* community, more or less, held control of the economic sector, as this sector was the only access to social rise that was left to them during the Mainlander authoritarian years. In addition, *benshengren* had the family connections in Southern coastal China provinces (Fujian in particular), and spoke some of the dialects (*minnanhua* or *kejiahua*).Yet, during the authoritarian years and at the beginning of the democratization, the budding opposition, first, the Minjindang as well as the reformist wing of the Guomindang (mainstream faction), next, was formed by Taiwanese (with some exception of course) putting pressure to call into question the long term goal of China's unification. In sum, from the middle of the 1980s, growing exchanges with China have allowed those who were pushing for the implementation of institutions representative of the island's population only to maintain their control over the national economy.

The question then arises whether the strong political differential can progressively die down, whether growing exchanges should foster a deeper integration between the two sides. In so doing, not only would political tensions be eased between the two governments, but Taiwan as a democracy could play a major part in triggering political changes on the Mainland. In fact, if one cannot deny that some common values are forged within transnational networks, both political and economic reasons hamper, for the time being, a conversion of cross-straits flows into a long-lasting process of integration.[86] As far as politics are concerned, the sovereignty dispute forbids any active commitment of Taiwan's political forces to put active pressure on the Chinese government so as to initiate a democratization process on the Mainland, or to be actively involved alongside Chinese dissidents. Quite the contrary, protecting Taiwan's democracy, that is protecting the autonomy if not the de jure independence of the state, requires a low profile attitude in this field.

As to economics, one must, above all, focus on the very motives of Taiwanese investors. The forming of a Chinese transnational economy relies on making the most of the border. Low production costs refers in fact first and foremost to social conditions, legal protection (or the lack of) in particular.[87] Hence, though it is not necessarily correlated, a stereotype of the *Taishang* has been formed[88] that runs counter any normative discourse on the values being spread through exchanges. This stereotype can be qualified, even called into question, by Chinese local bureaucrats or by scholars.[89] Yet, the very fact that it is often recalled is indicative of the nature of the border. Moreover, the elements forming this stereotype refer to the reasons displayed by the Taiwanese investors relocating in China. Often cited,[90] the possibility to resort to person-to-person relations (*guanxi*) can be pinpointed as corruption. Likewise, when the Taiwanese investor puts forward a comparative advantage in understanding the Chinese market, he is often compared to the exploiter capitalist,[91] even to a Mafioso.[92]

If one goes back to the state–society link in Taiwan, Chu Yun-han has argued that the Guomindang enjoyed a high autonomy because of its control over business associations: "As long as there is no alternative regime in sight, the KMT can effectively construct an unequal partnership with the business élite, in which the party-state élite set the limits on influence-buying and policy contestation."[93] And further: "when the business sector does not enjoy the option of shifting its support between competing parties, it is deprived of a vital bargaining power vis-á-vis the state."[94] However, the Chinese market offers this alternative. Certainly, there is no question about the strong collusion between the Guomindang leadership and the business élite that is coming out with democratization. But precisely, in the emergence of the "nascent class bias" (Chu Yun-han) that is replacing the old subethnic bias in Taiwan, cross-straits exchanges are playing an important part. The process at work would be that of state formation, in Lonsdale's terms: transnational forces support the state, benefit from it, and use it for their own ends. The articulation between transnational forces and governmental action is indeed "a contradictory process of conflicts, negotiations and compromises."

From the cross-straits relations' case, it appears that one should focus on the borders of power, instead of focusing on sovereignties,[95] even if it can be at the expense of a mutually exclusive sovereignties' vision of the world. Certainly, as democracy goes, more or less, hand in hand with the internationalization of economy, borders tend to be blurred. But at the same time, democracy is not only based on representative institutions of a territorialized population; it also offers new institutional channels for bargaining. Hence, it remains the main locus where power and society are (re)structured. Therefore, borders should be defined less as lines that can be materialized on geographic maps (object of governmental agreements or disagreements), than as the stake of negotiations between transnational and governmental actors. The mere existence of this stake—both for producing and controlling wealth—precludes reasoning in terms of a demise of the state, for it is constitutive of state "formation."

Notes

1. Among the works that have helped this chapter Chen, Te-sheng, *Liangan zhengjing hudong: Zhengce jiedu yu yunzuo fenxi* (Political and Economic Interaction Across the Taiwan Straits, An Analysis of Policy Interpretation and Implementation) (Taipei: Yongye, 1994); Chu, Yun-han, "Making Sense of Taiwan's Mainland Policy: A Political Economy Perspective," paper presented at the annual conference of the Association for Asian Studies, Chicago, 13–16 March 1997; Hsin-huang Michael Hsiao, and Alvin So, "The Taiwan-Mainland Economic Nexus: Sociopolitical Origins, State-Society Impacts, and Future Prospects," *Bulletin of Concerned Asian Scholars* XXVIII,1: 3–12; Leng, Tse-kang, *The Taiwan–China Connection: Democracy and*

Development Across the Taiwan Straits (Boulder, Co.: Westview Press, 1996); Tak-Wing Ngo, "Business Encirclement of Politics: Government–Business Relations across the Taiwan Strait," _China Information_ X, 2 (Autumn 1992): 1–18.

2. Charles E. Lindblom, _Politics and Market, The World's Political-Economic Systems_ (New York: Basic Books, 1977).

3. Ngo, "Business Encirclement of Politics."

4. The first Taiwanese investment on the Mainland dates back to 1983. Source: personal interview with Huang Chintan, vice-executive secretary, Investment Commission, Ministry of Economic Affairs, Taipei, September 30, 1999.

5. Though, in general, Taiwanese figures are by far more reliable than the Chinese ones, the latter should be preferred as far as Taiwanese investments on the Mainland are concerned since many firms do not declare their investments to the Taiwanese administration in order to get around the regulations. According to Taiwan statistics, up to June 2001 there were 23,415 approved cases of indirect investment on the Mainland: _Liangan jingmao_ (Straits Business Monthly), 115 (10 July 2001): 55.

6. About 70 percent for 1998. Personal interview with Kao Charng, Researcher, Chung-Hua Institute for Economic Research, Taipei, October 7, 1999.

7. The so-called three links concern trade _(tongshang)_, mail _(tongyou)_, and transports _(tongzhuan)_. Direct cross-strait transportation raises important issues, such as vessel registry (because resolution of registry issues will require cross-strait negotiations), or transport routes (because special inter-regional sea-lanes and flight routes have to be established).

8. Foreign registered PRC vessels can ship goods to Kaohsiung Port for transshipment to a third place.

9. In late March 2000, the Legislative Yuan passed the Act of Offshore Island's Construction (_Lidao jianshe tiaoli_). Article 18 of the Act exempts transport between Mainland China and Taiwan's offshore islands of Jinmen (Kinmen), Mazu (Matsu), and Penghu from restrictions (_xianzhi_) of the Statute governing the relations Between the People of the Taiwan Area and the Mainland Area (_Liangan renmin guanxi tiaoli_).

10. There were four indirect channels: through a company located in a third country; through investment in another company located in a third country; through a Taiwan company's branch established in a third country; through indirect remittance. On the "special case" category, see below.

11. Chen Shui-bian's election did not alter this policy dramatically. In his inaugural address on May 20, 2000, President Chen Shui-bian stated that as long as the CCP regime shows no intention of using military force against Taiwan, he would observe "the five no's" (not declare independence; not change the national title; not push for the inclusion of the "state-to-state" description in the Constitution; not promote a referendum on Taiwanese independence; and not seek to abolish the Guidelines for National Unification (_Guojia tongyi gangling_) adopted in 1991). As to the investment policy, the motto "patience over haste" has been replaced in 2001 by "active liberalization and effective management" (_jiji kaifang, youxiao guanli_). And in response to mounting demand from the business sector, the government lifted the longstanding ban on direct investment. It also dropped the US$ 50 million ceiling on single investment projects. The latter should be put into the special review category.

12. Source: personal interview with Shrive Chi, vice-chairman, Council for Economic Planning and Development, Taipei, September 29, 1999.

13. Some commodities that are shipped from Taiwan to China through Hong Kong do not pass through the Hong Kong customs as they are transferred in Hong Kong waters to another cargo vessel heading for China. Source: same.

14. Robert O. Keohane, and Joseph N. Nye Jr (eds), _Transnational Relations and World Politics_ (Cambridge, Mass.: Harvard University Press, 1972): xii.

15. In Jane Khana (ed.), _Southern China, Hong Kong, and Taiwan: Evolution of a Subregional Economy_, The Center for Strategic and International Studies, Significant Issues Series, XVII, 7 (Washington, 1995): viii.

16. Omae, Kenechi, "The Rise of the Region State," *Foreign Affairs* 72, 2 (Spring 1993): 78–87; also: *The End of the Nation-State: The Rise of Regional Economies* (London: Harper Collins, 1996); *The Borderless World: Power and Strategy in the Global Marketplace*, 2nd ed. (London: Harper Collins, 1994).

17. Saskia Sassen, *Losing Control, Sovereignty in an Age of Globalization* (New York: Columbia University Press, 1996), in particular, chapter one "The State and the New Geography of Power": 1–30.

18. Jacques Levy, "Une géographie vient au monde," (A Geography Comes into the World) *Le débat* (November–December 1996); Denis Retaillé, "La vérité des cartes," (The maps' truth) ibid.

19. Steve Smith, "The Self-Images of a Discipline: A Genealogy of International Relations Theory," in *International Relations Theory Today*, eds. Ken Booth, and Steve Smith (University Park: The Pennsylvania State University Press, 1995): 3.

20. See her seminal work: *The Retreat of the State: The Diffusion of Power in the World Economy* (Cambridge: Cambridge University Press, 1996).

21. Justin Rosenberg, *The Empire of Civil Society, A Critique of the Realist Theory of International Relations* (London: Verso, 1994); Michael Waltzer (ed.), *Toward a Global Civil Society* (Providence, Oxford: Berghahn Books, 1995); Ronnie D. Lipschutz, "Reconstructing World Politics: The Emergence of Global Civil Society," *Millennium Journal of International Studies* 21, 3: 389–420.

22. Andrew Hurrell, "International Political Theory and the Global Environment," in *International Relations Theory Today*, eds. Booth and Smith: 145.

23. This literature is almost as numerous as that positing a decline of the state as a result of globalization. Among the works that have oriented my own research: Linda Weiss, *The Myth of the Powerless State* (Ithaca: Cornell University Press, 1998).

24. Peter Evans, "The Eclipse of the State? Reflections on Stateness in an Era of Globalization," *World Politics* 50, 1 (October 1997).

25. Thomas Risse-Kappen, *Bringing Transnational Relations Back In, Non-State Actors, Domestic Structures and International Institutions* (Cambridge: Cambridge University Press, 1995): 5.

26. Certainly, this theory does include factors such as the economy, science, and culture, but nothing other than the state perspective gives full meaning to their role in international relations. More precisely, this theory argues that since violence is at the core of the interstate system, transnational relations do not significantly affect "high politics," whose business is security and war. Therefore, governments will always prevail in any direct confrontation with transnational actors.

27. Jean-François Bayart, "Avant-propos," (Foreword) in *La greffe de l'Etat* (The graft of the state), ed. Jean-François Bayart (Paris: Karthala, 1996): 6.

28. Yves Chevrier, "L'empire distendu: Esquisse du politique en Chine des qing à Deng Xiaoping" (The Loose State: An outline of Chinese politics from the Qing to Deng Xiaoping), in *La greffe de l'Etat*, ed. Bayart: 276.

29. Bruce Berman, and John Lonsdale, *Unhappy Valley, Conflict in Kenya and Africa* (London: James Currey, Nairobi: Heinemann Kenya, Athens (Ohio): Ohio University Press, 1992): 5. Underlined in the original. See also chapter 2 by John Lonsdale: "The Conquest State of Kenya, 1895–1905": 13–44.

30. Ibid., 15.

31. Ibid., 39.

32. Anthony Giddens, *A Contemporary Critique of Historical Materialism, Vol 2: The Nation-State and Violence* (Berkeley and Los Angeles: University of California Press, 1987): 205. Underlined in the original.

33. See, in particular, You-tien Hsing, "Building *Guanxi* Across the Straits: Taiwanese Capital and Local Chinese Bureaucrats," in *Undergrounded Empires, The Cultural Politics of Modern Chinese Transnationalism*, eds. Aihwa Ong, and Donald Nonini (New York and London: Routledge, 1997): 143–164.

34. Béatrice Hibou (ed.), *La privatisation des Etats* (States' Privatization) (Paris: Karthala, 1999).
35. Aihwa Ong, *Flexible Citizenship, The Cultural Logics of Tansnationality* (Durham and London: Duke University Press, 1999). In chapter 8, "Zones of new sovereignty," she argues that the industrializing states in Southeast Asia have responded to the challenges of globalization by also becoming more flexible in their management of sovereignty.
36. Gilles Guiheux, *Grandes entrepreneurs et grandes entreprises à Taiwan (1949–1990)* (Big entrepreneurs and large-size firms in Taiwan 1949–1990), Ph.D. Thesis, Ecole des Hautes Etudes en Sciences Sociales (Paris: 1996): 271.
37. Source: Ministry of Economic Affairs, Taipei. It was US$1.03 million for 1994 already.
38. Finance and cement. The group belongs to the Koo family.
39. US$3.5 million for this investment.
40. Source: *Liangan jingji tongjin yuebao* (Monthly Economic Statistics on Cross-Straits Relations), Ministry of Economic Affairs, Taipei, 19 (March 1994): 41.
41. The first investment was located in Shanghai, and amounted to US$5.1 million.
42. As members of the Guomindang's central committee were not allowed to travel on the Mainland, the picture must have been taken during one of Jiang Zemin's trip abroad.
43. This is for instance the case for Jeffrey Koo Jr, son of Jeffrey Koo (Koo Lien-sung), chairman of the Taiwan based Chinatrust Commercial Bank, and grandnephew of Koo Chen-fu, chairman of the Straits Exchange Foundation. The *Far Eastern Economic Review* reports that "Jeffrey Koo Jr. has used his golfing skills to build a network of powerful Chinese business leaders. He has closed relationships with Wang Jun, chairman of the state conglomerate China International Trust and Investment Corp.—better known as CITIC—and with He Ping, president of an army-run conglomerate, China Poly Group, and a son-in-law of the late patriarch Deng Xiaoping." (13 November 1997): 60.
44. Chevrier, "L'empire distendu," 262–395.
45. Rocca, "L'entreprise, l'entrepreneur et le cadre. Une approche de l'économie chinoise" (The Enterprise, the Entrepreneur and the Cadre: An Approach of China's economy), *Les études du CERI* 14 (April 1996); and "Le capitalisme chinois ou les paradoxes du flou," (Chinese Capitalism and Haziness' Paradoxes) *Pouvoirs* 81: 21–30.
46. Chung-Hua Jingji Yanjiu Yuan (Chung-Hua Institute for Economic Research), *Taishang yu waishang zai dalu touzi jingyang zhi diaocha yanjiu* (A Comparative Study of Foreign Investments in Mainland China) (Taipei, 1994): 25.
47. Source: interviews conducted in *Taishang*, Xiamen, October 1997, and Taipei, September and October 1999.
48. Source: same.
49. Source: same, and personal interview with Wu Hsing-hsin, deputy-secretary general, Straits Exchange Foundation, Taipei, September 22, 1999. For other examples of Taiwanese investors mobilizing their networks in order to protect their own interests, see Ngo, "Business Encirclement of Politics," 15–16.
50. The English translation is sometimes "Mainland-investing Taiwanese Business Association," closer to the Chinese name.
51. *Jiaoliu* (Exchange) 45: 68.
52. *Jiaoliu* 46: 66–69.
53. A senior advisor to the president, Ding Mou-shih, the Mainland Affairs Council chairman, Su Chi, the National Security Council deputy secretary-general, Hu Wei-chen.
54. For a thorough account on this subject, see: Chu, Yun-han, "The Realignment of Business-Government Relations and Regime Transition in Taiwan," in *Business and Government in Industrialising Asia*, ed. Andrew MacIntyre (St Leonards: Allen and Unwin, 1994): 113–141. For a historical overview as well as updated information on business associations in Taiwan (the article does not tackle the issue of cross-straits relations), see Gerald A. McBeath, "The Changing Role of Business Associations in Democratizing Taiwan," *Journal of Contemporary China* 7, 18 (July 1998): 303–320.

55. I am referring here mainly to the two major associations: the Chinese National Federation of Industries and the General Chamber of Commerce of the Republic of China.

56. For an overview, see Leng, *The Taiwan China Connection*, 88–89.

57. For works concluding a larger autonomy see: Harmon Zeigler, *Pluralism, Corporatism, and Confucianism: Political Association and Conflict Regulation in the United States, Europe, and Taiwan* (Philadelphia: Temple University Press, 1988), and Robert Wade, *Governing the Market: Economic Theory and the Role of Government in East Asian Industrialization* (Princeton: Princeton University Press, 1990); for a more shaded assessment, see Chu, Yun-han, "The Realignment of Business–Government Relations and Regime Transition in Taiwan."

58. Mark Granovetter, "Economic Action and Social Structure: the Problem of Embeddedness," in *The Sociology of Economic Life*, eds. Mark Granovetter, and Richard Swedberg (Boulder, Co.: Westview Press, 1992): 53–81.

59. In Granovetter's and Swedberg's words: "(…) economic action cannot, in principle, be separated from the quest for approval, status, sociability, and power." (Ibid.: 7).

60. "Un sens du désintéressement—l'affirmation que le profit n'est pas recherché pour lui-même—la reconnaissance d'une responsabilité sociale—la nécessité pour les grands patrons tai-wanais de 'rendre à la société' ce qu'elle leur a donné—et enfin la défense des intérêts nationaux—leur activité devant être patriotique." (A sense of unselfishness—the assertion that one does not seek profit for the sake of it—the recognition of a social responsibility—the necessity to 'return to the society' what it has given—and, finally, the defense of national interests—their activity must be patriotic." (Guiheux, *Grandes entrepreneurs et grandes entreprises à Taiwan*, 299).

61. On the fictitious nature of this privatization, see Françoise Mengin, "Une privatisation fictive: le cas des relations avec Taiwan," (A fictitious privatisation: the case of relations with Taiwan) in *La privatisation des Etats*, ed. Hibou, 197–223. "Private" relations are either the result of a trans-position of former relationships from the official to the nonofficial sphere when a substantial cooperation had been developed prior to the severing of diplomatic and consular relations (it was the case with Japan, the United States, Saudi Arabia, or South Korea, which have severed diplomatic ties with Taipei in 1972, 1979, 1990, and 1992 respectively), either relations that have been set up, as such, from the outset (with most European countries for example).

62. For a presentation of Koo Chen-fu's paradiplomatic activities, see Guiheux, *Grandes entrepreneurs et grandes entreprises à Taiwan*, 363–366.

63. See below.

64. Big businessmen account for one third of the SEF's board of directors: 13 out of 43 members. The others are 12 representatives of public enterprises or enterprises controlled by the Guomindang, six representatives of the government, five scholars, seven representatives of the media.

65. He had since been promoted "Senior Advisor" to the president.

66. The single nontransferable vote system according to which the majority of Taiwan's represen-tatives are elected enhances the part played by money in politics. On this issue, see: John Fuh-sheng Hsieh, "The SNTV System and Its Political Implications," in *Taiwan's Electoral Politics and Democratic Transition, Riding the Third Wave*, ed. Tien, Hung-mao (Armonk, N.Y.: M.E. Sharpe, 1996).

67. See Leng, *The Taiwan–China Connection*, 86.

68. See above.

69. Personal interview with Kao Ching-yuan, chairman, Tongyi, Taipei, October 7, 1999.

70. Among others: Tien, Hung-mao, *The Great Transition: Political and Social Change in the Republic of China* (Stanford: Hoover Institution, 1987); Tien (ed.), *Taiwan's Electoral Politics and Democratic Transition*.

71. For a good summary Leng, *The Taiwan-China Connection*, 64–70.

72. The two other conclusions drawn, on this matter, by Leng are that ethnicity and ideologi-cal factors have emerged as the crucial elements in Taiwanese politics, and that the true

manipulator of China policy was President Lee Teng-hui himself (Leng, *The Taiwan–China Connection*, 69).

73. Personal interview with Su Chi, chairman, Mainland Affairs Council, Taipei, September 22, 1999, and with Wu Hsin-hsing, mentioned above.

74. See, in particular, *Zili zaobao* (Independence Morning Post) (2 January 1994), and *Zhongguo shibao* (China Daily) (3 January 1994).

75. This is very well formulated by Leng Tse-kang: "Economic bureaucrats could formulate policies according to actual economic demands in an environment *insulated* from political concerns." Leng, *The Taiwan–China Connection*, 75. Emphasis added.

76. The question whether Taiwan's economy is overdependent on China's is very tricky, for the latter is also dependent on Taiwanese investments: in terms of employment in particular. According to Wu Rong-I (president, Taiwan Institute for Economic Research), in 1999, 8 million people were employed by Taiwan-invested companies on the Mainland (personal interview, Taipei, September 29, 1999). Leng Tse-kang for his part puts forward, for 1995, the figure of 3.9 million job opportunities (about 2.2 percent of Mainland China's nonagricultural employment): see Leng, Tse-kang "A Political Analysis of Taiwan's Economic Dependence on Mainland China," *Issues and Studies* 34, 8 (August 1998): 144. One should also mention Taiwanese investments' contributions to China's total export value: 14.4 percent for 1995 (Ibid.).

77. Source: personal interview with Shrive Chi mentioned above.

78. On July 22, 2000, the Minister of Economic Affairs, Lin Hsin-yi, stated that though the new government would not abandon the *jieji yongren* policy, it would review each industry in terms of its value to determine if it should remain in Taiwan. Basic infrastructural and high-tech industries that are currently prohibited to transfer to the Mainland should be gradually liberalized under the premise of national security. And investments in information technologies could be reviewed on a case-by-case basis. See: *Liangan jingmao* (Straits Business Monthly) 104 (10 August 2000): 51. See also above, note 11.

79. Which must be approved by the company's shareholders and board of directors.

80. Aihwa Ong puts it very well: "Yet if we consider state power as a positive agency, the issue is no longer one of the state 'losing control' but rather one of the state taking an active role in refashioning sovereignty to meet the challenges of global markets and supranational organizations." *Flexible Citizenship*, 215.

81. This investment was a twofold threat to Taipei's Mainland policy, as, on the one hand, it was calling into question the then ban on direct investment, and, on the other hand, it was damaging Taiwan's economic edge by undermining the whole petrochemical industry of the island.

82. *Far Eastern Economic Review* (22 April 1993): 75.

83. Ngo, "Business Encirclement of Politics," 14.

84. *Jiaoliu* 45: 57.

85. For subsequent development on this issue, see Françoise Mengin, "Taiwan: la question nationale et la démocratisation," (Taiwan: the national issue and democratization) in *Démocraties d'ailleurs* (Democracies from elsewhere) ed. Christophe Jaffrelot (Paris: Karthala, 2000): 587–616.

86. I don't want to open the debate here about the possible existence of a link between economic growth and democratization, as it has been set by some authors such as Seymour Martin Lipset, "Some social requisites of democracy: Economic development and Political legitimacy," *American Political Science Review* 53, 2 (1959): 69–105; Phillips Cutright, "National political Development: Measurement and Analysis," *American Sociological Review* 28 (April 1963): 253–264; Robert Wade, *Governing the Market* (Princeton NJ: Princeton University Press, 1990); or Samuel Huntington, *The Third Wave: Democratization in the Twentieth Century* (Norman: University of Oklahoma Press, 1991). This line of reasoning has been disqualified by Christophe Jaffrelot, "Comment expliquer la démocratie hors d'Occident?" (How to explain democracy outside the Western world?) in *Démocraties d'ailleurs*, ed. Christophe Jaffrelot, 12–19.

87. Interviews conducted with *Taishang* in Xiamen, October 1997, and in Taiwan, September 1997, and September–October 1999, all confirm this point.

88. This stereotype is analyzed in Joseph Bosco, "Taiwan Businessmen Across the Straits: Socio-Cultural Dimensions of the Cross-Straits Relationship," Department of Anthropology, Chinese University of Hong Kong, Working Paper No. 1, 1994; and Anita Chan, "The Emerging Patters of Industrialization Relations in China and the Rise of Two New Labor Movements," *China Information* IX, 4 (Spring 1995): 36–59. See also Aihwa Ong, *Flexible Citizenship*, 46–48.

89. Interviews with *Taishang* conducted in Xiamen, October 1997.

90. Same; and *Taishang fu dalu touzi zhuyi shixiang* (Points on which Taiwanese investors should pay attention to in the Mainland), Dalu weiyuanhui (Mainland Affairs Council), 1994.

91. See Anita Chan, "Regimented Workers in China's Free Labour Market. Military Discipline in one of Dongyuan's Shoe Factory," *China Perspectives* 9 (January–February 1997): 12–17.

92. Reporting on Taiwanese investors in Xiamen, Bosco aptly reminds one of Max Weber's words about the criticism directed at early capitalists (Bosco, "Taiwan Businessmen Across the Straits," footnote 4).

93. Chu, "The Realignment of Business–Government Relations," 133.

94. Ibid.

95. For a very interesting insight on the relation between power and sovereignty, based on a Foucauldian analysis, see Janet Roitman, "Le pouvoir n'est pas souverain," (Power is not sovereign), in *La privatisation des Etats*, ed. Hibou, 187–196.

INDEX